Women and Wars

University of Liverpool

Withdrawn from stock

For my daughter Mariel
And in loving memory of Edna Kaplan and Sara Ruddick

Women and Wars

EDITED BY CAROL COHN

polity

Copyright © Carol Cohn 2013

The right of Carol Cohn to be identified as Author of this Work has been asserted in accordance with the UK Copyright, Designs and Patents Act 1988.

First published in 2013 by Polity Press
Reprinted in 2013, 2014, 2015, 2016, 2017 (twice), 2018, 2019

Polity Press
65 Bridge Street
Cambridge CB2 1UR, UK

Polity Press
350 Main Street
Malden, MA 02148, USA

All rights reserved. Except for the quotation of short passages for the purpose of criticism and review, no part of this publication may be reproduced, stored in a retrieval system, or transmitted, in any form or by any means, electronic, mechanical, photocopying, recording or otherwise, without the prior permission of the publisher.

ISBN-13: 978-0-7456-4244-4
ISBN-13: 978-0-7456-4245-1(pb)

A catalogue record for this book is available from the British Library.

Typeset in 9.5 on 13 pt Swift Light
by Servis Filmsetting Ltd, Stockport, Cheshire.
Printed and bound in Great Britain by TJ International Ltd, Padstow

The publisher has used its best endeavours to ensure that the URLs for external websites referred to in this book are correct and active at the time of going to press. However, the publisher has no responsibility for the websites and can make no guarantee that a site will remain live or that the content is or will remain appropriate.

Every effort has been made to trace all copyright holders, but if any have been inadvertently overlooked the publisher will be pleased to include any necessary credits in any subsequent reprint or edition.

For further information on Polity, visit our website: www.politybooks.com

Contents

Boxes and Tables		vi
Abbreviations		viii
Contributors		xiii
Foreword by Cynthia Enloe		xv
Acknowledgments		xvii

1	Women and Wars: Toward a Conceptual Framework	1
	Carol Cohn	
2	Women and the Political Economy of War	36
	Angela Raven-Roberts	
3	Sexual Violence and Women's Health in War	54
	Pamela DeLargy	
4	Women Forced to Flee: Refugees and Internally Displaced Persons	80
	Wenona Giles	
5	Women and Political Activism in the Face of War and Militarization	102
	Carol Cohn and Ruth Jacobson	
6	Women and State Military Forces	124
	Jennifer G. Mathers	
7	Women, Girls, and Non-State Armed Opposition Groups	146
	Dyan Mazurana	
8	Women and Peace Processes	169
	Malathi de Alwis, Julie Mertus, and Tazreena Sajjad	
9	Women, Girls, and Disarmament, Demobilization and Reintegration (DDR)	194
	Dyan Mazurana and Linda Eckerbom Cole	
10	Women "After" Wars	215
	Ruth Jacobson	

Notes		242
References		250
Index		279

Boxes and Tables

BOXES

2.1   Definitions of gender-based and sexual violence   39
2.2   Changing gender roles in Afghanistan   40
2.3   Double work burdens   43
2.4   Becoming a forced wife in Sierra Leone   47
3.1   UN Security Council Resolutions on women, peace, and security   57
3.2   Sexual slavery: the "comfort women" of the Second World War   58
3.3   Obstetric and traumatic fistula   66
4.1   Additional Human Rights Conventions that pertain to the rights
      of forced migrants   83
4.2   Key terms: humanitarian assistance versus development aid   85
4.3   UNHCR Conclusion No. 39 (XXXVI) Concerning Refugee Women
      and International Protection   96
4.4   UNHCR definition of "women at risk"   97
5.1   The Committee of Soldiers' Mothers in Russia: from
      "maternalism" to anti-militarism?   110
5.2   Maternal practice as a *potential* resource for peace politics   111
5.3   Laura Bush on the US war in Afghanistan   115
5.4   The Women's Peace Camp at Greenham Common   119
6.1   The "double whammy" for US military women   142
6.2   Sexual assault and abuse in the North Korean military   144
8.1   (Where) have women appeared in peace agreements?   177
8.2   Sudanese women in the processes of building peace   179
8.3   Issues addressed by UN Security Council Resolution 1325   184
8.4   1325 in practice: the case of Afghanistan   185
8.5   After the peace agreement: women building peace in Aceh   191
9.1   DDR processes: who does what?   199
9.2   A woman commander speaks on DDR in Burundi   203
9.3   The Women in Crisis Movement: a response to the challenges of
      reintegration   208
9.4   Skills developed by women members of armed opposition
      groups in Africa   211
10.1 United Nations Peace Support Operations: where and who?   220

10.2 Where are the women in PSOs? 223
10.3 Gaps between gender rhetoric and funding 230
10.4 Land reform in Mozambique: the battle to protect women's rights 234
10.5 Returning to normal life or encountering backlash? 238
10.6 Peace-building in postwar Kosovo 239

TABLES

6.1 Proportion of women serving in state militaries around the world 131
6.2 Examples of countries where women may serve in at least some combat roles 139
7.1 Women and girls inside armed opposition groups 1990–2011 149
10.1 Who does what in the postwar environment? 219

Abbreviations

AIDS	Acquired Immunodeficiency Syndrome
Al-Shabaab	Harakat al-Shabaab al-Mujahideen (Somalia)
AMB	al-Aqsa Martyrs' Brigade
ASC	Assembly of Civil Society (Guatemala)
AUC	United Self-Defense Forces of Colombia
AusAID	Australian Agency for International Development
BASIC	British American Security Council
BBC	British Broadcasting Corporation
BCPR	Bureau for Crisis Prevention and Recovery (United Nations)
BINGO	big international nongovernmental organization
CDF	Civil Defense Forces (Sierra Leone)
CEDAW	Convention on the Elimination of All Forms of Discrimination against Women
CHRGJ	Center for Human Rights and Global Justice
CIA	Central Intelligence Agency
CNDD-FDD	National Council for the Defense of Democracy/Forces of Defense of Democracy (Burundi)
CPC	Civilian Protection Component (Mindanao)
CRC	Convention on the Rights of the Child
CRSV	conflict-related sexual violence
CSMR	Committee of Soldiers' Mothers of Russia
CSO	civil society organization
DDR	disarmament, demobilization and reintegration
DFID	Department for International Development (UK)
DPA	United Nations Department of Political Affairs
DRA	Dutch Refugee Association
DRC	Democratic Republic of the Congo
ECOWAS	Economic Community of West African States
EPLF	Eritrean People's Liberation Front
EU	European Union
FAD	Feminist Approach to Development
FAO	United Nations Food and Agriculture Organization
FARC	Fuerzas Armadas Revolucionarias de Colombia – Ejército del Pueblo
FMLN	Farabundo Martí National Liberation Front (El Salvador)

FORO	Foro Nacional de la Mujeres (Guatemala)
Frelimo	Frente de Libertação de Moçambique
FRODEBU	Front pour la Démocratie au Burundi
GAD	Gender and Development
GAFM	Gender and Forced Migration
GAM	Free Aceh Movement
GBV	gender-based violence
GDP	gross domestic product
GRP	Gender and Reparations Project
GWG	Gender Working Group (Aceh)
HIV	Human Immunodeficiency Virus
HRW	Human Rights Watch
IANSA	International Action Network on Small Arms
IASC	Inter-Agency Standing Committee
IAWG	Interagency Working Group
ICC	International Criminal Court
ICCPR	International Covenant on Civil and Political Rights
ICERD	International Convention on the Elimination of All Forms of Racial Discrimination
ICESCR	International Covenant on Economic, Social and Cultural Rights
ICM	Intergovernmental Committee for Migration
ICRC	International Committee of the Red Cross
ICTJ	International Center for Transitional Justice
ICTR	International Criminal Tribunal for Rwanda
ICTY	International Criminal Tribunal for the former Yugoslavia
IDDRS	Integrated DDR Standards
IDF	Israeli Defense Force
IDMC	Internal Displacement Monitoring Centre
IDP	internally displaced person
IFI	international financial institution
ILO	International Labor Organization
IMF	International Monetary Fund
IMT	International Monitoring Team (Mindanao)
IOM	International Organization for Migration
IRB	Immigration and Refugee Board of Canada
IWGRW	International Working Group on Refugee Women
IWNAM	International Women's Network against Militarism
JPuD	Women's Peace Network (Aceh)
JPuK	Women's Policy Network (Aceh)
LoGA	Law on the Governing of Aceh
LRA	Lord's Resistance Army (Uganda)
LTTE	Liberation Tigers of Tamil Eelam
MARWOPNET	Mano River Women's Peace Network

MDRP	Multi-Country Demobilization and Reintegration Program
M4P	Mothers for Peace
MIRF	Moro Islamic Revolutionary Front
MoU	Memorandum of Understanding
MP	Member of Parliament
MPC	Mindanao Peoples Caucus
MWC	International Convention on the Protection of the Rights of All Migrant Workers and Members of Their Families
NATO	North Atlantic Treaty Organization
NGO	nongovernmental organization
NKHR	North Korean Human Rights
NIWC	Northern Ireland Women's Coalition
NMA	Naga Mothers' Association
NORAD	Norwegian Agency for Development Cooperation
NSAG	non-state armed group
NWUM	Naga Women's Union of Manipur
OCHA	United Nations Office for the Coordination of Humanitarian Affairs
OSCE	Organization for Security and Co-operation in Europe
OSRSG/CAC	Office of the Special Representative of the Secretary-General for Children and Armed Conflict
PCR	post-conflict reconstruction
PIJ	Palestinian Islamic Jihad
PKK	Kurdistan Workers' Party
PLA	People's Liberation Army (China)
PMS	premenstrual syndrome
PMSC	Private Military and Security Company
POP	people-oriented planning
POW	prisoner of war
PSO	peace support operation
PTSD	post-traumatic stress disorder
RAWA	Revolutionary Women of Afghanistan
RCD	Rassemblement Congolais pour la Démocratie
Renamo	Resistência Nacional Moçambicana
RUF	Revolutionary United Front (Sierra Leone)
SADF	South African Defense Force
SALW	small arms and light weapons
SDN	Sub-Committee on De-escalation and Normalization (Sri Lanka)
SEA	sexual exploitation and abuse
SGI	Sub-Committee on Gender Issues (Sri Lanka)
Sida	Swedish International Development Agency
SIHRN	Sub-Committee on Immediate Humanitarian and Rehabilitation Needs (Sri Lanka)

SPLA	Sudanese People's Liberation Army
SPLM	Sudanese People's Liberation Movement
SPLM/A	Sudanese People's Liberation Movement/Army
SPM	Sub-Committee on Political Matters (Sri Lanka)
SRSG	Special Representative of the Secretary-General
SSNP	Syrian Socialist National Party
SSR	security sector reform
SSWC	Save Somali Women and Children
STD	sexually transmitted disease
STI	sexually transmitted infection
TB	tuberculosis
TCC	Troop Contributing Country
TNT	trinitrotoluene
UK	United Kingdom
UN	United Nations
UNAMID	African Union/United Nations Hybrid operation in Darfur
UNDDR	United Nations Disarmament, Demobilization and Reintegration
UNDP	United Nations Development Programme
UNDPKO	United Nations Department of Peacekeeping Operations
UNECHA	United Nations Executive Committee on Humanitarian Affairs
UNESCO	United Nations Educational, Scientific and Cultural Organization
UNFPA	United Nations Population Fund
UNGA	United Nations General Assembly
UNHCR	United Nations High Commissioner for Refugees
UNICEF	United Nations Children's Fund
UNIFEM	United Nations Development Fund for Women
UNITA	National Union for the Total Independence of Angola
UNODA	United Nations Office for Disarmament Affairs
UNRWA	United Nations Relief and Works Agency
UNSC	United Nations Security Council
UNSCR	United Nations Security Council Resolution
URNG	Guatemalan National Revolutionary Unity
US	United States
USA	United States of America
USCRI	United States Committee for Refugees and Immigrants
USDOD	United States Department of Defense
VA	United States Department of Veterans Affairs
WAD	Women and Development
WCRWC	Women's Commission for Refugee Women and Children
WFP	World Food Program
WHO	World Health Organization

WICM	Women in Crisis Movement
WID	Women in Development
WIFM	Women in Forced Migration
WILPF	Women's International League for Peace and Freedom
WREI	Women's Research and Education Institute
WSP	Women Strike for Peace
WTO	World Trade Organization

Contributors

Carol Cohn is Director of the Consortium on Gender, Security and Human Rights and Professor of Women's Studies at the University of Massachusetts Boston. Her major research interests include gender and armed conflict, the gendered discourses of US national security elites, and gender mainstreaming in international security institutions.

Malathi de Alwis teaches in the Faculty of Graduate Studies, University of Colombo, Sri Lanka. She has a PhD in Sociocultural Anthropology and is currently working on postwar processes of memorialization and reconciliation. She is a co-founder of several feminist peace groups and a member of the Women in Conflict Zones Network (WICZNET).

Pamela DeLargy managed the United Nations Population Fund's (UNFPA) humanitarian programs for almost a decade, advocating for attention to women's health in humanitarian settings across the world. She played a lead role in the development of UN responses to sexual violence in conflicts. Currently, she is the UNFPA Representative in Sudan.

Linda Eckerbom Cole is the co-founder and executive director of Community Action Fund for Women in Africa, a non-profit organization working with women and girls in conflict and post-conflict areas.

Wenona Giles teaches at York University, working in the areas of gender, migration, refugee issues, ethnicity, nationalism, work, globalization, and war. She coordinated the international Women in Conflict Zones Research Network and recently completed an international research project concerning protracted refugee situations. She is now working on an international collaborative research endeavor to bring higher education degree programs to long-term refugees in camps.

Ruth Jacobson is a former Lecturer at the Department of Peace Studies, University of Bradford in the United Kingdom. In the mid-1980s, she lived and worked in a war zone in Mozambique where she saw the impact on women and girls at close quarters. Subsequently, she has contributed to feminist organizing in the field of humanitarian relief and post-conflict organizations.

Jennifer Mathers is a Senior Lecturer in the Department of International Politics at Aberystwyth University. Her major areas of research and teaching include gender and conflict; from 2007–2010 she edited *Minerva Journal of Women and War*.

Dyan Mazurana is Associate Research Professor at the Fletcher School of Law and Diplomacy, and Research Director at the Feinstein International Center, Tufts University. She works with a variety of governments, UN agencies, human rights, and child protection organizations regarding improving efforts to assist youth and women affected by armed conflict, and has worked in Afghanistan, the Balkans, southern, west and east Africa, and Nepal.

Julie Mertus, Professor of Human Rights and Director of the Program on Ethics and Peace at American University, has extensive experience working on gender and conflict issues for a number of governmental and nongovernmental human rights and humanitarian organizations from Albania to Zimbabwe.

Angela Raven-Roberts has managed humanitarian and development programs for organizations including Oxfam America, Save the Children USA, and UNICEF, working in countries including Papua New Guinea and Ethiopia. She holds a PhD in Anthropology, and oversaw the design of the first Master's of Arts in Humanitarian Assistance (MAHA) degree in the USA, at Tufts University.

Tazreena Sajjad is a Professorial Lecturer at the School of International Service at American University. Her research interests include human rights and conflict, transitional justice, humanitarian intervention, human rights in states of emergency and gender and armed conflict. She has also worked as a human rights practitioner and researcher in Afghanistan, Nepal, and Bangladesh.

Foreword: Gender Analysis Isn't Easy

I can't tap dance. I watch old Fred Astaire movies and think, "He makes it look so easy." There are many things I haven't learned how to do – to do calculus, to speak Turkish. Thanks to the hard, patient tutoring of so many feminist friends and colleagues, what I have learned how to do is gender analysis. Of course, friends continue to teach me – I'm not "there" yet.

That is, gender analysis is a *skill*. It's not a passing fancy, it's not a way to be polite. And it's not something one picks up casually, on the run. One doesn't acquire the capacity to do useful gender analysis simply because one is "modern," "loves women," "believes in equality," or "has daughters." One has to *learn* how to do it, practice doing it, be candidly reflective about one's short-comings, try again. To develop gender analytical skills, one has to put one's mind to it, work at it, be willing to be taught by others who know more about how to do it than you do. And, like any sophisticated skill, gender analysis keeps evolving, developing more refined intellectual nuance, greater meth-odological subtlety. One has to get to the point where one can convincingly describe the processes of gender analysis and its value to others, including to those who are skeptical, distracted, and stressed out. It takes myriad forms of energy to do gender analysis and to convince others of its necessity.

Carol Cohn and her smart contributors, first, are offering us a sophisti-cated, up-to-date gender analytical tool kit. Second, they are showing us what can be revealed if we learn how to use that gender analytical tool kit.

It's always more engaging to learn a new set of skills if your guides can show you exactly what you'll see with these tools that you would otherwise miss – and why those new findings matter. For instance, using their gender analytical skills, these contributors expose the diverse forms of violence wielded during wars: guns and bombs aren't the only weapons. They pull back the curtain on the differences between girls' and boys' experiences of being made to serve in adult men's fighting forces. "Children" turns out not to be a very useful category when trying to rebuild any society after a war. Cohn's contributors also show us why we will never usefully understand armed conflicts if we stubbornly focus our attention solely on the immediate war zone; we have to learn how to do gender analyses of refugee camps, of markets, of peace negotiations. Their gender analytical skills make it clear, too, that the months and years so comfortably labeled "postwar" in practice are riddled with wartime ideas about men-as-actors and women-as-victims, misleading ideas that serve to perpetuate the very conditions that set off the conflict in the first place.

The contributors whom Carol Cohn has brought together are among the most experienced users of gender analytical skills in the globally important (and maddeningly complex) field of war, armed conflict and postwar peace-building. Their experiences are of using their gender analytical skills while in the midst of confusing relationships "on the ground." These are analysts who've been in refugee camps where water is short, collecting firewood is risky, power hierarchies are dysfunctional, and donors' attention spans are short. They are analysts who have sat in long hearings where diplomats with no mud on their shoes decide whether or not a Gender Unit in a peacekeeping operation will get a decent budget. They have talked to women quite reasonably afraid to describe what actually happened to them and their daughters when rival male soldiers swept through their villages. They have met with local women's groups who have tried to get local male military commanders to listen to their proposals. In New York and capital cities, these gender analysts have lobbied government, nongovernmental organizations, and UN agencies to put aside their usual "only men really matter" ways and, instead, to take women seriously when they evaluate their policies' outcomes, when they write their peacekeepers' mandates, and when they allocate their funds.

Thus, as readers, we each can read *Women and Wars* with the triple aims of acquiring new gender analytical skills; finding out what the causes and dynamics of armed conflict look like if we view them through a gendered lens; and learning how to convince others to adopt these crucial gender analytical skills. This is the sort of book you'll want to make notes on, quote to others, take with you in your knapsack.

Cynthia Enloe

Acknowledgments

No piece of intellectual work is ever solely the product of one mind, and this is perhaps nowhere more true than in the case of a textbook designed to introduce readers to the tremendously rich literature about women and war. This book would not exist without the indefatigable efforts of activists, scholars, and practitioners around the world who work to prevent wars or to bring them more swiftly to an end, to expose wars' gendered workings, and to construct a less violent, more just world. It has been my pleasure and privilege to get know many of them, and to read and read about many more; I deeply regret that this book cannot begin to do justice to the complexity of their thinking or to the courage of their work, but I am enormously grateful for all they have taught me, and hope that they find at least some of it reflected in these pages.

So many friends and colleagues have contributed to the ideas in this book, it will be impossible to thank them all. But I must start with two friends, Cynthia Enloe and Sara Ruddick, with whom I have been in rich dialogue for so long that my thinking often feels like an extended conversation with each of them. There are no adequate ways to describe what their friendship, nuanced thought, fearless originality, intellectual honesty, and personal generosity have meant to me.

I am tremendously grateful, too, to Ann Tickner, from whom I have learned so much. She has also been a generously supportive friend and colleague, and a vitally important contributor to this journey. More recently, friendship and collaboration with Malathi de Alwis and Ruth Jacobson has stretched and enriched me both intellectually and personally. My work is also enriched by the writings and friendship of Spike Peterson, Ann Runyan, Jindy Pettman, and many other wonderful colleagues in the Feminist Theory and Gender Studies section of the International Studies Association.

I am deeply grateful to Felicity Hill for bringing me into the "women, peace and security" advocacy networks that have coalesced around UNSCR 1325, and for the world that opened up to me. I appreciate her great generosity in all that she taught me, as well as her political acuity, wicked wit, and the kitchen table conversations. Jennifer Klot has been an invaluable guide to the UN system, and has taught me a tremendous amount – perhaps even more than I really wanted to know – about the policy, political and analytic challenges of addressing issues of women and war at the UN. In and around the UN, I have also been lucky to have the friendship and education offered by, among others, Sheri Gibbings, Sylvia Hordosch, Maha Muna, Nadine Puechguirbal, Kristin Valasek, and my sisters in the NGO Working Group on Women, Peace and Security. Additionally, it has been a great pleasure and honor to learn from colleagues such as Balghis Badri, Cynthia Cockburn, Luz Méndez, Ndeye Sow, and Dubravka Zarkov.

I have benefited from a very supportive institutional home in the time I have worked on this book. I wish to thank my faculty and administrator colleagues at the University of Massachusetts Boston, including Ann Blum, Elora Chowdhury, Amani El Jack, Jean Humez, Rajini Srikanth, Dean Donna Kuizenga, and Provost Winston Langley for their friendship, support, vision, and wonderful scholarship. Most critically, I owe an enormous debt of gratitude to my Associate Director at the Consortium on Gender, Security and Human Rights, Sandra McEvoy, who has been exceptionally generous, skilled, committed and hardworking in keeping all of the moving parts of our complex program functioning and making such a success of it – enabling me to pour the necessary time and energy into this manuscript. She is a valued interlocutor, scholar, co-teacher, and all-around co-conspirator who enriches every dimension of my and the Consortium's work.

This book has truly been a collective effort. The idea for it was hatched between Louise Knight, of Polity Press, and Laura Sjoberg, who brought me into the project. I am grateful to Laura for the extensive work she put into the early stages of this project, and to Louise, Emma Hutchinson, and David Winters at Polity for their support and guidance throughout the development of this book, and for their patience. The early stages of this project also benefited greatly from the collective wisdom of the "April 11th group," which came together to brainstorm the conceptual framework for the book; participants included Dinu Abdella, Cynthia Enloe, Ruth Jacobson, Ramina Johal, Milkah Kihunah, Jennifer Klot, Dyan Mazurana, Sandy McEvoy, Julie Mertus, Sonali Moonesinghe, Selma Scheewe, and Laura Sjoberg.

I am most grateful to the contributors, not only for their excellent work, but for sticking with this project through delays and innumerable editorial requests. Additionally, Malathi de Alwis, Cynthia Enloe, Ruth Jacobson, and Dyan Mazurana have been treasured compatriots throughout this process, offering moral and intellectual support when it was needed most.

Many colleagues generously shared their time and expertise, reading and commenting on various drafts. In particular, I'd like to thank the following people for their very useful feedback on one or more chapters: Megan Bastik; Joshua Chaffin; Catia Confortini; Malathi de Alwis; Bina D'Costa; Marsha Henry; Sandra Krause; Sarah Masters; Megan Mackenzie; Sandra McEvoy; Dyan Mazurana; Luz Méndez; Nida Naqvi; Isis Nusair; Laura Sjoberg; Inger Skjelsbæk; and Elisabeth Wood. I am also grateful to Polity Press's two anonymous reviewers for their very helpful comments.

In working to produce a book that is accessible and useful to both undergraduate and graduate students, it has been a great gift to have Consortium interns and students who were willing to read and offer comments on drafts of chapters. In particular, I would like to thank Emily Baum, Katie Davis, Chloe Diamond-Lenow, Cassandra Hawkins, Laura Matson, Mary Helen Pombo, Marie Puccio, Harin Song, Helena Wahlstrom, Jill Williams, Ayala Wineman, and the students of the Fall 2010 Honors Seminar 380-02 at UMass Boston. Additionally, valuable research and manuscript production assistance was also provided by Consortium interns Jane Lief Abell, Emily Campbell, Hyomi Carty, Gina Choi, Alexa Cleary, Brenna Doyle, Delia Flanagan, Mary Glenn, Jodi Guinn, Cassandra Hawkins, Mallory Hennigar, Wendy Jepson, Tavish MacLeod, Laura Matson, Shannon Nolan, Mary Helen Pombo, Anya Priester, Hannah Roberts, Jillian Rubman, Kelsi Stein, Cara Wagner, Jill Williams, and Ayala Wineman.

Critically, there are two main people whose support in the preparation of this manuscript has been extraordinarily generous and skilled, and whose loyalty and endless hours of hard work far surpass anything I could ever repay. Azure Mauche has been the citation wizard, the reference detective, the bibliography queen – a tremendous challenge in a book with multiple contributors situated around the world. I am enormously grateful to her for taking on this demanding, frustrating task in the midst of a complicated and demanding life (and claiming to enjoy it). Caitlin Lucey has been a partner *extraordinaire* in every aspect of getting this manuscript done. Her dedicated and tireless efforts have included multiple readings of every chapter, resourceful research assistance, proofing, formatting, and checking and double-checking everything. She has been intellectual sounding board, technical problem-solver, and morale booster, with the focus of a laser and the patience of a saint. I am in awe, and enormously grateful.

It is customary to "last but not least" thank one's family; the incommensurability between that formulation and what one's closest family members both give and put up with is hard to fathom. My family's love, support, understanding, and forbearance have meant the world to me. I owe special words of appreciation to my grandmother Edna, an extraordinary human being and activist, whose 1916 high school valedictory speech on "Women in the Current War Effort" still tickles and teaches me; to my mother Helen, who taught me more than I can say; and to my daughter Mariel, for all the joy.

CHAPTER 1

Women and Wars: Toward a Conceptual Framework

Carol Cohn

This is a book about the relationships between women and wars: the impacts wars have on women, the ways women participate in wars, the varying political stances women take toward war, and the ways in which women work to build peace.

There is an old story about war. It starts with war being conceived of as a quintessentially masculine realm: in it, it is men who make the decisions to go to war, men who do the planning, men who do the fighting and dying, men who protect their nation and their helpless women and children, and men who negotiate the peace, divide the spoils, and share power when war is over.

In this story, women are sometimes present, but remain peripheral to the war itself. They raise sons they willingly sacrifice for their country, support their men, and mourn the dead. Sometimes they have to step in and take up the load their men put down when they went off to fight; they pick up the hoe, or work in a factory producing goods crucial to the war effort – but only as long as the men are away. To the men in battle, they symbolize the alternative – a place of love, caring, and domesticity, and indeed, all that is good about the nation which their heroic fighting protects.

The gendered reality of war is far more complex than this old story portrays. War itself is more complexly gendered than this masculinized story allows, and women's role in and experience of war is far more integral and varied. In this book, we will show that one cannot understand either women's relation to war or war itself without understanding gender, and understanding the ways that war and gender are, in fact, mutually constitutive.

Which women? Which wars?

The starting point for thinking about women and wars must be that women's experiences of war and their relations to war are extremely diverse. Women both try to prevent wars and instigate wars. They are politically supportive of wars, and they protest against wars. Women are raped, tortured, maimed, and murdered, they are widowed, the children they have nurtured are lost to violence; but women are also members and supporters of the militaries and armed groups that commit these acts. Women stay home, resolutely striving to sustain family and community relationships; and women are displaced, living in camps without any of the structures that they have built to make life possible. Women are empowered by taking on new roles in wartime, and disempowered by being abducted from their homes and forced into armed groups or military prostitution. When the war is over, women work to rebuild their communities, and women are ejected from their families and communities because they have been raped, or been combatants, or lost a limb to a landmine.

The diversity of women's experiences of and relations to war is due to both diversity among women and diversity among wars. "Women," of course, are not a monolithic group, but instead individuals whose identities, options, and experiences are shaped by factors including their age, economic class, race, clan, tribe, caste, ethnicity, religion, sexuality, physical ability, culture, geographic location, state citizenship and national identity, and their positioning in both local and global economic processes. Their relations to war are shaped by, but not reducible to, these multiple factors; they are also thinkers who make their own sense of the multiple social, cultural, economic, and political forces which structure their lives. The multiplicity of these factors and the sense women make of them gives rise to contradictory interests among women, and even within any particular woman. This means that attempts to generalize about "women and war," while in some ways unavoidable in a book of this kind, always run the risk of doing conceptual violence to the realities of women's lives. And that we must, at a minimum, reject comfortable assumptions such as "women are naturally more peaceful than men" or "women are war's victims," and instead commit to exploring the specificity of different women's relations to wars and the multitude of factors which shape those relations.

This, in turn, requires paying attention to the specificity of wars. Wars are neither a uniform phenomenon, nor a uniformly gendered phenomenon. They vary along many dimensions including the weapons, tactics, and strategies employed, the political motivations and goals, the global economic and political relationships within which they are embedded, the kinds of militaries and armed groups engaged in the fighting, the number, range, and type of other actors involved in the conflict, and the resources available for recovering from war.

Thus, understanding that there is great breadth and diversity of women's experiences of war is a critical first step, but we also need more than a catalogue of what women do and what happens to them. In order to understand the specificity and complexity of women's different experiences of and actions in war, we need to start by understanding the contexts within which that experience is embedded, the series of interlocking systems, relationships, and processes which constitute the conditions under which women act. These include the gender systems within which women live; the specific kinds of wars being fought; and the wider set of actors and economic, political and social processes, from local to global, which shape both women's lives and the societies within which they live before, during, and after war.

Our approach to thinking about gender

"Gender" is a complex term which has been employed in many different ways by scholars, policy makers and activists; unfortunately, this means that when any two people use the word "gender," they may not be sharing a common understanding at all. For many policymakers in international institutions, for example, "gender" is often little more than a more "neutral-sounding" word for women; so when they refer to "gender issues" they really mean those things they think of as "women's issues," and when they talk about something like "gendering peacekeeping," they are most likely referring to adding women to peacekeeping forces or addressing women's needs during a peace-keeping mission. For others, however, "gender" is taken as referring to *both* men and women, and a "gender issue" might, for example, be the problem of how to disarm male fighters at the end of a war if their identities as men are bound up with possessing and using guns. In answering that question, a feminist economic researcher who sees "gender" as a structural, material relationship between men and women would likely come up with different solutions than a feminist sociological theorist who understands "gender" as a "situated accomplishment." If, as this book shows, gender is a crucial factor both in how women and men experience wars *and* in war itself, it is critical for us, at the outset, to unpack some of the meanings of gender that will prove analytically useful to the study of women and war.

Gender as structural power relation

Among the many different uses and meanings of the word "gender," one common place to start is to understand that gender is a social structure which shapes individual identities and lives. It shapes how people see themselves and are seen by others. It shapes the kinds of daily activities and paid work in which people are likely to engage. It shapes the kinds of material and cultural resources to which they have access, and the kinds of power and authority they might wield.

But gender not only structures our lives as individuals; it also shapes, and is shaped by, the institutional and symbolic universe we inhabit, and the material processes – such as economic growth or decline, "globalization," militarization, or climate change – which constitute the context and conditions within which our lives play out. This is because gender is not simply a set of ideas about male and female people and their proper relations to each other; gender is, more broadly, a way of categorizing, ordering, and symbolizing power, of hierarchically structuring relationships among different categories of people, and different human activities symbolically associated with masculinity or femininity. So, as will be shown later in this chapter and throughout the book, the institutions that are constitutive of the wider economic, political, social, and environmental processes formative of war are themselves structured in ways that both draw on and produce ideas about gender, that rely on gendered individuals in order to function, and that are permeated with symbolic associations with gender in their practices and conceptions of their missions.

In understanding the many different meanings of gender, as well as the ways they are linked, the conceptual lynchpin that holds them all together is this: gender is, at its heart, a structural power relation. Just as colonialism, slavery, class, race, and caste are all systems of power, so is gender. Each rests upon a central set of distinctions between different categories of people, valorizes some over others, and organizes access to resources, rights, responsibilities, authority, and life options along the lines demarcating those groups.

There are many different ways of talking about a system that structures power relations along the lines of gender difference. One of the first to gain prominence was the word "patriarchy." Although the literal meaning of the word is "rule of the father," patriarchy is generally taken to have a broader meaning. A patriarchal system is one in which not only are fathers the heads of families, with authority over their wives and children, but also where men exercise power and dominate women through control of society's governmental, social, economic, religious, and cultural institutions. While some writers are reluctant to use the word, either due to worry that it will scare readers or because they feel that it does not adequately address the nuances of gendered power relations, others see its sustained value in its foregrounding of power, which can sometimes seem to disappear in discussions about "gender." One of the foremost scholars on women and war, Cynthia Enloe, states, "Patriarchy allows you to talk about the relationship of constructed masculinities and constructed femininities, over time and in relationship to each other and as they relate to structures of power. If you just use 'gender,' then you can, in fact, never ask about the power relationships that both construct masculinity and femininity and relate them to each other unequally."[1]

Other gender analysts attempt to ensure the centrality of power to discussions of gender by talking about "gender subordination," a term which they see as useful in pointing to the male–female gender binary, as well as to the ways in which *within* each category there are gendered hierarchies. Others find "gender system," "gender order," and "gender hierarchy" to be useful in pointing to the complexity of hierarchical gender statuses both between and among men and women. R. W. Connell (1987), for example, has focused attention on the multiplicity of masculinities that exist, finding that "hegemonic masculinity" not only helps legitimate men's power vis-à-vis women, but also legitimates some men having greater power than other men, those with "subordinate masculinities." Still other writers employ the concept of "masculinism," "the ideology that justifies and naturalizes gender hierarchy by not questioning the elevation of ways of being and knowing associated with men and (hegemonic) masculinity over those associated with women and feminism" (Hooper 1998, p. 31).[2]

Whichever specific term is used to connote gender as a structural power relation, there are two key points to keep in mind for the purposes of this book. First, it is important to notice that in no case is gender ever reduced to a monolithic picture of one unified category of people, men, having power over another unified category of people, women. Instead, each of these terms points to the necessity of seeing that there are not only power differentials *between* each category, but also *within* each. This is because gender never stands alone as a factor structuring power in a society, but rather is inflected through, and co-constituting of, other hierarchical forms of structuring power, such as class, caste, race, ethnicity, age, and sexuality. It is the intersections of these structures that produce multiple masculinities and femininities, and concomitant power differentials, *within* each category.[3]

Second, we need to remember that the many different phenomena which the word "gender" is used to encompass become coherently linked only when they are seen as facets of the way in which gender functions as a system of power. So three key phenomena we will shortly examine in this chapter – gendered identities, gendered social structures, and gendered symbolic meanings – should not be understood in isolation, but rather as three co-constituting aspects of *gender as a social system which structures hierarchical power relations*.[4] Further, the interrelations between them are critical to understanding why women's – and men's – experiences of war can only be understood through the lens of gender analysis.

Gendered power relations and the relation of sex and gender

A system which empowers some categories of people at the expense of others requires political, social, economic, cultural, legal, and educational institutions which actualize and undergird this distribution of power. It also requires an ideology that justifies that unequal access; it has in some way to "make sense" or to appear legitimate that some people have access to resources, or even to rights over their own bodies, which others do not. Typically, this involves a set of beliefs about what each category of person is like. Both colonialism and slavery, for example, have relied on racism, a system of belief which posits supposedly "biologically" distinct racial categories (with, at the most, only marginal relation to physiological fact), and attributes different characteristics as inherent in people in each category. The characteristics belonging to each are not only seen as distinct but also distinctly coded as opposites, one inferior and one superior, and as less and more suited to different kinds of work, different life options, and different access to power. So the arrangement of power in which colonizers have the right to govern the colonized and to exploit and expropriate both their natural resources and labor only appears legitimate if the people who are colonized are understood as racially inferior – primitive, childlike, heathen, uncivilized, ignorant, and thus unfit for governing themselves – and the people who colonize are understood as their racial superiors with an "opposite" set of characteristics – advanced, mature, god-fearing, civilized, intellectually superior, and beneficent, and thus well-suited for having power over others "for their own good."

In a parallel manner, men's greater access to power and resources than women's has long relied for its justification on a set of beliefs about men's and women's reputedly biologically based characteristics. *If* men are believed to be stronger, more rational, more in control of their emotions, smarter, independent, tougher, better able to make and stick to a decision, courageous, more aggressive and thus willing to fight when necessary, more active, better at math and science, more oriented toward achievement and changing the world in which they live, while women are believed to be weaker, irrational, governed by their emotions, less intelligent, dependent, soft, indecisive, timid, passive, bad at math and science, and much more interested in domestic relationships than in public life, *then* it might appear to make the most sense for men to be in charge. These beliefs would suggest that in the public sphere of industrialized states, men would be better skilled than women at running governments, corporations, factories, religious and educational institutions; in the family they would be better suited to make the decisions, control the finances, and control and protect women and children (who are both seen as unable to protect themselves).

There are two key things to highlight in thinking about this system. First, that blatant inequality – that is, men's and women's unequal access to power, authority, and resources – is not only legitimated, but also made to appear natural and unremarkable, by a belief system that divides humans into two categories, male and female, and then sees a huge range of different characteristics as residing *within the individuals* in each group. This way, men's dominance of political, economic, and social institutions is seen as simply a result of their inherent *individual* capacities (and women's lack of those capacities), rather than as a result of *social structures* which systematically advantage men and disadvantage women.

Second, it is critical that the different characteristics attributed to males and females are seen to be based in their respective *bodies*, for if the differences are seen as biological, then male dominance is seen not only as "natural" but also unchangeable. Although feminist theorists have challenged the belief that the body is somehow a simple biological given, independent of culture, and unchanging, it remains true that for many people, that which is seen as biologically based is seen as "natural" and immutable.

It was in response to this set of social beliefs underlying male dominance – that it is legitimate because it derives from biologically based differences between males and females – that the concept of gender (in its nongrammatical usage) was first developed. Feminist social scientists and historians observed that, although male and female biological difference is relatively consistent, what societies believe about what men and women are "naturally" like varies substantially across cultures and through history. So the term "gender" was used to mark and make visible a distinction between the biological differences between males and females (or "sex" difference) and the socially constructed meanings ascribed to those differences ("gender"). Gender is constructed through a process in which humans are divided into categories (male and female) and a multiplicity of dichotomously conceived traits, characteristics, and meanings are associated with each category, which is then conceived as the opposite of the other (masculinity and femininity). Critically, the meanings attached to each category are not neutral; rather, those coded as masculine are consistently valorized over those coded as feminine, and those individuals and activities marked as masculine are considered to have more status and value than those seen as feminine. So if before the concept of gender was developed it was widely taken for granted that what we expect men and women to be like – their personalities, the kind of work they do, the roles they take in family and community life – flows directly from their biological sex, the concept of "gender" interrupts that (too) easy equation. Gender insists that, however much is biologically given, societies construct a much greater set of differences than biology dictates, and that those socially constructed differences, in turn, legitimate a social order based on the domination of men over women, and some men over other men.

This distinction between "sex" and "gender" – between what appear to be unvarying biological sex differences and the far more varied social constructions of masculinity and femininity – is pivotally useful, but has also been somewhat complicated in recent years. Although it has been true throughout history that most (although not all) societies have understood people to be either "male" or "female" on the basis of a set of biological characteristics including appearance, reproductive anatomy, and reproductive capacity, we now know that sex categories are not that simple. In fact, it is estimated that in at least 1 percent of births there are morphological features which make it difficult to see the infant as clearly a member of either biological sex category (Chase 1998; Diamond & Sigmundson 1997; Fausto-Sterling 2000); instead, they are biologically intersex. So the idea that there are only two biological sexes must itself be understood as a social construction.

What is significant to us in a book about women and wars, however, is that in most societies there is a taken-for-granted belief that there are (only) two sexes, and that one's seemingly "natural" and self-evident membership in either group (sex) brings with it a vast array of meanings, options and constraints (gender) beyond that which biology itself dictates. The imputed character traits, capacities, strengths, and weaknesses are seen then to be appropriately shaping the relations between the sexes, as well as the kinds of work each does, the activities each engages in, and the kinds of resources, power, and authority each can or cannot access. And it is these social facts, these social arrangements as they intersect with other social structures, such as class, caste, race, and ethnicity, which are the most important shapers of women's (and men's) experiences of war. Together they constitute: the conditions of women's lives before wars start; the practices women engage in and vulnerabilities they experience during war; the ways in which women will be viewed in war by everyone from enemy soldiers and political leaders to humanitarian assistance workers and policy makers; and the resources women can call upon to deal with wars' consequences.

One powerful way to see these connections between gendered social arrangements and women's experiences of war is to think about women's oft-focused-upon vulnerability in war. One can start by thinking about gendered divisions of labor; if gathering firewood and fetching water for the household are viewed as "women's work," for example, women will, during a war, be more vulnerable to rape, as these responsibilities take them to areas outside their villages or camps where they are isolated and more easily attacked. If taking care of children, the sick and the elderly is seen as "women's work," it will be harder for women than for men to quickly flee a village that is about to be raided and torched. If the gender arrangements of a society place men but not women in the paid labor force of the formal economy, and/or allow men but not women to own land, the women left behind when men depart to fight or die in battle will have little access to resources to support their families; this leaves them vulnerable to a variety of socially, economically and sexually exploitative relationships. In each of these cases and many more through-out this book, it is not a woman's biology that is the principal shaper of her experiences of war, but the gender arrangements within which she lives. So in seeking to understand "women and wars," it will be crucial to always be viewing women through the lens of gender analysis.

Gendered selves

If gender is not simply a pure manifestation of biological sex difference, but rather a social construction, how do people come to believe the specific things they do about what women and men, and girls and boys, are and should be like? And if gender is understood as a structural power relation, why do so many females and males accept it as both natural and reasonable that men (as a group) have more power than women? How do they come to experience themselves and their own identities in alignment with ideas about masculinity and femininity that would make this feel acceptable?

Theorists and researchers in different disciplines have come up with a multiplicity of answers to these questions. While an exhaustive exploration of their theories is beyond the scope of this book, several points are worth highlighting as they are helpful to us in understanding the gender relations that shape women's experiences of war.

Most critically, scholars' ideas about the nature of gender identity have undergone significant changes in the past several decades. Early western psychoanalytic conceptions saw the development of a coherent and stable gender identity as a product of the family relationships of early childhood;

one's actions then are seen as emanating from, and expressions of, that sol-
idly internalized, fixed identity. Early western sociological theorists of gender
saw gender identity less as constituted within the psychodynamic relations
of the family, and more in children learning "sex roles" via socialization by
family, friends, educational and religious institutions, and the mass media,
all of which communicate the behaviors, interests, abilities, personality characteristics, and attitudes seen as appropriate and desirable for each sex. While
it is acknowledged that what is seen as appropriate for each role can change
over time, this theorization, like psychodynamic theories, still sees gender
identity as internalized, coherent, and resistant to change, and has difficulty
accounting for the multiple masculinities and femininities that exist within
any given society – or individual.

In contrast, more recent conceptualizations of gender identity see it more
as a "doing," more like a performance, than a "being." That is, rather than an
internalized identity which is established at an early age and then becomes
the source which shapes one's actions, gender is seen as something fragmented and fluid that we are each producing, enacting, performing, on a
daily basis (Kessler & McKenna 1978; West & Zimmerman 1987; Butler 1990).
Gender is understood as a "situated accomplishment," meaning that in any
setting (e.g., family, community, sporting event, workplace, state military
or non-state armed group) there are specific social practices and discursive
codes which shape our understandings of how to be a man or woman in that
setting. We "do" or accomplish gender in that setting through social interactions in which we are responsive to context-specific expectations of masculinity and femininity and to the knowledge that others will hold us accountable
for doing so (West & Zimmerman 1987). A man who is an army drill sergeant,
for example, will likely "do masculinity" one way when he is interacting with
new recruits, a different way when he is interacting with his superior officer,
and a third way when interacting with his wife, and yet another way when
interacting with his newborn infant. Not only is he responding to different
social expectations and patterned practices in each setting, he is also aware
that if he fails to "do masculinity" differently in those four settings, others
will hold him accountable – perhaps, for example, calling child protective
services if he treats his infant the way he treats his new recruits, or removing him from his job if he treats his recruits the way he does his infant, or if
he talks to his superior officer the way he does his recruits. If he is also from
a social group that is different from the dominant one in his workplace, for
instance, a different class, race, religion, or sexuality, the distance between
the masculinities he enacts as he moves between the different settings and
relationships of his daily life are likely to be even greater and more complex
to negotiate.

This conception, then, transforms the ways in which we understand gendered selves; gender is not a unitary, coherent, unalterably fixed identity, but
rather more fluid, contingent, and fragmented, something that is continually

being produced in accordance with the multiple social settings and structures within which we live. At the same time, our actions are producing, reproducing, and sometimes altering those social structures. So if a man is part of an armed group committing a gang rape, he knows what is expected of him as a "real man" in that setting, that his masculinity will likely be scathingly impugned by the men he is with if he resists their pressure to participate, possibly with long-term negative consequences. At the same time, his actions and those of his peers are themselves part of what produce and reproduce the meaning of masculinity in that armed group.

This conception of gender also helps shift from a frame of unitary, opposed categories of masculinity and femininity to a more complex vision of multiple masculinities and femininities. For our purposes, it is not only important to see that any individual "does" (or "performs") masculinity and femininity in multiple, context-specific ways, but also to emphasize that the variety of culturally available masculinities and femininities are related to multiple structures of power and inequality. In thinking about Connell's concept of "hegemonic masculinity," we need to remember the doubled way in which it is hegemonic. First, it is hegemonic in the sense that it is the dominant, culturally glorified form of masculinity in a particular cultural, social and historical setting. It is also hegemonic in the sense that the characteristics attributed to hegemonic masculinity are those that act as the justification for some men having power over other men and over women. Hegemonic masculinity and subordinated masculinities will always have embedded within them not only gender, but a given society's other forms of structuring power, such as race, ethnicity, class, caste, religion, age, physical ability, and sexuality. Further, many of the ways that the subordinate groups in each of those systems are characterized bear striking similarities to the ways in which women, in general, are characterized. In comparison to the dominant group, they are seen as less rational, less dependable, less strong, less courageous, less moral, less civilized, more childlike, closer to nature than to culture, less suited to govern themselves – and thus, a priori, feminized. Or, put differently, there is no form of gender, of masculinity and femininity, that is not marked by these interlocking structures of power – no such thing as gender uninflected by, for example, race, class, or sexuality – exactly because these differentially valued masculinities and femininities underwrite and legitimize power differentials and inequality.

Why is this last point particularly important to the study of war? If war hinges on disempowering one's opponent, and gender difference encodes power, then manipulating gender can be deployed as a tactic of disempowering. In other words, it has the effect of making not just men but their *manliness* a target. This can and does take many forms. A crucial part of training troops to be willing to fight and kill, for example, entails denigrating and objectifying "The Enemy," and this process is typically facilitated through racialized, ethnicized, effeminized, dehumanized representations of one's opponents.

Another example can be found in some combat and prisoner-of-war situations, where combatants may be taught that one of the most effective ways of disempowering an opponent is by "unmanning" him via tactics such as sexual assault or humiliation, both of which are seen to feminize him; Abu Ghraib stands out as one recent and well-publicized instance of this practice (Nusair 2008). A third example of attempted disempowering via targeting a man's manliness, rather than simply the man himself, can be seen in the use of the rape of women as a tactic of war. Because a core aspect of hegemonic masculinity in most societies is men's control over and protection of their wives and daughters, the rape of male opponents' women can be seen as an effective way of unmanning/disempowering these men. In all three of these examples, a contest of power is played out through the medium of multiple masculinities, where the attempt to reduce one's opponent's power by attacking his (hegemonic) manliness – that is, via racialized, ethnicized, feminized, subordinated masculinities – becomes a weapon of war.

Gender as a meaning system

To this point, we have been talking largely about gender as it relates to male and female persons, and the ways their relationships are structured. This includes not only the social construction of the masculinities and femininities expected of and available to sexed bodies, but also the links between those constructions and the roles and activities expected of and available to women and men (and girls and boys), the gendered division of labor in a society, and the differential access to power, authority, and resources which those socially constructed differences underwrite and appear to legitimate.

But the meanings encoded in "masculinity" and "femininity" are not only located in the relational structures of people's lives. Critically, gender functions more widely as a discourse, a set of symbols, a system of meanings.[5] Gender constitutes a central organizing discourse in all societies we know of, "a set of ways of thinking, images, categories and beliefs which *not only* shape how we experience, understand and represent ourselves as men and women, but which *also* provide a familiar set of metaphors, dichotomies and values which structure ways of thinking about other aspects of the world, including war and security" (Cohn & Ruddick 2004, emphasis in original). When we think about objects, activities, professional norms and practices, occupations, academic disciplines, or any field of human endeavor or aspect of the world we inhabit, our perception of it is shaped through these gendered meanings, and the symbolic gendered associations have consequences. Because gender is not neutral, because that which is associated with masculinity is consistently valued and rewarded above that which is associated with femininity, it appears "natural," for instance, that childcare workers make less money than police officers, or that people in the "hard" sciences have better salaries than those in the "soft" sciences. Or that mainstream economists consistently overlook and undervalue women's labor in families, communities, and the informal economy in comparison with men's (and women's) work in the formal economy.

A classic example of both symbolic gender coding and its negative consequences can be found, unfortunately, in the meanings associated with "war" and "peace" themselves. Quite aside from, and separable from, the practical matter of the sex of the people who participate in war and peacemaking, war and peace are profoundly gendered *at a symbolic level*. War is associated with action, courage, seriousness, destruction, weapons, explosions, violence, aggression, fury, vengeance, protection, mastery, domination, independence, heroism, "doing," hardness, toughness, emotional control, discipline, challenge, adrenalin, risk – all terms which are coded "masculine" in most cultures. Peace, in contrast, is associated with passivity, domesticity, family, tranquility, softness, negotiation, compromise, interdependence, nonviolence, a "being" rather than a "doing," a lack of action, excitement, challenge and risk, an absence rather than a presence – all, in short, coded "feminine" in most cultures.

That the "masculine" is valued so much more highly than the "feminine" can then perhaps help make sense of some phenomena that should otherwise appear surprising. Although most people would probably say they prefer peace to war and agree that it is important to know how to solve conflicts without the use of violence, in the USA and most other countries, war studies (also known as "security studies") has a much higher status and far more resources than peace studies. Security studies is seen as hard-nosed, serious, realistic, and important, while peace studies is often viewed as soft, idealistic, and insignificant. Similarly, billions of dollars are invested in developing weapons, strategies, institutions, and people skilled in the use of armed violence; in comparison, there is almost no investment in developing tools, strategies, institutions, and people skilled in the use of nonviolent methods of conflict resolution and conflict transformation. War is seen and felt to be an effective (if regrettable) mode of achieving goals, while nonviolent methods are seen and felt to be ineffective, despite much historical and contemporary evidence belying both assumptions.

Gender coding is visible throughout multiple phenomena associated with war, and is consequential throughout. In humanitarian assistance organizations, for example, as in any other organization, some realms of activity are more masculinized and highly valued than others, and this has important implications for how the organizations carry out their work and the effects they have in communities. Suzanne Williams (2002), writing as a policy advisor on gender, human rights and conflict at Oxfam, shows the ways in which "Oxfam's organizational imperatives are both conceptualized and implemented" in a way that is dichotomized and gendered, metaphorized as "hard" and "soft." "Hard" interventions are those that are primarily technical, perceived as urgent, and visibly show fast and quantifiable results – such as the work of engineers who bring clean water to a refugee camp. "Soft" interventions are those which are more social than technical, longer term, where both the inputs and results are less quantifiable – such as work addressing so-called "women's issues," health, disability, or hygiene promotion. The greater value accorded the masculinized "hard" over the feminized "soft" shapes the ways actions and programs are perceived, appraised, and rewarded – both within the organization, and externally – as the "hard" attracts more of the funding. According to Williams (2002), this "becomes a self-perpetuating cycle of highly gendered systems of value and reward, which affects not only the nature of interventions but the staff responsible for them" (p. 91).

Another example of this consequential symbolic coding concerns the attention given to the potential and real harms created by different types of weapons. Nuclear weapons draw far more attention from researchers, theorists, policy makers, politicians, and arms controllers in the global North than small arms and light weapons (SALW) do, despite the undeniable fact that SALW are the source of far greater, pervasive human suffering – as well as both state and human insecurity – around the world. How are we to understand this? Cohn and Ruddick (2004) suggest that any attempt to explain it would be incomplete without taking account of the workings of gender discourse. Nuclear weapons are cataclysmic, while SALW are quotidian. Nuclear weapons are advanced; involve high level science, math and engineering; and require large, complex, hi-tech delivery systems to deploy. By comparison, SALW are technologically simple; easy to produce; and their use requires only human bodies, not complex hi-tech systems. Nuclear weapons are massively powerful and destructive; working on them is seen as concomitantly "serious" and important. The scale of destructive and explosive power of SALW is comparatively tiny, even though they can cause terrible injury. Nuclear weapons require high levels of education, skill and expertise to manage; SALW in many instances require such low levels of education, skill, and expertise that a drugged, illiterate child can use them, and with deadly effectiveness. Nuclear weapons are designed to be used from a great distance, without personal engagement with the tortured human effects, and are apprehended through highly complex, abstract theorizing with a premium on being "hard-nosed" and "free of emotion"; SALW are designed to be used far closer to the women, men, and children whose bodies they will tear apart, and they neither require fancy abstract theoretical footwork for their utility to be apprehended, nor offer the same kinds of opportunities for it. Nuclear weapons are reputedly the ultimate arbiter of (state) power and the ultimate deterrent/protector against a powerful foe; SALW offer no affiliation with that scale of power for the professionals who might choose to work on them. In short, in the cultures that produce them, nuclear weapons bear a striking isomorphism with hegemonic masculinity (Cohn 1987, 2003). Small arms and light weapons simply do not measure up. While small arms and light weapons may be intimately and intricately enmeshed with the masculinities of the combatants who use them, they are certainly subordinated in the imaginations and attractions of most of the men of the theorizing, policy-formulating, and regulating classes of the global North. That work on SALW seems not to tap the same allure of hegemonic masculinity and is not accorded the same status of ultimate seriousness by these men results in astonishingly little serious attention being given to what are appropriately called "weapons of mass destruction in slow motion" – the small arms and light weapons that women and men in conflict-affected areas around the world are desperate to see removed, destroyed, and prevented from reinfecting their communities (Cohn 2002; Cohn et al. 2005).[6]

A third war-related example of where symbolic gender coding is overtly consequential for women, and one that has been the subject of much fruitful feminist analysis, is in discourses of nationalism and other forms of collective identity (e.g., Jayawardena 1986; Yuval-Davis & Anthias 1989; Kandiyoti 1991; Yuval-Davis 1997). Nationalist ideology frequently symbolizes the nation, the homeland, as a woman; it is the (symbolic) body of the woman/mother/land that the male citizen soldier must protect against violation, penetration, conquest. Conversely, (physical) women and their bodies are seen as the repository and reproducers of national, racial, ethnic, tribal, or religious identity – they are the vessels through which men of the nation or other collectivity can (re)produce new members of the group; thus, their bodies are the territory over which men must have control in order to assure the continuation of their national identities, bloodlines, and their familial and national honor. That the symbolic gender coding of nation-as-woman and woman-as-nation has (often terrible) consequences for women has been horrifically apparent in the use of mass rape as a tactic of "ethnic cleansing" and genocide. Whether in Bosnia, Rwanda, Darfur or Bangladesh, the targeting of women for rape only "makes sense" (within the twisted logic of war) because of the association of woman and nation; without that, rape would be a form of individual torture, of promoting terror, but it would not be perceived as having the power to attack and destroy a national, ethnic or tribal group. Nor, concomitantly, would "the need to protect women's religious or ethnic purity" be as readily available as a way to legitimize war, as it was employed, for example, in the 1947 Partition of India (Butalia 2000).

Although these three examples are but a small sample, they begin to suggest something about the pervasiveness of gender as a symbolic system across diverse fields of human endeavor and institutional structures. This is understandable if we return to our discussion of gender as a structural power relation, in which masculinities and femininities become a way of categorizing, ordering, and symbolizing power. As such, gender provides a core metaphor and system of meanings available to underwrite, legitimize, and "naturalize" any other hierarchical structuring of relationships between different categories of people and different human activities, as well as between humans and nature.

Feminist analysis of gender as a meaning system adds a new dimension to our understanding of the multiple systems of structuring power. In my earlier discussion of intersecting power hierarchies, I noted that any analysis of the factors shaping a woman's or man's experience of war needs to ask where they are situated in the multiple axes structuring power in their society, including not only gender but also, for example, race, ethnicity, caste, and class. But gender does not only *intersect* with other structures of power; it *infuses* them. Because gender is itself a primary way of signifying power (Scott 1986), it provides a central organizing set of metaphoric associations that help to naturalize the structured inequality of other hierarchical power structures. For example, as postcolonial feminists have shown, colonial and postcolonial racial hierarchies are legitimated in part through the portrayal of the subordinated "other" as feminized, that is, as weak, effeminate, passive, irrational, and lacking the moral fiber of the colonizer.[7] In the context of war, whether it is a war of national liberation or a civil war, the fissures of political and economic inequality that underlie the conflict will evoke multiple gendered associations, as men in the effeminized national, racial, ethnic, or religious group fight not just for political independence, autonomy or self-rule, but also, given the gendered significations of power, for their own manhood as well.

Gendered institutions

There is one more facet of gender that needs to be central to any attempt to understand women and wars – the concept of "gendered institutions."[8] State militaries, armed insurgent groups, private military and security companies (PMSCs), multilateral security institutions, national diplomatic corps, arms manufacturers, development assistance agencies, international financial institutions, humanitarian relief organizations, local and international nongovernmental organizations, parliaments and transitional governments, foreign ministries and defense ministries, courts and police forces, families, educational systems, and religious institutions – all of these shape the conditions within which women experience war, try to survive, and attempt to build peace. And all of them are gendered, in multiple senses. They each have gendered divisions of labor and power within them. They also each have built into them presumptions about gender – both gendered identities and gender as a symbolic system – that shape the way they conceive their missions and envision the most effective ways of carrying out those missions. They each rely on workers and family members to have the gendered identifications and self-perceptions that make the institutions' gendered roles, work practices and power dynamics feel acceptable, rewarding, even alluring. And they not only rely on but also are productive of ideas about appropriate masculinities and femininities which in turn have a wider cultural impact than the bounds of the institution itself. Ultimately, it is these institutions that constitute the material, organizational, and social practices which, in dynamic interaction with gendered identities and gendered discourses, are the daily, nitty-gritty producers and reproducers of hierarchical gendered power relations.

The chapters of this book will demonstrate numerous ways in which institutions are gendered. For the purposes of this introduction, we will look in a bit more detail at only a few. Perhaps one of the most obvious is the gendered division of labor – what is the distribution of different kinds of male and female workers, and what kinds of work are they doing? Where are the men and women of different races or ethnicities, classes or castes, and sexualities, and how does that distribution map onto pay, status, and power? Classic examples include low-paid female clerical staff supporting well-paid male executives, or women clustered in the human resources department of a multinational engineering firm or in the human rights office of a peacekeeping operation, or women peace activists doing a huge amount of the grunt work in mixed-sex peace organizations whose publicly visible, titular leaders are men. While these and other models may exhibit somewhat more permeability than they once did, overall, patterns of gendered, racial, and ethnicized divisions of labor within organizations are still easily discerned. And even in those institutions that have a predominantly female labor force – for example, primary schools, garment industry sweatshops, sneaker factories, or commercial flowers-for-export farms – the positions with the most power and pay are still overwhelmingly held by men from dominant social groups.

When these differential employment patterns are noticed, it has been common to locate the cause either as discrimination by employers (e.g., "we can't promote that African American man to this executive position because he doesn't think the way we do") or as lack of capacity or interest on the part of the lower paid, lower status worker (e.g., "women can't be in combat positions because they lack upper body strength," or "the reason we can't recruit more women in peacekeeping operations is because their first priority is their families"). What all of these explanations share is that they treat the organizational *structure* itself as neutral, and locate the cause for the gendered division of labor, authority, and reward in *individuals* interacting with that putatively neutral structure.

Feminist theorists of gendered organizations, however, show that it is a mistake to look only at individuals' motivations. They argue that organizational structures, cultures, and practices are already themselves deeply gendered, and that it is the presumptions about gender ingrained in those structures, cultures, and practices that will shape whether a person is perceived as sufficiently competent, qualified, motivated, and well suited for a task or job. How can an organizational structure simultaneously appear neutral and be deeply gendered? One key to understanding this is to remember that most organizational structures have been built and run by men, and that, in most societies, men are the "default" category, the category associated with generic personhood. In this situation, when men are thinking about the work that their organization must do and how to accomplish it, the "modal worker" they are imagining is usually also a man – that is, someone with both a male body and (heterosexual) male social relations – and they organize work structures and practices in a way that fits that modal worker. If, for example, you are assuming the workers on submarines are young male sailors, that will shape everything from the toilet-seat-to-urinal ratio to the size and weight of the storage containers and toolboxes you engineer. Or if you are developing a set of work expectations in a law firm or in a department at the Pentagon, and you assume that your modal worker will be an able-bodied heterosexual man, it will seem perfectly reasonable to structure the work in a way that relies on workers being at work until late at night. This is because the conventional gendered expectations for heterosexual men is that their social relations will include having a family, but they will not have the responsibility to go grocery shopping, cook dinner, supervise homework, get the kids to bed, and prepare everyone's lunches for the next day.

Of course, men are not posited as the modal worker in all positions within an organization; assumptions about female bodies, characteristics, and social lives often lead to the envisioning of low-level "support" jobs, such as secretaries, childcare or elder-care workers, or low-wage sweatshop workers, as women. But overwhelmingly, the ideal type of employee doing the "serious" work, the employee or manager these women are meant to support, has the characteristics of a man.

What is most tricky here is that this process of basing most organizational structures and practices on an assumed male worker is not especially conscious or visible. That is, a senior manager or high-ranking officer, or engineer does not look around and say "how can I get this job done by men?" He simply says "how can I get this job done?" and assumes that the modal good worker will have the characteristics of a man – without necessarily being aware that he is thinking about gender at all. So the organizational structures and work practices that are developed come to simply be seen as the *right* way or the *best* way to do it – full stop – rather than as one, *arbitrary* way tailored to the particular bodies, needs, and social relations of one subgroup of humanity.

What is especially pernicious about this from a gender equality perspective is that once those (invisibly gender-specific) "best ways" to do things are established, any deviation to better fit the body or social life of a different subgroup is automatically perceived as lesser, an "accommodation to special needs," a "lowering of standards," a reflection of the lack of capacity, qualification, or motivation of the person in the (deviant from the able-bodied, heterosexual male norm) subgroup – whether or not these different ways of doing things are, in fact, in any objective sense, inferior. So women sailors are perceived as deficient, inferior, if they can't hoist 100 lb storage containers, despite the fact that there is no inherent reason for those containers to be 100 lb, and that having 50 lb containers not only works just as well but also helps lower the number of back injuries among male sailors. And women officers who reject the macho work culture of competing to see "who stays at the Pentagon the latest," and who work efficiently to accomplish more than their male counterparts before leaving at seven rather than nine or ten, are still perceived as "lacking commitment." The fact that a particular *action* (staying long hours) has come to be seen as the sign of a particular *characteristic* (commitment) is not recognized as arbitrary or gender specific – it is simply seen as a natural and neutral indicator of what it means to be committed.

What this means for women in the context of war is profound. The most obvious example might be women in militaries and armed groups, but it applies to any of the organizations referenced at the beginning of this section. If organizations are gendered (masculine) in their structures, cultures, and work practices, if "doing the job right" is (invisibly and arbitrarily) synonymous with "doing it like a man," many women will appear as though they are deficient, they "just aren't qualified," they require "special treatment," or they are lowering organizational standards – even when they are, in fact, getting the job done well (although perhaps upon occasion in a somewhat different manner). Their differences will always be perceived as signs of inadequacy, rather than simply as variation, or even as potential sources of ways to improve the organization's functioning.

So a woman newly entering the parliament of a transitional postwar government, for example, might experience herself in a real double bind. She will appear incompetent if she does not adopt the work practices, priorities, and assumptions that have been developed by the men who have established the norms; but if she adapts to those norms, she may be unable to advocate for any of the priorities she wanted to fight for. Or a woman who has devoted years of hard work to attain a mid-level position in a highly masculinized organization, such as the Department of Peacekeeping Operations or the Department of Political Affairs at the United Nations (UN), will likely face similar challenges. Her success in modally male roles has most often been based not only on extremely hard work, but also on her willingness to adopt the gendered assumptions, values, and worldviews that are held by men who succeed in the organization. If she were to decide to raise what are perceived as "women's issues," she would jeopardize the respect and credibility as a "serious" professional that she worked so hard and so long to establish.[9] Or, a third example, the staff of a UN Secretary-General who are charged with vetting candidates for leading peacekeeping operations or the facilitator/mediator of a formal peace negotiation might feel justified in saying that it is too hard to find any "qualified" women candidates because they are unaware and unquestioning of the masculinist assumptions built into their conceptions of "qualified."

To this point, we have been talking about the ways in which what appears neutral is actually gendered, thus disadvantaging women who don't live up to apparently "neutral, objective" standards which are actually often based not on what is most functionally necessary or efficient, but rather on assumptions about the way people with male bodies and heteronormative social lives would be expected to do them. There are, of course, some institutions where the gendered presumptions are not implicit and opaque, but rather explicit and overt. Perhaps the quintessential example of this is the armed forces, in which the identity of soldier or warrior is seen as isomorphic with being a "real man." In this context where successfully filling the role is synonymous with proving one's manhood, women face a complex set of challenges when they try to simultaneously "do soldier" and "do gender." Any form of femininity a woman enacts threatens to mark her as "not a real soldier"; however, if she fails to "do femininity," she is "not a real woman," a "dyke," a "bitch." So women in militaries have to give a lot of thought to how to manage their presentations of self as both woman and competent worker (soldier/real man), given that the two are seen as inherently antithetical (Herbert 1998). Whether the difficulties they face are more or less extreme than those faced by women in other organizations that are equally gendered, but perhaps less visibly so, is an interesting question. But in either case, women pay a high price for the fact that what come to be thought of as "neutral, objective" standards and modes of functioning are actually premised on male bodies and social lives, as well as on masculine values and interests.

If institutions have gendered presumptions built into their structures, practices, and values, it follows that in order to function effectively they must rely on workers and family members to have the gendered identifications and self-perceptions that make the institutions' gendered roles, work practices, and power dynamics feel acceptable, rewarding, even alluring. And if, as argued earlier, gender is not simply a unitary identity that is socially constructed in an individual once and for all, but rather a more dynamic and complex set of enactments that are context-specific, it follows from institutions' reliance on gender that they must constantly be engaged in processes of managing, producing, and, as needed, altering ideas about appropriate and valued masculinities and femininities. As Cynthia Enloe (1988, 1990b & 2000) so brilliantly shows us, militaries not only employ and manipulate ideas about masculinity to accomplish their ends but are equally dependent upon manipulating ideas about femininity as well – and they put tremendous amounts of thought, energy, and effort into the process. Dyan Mazurana (chapter 7 in this volume) builds on Enloe's analysis to show how power is wielded in the efforts to construct and mobilize the kinds of militarized and gendered identities required for the functioning of non-state armed groups.

So at the same time as institutions rely on particular ideas about gender in order to function, they are also producers of ideas about appropriate masculinities and femininities – and these, in turn, have cultural and structural impacts beyond the bounds of the institution itself. Carefully thought-through military recruitment campaigns, for example, not only deploy images of a particular kind of masculinity in order to attract young men for whom proving their masculinity is appealing; those images circulate in a wider population than only the men who choose to join, culturally valorizing that particular version of militarized masculinity as one worth aspiring to for any man, and as being attractive to any woman. And, as Enloe (2000) demonstrates, it is not only in recruitment campaigns but throughout multiple cultural sites, from soup cans to fashion shows, that the attractiveness of militarized gender identities is produced.

A different kind of example of the way in which institutions are not only internally gendered in their structures and functioning but also, externally, (re)productive of both gender ideology and structural gendered inequalities beyond their own borders can be seen if we return to thinking about refugee camps. A characteristic of institutions that take men as the default assumption both in their own staffing and in their work practices is that they often fail to think about women's needs, priorities, or interests – or even to talk to and ask women about them. This may help make sense of something that would otherwise seem inexplicable: despite the fact that the preponderance of the population in refugee camps are women and children, and that it would seem self-evident that women and adolescent girls need some kind of supplies to handle their menstruation, a 2000 study by the UN High Commissioner for Refugees (UNHCR) revealed that many UNHCR staff were not including any sanitary supplies in the relief packages given to female refugees (Rehn & Sirleaf 2002, p. 37). Although the efforts of women's advocates both outside and within the UN have finally led to more gender-sensitive practices in refugee camps, the example remains an excellent illustration of the ways that the actions (or inactions) of a gendered institution not only function to reproduce ideas about gender (e.g., "women are disabled some days of the month and cannot be counted on") but also to reproduce and even intensify structural gender inequality itself. Without menstrual supplies, women and adolescent girls will remain confined to their tents or huts during their periods, so they will on a regular basis miss school, agricultural activities, and whatever literacy, income-generation or other kinds of capacity-strengthening activities there might be; indeed, they may even have to drop out of them. In other words, the gendered practices of UNHCR staff produced not just short-term inconvenience but longer-term disadvantage, as they contributed to denying women and girls the skills and resources that could enable them to improve their life options once they left the camps.

Our approach to thinking about war

Most people do not bother to ask the question, "What is war?" because they have a sense that they know it when they see it. Pushed to answer, they might describe war as an armed violent conflict between states or sub-state actors, which starts when the first shot is fired and ends when the gunfire stops, whether due to military defeat or a negotiated settlement. Viewed from the perspectives of both women's experiences and feminist analysis, however, this picture of war requires substantial revision.

The experiences of women and the boundaries of war

When looked at from the perspective of women's lives, it becomes apparent that the category "war" itself is problematic. The idea of war as a discrete event with a clear location and a distinct beginning and end does not stand up to scrutiny when we examine women's experiences "before," during, and "after" war, nor when we think about what is required to wage war.

Women's firsthand accounts of war and feminist analysis of war both emphasize that war is neither spatially nor temporally bounded.[10] Rather than seeing war as an aberrant event which suddenly "breaks out" of an otherwise peaceful context, war is seen as a creation and creator of the social reality in which it thrives. War's violence is seen as part of a "continuum of violence" that women experience (Cockburn 1998, p. 80); while it may be a magnification or distortion of "peacetime" violence, it nonetheless draws upon and reflects other social practices. Weapons of violence, and representations of those weapons, travel through interlocking institutions – economic, political, familial, technological, and ideological. These institutions prepare some people but not others to believe in the effectiveness of violence, to imagine and acquire weapons, to use and justify using force to work their will. They prepare some but not others to renounce, denounce or passively submit to force, to resist or accept the war plans put before them.

Practically, feminists see war as neither beginning with the first gunfire, nor ending when the treaties are signed. Before the first gunfire is the research, development and deployment of weapons; the maintaining of standing armies; the cultural glorification of the power of armed force; and the social construction of masculinities and femininities that supports a militarized state (Cohn & Ruddick 2004, pp. 410–11).

When peace agreements are signed, although they may end the organized armed violence, wars are anything but over. Villages, towns, and cities may be in ruins, agricultural land poisoned with chemicals or peppered with landmines; roads and bridges impassable, hospitals and schools mere piles of rubble. The rent social fabric of community and nation will take painstaking reweaving, the wounded bodies and psyches of both fighters and their victims may be beyond repair or require years of careful tending. A surfeit of arms on the streets and in homes threatens to escalate street crime and domestic violence to new levels of lethality. Ex-combatants trained to kill with gun or machete, to destroy what they fear and take what they want, represent an enduring threat to family and community unless psyches are healed, nonviolence (re)learned, and means of livelihood are found. Often, "peace" brings increased levels of sexual violence against women and girls, and leaves female- and child-headed households struggling to subsist in a world where rights and resources redound only to men.[11]

Refusing the conception of war as a discrete event, though, is not to say that there is no difference between war and peace, or that it is not important to attend to the specific extreme violences that are part of active armed conflict. On the contrary, as Margaret Urban Walker (2009) argues, we deny the reality of women's experiences if we fail to acknowledge that even the same kind of violent act, such as rape, will be experienced differently and have different meanings and consequences, depending on whether it occurs in private as a part of a familiar domestic social relation, or in public as part of armed conflict. Nonetheless, attention to women's lives helps us to see that the familiar binary of "war and peace" obscures a far more complex reality, and obliges us to problematize the images and assumptions built into terms such as "post-war" or "post-conflict."[12] Our study of women and war, then, cannot look only at (what is conventionally understood as) war itself, but must also analyze the processes and institutions that are productive of both war and gender, and the ways in which those two are intertwined.

War and gender

Something about war that is so taken for granted that it has, until recently, entirely escaped analysis in the mainstream international relations literature is that war is a profoundly gendered practice, both at a practical and symbolic level.[13] Practically, although both men and women experience many of the same phenomena, such as sexual assault, injury, torture, displacement, loss of livelihood, and the death of loved ones, they do so in related but distinct ways. The differences in how they experience these are due to many of the different facets of gender relations, including: men and women are differently embodied; because they symbolize different things to their communities and their opponents, they are targeted differently and their injuries have different social impacts; they have different responsibilities to their families and communities, and thus end up differently in harm's way; their different livelihoods, access to the cash economy, and ability to own and inherit property all impact the resources they can access to aid in recovery.

War fighting itself has historically been seen as a practice engaged in predominantly (although not solely) by men; it is also symbolically and practically linked to norms of masculinity. That is, it is a practice which – on the surface at least – relies on combatants' strength, toughness, courage, aggressiveness, and violence. It is a sphere in which both state militaries and armed militias promise to make men out of boys; where being "a good soldier" is synonymous with having the characteristics of being a "real man"; and where "male bonding" is seen as crucial to a fighting unit's effectiveness.

Despite this deep association with masculinity, however, women's labor has always been central to war making. State militaries have historically depended on women as everything from nurses, clerical workers, sex workers, faithful wives, and patriotic mothers to pilots and trainers of pilots, drivers, teachers and workers in war industries – and now the roles women play directly in militaries are far wider.[14] Armed groups depend on women and girls as combatants, porters, messengers, spies, weapons smugglers, cooks, sex slaves, and "bush wives." Nonetheless, women's roles have consistently been either unacknowledged or represented as tangential in order to protect war's "masculinity."

Many feminists, while analyzing the ways in which war is gendered, at the same time challenge the view that it is "naturally" so. In particular, they challenge the view that male biology leads men to be "naturally" warlike, pointing out first how much work it takes to get men to be willing to kill and to risk their own deaths. Basic training, which aims at breaking down men's individual identities and reconstructing them as soldiers; training and drilling, which aim at bypassing conscious thought and making the use of weapons a rote process; and the emphasis on creating bonded units which motivate men to fight and kill out of love and loyalty to their buddies, rather than out of supposed aggressive impulses directed at the enemy – all of these belie the idea that warfare is somehow a natural outgrowth of male characteristics.

Feminists also point out that much of war's execution requires activities and attitudes that are far from the picture of violent, aggressive masculinity that is seen as isomorphic with war. Soldiers in state militaries must be subservient to their leaders and obey orders. They must be their own housekeepers, ironing their own clothes, sewing on their own buttons, and keeping their own quarters spotless. They must care for and help each other in a web of interdependence. Although some soldiers are in direct combat roles, the vast majority of soldiers in state forces spend their days cooking and cleaning; ordering, transporting and storing supplies; gathering information; maintaining their equipment; communicating with others; arranging entertainment and recreation, and carrying out the many more not overtly aggressive activities that are required for militaries to function. In other words, rather than being embodiments of masculine violence, many of the actual activities soldiers engage in would be culturally coded as "feminine," were they not taking place within an institution which is itself coded hyper-masculine.

Viewed in this light, war's masculinity can be seen not as a "natural fact," inherent in war, but rather as a carefully produced and policed social construction. This was articulated with stark clarity by the (then) commandant of the US Marine Corps, General Robert H. Barrow, in the context of US debates over whether women should be allowed in combat positions:

> War is a man's work. Biological convergence [i.e., deploying women] on the battlefield would not only be dissatisfying in terms of what women could do, but it would be an enormous psychological distraction for the male who wants to think that he's fighting for that woman somewhere behind, not up there in the same foxhole with him. It tramples the male ego. When you get right down to it, you have to protect the manliness of war.[15]

Arguably, the vehemence of opposition to allowing openly gay men to serve in the US military can be seen as rooted in the same need to protect the "manliness of war" and, thus, of the identity of the soldier; if men who are seen as "not real men" can be good soldiers, being a member of a military can no longer be a guarantor of manliness – that is, of hegemonic (heterosexual) masculinity (Cohn 1998). In this light, manhood, rather than being the prerequisite for a soldier, can be seen to be its reward.

Which wars? Which global processes?

All wars are deeply gendered, in the preparations made for them, the kinds of masculinities and femininities required to support and conduct them, the effects they produce, and the processes that attempt to recover from them. Understanding the specific ways in which any particular violent conflict is gendered will not only help us better understand the experiences women and men have of that war; it will also enable us to have a more realistic and accurate understanding of the war itself.

This book is largely focused on recent and current wars. Many analysts believe that there has been a fundamental change in the nature of warfare since the end of the Cold War. In organizations such as the UN and humanitarian NGOs, and among humanitarian specialists, terms such as "complex political emergencies" or "protracted emergencies" are used to denote armed conflict-related disasters of prolonged duration with complex causes and sets of actors, high degrees of infrastructural and social breakdown, and high degrees of civilian involvement (whether as "collateral damage" in the overall breakdown, or as targets, or as perpetrators). Another influential framing of the nature of current wars comes from Mary Kaldor (1999), who coined the term "new wars" (p. 1) to mark what she asserts are three major ways in which current wars are distinct from earlier ones. She sees major changes in: (1) war's goals (from geopolitical, state-centric goals, often framed ideologically, to goals framed more in terms of particularistic identity politics); (2) war's methods (from territory conquered and controlled physically by state-based, centralized military organizations, or, in the case of guerilla warfare, by capturing "hearts and minds," to territory controlled through the use of spectacular violence to create fear and through destroying whatever makes that territory habitable); and (3) war's financing (from centralized and state-based to decentralized and dependent on external resources, including "remittances from the diaspora, 'taxation' of humanitarian assistance, support from neighboring governments, or illegal trade in arms, drugs, or valuable commodities such as oil or diamonds or human trafficking" (Kaldor 1999, pp. 6–10). This last change reflects the role of economic globalization in weakening the control of state regulation and facilitating the flow of licit and illicit trade across borders.

Some writers have questioned how analytically useful it is to stress the discontinuities between current and earlier forms of war. For one thing, talking about "new wars" tends to obscure the existence of some major current wars, such as those in Iraq and Afghanistan, which are not the wars this model was designed to explain. Critics also contest the idea that the purposeful strategic targeting of civilians is somehow new, and point to many earlier examples (the routine civilian massacres of Genghis Khan, the tactics of the Crusaders, the fire-bombing of Dresden and atomic bombing of Hiroshima and Nagasaki prominent among them). Some also argue that the civilian/combatant binary is an artificial one (Slim 2008) – one which relies for its construction and naturalization on gender (Carpenter 2005, 2006a; Kinsella 2006). Dubravka Zarkov (2008b, 2008c) offers a particularly trenchant critique of the conceptual and political problems which inhere in some of the analyses stressing current wars' discontinuities from former ones.

Without entering the debate about how new the "new wars" are, it is nonetheless possible to highlight several important aspects of many of the twenty-first century wars in which women are enmeshed. Many current armed conflicts are characterized by: blurred lines between civilians and combatants; high civilian casualties; the direct targeting of civilians; the deliberate targeting of social, political, and economic infrastructure (including health care, education, transportation, and food distribution systems); and the strategic targeting of the most basic means of life and livelihood (e.g., villages and fields are burned, wells poisoned, and cattle killed or stolen). These armed conflicts, unsurprisingly, also often result in mass displacement. And they frequently have very high levels of sexual violence and other forms of extreme interpersonal violence and cruelty. At the risk of stating the obvious, when we think about women's experiences, each of these dimensions of war results in high casualties and terrible suffering.

While some wars still pit the armies of state against state, many more do not. Instead, they involve a complex decentralized set of armed actors within a state, including but not limited to: state-organized militaries, proxy forces and militias, armed insurgent forces and rebel groups, mercenaries and private military forces, and arms traffickers. Despite this, it is a conceptual mistake to think of these wars as intra-state only, for several reasons. First, the wars' violence is typically not contained by state borders; refugees and armed groups frequently flow across borders, straining and destabilizing neighboring countries and widening the spread of armed violence. Further, even without physical border crossings, governments of neighboring countries or far-distant ones may, for their own political reasons, be financially and logistically supporting armed groups (examples include Afghanistan, Democratic Republic of the Congo, Eritrea, Iraq, and Sudan).

It is also a dangerous simplification to think of these wars as "intra-state" because these conflicts are caused, fueled, and sustained by (and contribute to) dynamics that are not only local, but also national, regional, and global in scope.[16] The economic, social, and political distortions produced by colonial histories, the magnification of destruction caused when local conflicts were taken up as proxy wars during the Cold War, and the ravages of neoliberal economic policies imposed by international financial institutions have left legacies of poverty, inequality, violence, exploitation, minimal to nonexistent social support, and weak states rife with corrupt actors. The globalization of capitalist production, trade, and finance leave many countries without the power to regulate their own economies, with ever-increasing gaps between rich and poor, and with whole sectors of the population permanently without the possibility of supporting themselves and their families. It also leaves much of the countries' wealth in the hands of transnational corporations who work with client local elites to ensure the stability that is essential for their extraction of raw materials and production for export. Ensuring stability, however, in the context of great poverty, exploitation, environmental degradation, and the destruction of traditional means of subsistence requires repression, which is bought with ever-increasing militarization. Indeed, as feminist scholars have prominently argued, the current forms of economic globalization and increasing militarization are necessarily inextricably linked (Enloe 2007; Peterson 2008; Zarkov 2008a).

Insurgent groups seeking social transformation or state control fund their activities (now that Cold War patronage is no longer available) through the development of shadow economies, relying on control and exploitation of gold, diamonds, minerals such as coltan, and other natural resources such as timber, as well as through trafficking in drugs and humans. Control of the land that contains the natural resources requires displacing those who live there, and a quick, cheap method is through the extreme violence and mutilation, sexual and otherwise, that sows terror. Labor is needed as well, so abduction, slavery, and human trafficking become another crucial dimension of the shadow economies. The wealth produced in these economies not only funds the purchase of arms and the support of fighters; it also makes many warlords, leaders of insurgent groups and organized criminals rich, significantly reducing their motivation to bring war to a swift end. But they are not the only ones getting rich off of shadow economies, which cannot exist except as part of transnational political and economic processes, both legal and illegal, and the involvement of multinational (largely northern-based) corporations, and the state militaries, non-state militias, and private military companies that support them.

A brief look at one small element of an extremely complex conflict situation will illustrate. The mining of coltan, a mineral used in cell phones, laptop computers and other electronic devices, has been one of the (many) sources of funding for and profit from war in the Democratic Republic of the Congo (DRC). According to a 2001 UN report on the illegal exploitation of natural resources and other forms of wealth in the DRC (UNSC 2001), Rwanda and Uganda, and their proxy militias, have been the primary exploiters of the DRC's coltan. Both governments – along with six of the nine other governments involved in the war in the DRC – have been supported by US military aid in the form of weapons transfers and military training; China and France are the other two biggest arms suppliers to the region (Hartung & Moix 2000). But the exploitation of coltan requires more than military resources; it requires buyers. The UN report identifies multinational corporations as the engine of the conflict, and lists, among them, multiple US-based companies (including Cabot Corporation, OM Group, AVX, Eagle Wings Resources International, Trinitech International, Kemet Electronics Corporation, Vishay Sprague), as well as corporations based in other countries, including Germany, China, and Belgium. Once they process the coltan, it is sold to corporations such as Alcatel, Compaq, Dell, Ericsson, Hewlett-Packard, IBM, Lucent, Motorola, Nokia, and Sony for use in consumer electronics.[17]

Even this briefest of snapshots of but one among many economic elements of war in the DRC (and of none of its formative historical antecedents) quickly makes apparent the folly of simplistic portrayals of this (or any) conflict as simply "an intra-state conflict fueled by age-old ethnic animosities and particularistic identities." This snapshot should also jar any of us whose main picture of the war in DRC comes from media representations of the horrific numbers of women who have been systematically gang-raped, tortured and mutilated.[18] Typically, the image of men and masculinity evoked in these representations is that of a local militia member – African, young, poor, violent, brutal, inhuman, "uncivilized," perhaps drugged, deeply misogynistic, soulless. But what are the images of men and masculinity that are implicit in the fragmentary picture of the coltan trade just above? They include men not only from DRC, but also Rwanda, Uganda, the USA, Europe and Asia – middle-class and middle-aged businessmen and government officials, whose hands are never (physically) bloody, who are upstanding members of their communities, some of whom are the military heroes, corporate wizards and technological masters of the universe so widely culturally admired. They are not the men whom we normally associate with the inexplicably brutal rape "over there." But unless we understand the interrelation of *all* of these masculinities and more, we cannot, in fact, understand those rapes.

In sum, if we want to understand the multiple relations of women to wars, we need to always ask the question: what is the context within which war takes place, within which people fight, suffer, survive and recover? Answering that question will require not only attention to the specificity of local histories and prewar gender relations, but also analysis of the global processes – historical, political, economic, and social – within which they are embedded. Intertwined processes of neoliberal economic restructuring, the globalization of production, trade and financial markets, and increasing militarization will all be at work; the intricacies of their roles as drivers and shapers of particular conflicts will need to be traced, including their shifting (and sometimes contradictory) impacts on women, men, and gender relations in a conflict-affected area, which in turn feed into the dynamics of war. And, as argued above, these impacts must be understood not simply as tangential, collateral effects of processes and institutions that are somehow free of gender themselves. Instead, the institutions which constitute these processes – be they militaries, militias or PMSCs, arms manufacturers or dealers, global corporations or international financial institutions, criminal traffickers of drugs and people, or international trade regulators – are thoroughly gendered themselves. They both rely on and produce particular ideas about masculinities and femininities in order to function, and their valorization of people, ideas, interests, priorities, and practices associated with masculinity over those associated with femininity has constitutive effects on their missions, their organizational practices, and their impacts on women, men, communities, economies, and nature itself.

Women's experiences in war through the lens of gender analysis

All humans are vulnerable in the face of war. There is no one who enters a war with body and mind, family and community, fully shielded by impermeable armor. It is the human condition in the twenty-first century – the fragility of our flesh against the destructiveness of our weapons, and against the power of our institutions to mobilize, construct, and manipulate the identities and ideologies that make us willing to inflict terrible harms on other human beings – or to have others do it in our name.

The theme of women's vulnerability in war seems, at times, to eclipse this universality. It reverberates across centuries and cultures in the age-old war narrative of heroic men fighting to protect vulnerable women, children, and nation. It echoes through the chambers of international policy elites, as they intone their commitment to implement Security Council Resolution 1325 on Women, Peace and Security. And it is voiced by women activists and feminist scholars who insist that we attend to the disastrous effects of war on women, even while we see also the agency, ingenuity, courage, and, yes, steadfast heroism that women muster daily in its midst.

Women's vulnerabilities, like men's, cannot be understood without attending to the particular historical, political, economic, social, and cultural processes that constitute a specific armed conflict and their positions in it. All of those processes are neither independent of gender, nor simply intersecting with gender, but are themselves gendered in both material and symbolic ways, all with practical effects.

Women's vulnerabilities, like men's, also cannot be understood without a multilayered gender analysis, an analysis which moves us away from careless ontological assumptions about women as a "naturally" vulnerable group to a clear-eyed assessment of the manifold ways in which gender, as it intersects with and inflects through other structures of power, plays out in embodied lives – amplifying the vulnerabilities of some while allaying those of others.

The moment that gender is understood as a way of organizing differential access to power, resources, and authority, it becomes clear that no aspect of war's impact on women, women's impact on war, or even war itself can be fruitfully understood, or changed, without a gender analysis. Even something that may at first appear to be ineluctably biological – women's vulnerability to rape in war, for example – is so deeply and multiply constituted by gender that any attempt to address it without a multifaceted gender analysis can only be deeply flawed and utterly inadequate.

Throughout this chapter, as we have explored some of the multiple elements which interactively constitute gender as a structural power relation, including gendered selves/identities, roles/divisions of labor, ideologies, discourses, symbolic meanings, practices and institutions, we have been encountering some of the dimensions of gender that construct women's vulnerability in war. Again, the ways these elements of gender manifest themselves will be context-specific, and women of different classes or geographic locations, for example, will be differently, and to varying degrees, vulnerable. Nonetheless, it is worth refocusing on some of the prevalent ways in which it is gendered power relations, in all their complexity and multidimensionality, which are at the heart of women's vulnerability in war, including the following:

- Gendered roles and divisions of labor, as the "women's work" of gathering firewood and fetching water, leave rural women in many conflict-ridden regions isolated and vulnerable to attack; and the "women's work" of caring for children, the sick, and the elderly leaves women more vulnerable because they are too encumbered to flee quickly.
- The patriarchal presumptions that view women as men's property, men's control over "their" women as a marker of manhood, and women's sexual "purity" as central to patriarchal family honor have the effect of constructing the rape of a woman as a way to attack male opponents, thus making women more highly valued targets.
- The symbolic framing of woman as repository and reproducer of ethnic, national, religious or other collective identities – at the same time as patrilineal descent systems render her unable to pass on her group identity to her children – constructs the rape of a woman as a way to undermine, "ethnically cleanse," or commit genocide against a population.
- These same gendered constructions not only make women more prone to attack; they also increase women's vulnerability *after* an initial sexual assault. If masculine identity or family or group honor cannot tolerate "their" women's sexual violation or "their" women's giving birth to children of "the enemy," women are likely to be cast out, losing the protection of familial social and economic relationships. Lacking places to go and means of livelihood, especially if patriarchal rules of inheritance do not allow women to own property, those women will more likely fall prey to additional violent sexual assaults or exploitative relationships.
- If prevalent gendered meanings include constructions of male sexuality as

heterosexual and as a constant overwhelming force that "naturally" must have an outlet – and this is combined with a vision of women as objects of male desire rather than subjects of their own, and with a normative belief that sees women as lesser beings than men – it is easier for men to feel legitimate in committing acts of sexual violence.

• If militaries and armed insurgent groups are gendered institutions which rely on ideas about valued masculinities and devalued femininities for their very ability to function, they will both attract and produce men with heavy investments in "manly" behaviors and in never appearing weak/feminized/subordinately masculine. And if gender is a "doing" rather than a "being," a context-specific accomplishment rather than established once and for all, the context of para/military rape will be one in which the hegemonically masculine status of a man who does not participate will be in jeopardy. This, too, amplifies the likelihood of women being the victims of sexual violence.

This list could be much longer; these are but a few of the examples that might have been chosen. But they start to illustrate that a multilayered gender analysis is critical to understanding not only women's vulnerabilities, but their experience and agency as they: endure, and sometimes commit, extreme violence; face displacement; participate in fighting forces; organize and take political action; and work to recover from armed conflict and to make, build, and sustain peace.

A guide to the chapters

The first set of chapters in this book aims to give the reader a nitty-gritty sense of what happens to women during wars – of the effects of war's violence and disruption on women's daily lives, and how women adapt to changing circumstances. As stressed in this introduction and throughout the book, to really have a sense of what happens to women, and what their options are, we must always pay attention to the specific context of any given war, and the war's impact on evolving gender relations. What these three chapters aim to do is to delineate some of the key issues, processes, and dynamics that may be traced with more specificity when looking at individual wars. For example, wars regularly have effects on livelihoods – the ways people make a living/sustain themselves and their families (chapter 2), on women's health (chapter 3), and on where and how people live, as displacement is a common feature of most wars (chapter 4).

As we have stressed, how each of those affects women depends not only on preexisting gender relations but also on the broader political, economic, and social processes out of which wars arise and in which they thrive. In **chapter 2**, "Women and the Political Economy of War," Angela Raven-Roberts discusses the importance of situating wars in the globalized political economic relations which shape the causes and consequences of contemporary armed conflict. This approach helps us move from seeing wars as isolated outbreaks of armed violence to being better able to analyze the dynamics which drive and sustain wars; this, in turn, enables us to deepen our understanding of the specific ways in which gender relations are disrupted and transformed. Raven-Roberts focuses on the gendered effects of wars' disruptions of formal economies and livelihood systems, and women's vulnerabilities and opportunities in illicit and informal economies, and the role of the militarization of livelihoods in transforming masculinities.

In **chapter 3**, "Sexual Violence and Women's Health in War," Pamela DeLargy discusses the incidence of rape in wartime, and other forms of sexual violence and exploitation. She addresses both the explanations for and consequences of sexual violence, looking at its short- and long-term implications not only for the women themselves, but also for their communities. As wartime sexual violence has lately been receiving increased global attention, DeLargy also looks at the development of response and prevention policies within the international health, human rights, and security communities, and at some of the unforeseen challenges and unintended consequences of their actions. The chapter then reviews some other important health risks for women in war, focusing particularly on reproductive health.

Chapter 4, "Women Forced to Flee: Refugees and Internally Displaced Persons," by Wenona Giles, looks at processes of wartime displacement and the experiences of women as refugees, internally displaced persons (IDPs), and persons displaced in urban areas. The chapter examines the question of who is forced to flee their homelands and why, looking for the causal roots of displacement, including the use of displacement as a tactic in war. The gendered causes and experiences of displacement and exile for women and girls are examined, specifically looking at long-term displacement, internal displacement, resettlement, and repatriation; the failure of humanitarian aid organizations to respond to the gender dimensions of need and capacity in these various settings is also explored. Giles then describes feminist approaches to the development of the refugee protection regime from the 1970s to the present.

As will be clear when reading this first set of chapters, it is critical to beware of categorizing women as *either* victims *or* agents during war; it is a false dichotomy with deleterious effects. While of course it is true that wars visit exceedingly terrible experiences upon some women (i.e., they can be "victims"), it is equally true that those same women will draw upon the internal and external resources they have to deal with to try to improve their situations (i.e., they have "agency") – it is not either/or. Intellectually, if we fail to fully understand this and see women only as passive victims, it will hobble our efforts to imagine the lives of war-affected women. Politically, when policy makers fail to understand this, they create paternalistic policies which condemn sexual violence but too often fail to take women seriously as political actors. Practically, when humanitarian organizations fail to fully understand this, it leads to international interventions that make women the passive recipients of goods or services, but fail to draw on women's own strengths and capacities to create longer-term, sustainable solutions.

All in all, it would be best to discard the victim–agent dichotomy, and to think instead about both the challenges and opportunities that women confront, and the agency they have and constraints they face in responding to these. This is perhaps particularly important as we turn to the next group of chapters which discuss women who take political action, supporting or resisting war and militarization, and women who are in state militaries or non-state armed opposition groups. Although someone subscribing to the victim–agent dichotomy might too facilely see the previous three chapters as about women as victims and these next three as about women as agents, it would be a mistake. In fact, some of the women in these next chapters are the same as those we met in the earlier chapters, in the sense that they will have had similar experiences; for example, the woman who decides to join either an armed insurgent group or a women's peace organization may make that choice because she has been subjected to sexual violence by men in state militaries. So in these, as in all of the book's chapters, we need to maintain a kind of doubled vision, looking for the multitude of structural and individual factors that shape women's experiences, opening up or restricting their options – and simultaneously attending to women's agency as they make decisions about how to deal with the hand they have been dealt.

In **chapter 5**, "Women and Political Activism in the Face of War and Militarization," Carol Cohn and Ruth Jacobson explore different forms of women's organized collective action in response both to specific wars and to militarization and war systems more broadly. The chapter argues that women's actions never exist somehow in and of themselves as the political acts of (gender-neutral) citizens, but rather are always perceived and represented through a discursive context including dominant tropes of "women's peacefulness" and "the protector and protected." It explores the political impacts of these tropes, as well as the ways that women activists both deploy and subvert them. In this context, the chapter looks at: maternalist political action, both in support of wars and in opposing wars and repressive regimes; feminist transnational political organizing against militarization and nuclear weapons; and women's political action in response to nationalist conflict.

Chapter 6, "Women and State Military Forces," by Jennifer Mathers, begins by noting that the presence of women in state militaries is unsettling to conventional war narratives. Women in militaries challenge assumptions about appropriate roles for men and women within a society and about the nature of masculinity and femininity. The chapter explores some of the key relationships between women, men, militaries, societies, and gender. It looks at the role of militaries in constructing ideas about gender, and the gendering of military institutions themselves, including the debates about women in combat. It examines the experiences of women who serve as soldiers in state militaries, exploring issues including their recruitment, the ways in which they negotiate their conflicting identities as women and soldiers, and the discrimination and abuse which they suffer from male soldiers. The analysis goes beyond women *in* militaries to explore women *and* militaries – that is, to look at some of the many ways that civilian women's lives can be affected by both militaries themselves and processes of militarization.

Although the integration of large numbers of women into state militaries is a relatively recent phenomenon, significant numbers of women and girls have long participated in armed insurgencies and wars of national liberation. **Chapter 7**, "Women, Girls, and Non-State Armed Opposition Groups," by Dyan Mazurana, explores examples from around the world of women's and girls' participation in a variety of kinds of non-state armed groups (NSAGs), including as members of national liberation forces and armed opposition groups and as terrorists. It focuses on gender analysis of: how and why women are pressed into NSAGs or choose to join; women's varied roles within these groups and the effects of women's participation on women themselves, on the tactics and ideologies of the NSAGs, and on the wider social and political structures of the society when the armed conflict ends. It discusses the variety of roles played by women in the hierarchical structure of non-state armed groups, and tracks how and why insurgencies' use of women and girls shifts over time. Most importantly, the chapter shows how those groups are aware of and struggle to manipulate gender (both femininity and masculinity) in an attempt to strengthen their armed struggle against the state.

The final three chapters of the book look at some of the processes involved in ending the period of acute armed violence and beginning the challenging and always incomplete work of trying to build a sustainable peace. This is a critical moment for women and for gender relations. The earlier chapters showed multiple ways in which wars stress, fray, and disrupt preexisting gender relations, at times burdening women with the need to take on "men's" work or making their bodies the terrain on which war is fought, but at times also offering the fluidity and instability for women to take on newly empowered roles and build new senses of self. When wars end, women and men return to their communities, or end up in new ones, and postwar states solidify into new forms. At every step of those processes, decisions are being made – by everyone from the most powerful international institutions to the most local-level humanitarian assistance worker or member of a local council. The chapters that follow explore some of those profoundly gendered processes, and their implications for women.

In **chapter 8**, "Women and Peace Processes," Malathi de Alwis, Julie Mertus and Tazreena Sajjad analyze women's participation in both formal and informal peace processes, and the relation between the two (or lack thereof). They argue that, in order to understand peace processes, our focus must be much broader than the peace table, both temporally and spatially; we need to examine not only the formal and informal processes that lead up to formal negotiations, but also the roots of the conflicts, what the political stakes are, and the roles of multiple parties besides the direct "parties to the conflict," including neighboring states, regional alliances, international bodies, and UN organizations. Crucially, regarding women's participation, they show the importance of going beyond the questions of why and how to add women; we must also be cognizant of the ways that the institutional processes which determine who participates, how peace agreements are drafted, what they contain, and how they are honored, monitored, and implemented are themselves already gendered. UN Security Council Resolution 1325 and its successor resolutions are meant to be tools to intervene in those processes; the authors examine their viability in fostering effective change, highlighting dilemmas of women's representation and effectiveness.

One crucial part of the transition from war to peace is the disarming and disbanding of armed groups and the reintegration of fighters back into civilian life. In **chapter 9**, "Women, Girls, and Disarmament, Demobilization, and Reintegration (DDR)," Dyan Mazurana and Linda Eckerbom Cole explore the question of why DDR has traditionally focused on the needs and security of adult male ex-combatants and overlooked women and girls. It starts by looking at the sociopolitical context in which many DDR programs occur, and introduces the reader to what official DDR processes entail and the actors who carry them out. It then looks at when, where, and why women and girls are so often excluded from DDR programs, as well as why some might choose not to participate in them. The gender-specific challenges women and girls face during peace negotiations and as they attempt to reintegrate into civilian life are explored. Ultimately, the role of gendered assumptions, both within armed opposition groups and also among the DDR planners and programmers themselves, are shown to have decisive impacts on women's and girls' involvement in DDR.

Chapter 10, "Women 'After' Wars," by Ruth Jacobson, follows through the thematic and empirical threads of the earlier chapters, exploring questions such as what happens when women forced to flee (see chapter 4) return home? Or, how does the particular model of liberal democracy advocated by international donors impact women who have forged a public or political voice through the crucible of armed conflict? Thus, the chapter looks at a range of institutions that shape the postwar lives of women and girls, from global financial institutions to regional, national, and much more local institutions in the conflict-affected society. It starts with a look at the analytical and methodological challenges of discussing "post-conflict" societies, followed by a look at some of the principal gendered elements of the "first stage" environment, such as peace support operations and the return of displaced populations. It then focuses on the role of international institutions, particularly the international financial institutions (IFIs), which have the power to

shape multiple economic, social, and political dimensions of postwar societies by imposing policies on nation-states which are often, at the end of war,
in dire need of international funding. It also examines postwar political transformations known as "democratic transition," which demonstrate another
way in which the international community impacts the shape of the postwar
state. Jacobson's examination of these processes highlights the ways in which
they often have the effect of marginalizing or even disempowering the very
women who sustained the socioeconomic fabric of their communities during
the conflict. Unfortunately, women have also tended to be marginalized in
another sphere of postwar recovery – the quest for justice – as Jacobson finds
when examining various forms of truth commissions. The chapter's final
section looks at the phenomenon of postwar "backlash" against women, and
then at women's agency, despite all the challenges, in building a sustainable
peace.

CHAPTER 2

Women and the Political Economy of War

Angela Raven-Roberts

In 2003, during the height of the civil war in Liberia, two women, one Christian and one Muslim, began to organize a series of daily demonstrations and protests outside the US embassy in Monrovia close to the presidential palace of Charles Taylor. Their intention was to embarrass the fighting warlords and call attention to the costly impact of their fighting on all communities in Liberia – especially on women and children, who were suffering terrible atrocities, rape, violence, and loss of education and livelihood caused by the general breakdown of all sectors of Liberian society. These women's protests grew in size and number, finally forcing the rebels and government into a peace accord and the formation of a transitional government which restored peace and organized elections. The outcome was the election of a very well-known Liberian peace activist, Ellen Johnson Sirleaf, who became Liberia's first woman president.

Every year, armed conflict kills and injures thousands of people and damages the livelihood systems and communities of hundreds of thousands more. Wars destroy long-evolved bonds of trust among individuals and within communities, and leave communities devastated both directly, in "war-torn" societies, and indirectly, as the impacts of war and conflict "ripple" out from the centers of fighting in the form of economic disruptions, refugee flows, infrastructural damage, and political instabilities. The ways that war and conflict affect livelihoods, health care, domestic violence, household stability, interpersonal relationships, and a myriad of other "everyday" experiences have been under-explored in traditional studies of war and violence, even and especially as war is changing in the twenty-first century.

Increasingly, however, we are learning more about war's gender-specific effects. We know, for example, that women die at higher rates than men from the indirect effects of war on health and social services; indeed, rigorous studies on the impact of armed conflict on life expectancy show that "over the entire conflict period, interstate and civil wars on average affect women more adversely than men. . . . [Among] civil wars, we also find that ethnic wars and wars in 'failed' states are much more damaging to women than other civil wars" (Plumper & Neumayer 2006, p. 723). We are also learning more about the gender-specific ways in which women experience wars, including but not limited to: enduring increases in sexual violence; dealing with the physical, emotional, and economic challenges of widowhood; feeling economic changes and unemployment more acutely than their male counterparts; coping with damage to or destruction of the local community support structures and networks on which their and their families' lives depend; and enduring gender-specific threats to health and physical security. Many of the ways that women (especially women civilians) experience war differently than men are removed from the traditional "battlefield" physically, and sometimes temporally. Knowing this, we will need to look at the impacts of war more broadly than many other texts do if we want to know what happens to women in wars.

Of course, though, we want not only to know *what* happens to women in wars, but also to gain a more thorough understanding of *why*. In all communities, there is a range of socially constructed, gendered behaviors, roles, power relations, and ideologies that structure the daily lives of men and women, and these are inflected through other social categories such as ethnicity, race, class, caste, religion, or age. Differences in how people experience war have to do with social positioning – between men and women, as well as among them. So it is essential to understand the underlying social structures – how a society is organized – before a war in order to understand war's impact on people during and after. This is not only because people's social locations are likely to shape their relations to war (for example, in the USA, a working-class student without the money to pay college tuition is more likely to join the military than a middle-class student who has a broader array of economic options) but also because the social relations, power structures, divisions of labor, and social and economic infrastructure which constitute the conditions of people's lives are all also likely to be transformed. That is, armed conflicts not only feed off the power structures and inequalities that exist within societies; they also affect and sometimes reshape those power structures at the community, family, and household levels.

In order to understand the gendered impacts of war, including the ways in which war unevenly affects differently located women and men, we need to understand the gendered relations and ideologies and (their intertwining with) other social structures which prevailed before the war. And we also need to understand the nature of the war itself – and the local and global political and economic relations which shape its specific forms of violence. This chapter, then, will look at some of women's nitty-gritty experiences of war and the ways that wars both magnify and reshape gender inequalities. But it will do so while contextualizing those wars in the globalized political economic relations which shape the causes and consequences of contemporary armed conflict.

This chapter will review key issues in the current analysis of contemporary conflicts. It will explore how a political economy approach to war can deepen our understanding of the gendered impacts of war and the specific ways in which women are involved as agents as well as victims, and as winners as well as losers, in the complicated trajectories of war and violence.

Where are the women?

The study of contemporary armed conflict and political violence has attracted and is informed by a wide variety of disciplines that attempt to define war's characteristics and account for its impact and long-term consequences. Apart from political science and international relations, the study of armed conflict, peace, and related topics is of interest to sociology, anthropology, psychology, development studies, geography, environmental studies, public health and the medical sciences, as well as international law and security and cultural studies.

War studies have also been of interest to feminist scholars. Over the last twenty years, a considerable body of feminist literature and analysis has developed which critiques standard theories of war. It also offers a more nuanced explanation of how men and women, and the constructions of masculinities and femininities, are shaped by armed violence, and how they respond to conflict and manage its consequences. Feminists are also involved in attempting to construct analytical frameworks for understanding and making "sense" of war economies and their impact on the complexities of gender-based violence and torture in conflict situations (see Text Box 2.1).

There are, as this book portrays, diverse approaches within feminist analysis itself that contribute a range of perspectives to the analysis of war. Because the majority of conflicts are taking place in the regions of the global South, the contributions of postcolonial feminists are critically important, concerned as they are with reviewing the dynamics of colonial relations and the impact of imperialism on the various regions affected by war. At the same time, it is also important to consider the evolution of processes of militarization and gender ideologies within the "metropole" or heartlands of the global economy.[1] What will be of significance is the ways in which the discourses of feminists who analyze western institutions and ideologies are able to interact or interface with those reviewing specific geographic localities. In particular, it is important to avoid essentializing the experiences of "Third World Women" and representing them as a homogenous category with no acknowledgment of differences and aspirations based on class, race, history, and location.

The question that serves as a title for this section, "Where are the women?" is one that Cynthia Enloe has consistently asked when looking at war and militarization, and has inspired other feminists to ask. In her most recent book, *Nimo's War, Emma's War: Making Feminist Sense of the Iraq War* (2010), Enloe discusses eight women (Nimo, Maha, Safah, Shatha, Emma, Danielle, Kim, and Charlene) in the war between the United States and Iraq, and examines the very different ways in which those eight women experience the war. Among the Iraqi women, Shatha is an Iraqi legislator navigating fierce domestic and international political and economic challenges; Nimo runs a beauty parlor where war is a constant physical and economic concern, as well as a topic of

Box 2.1 Definitions of gender-based and sexual violence

Gender-based violence (GBV)

In 1993, the UN Declaration on the Elimination of Violence against Women offered the first official definition of gender-based violence. Article 1 of the Declaration states gender-based violence or "violence against women" is "any act of gender-based violence that results in, or is likely to result in, physical, sexual or psychological harm or suffering to women, including threats of such acts, coercion or arbitrary deprivation of liberty, whether occurring in public or in private life" (UN 1993).

Article 2 states that the definition of GBV should "encompass, but not be limited to . . . physical, sexual, and psychological violence occurring in the family, including battering, sexual abuse of female children . . . dowry-related violence, marital rape, female genital mutilation and other traditional practices harmful to women, non-spousal violence and violence related to exploitation . . . physical, sexual and psychological violence within the general community, including rape, sexual abuse, sexual harassment and intimidation at work, in educational institutions and elsewhere, trafficking in women and forced prostitution [and] physical, sexual and psychological violence perpetrated or condoned by the State . . ." (UN 1993).

The 1995 Beijing Platform for Action expanded on this definition, specifying that it includes: violations of the rights of women in situations of armed conflict, including systematic rape, sexual slavery and forced pregnancy; forced sterilization, forced abortion, coerced or forced use of contraceptives; prenatal sex selection and female infanticide. It further recognized the particular vulnerabilities of women belonging to minorities; the elderly and the displaced; indigenous, refugee and migrant communities; women living in impoverished rural or remote areas, or in detention (UN 1995).

Sexual violence

"Sexual violence is an overarching term used to describe '[a]ny violence, physical or psychological, carried out through sexual means or by targeting sexuality.'[2] Sexual violence includes rape and attempted rape, and such acts as forcing a person to strip naked in public, forcing two victims to perform sexual acts on one another or harm one another in a sexual manner, mutilating a person's genitals or a woman's breasts, and sexual slavery" (HRW 2003, p. 2).

conversation; Maha deals with being widowed by the war; and Safah navigates coming of age in a conflict-ridden society after surviving a massacre. Among the American women, Emma, the mother of a soldier and a potential army recruit, confronts the contradictions of military recruiting; Danielle serves as a soldier; Kim "fights her own war" at home, managing her family while her husband is away and providing support to other military families; and Charlene picks up the pieces when the war leaves her as the sole income-earner for a three-generation household and as the caretaker for her son, an injured war veteran.

Asking the question "Where are the women?" not only helps us see the specificity of different women's lives in war; it also reveals that we need to *look at war* differently to see its gendered features and gendered impacts. Too often, studies of war look only at the political decision making that starts and ends wars, what happens on the battlefield between combatants with

Box 2.2 Changing gender roles in Afghanistan

In Afghan society, it was tradition that men were the main wage earners and protectors of the family and women worked in the home, taking care of the children. There was a period between the 1940s and the 1970s when education of women was encouraged and women had freedom of movement and work. This changed after the overthrow of the communist regime, and under the strict rule of the Taliban, who enforced restrictive laws on women, forcing them to wear the burqa and forbidding them to work outside the home or even move around in public without being accompanied by a male relative. The Taliban also controlled men, enforcing some restrictions on men's own movements, as well as on what they could wear, the length of their hair, leisure activities, music, and dancing, among other activities, generally imposing a reign of fear over anyone seeming to break (the Taliban's interpretation of) Sharia law. In the current situation, roles are changing again, with some attempts by NGOs, the UN, and other development organizations to target education and economic opportunities for women to counter their previous discrimination. However, similar opportunities have not been created for many men, who now have become the homemakers and feel resentful and disempowered and assert their sense of masculinity through domestic violence or rejoining militant groups.

weapons. Looking for women in war means that we have to see war as an event that takes place not only during the armed hostilities themselves, but across a much wider temporal frame; we need to analyze the social, cultural, political, and economic dynamics and inequalities that precede the outbreak of warfare, and the after-effects that can play out over generations. It also means that we need a wider spatial frame; we need to explore a broad range of locales from households, communities, businesses, towns, cities, countries, and regions, right up through the political and economic processes which are referenced by the term "globalization," i.e., the many ways in which shared international economic and political processes impact countries (see Text Box 2.2). In the next section, we will turn to political economy as a useful tool in our quest for developing this more comprehensive approach.

Political economy as an approach to understanding war and gender

A political economy approach to conflict seeks to understand the relationship between violence and processes of political and economic power. The added value of this approach is that it seeks to widen the context of a given crisis beyond its immediate cause to deepen our understanding of who may be benefiting from the violence as well as appreciating more deeply the various and specific ways in which those who are targeted by the violence are affected. From a gender perspective, this approach can help heighten the specific ways in which patterns of inequalities in political and economic structures and institutions are both shaped and exacerbated during armed conflict and how women's access to power and resources may be affected. At the same time, it helps explain how the social constructions of identity, especially of forms and attributes of masculinity and femininity, are deeply informed by and embedded in the interaction of processes of militarization and political, social, cultural, and economic change.

A gender-conscious political economy approach thus attempts to present a holistic view of the interrelatedness or interconnectedness of different social and economic processes. It is an approach that attempts to capture the totality of the context of war; it brings together historical as well as contemporary factors and causes, and better situates a rationale and motive for acts of violence, or individual or state-sponsored terrorism. A political economy approach can also help explain how war itself can have economic and political justifications and be used to create economic gains and sustain political power (Cramer 2006, p. 329). This approach can also help broaden the linkages between local-level historical and social processes and their interconnectedness to international or global processes. This issue is of special relevance to the understanding of many current conflicts that are often explained away as either emanating from local "tribal or ethnic hatreds" or as the result of irrational behaviors and acts of embittered and socially excluded communities or groups, such as marginalized youth.

Many of the wars that we look at in this chapter and the book as a whole are wars that have taken place since the end of the Cold War. The 1990s saw an escalation of armed conflicts and "state failure." These can in part be attributed to two decades of the "hollowing out of the state" that resulted from the neoliberal restructuring of economies in the global South, perhaps especially the debilitating effects of structural adjustment programs on African countries.[3] (See chapter 10 for a more detailed discussion of neoliberal economic policies and their effects.) In Europe, a major causal factor in the rise of armed conflicts was the fall of the Soviet Union and the tensions caused by competing new elites in the emerging states of the post-Soviet empire.

In this post-Cold War period, many conflict-affected areas have been characterized by violence targeted at civilians and their livelihood systems, the flagrant abuse of human rights and humanitarian law, the availability of a steady supply of small arms and light weapons, the use of extreme tactics to displace communities and plunder their assets, and the development of sophisticated parallel or "war economies" (Kaldor 1999; Duffield 2008; Keen 2008). Some researchers have explained the emergence of these parallel structures as being a rational approach to the impacts of and marginalization caused by globalization, and to the demise of the formal state-system welfare and protection institutions. These are being replaced by informal systems of governance built around coalitions of criminal networks (national and local), traffickers, mercenaries, militias and even, inadvertently, international relief agencies whose assets could be looted to help feed the system. These entities, labeled as "Emerging Political Complexes" (as counterpoint to the humanitarian agencies' own definitions of "Complex Political Emergencies") (Duffield

2001), are able to control populations and large resource-rich regions and to link into the international market through criminal networks to sustain themselves.

War's rupture of livelihood systems

Examination of political economies of war shows that one of the most affected areas of community life is the damage caused by war to livelihood systems. ("Livelihood systems" refers to the various ways in which people "earn a living"; rural livelihoods, for example, include methods such as farming, fishing, or working on coffee or tea plantations as laborers.) Livelihood systems can either be subject to inadvertent damage from conflict or, more commonly, can also be the target of deliberate destruction and "asset stripping," i.e., the robbing of people's resources via means such as burning their crops, stealing their cattle, and destroying their work implements. Marketing and transportation systems are often destroyed and damaged. People are forcibly kept on the move in order to prevent them from returning to their homes and recovering their assets. Families are forced to split up, disperse, enter into refugee or internally displaced person (IDP) camps and to develop alternative ways of earning a living which can result in unhealthy consequences and outcomes.

The damage done to livelihood systems has intensely gendered impacts because livelihood is an arena where gendered relations and ideologies are very pronounced at the community as well as the household and personal levels. In many societies, there are clear sexual divisions of labor within the household or what is known as the "domestic" or "reproductive" economy.[4] For instance, in many agricultural production systems there is a clear sexual division of labor, e.g., men do the plowing, women take care of the milking; women go to the market when it is a chore and men go when it is a privilege; women can do maintenance agricultural labor and men can participate in sowing and harvesting. Often, only men can own land, only men can inherit household assets such as animals and farm tools, only men can obtain credit from state institutions, and only men can represent "the family" when it comes to getting welfare or relief benefits. In pastoralist societies, this sexual division of labor is often very pronounced and includes clear labor-role assignments, extending down to the roles of children: small boys help take care of small animals and younger male adolescents can be sent off for several months at a time to "cattle camps" or seasonal pastures where they live and oversee their family herds. Girls, too, look after small animals, but also help with milking and make household items from animal products, e.g., spinning wool and sewing leather shoes.

In wartime, the normal division of labor within the household is severely disrupted and added burdens are put onto each member of the family (see Text Box 2.3). Children can be forced into more intense productive roles, or

Box 2.3 Double work burdens

As a result of armed conflict and the loss of men to the battlefront or death, women have both to work at home to raise the family and also to seek outside employment to secure an income. In countries such as Uganda, Sudan, and Somalia, women have to take on work normally done by the men, such as farming, trading, and making handicrafts for sale. These roles may often give them some sense of power and independence. However, this is often lost when the men return home and reclaim these activities. If the male of the household is dead, children are pulled out of school to share the labor, resulting in the children's marginalization and their loss of educational possibilities.

even be kidnapped, or sold into slavery to earn money for the household or to repay debts; girls may be forcibly married for the same reason. Men may be forced to migrate or join militias and women have the added burden of taking over their activities. If a male family head of household is away or killed and his wife cannot access credit or cannot arrange for other males to help with plowing the land, then her own and her family's chances of survival are compromised. For example, in the conflict in the 1990s in Bosnia, many women found themselves as heads of agricultural households due to the loss of their husbands either temporarily as soldiers or permanently as war casualties. Many of those women were needed to run their family farms despite the loss of their houses, infrastructural damage that made the sale of agricultural goods much more difficult, the placement of landmines on their property against their will, and the obliteration of more than half of their livestock. These difficulties were exacerbated as many households took in children orphaned by the war, which increased both mental and economic stresses on their households. Many other female-headed households folded under the dual economic pressures of war and gender inequality.

At the same time, changes in formerly strict divisions of labor can result in women taking advantage of new situations. A woman might, for example, be able to gain access to resources which were previously unavailable to her, and then use them to secure a micro-credit loan to start a small income-generating activity. She might be able to trade or to save money on her own without having to share or hand it over to the head of the household. Often women can also take on jobs that were formerly construed as being "men's work," such as setting up a small business.

Another area of livelihood systems that can be ruptured by armed conflict and displacement, with important gender ramifications, is what is known as "social insurance" or family-coping strategies. These are the systems that households have developed over time to deal with crisis situations. For example, in many agricultural communities in Africa there are systems for borrowing money, labor, or work animals from other members of the family and larger networks of extended kin. People in these networks may also help support each other by offering accommodation during displacement and exchanging information on sources of employment and other useful services that go to support family survival. However, during wartime, the families and friends women would rely on or borrow from are often experiencing similar problems. Savings and other accumulated forms of wealth such as land, fruit plantations and animal herds are frequently targeted and either looted or destroyed, and this further erodes the family ability to survive and weather a crisis. The loss of income and assets means that there is nothing to share and no ability to repay debts or return reciprocal favors. In those cases where traditionally it is only men, not women, who could access these networks, women are further at risk of complete destitution during a conflict situation.

Not only does war deplete the assets that network exchanges rely upon; wartime also makes these support networks much harder to maintain. Pre-conflict, many of these networks are maintained by women's social interactions, but these may be severely constrained by male (or even older female) family members in times of war when domestic oppression is likely to increase and households are also likely to be more cautious about their interactions lest they interact with another household that is a threat to them. Displacement creates even more radical ruptures of long-established community relationships. For example, organizations working with women in Palestinian refugee camps in Lebanon note that one of the most lasting impacts of resettlement on Palestinian families is the destruction of their support networks, which previously allowed families and communities to have a level of social insurance when they fell on hard times. Resettled families, from Lebanon to Thailand to Iceland, have trouble re-establishing those networks that had previously been so vital to their survival.

Gendered livelihoods in war's informal and illicit economies

The economic effects of war are often felt the most severely at the margins of social and political life because many of the poorest people in conflict-ridden societies have few marketable skills they can redeploy when they are in a crisis situation. At the same time, lack of formal education can limit people's access to information they need for survival, such as information about where sources of relief can be obtained, information about market conditions and prices, and above all information about their rights and opportunities to legally claim entitlements.

The effects on livelihood systems are felt all the more strongly at the family level as a result of the eroding of formal economies that stems from armed conflicts. Infrastructure is a casualty of war. Some infrastructure damage is incidental, but much of it is purposive. Transportation systems are hit and ports, railways, roads, bridges, and warehouses are damaged or destroyed. Healthcare and education systems, utilities, and communications are targeted and lose the ability to function. As a result, large and small businesses will close down or leave the country and the formal economic system will tend toward collapse, leaving hundreds of workers destitute and without a livelihood. Infrastructure in communities is also purposefully targeted. Militias can block roads and withhold essential supplies, outside humanitarian aid can be delayed or itself subject to looting and destruction.

So during and after war, people are forced to rely on alternative strategies, such as petty trade or even bartering or exchanging goods and services in what is known as the "informal economy." Many activities will involve semi-legal activities. The globalized black market economy becomes entwined with the remnants of the formal economy and creates conditions in which many people come to make a living. These activities constitute part of what Foucault has termed "tolerated illegalities,"[5] which people are forced into and which have been socially accepted as necessary survival strategies.

These illicit economies are important not just for trade in resources such as timber, rubies, diamonds, coltan, gold, and human beings, but also for the day-to-day survival of civilians themselves. Civilians caught up in these conflict zones, without the chance of working in the formal economy, have to manage and plan their own livelihood strategies within these emerging illicit and parallel economies. This participation fluctuates both in its type and in its influence on wars and conflicts. For example, in Mexico, it is estimated that almost 30 percent of the workforce works in the informal sector, with a substantial percentage of those people working in illicit economies, such as the drug trade, human trafficking, copyrighted material copying and theft, and the sex industry. The involvement of such a large sector of the economy in illicit economies is both a result of conflict and a cause of it, especially in the areas the government struggles to control.

Unfortunately, and of special significance for gender relations, a key feature of illicit economies is the re-commoditization of women and children as "resources" to be trafficked and exploited. They are commodified in a number of ways, including as indentured servants and sex workers. That women are especially vulnerable to this kind of commoditization is not a "natural" fact, but a social one, rooted in the gendered economic and social structures which precede the conflict itself, as well as the gendered ideologies bound up in militarization.

Economically, when war breaks out, many women are already in a precarious position. Even before war has weakened formal economies, women's access to them in most places tends to be far more limited than men's. To the extent that women do have access to the formal economy, their employment is often concentrated in government or government-supported service sector positions, in areas such as education, health care and social services. As these are also the very sectors that were diminished or dismantled under structural adjustment programs (see chapter 10), many of these formerly employed women have lost their jobs by the time the war starts, and lost access to the financial and social provisioning resources which, even if small, would afford them more options.

Second, to the extent that women are part of household economies with a defined gendered division of labor and access to resources, men's absence – because they have fled for their safety or to try to find work, or they have been abducted into or voluntarily joined an armed group, or because they have been killed – leaves women and their families in an even more precarious position. And this is magnified by various kinds of gender inequality. If, for example, women are denied the right to own land and other property, access to credit, education, or means of transportation, the resources they can marshal are painfully constrained. Finding sources of income from such a politically and socially subordinate position in a war-torn economy is made even more difficult by infrastructural obstacles; as, for example, when women looking for new sources of income and support encounter cities, towns and roadways damaged by the conflict. Or when healthcare systems have been destroyed and care of a sick family member requires a woman's constant presence.

The intensification of sex industries in war economies also intensifies women's vulnerabilities. While in many cultures children and women (as wives) are normally considered as assets to the household economy, they now become liabilities subject to kidnapping and sexual exploitation. The ready availability of guns that move through and flood illicit economies make the dangers of both all the greater. And although the presence of international agencies in conflict zones can provide aid, the effect is not an unadulterated benefit for women, as the agencies and their personnel themselves become magnets for black marketers, drug and human traffickers keen to sell their wares.

Finally, the commoditization of women is compounded by gender ideologies that represent the presence of women and young girls willing to exchange sex for money as "natural." Thus, soldiers, peacekeepers, and humanitarian workers, all of whom are charged with the duty to protect civilians, appear not to see their own actions when they buy or barter for sexual services as a violation of that duty.

Many people who think about war *see* the sex trade and human trafficking, but regard it as a natural by-product of war making and war fighting. In reality, it is neither natural nor a by-product – rather, it is a key link in the chain of the gendered political economy that produces, sustains and is produced by war and conflict. In war-torn Kashmir, for example, not only have Kashmiri women turned to the sex industry in the absence of other economic opportunities, but the occupying Indian military has imported prostitutes to Kashmir to tend to what they see as the "genuine and natural needs" of Indian soldiers, with an eye toward decreasing high incidences of soldier violence, mental instability, and suicide (*Daily Mail* [Pakistan] 2009). In other words, not only does the Indian military see women's service as prostitutes as natural, it sees it as beneficial to the mental and physical health of the soldiers serving in the conflict zone. To hold this understanding, the Indian military has to see sexual servitude as nonviolent itself, and it must see women's involvement in wartime prostitution as a natural part of the political economies of war and an integral part of the process of fighting. The Indian military recruited professional prostitutes *for soldiers,* counted them as members of the military, gave them basic military training, and put them on a strict regimen of medical checkups to make sure that they remained healthy. Understood as such, wartime sex trades are not just an anomaly or an effect of war but are a crucial part of the political, economic, and sexual production of conflict.

Even in the face of this tremendously intensified commoditization of women in illicit economies, it would be a mistake to view women simply as passive victims. Women are constantly trying to figure out how to manage and make the best decisions and choices they can while under extreme constraint, and often in horrific circumstances. Though their options are riddled with gender discrimination and molded by the gendered nature of the making, fighting, and funding of wars, one of the decisions women are sometimes in the position to make is to participate in illicit economies. While there are political, economic, and survival threats that come from participation in illicit economies, often the women (and men) who engage in these activities are likely to suffer less economically in war than those who cannot or will not enter into those economies.

Women also make decisions to distribute scarce resources among their families, to stay in homes in conflict zones, or to flee to refugee camps or neighboring states. Some women choose to cooperate with insurgent groups for reasons ranging from political and ideological commitments to their own assessments that cooperation is the best way to ensure their physical security and/or their children's. Some women have become forced wives (also known as "bush wives") to such groups in an effort to avoid more brutal wartime sexual violence (see Text Box 2.4).

Becoming a forced wife or establishing some other nominally cooperative

Box 2.4 Becoming a forced wife in Sierra Leone

In Sierra Leone, Fatmata Jalloh was one such forced wife. She remembers that she was a pre-teen selling pancakes on the side of the road to contribute to her family's income when a rebel soldier threatened to kill her unless she agreed to go with him as his "wife." She spent the next two years as a domestic and sexual slave of her "husband," where she cooked for him and cleaned for him, while he protected her from the conflict and provided her with food and shelter. Fatmata explains now that there was no way that she could have left her "husband," since he would have likely killed her, and even if he had not, she would have had no access to food or shelter and would have been vulnerable to other male fighters. In reaction to the stories of Fatmata and others, the Special Court for Sierra Leone ruled that forced marriage is itself a war crime (in addition to the wartime rape that takes place inside of forced marriage) since it involves not only sex but other services and combines wartime rape with essentially indentured servitude. (See Moore 2008) way of dealing with men fighting wars is not the only coping mechanism women use. Some women find that work in the sex trade is their only way to support themselves or their families. Some find ways to capitalize on the fragility and openness of war economies; new opportunities for trade across battle lines, for example, may enable women to sell products and take over economic activities traditionally held by men. Some women become soldiers in state militaries or militias. They join for a variety of reasons which may include: patriotism; nationalism; the economic stability that soldiers' salaries often provide; the (relative) personal safety that comes with having a weapon and the protection of the rest of the state's military; an interest in changing their own status through the educational and resource benefits of military training; and/or a careerist desire to be a soldier. (For a more detailed discussion of women's experiences in state militaries, see chapter 6.)

Women also join non-state armed groups during times of conflict, as fighters or as support personnel. While they may do so under greater or lesser degrees of duress, joining may provide them with a replacement community (and/or family) for the one destroyed by the conflict, a communal source of income and/or food, and a level of protection that neutrality would not afford. In addition, many women join because they support the political causes of these groups, particularly when the groups' agendas include a formal call for gender equality and offer the hope of a new future of equality in a newly founded state. Women who fought in the liberation struggles of countries such as Nicaragua and Eritrea in the 1970s and 1980s enjoyed a marked change of status from their former position as marginalized women – they fought as equals alongside men, achieving high military positions and status. (For a more detailed discussion of women's experiences in non-state armed groups, see chapter 7.) However, after the wars many of these same women found themselves relegated to their former positions, as, in the competition for jobs in the new states they had fought so hard to establish, men once again dominated economic space and women were expected to go back to their prewar roles.

In short, while some women join state or non-state military groups as a coping mechanism or a last resort, other women join them (despite their heavily gendered structures) for political reasons, or economic reasons, seeking an alternative livelihood in resource-scarce situations. Still, these decisions cannot be understood as gender-neutral (that is, precisely the same as nominally similar decisions made by men) because they always take place within the constraints of gendered social, political, cultural, and economic structures, and within gendered conflicts.

At this point, it is important to make something that is *implicit* in the above section more *explicit*. As is evident when we look at many of the forms in which women can find a way to subsist within the political economies of war, it is crucial to understand that these livelihood options are not only illicit or informal, but also heavily militarized.

Militarization and the shifting terrain of gender

No examination of the gendered political economies of war would be complete without a review of the impact and effects of processes of militarization as they evolve and are transformed or mutated from the formal international level to informal local-level processes and institutions. Militarization has been described by Cynthia Enloe (2000) as: "a step by step process by which a person or thing gradually comes to be controlled by the military or comes to depend for its well-being on militaristic ideas" (p. 3). Enloe's work has been essential in charting the gendered and transnational connections which have bound industrial and commercial enterprises as far as the Philippines, Japan, and South America to the military-industrial complexes of the United States.

The concept has been elaborated further to describe the ways in which militaristic values and priorities have shaped actual strategies and means of making a living during conflict. The term "militarized livelihoods" is introduced by Lautze (2008) in describing the livelihood systems of regular soldiers in the Ugandan army. Lautze notes that there are intricate economic contradictions in war-torn areas, where soldiers at once support their families and need their support; where steady sources of income are often only found in militaries; and where patronage relationships spread violence, even while the itinerant lifestyle of soldiers and the stresses of frequent relocation of army families produce distinct relationship, social, health, and financial liabilities. The significant point here is that, by focusing on the ways in which militarization informs and shapes all actors in a conflict zone, from the insurgents, soldiers, and civilians, to all members of their community, as well as those involved in humanitarian intervention and peacekeeping, one can track the insidious economic, military, and political processes that infect social and everyday life at the local level.

In the context of destroyed or dysfunctional institutions, militarization becomes the defining principle which governs local-level politics, the local economy and even culture. Militarization sets up interlinked systems, reacting and responding to each other. People are driven into militias or soldiering to find protection or to earn a living, as well as perhaps to avenge or revenge former grievances. Both formal and informal military and militia systems offer consistent sets of organization, hierarchy, and a feeling of belonging to something. Both offer certain bonds of fellowship and a common identity and valorization of self, which is all the more important to people in times of conflict and disorder. The influence of both systems goes deep into the community, as the rest of life is informed and shaped by the strategies and outcomes of militarized processes.

Militias, insurgents, and armies in the deepest forests of Southeast Asia, the mountains of the Caucasus, the islands of the Pacific, or conflict zones in Africa and South America are networked into the global economy through the illicit trade in small arms (i.e., guns and other weapons that can be easily carried and concealed, and are not only easy for adults to use but for children and youth as well). They may inhabit failed states with no access to international markets for formal trade items, but globalization provides the only link between these local groups and the wider world through arms trafficking, drugs, communication equipment, and, most importantly, transnational cultural commodities such as CDs, videos, and DVDs. These cultural exchanges and influences have also been identified by researchers as playing a key role in the shaping and informing of new forms of youth and militarized identities and perhaps also influencing a certain glorification of violence and misogynist behavior (Reno 1998, p. 257).

It is in this nexus – of the practical reworking of male and female roles and identities that is always a part of war; the militarized institutions and processes that have replaced failed state institutions; and the economic, military, and cultural networking of local groups in the global economy – that one could perhaps locate new emerging processes of patriarchy and, in particular, a "predatory patriarchy." A predatory patriarchy is not only a reworking of male and female identities but, more significantly, a reconstruction of masculinities infused with and constituted through violence and aggression. These constructions distort, override, and replace traditional constructions of male identity as well as traditional values governing relationships between men and women, and even between generations.

The processes of militarization amongst the Dinka of Southern Sudan, for example, have led to profound changes in intergenerational relationships and respect for the elderly, adherence to laws regarding the treatment of noncombatants in conflict, and even the institution of marriage itself (Jok 2001, pp. xv, 211). Women come to be viewed by armed groups not only as workers, sex slaves, and servants, but also as the collective "womb" to reproduce and ensure the continuity of the group itself and reproduce other warriors. This change in perspective toward women may account for the increase in violence toward them both from within the group and, most especially, from the enemies of the Dinka who attack Dinka women not just as individuals, but as military assets and as symbols of the warrior enemy's "honor." This is but one instance of what has become a familiar pattern. In wars that are constructed along and through what are seen as ethnic, racial, religious and/or national differences, women come increasingly to be seen as biological and social reproducers of group members needed for defense, as signifiers of group identities, and as agents in political identity struggles (Peterson 1999).

Male identity as it has been shaped by protracted conflict – or, more accurately, the identities of young males in the global South – has also recently become the focus of political and intellectual attention. Across the globe, there is a concern about the nature of male youth violence, especially violence meted out to internal community members as well as enemies. The attraction of youth militias to the violent role models in Hollywood films or "gangsta" rappers or "rude boys" of the reggae genre has been much commented upon and attributed to the spread of new technologies of communication and globalized popular culture (Richards 1996). At the same time, there is a new genre of analysis that equates these actions with a "crisis of masculinity," a crisis that arises from and mirrors the crisis in economic, social, and cultural life that has been perpetrated across many regions of the world first under colonialism and then due to neoliberal restructuring of economies.[6]

The issue of "crisis of masculinity" is at the heart of masculinity studies, a subfield of gender studies, which has drawn attention to the impact of history and social change in the definitions of masculinity and femininity (Disch 2000). This is of particular relevance to those communities that have experienced colonial subjugation. Colonialism, globalization and contemporary conflict will have significant impacts on manifestations of masculinity and identity roles both in the private and public sphere (Vlassenroot & Van Acker 2000; Dolan 2002). Analysis of rampant sexual violence occurring in a particular community, then, will require tracing earlier contexts of gender relations between men and women in that community, and the ways in which masculinity and femininity were expressed and defined in preceding periods. Tracking the emergence of virulent or predatory masculinities, like tracking the processes of militarization, also involves the review of the impact of internal and external factors on youth socialization processes, given particular forms of political and economic disempowerment. A consideration of changing notions of sexuality itself is also important to factor into these debates.[7] At the same time as tracing these large-scale social processes, though, it is also key for those wishing to understand the emergence of malignant forms of masculinity to research why some men are able to resist and do not exercise or manifest normative violent masculinities.

New research from the Democratic Republic of the Congo (DRC) (Baaz & Stern 2008, 2009; Meger 2010) and Northern Uganda (Finnström 2008; Coughtry 2011) has provided useful information on the complex ways in which local populations have responded first to the impact of colonialism, which affected land tenure and local governance systems, and then to the patronage systems of postcolonial leaders which led to the emergence of new elites and entrepreneurs who manipulated access to governance and production systems to suit their own interests. In the DRC after the fall of President Mobutu,[8] newer power complexes emerged to fill the protection and governance gap based around real or reconstructed ethnic loyalties. These kinds of historical processes have impacted intergenerational relations and constructions of childhood and masculinity and femininity and the expectations and aspirations arising from them. The involvement of male youth in new militias has also resulted in a reworking of status and authority within families as sons have overthrown fathers, and the use of violence is legitimized to enforce power, control, and masculine identity within both the household and the community.

Gender analysis that crosscuts historical, anthropological, and political economy inquiries may help make sense of the staggering rates of rape and other forms of sexual violence in parts of the DRC. These kinds of analysis can also be helpful in avoiding some of the racist narratives that have been developed around youth and violent conflicts, especially in Africa. Finally, they could contribute to the development of more imaginative ways of dealing with young male militia members accused of violence; responses that can factor in and address the processes of their own disempowerment and how those become encoded in malignant forms of masculinity may be more effective than merely punitive approaches that might provoke further violence and resentment.

However, there is also a danger here. To the extent that the "crisis of masculinity" literature focuses on male youth violence as a threat to state stability, it tends to pay less attention to its effects on women and girls, or to female youth altogether. Further, if the "crisis of masculinity" is framed as deriving from young males' lack of access to the forms of empowerment and resources that traditionally defined male roles, the "policy solution" may be seen simply as finding ways to re-empower men. While that might result in greater state stability, would it transform "predatory patriarchies" back into somewhat less perniciously violent patriarchal forms? And even if it did, for whom, exactly, is that a good solution?

Conclusion

This chapter began with a story of how women, severely affected by war, were nonetheless able to mobilize and draw attention to their plight and actually exert social and political power to effect change, create peace, and move a country out of violence. Women, as the chapter shows, are not just wars' victims but also its fighters: they are hit hard economically, socially, physiologically, and psychologically, but still must act; they are faced with substantial hardship but also with some opportunities. They have to navigate the impact of war on the household economy as well as on the formal economy, seeking to adapt to the changes and to take advantage of any opportunities these changes may offer.

The key message of this chapter is that it would be a mistake to think that women experience wars as men do, and to conclude that gender-neutral analysis is a useful and appropriate tool. Women need to be understood as participants, as protestors, as agents making the best of bad circumstances, even while they are also war's victims. At the same time, war changes and challenges men's roles and identities, which in turn also has profound impacts on their relationship to women, including on their marital relations, household burden-sharing, and the ways each looks to the other to fulfill nurturance or protection roles within the family or within the bounds and cultures of their society.

Therefore, when we ask "Where are the women?" in war, it leads us to see a lot of things that traditional understandings both of war and of women's and men's experiences of war would render invisible. It leads us to see that wars are not just military but political and economic, and that the political economies of war often reach far beyond the immediate locations and times of the fighting that are usually taken as defining where wars happen and when they start and end. By specifically focusing on war's impact on women, their roles and their identities, one can also disaggregate and drill deeper into the impact of war on men. The result is a deeper understanding of the overall profundity of violence, and the ways armed conflict challenges, changes, and distorts all social and cultural norms. Above all, this wider vision of war and its impacts makes clear the necessity of preventing wars.

QUESTIONS FOR DISCUSSION

1   Contrast and compare some of the key ways in which men and women are affected by war physically, emotionally, and economically.

2   How have women been able to respond to the changes and challenges caused by conflict and displacement?

3   Discuss why "male identities" would be threatened by women taking over men's roles whilst they are away in battle. Why would this cause tension in the families when men return from war? How do you think these tensions should be addressed?

SUGGESTIONS FOR FURTHER READING

Clarke, Yaliwe (2008) "Security Sector Reform in Africa: A Lost Opportunity to Deconstruct Militarised Masculinities?" *Feminist Africa* 10: 49–66.
Federici, Silvia (2000) "War, Globalization and Reproduction." *Peace & Change* 25(2): 153–65.
Marchand, Marianne H., and Runyan, Anne Sisson (eds) (2011) *Gender and Global Restructuring: Sightings, Sites and Resistances*, 2nd edn. New York: Routledge.
Morgan, David (2006) "The Crisis of Masculinity," in Kathy Davis, Mary Evans, and Judith Lorber (eds.), *Handbook of Gender and Women's Studies*. London: Sage, pp. 109–24.
Peterson, V. Spike (1999) "Sexing Political Identities/Nationalism as Heterosexism." *International Feminist Journal of Politics* 1(1): 34–65.
Shepherd, Laura J. (2008) *Gender, Violence and Security: Discourse as Practice*. London: Zed Books.

CHAPTER 3

Sexual Violence and Women's Health in War

Pamela DeLargy

While armed conflicts can bring harm to anyone, men, women, girls, and boys may confront very different dangers. War has particular risks for the health and safety of women and girls, deriving from both social and biological factors. When conflicts involve (or even target) civilians, these risks can multiply. Whole communities are uprooted and forced to abandon their homes and belongings to seek safe haven. Depending on the type of warfare, they may be forced to flee numerous times, never able to re-establish stability within the family or engage in normal livelihoods. They often end up in crowded, unsanitary, and insecure environments, without even the most basic of services.

Women and girls bear the burden of insecurity and loss of access to health care in ways that have both immediate and potentially long-lasting implications. The lack of reproductive health care can have devastating implications for pregnant women and lead to untreated sexually transmitted infections (including HIV) or inability to prevent unwanted pregnancies. Lack of basic security provides a milieu for sexual violence, which has both immediate and long-lasting health and psychological effects. In most societies, women and girls are the caregivers for both the elderly and the very young; this can make it difficult to flee a life-threatening environment and can also add tremendous physical and psychological stress during a crisis. Even if their lives are not threatened, displacement can leave girls without basic menstruation supplies, malnourished (contributing to later anemia and pregnancy complications) or vulnerable to sexual exploitation by those providing relief supplies.

Of course, women experience war in many different ways, depending on the type and intensity of conflict as well as their differing roles, social status, and relationships. During the 2011 war in Libya, for example, a Bengali guest worker may have had fewer resources for escaping urban warfare than a middle-class Libyan woman whose family could drive to a border; however, the Libyan woman's ethnicity or political affiliation may have put her at special risk of attack. Even with these differences, though, women have a number of risks in common. This chapter outlines these risks and some of their short- and long-term implications for women and their communities. We begin by examining sexual violence – as a serious threat to the health and well-being of women and girls; as a destroyer of cultures and communities; and as a peace and security issue. We also describe the increasing global attention to sexual violence in wars and the corresponding development of response and prevention policies within the international health, human rights, and security communities. Some of the most difficult challenges to understanding and responding to sexual violence are also summarized. The chapter then reviews some other important health risks for women in war, particularly reproductive health risks.

Sexual violence in war: an age-old problem of contemporary concern

Never have I heard or read of such brutality. Rape! Rape! Rape! We estimate at least 1000 cases a night and many by day. In cases of resistance there is a bayonet stab or a bullet. We could write up hundreds of cases a day . . . .

From the diary of an American missionary in Nanjing, China (McCallum 1937, as cited in Hu 2000)

The atrocities these women have suffered distil evil into its basest form. . . . The US condemns these attacks and all those who commit them and abet them. And we say to the world that those who attack civilian populations using systematic rape are guilty of crimes against humanity.

US Secretary of State Hillary Clinton, speaking to Congolese women, August 11, 2009 (Clinton 2009)

Rape in wars in Africa has had a lot of attention in recent years, but it is not just an African problem. Conflicts with high levels of rape between 1980 and 2009 were most numerous in sub-Saharan Africa. But only a third of sub-Saharan Africa's 28 civil wars saw the worst levels of rape – compared with half of Eastern Europe's nine. And no part of the world has escaped this scourge.

The Economist, "War's Overlooked Victims" (*The Economist* 2011)

Sexual violence against women in war seems to have existed since human beings began waging war on each other. In her 1975 book, *Against Our Will*, Susan Brownmiller was the first to chronicle evidence of rape in the Homeric epics, in writings on the Crusades, the American and French revolutions, and on through the Vietnam War. Indeed, for centuries the issue was treated as an unfortunate but inevitable phenomenon, not worthy of much attention. The abduction and rape of tens of thousands of women during the partition of India and Pakistan in 1947 was seen as mere "collateral damage" in that conflict. In 1971, the rape of even more women followed during Bangladesh's independence war with Pakistan, again to little global outcry.

But history shows that wartime rape is not inevitable; in some wars it is prevalent and in others not. Some armed groups condone sexual violence and others do not. And even within a single armed group or a particular unit, some combatants commit sexual violence; others do not.[1] Indeed, there is also historical evidence of sanctions against rape in warfare, ranging from the death penalty imposed for rape by Richard II in England in 1325 to the

FARC's execution of its own members who commit rape in Colombia today (see chapter 7 in this book).

Today, tacit acceptance of sexual violence in conflicts is no longer the standard response. Perceptions have changed dramatically over the past two decades; the widespread systematic rape in the Balkans and the sexual assault on almost a quarter of a million Rwandan women horrified the international community. Kosovo, East Timor, Liberia, Sierra Leone, and Darfur followed, all conflicts in which sexual violence was systematically used as a tactic of war. Contemporary international media coverage and the growing involvement of celebrity activists have raised awareness about the horrific levels of sexual violence and torture suffered by women and girls in eastern Congo. The UN Secretary-General regularly speaks out about the situation, and the US government has established a massive foreign assistance program to help rape survivors there and to strengthen security for women (Kelly 2009). Policy makers, human rights activists, health providers, and military and religious leaders have all begun paying attention to the issue. The UN Security Council has passed landmark resolutions (see Text Box 3.1) on sexual violence in war as a security issue, and humanitarian agencies are engaged in dozens of initiatives to raise awareness of the issue, with hopes of protecting women in war zones and ending impunity for perpetrators.

But what does sexual violence in war mean, exactly? It can mean many things, depending on the type of conflict and the patterns of violence within it. It can mean rape, either opportunistic, as in a village where girls have no protection, or as a purposeful, systematic tactic of war, designed to demoralize a whole community, terrorize people into leaving their land, and/or humiliate men by proving they cannot protect their families. It can mean sexual torture, a means to terrify a population into submission or to extract information. It can mean sexual slavery, such as abduction of women or girls to cook and provide sexual services within non-state armed groups, or the abduction of women to sexually service soldiers in state militaries, as in the case of the so-called "Comfort Women" in the Second World War (see Text Box 3.2). It can mean sexual exploitation, such as the pressure on women to exchange sex for humanitarian relief or protection. It can mean forced pregnancy, as a means to "dilute" the bloodlines and ethnic identity of the enemy. It can mean forced termination of pregnancies or sterilization to prevent reproduction of a population group. It can mean rape or sexual torture of boys and men to humiliate them and break their ties to the community or to other combatants.[2] In some conflicts, all of these kinds of sexual violence may exist simultaneously; in others, different manifestations may arise at different stages of conflict. Although not every conflict includes widespread sexual violence, all too many do. And the dynamic of sexual violence may itself actually perpetuate conflicts, because it touches on the highly charged notions of family honor and integrity, often starting cycles of revenge and retaliation.

Box 3.1 UN Security Council Resolutions on women, peace, and security[3]

Since October 2000, the UN Security Council has adopted five resolutions on women, peace, and security. While the first, 1325, addressed a range of issues from sexual violence to a more equal decision-making role for women in conflict prevention, conflict resolution, peace processes, peace-building and governance, three of the follow-on resolutions have focused more narrowly on sexual violence. A sixth resolution, 1983 on HIV/AIDS, also links efforts to combat HIV/AIDS with campaigns against sexual violence and for the rights of women.

- **Resolution 1325** (2000) was the first UN Security Council Resolution (UNSCR) to link women to the peace and security agenda. It recognizes that women are disproportionately affected by conflict and calls for their active participation at all levels of decision making in conflict prevention, conflict resolution, peace processes, post-conflict peace-building, and governance. UNSCR 1325 further calls for the effective protection of women from sexual and gender-based violence in conflict settings, for the mainstreaming of gender perspectives in all aspects of peace operations, and for the promotion of women's rights and gender equality.
- **Resolution 1820** (2008) was the first UNSCR to recognize conflict-related sexual violence as a matter of international peace and security. It calls for armed actors to end the practice of using sexual violence against civilians to achieve political or military ends, and for all parties to conflict to counter impunity for sexual violence and provide effective protection for civilians. It also calls on the United Nations and peace operations to develop mechanisms to prevent and respond to sexual violence, including through the training of personnel, the deployment of more women to peace operations, the enforcement of zero-tolerance policies and the strengthening of the capacities of national institutions.
- **Resolution 1888** (2009) strengthens the implementation of UNSCR 1820 through establishing effective support mechanisms. It calls for the appointment of a Special Representative of the Secretary-General (SRSG) to coordinate UN efforts to address conflict-related sexual violence, as well as for the rapid deployment of teams of experts and advisors to situations of concern. UNSCR 1888 also calls for the inclusion of the issue of sexual violence in peace negotiations, the development of approaches to address the effects of sexual violence, and improved monitoring and reporting on conflict trends and perpetrators.
- **Resolution 1889** (2009) addresses obstacles to women's participation in peace processes and peace-building, as prescribed in UNSCR 1325. It calls for the UN Secretary-General to submit to the Security Council a set of indicators for use at the global level to track implementation of UNSCR 1325.
- **Resolution 1960** (2010) provides an accountability system for implementation of UNSCRs 1820 and 1888. It mandates the Secretary-General to list in the annexes to annual reports those parties credibly suspected of committing or being responsible for patterns of sexual violence in situations on the Council's agenda. Relevant sanctions committees may take action against listed parties. UNSCR 1960 also calls for the establishment of monitoring, analysis, and reporting arrangements specific to conflict-related sexual violence.
- **Resolution 1983** (2011) builds on the first Security Council action on HIV/AIDS, UNSCR 1308 (2000). It addresses HIV/AIDS programs in peacekeeping in the context of security sector reform, disarmament, demobilization, and reintegration processes, with particular attention paid to women and girls. It calls for the linkage of efforts to combat HIV/AIDS with campaigns against sexual violence and for the rights of women.

> ## Box 3.2 Sexual slavery: the "comfort women" of the Second World War
>
> During the Second World War, the Japanese Imperial Army abducted and held thousands of women from China, Korea, and the Philippines in sexual slavery in camps to serve Japanese soldiers.[4] Yet the International Military Tribunal for the Far East, held in 1946 to investigate and prosecute war crimes, did not include this violation. For almost fifty years, surviving "comfort women" had no formal recognition of the crimes committed against them. Then in 2001, a ten-year campaign by civil society in countries around the world resulted in the Women's International War Crimes Tribunal for the Trial of Japan's Military Sexual Slavery, which gathered testimony from survivors, former military officers and others, and proved that the enslavement of the women was an orchestrated policy of the Japanese government and a violation of international law. The judgment recommended that Japan officially recognize responsibility and compensate the survivors. The case is significant for bringing the language of sexual slavery into later legal deliberations on international criminal conduct and the law of war. But it is also famous for finally giving those who suffered a sense of justice.

International law

International humanitarian law applies in times of armed conflict to protect people and regulate the means of warfare. The most important of these laws are the so-called Geneva Conventions of 1949 and their Additional Protocols.[5] These are binding on both governments and non-state actors and require that the parties to an armed conflict differentiate between civilians and combatants and make provisions to protect civilians. The Geneva Conventions accord women specific status and protection related to their role in childbearing and their needs for privacy, and also prohibit sexual violence, now considered a war crime. However, it was not until the International Tribunals after the wars in former Yugoslavia and Rwanda that the first prosecutions of rape as a war crime were pursued.[6] The specific mention of sexual violence in the statute which established the International Criminal Tribunal for the former Yugoslavia (ICTY) was a milestone for recognition of rape as a serious crime (Engle 2005). In 1996, the ICTY issued the first international criminal indictment for sexual violence against women. At around the same time, the International Criminal Tribunal for Rwanda (ICTR) for the first time specifically included rape and torture as "crimes against humanity," a term which had originated in the 1907 Hague Convention.[7] Mass rape was also first raised as a factor in genocide in the ICTR when the judge ruled that sexual violence could constitute genocide if committed with the intent to wholly or partially destroy a particular group. In the trial of small-town mayor Jean-Paul Akeyesu, the court observed that the rape of Tutsi women resulted not only in physical and psychological destruction of them as individuals, but also of their families and communities.[8]

The International Criminal Court (ICC), established in 1998 and whose authority entered into force in 2002, further established rape and other forms of sexual violence as international crimes and established special procedures for protection of victims and witnesses during prosecutions (Park 2007). When the ICC was being established, it was not a foregone conclusion that the so-called Rome Statute (which established the court) would include attention to rape. But women's groups around the world organized a successful global advocacy campaign to ensure that the Court would both prosecute sexual crimes and also protect those who testified.

Although international law is now very clear that rape in war is a serious crime, the application of such law is far from guaranteed. Concerns about international law are usually not in the forefront of combatants' or their leaders' minds, and not all countries have agreed to the jurisdiction of the ICC. The US, for example, is not a signatory. Others who *are* signatories have not always abided by ICC decisions; Sudan, for example, has not recognized the ICC's indictment of President Omar Al-Bashir as legitimate, and neighboring countries he has visited have also refused to extradite him. Many members of the African Union feel that the ICC has unfairly focused attention on African leaders, despite similar violations in other regions.

While many countries coming out of war where rape was prevalent (such as Bosnia) seem to want to deny it, some others have recognized that the issue must be dealt with openly as part of the recovery and peace-building process. The Special Court for Sierra Leone, established after the war to prosecute atrocities, ruled in 2008 that abduction of women and girls as so-called "bush wives" for combatants was a crime against humanity. In Liberia, a special court was established to deal with the continuing high levels of violence against women and included provision for survivors to be able to testify without being seen by the alleged perpetrators.

Other instruments and conventions, which are considered "soft law," also provide a basis for the rights of women and girls to be protected against sexual violence. The most notable is the 1979 Convention on the Elimination of All Forms of Discrimination against Women (CEDAW) which includes gender-based violence as a form of discrimination. The later Declaration on Elimination of Violence Against Women (1993) sets out very specific prohibitions against a wide variety of types of violence against women, including rape, sexual assault, trafficking, and female genital mutilation. Although not legally binding, they do provide a strong moral basis for holding signatory states accountable. In 1994, the UN established the post of Special Rapporteur on Violence against Women to monitor the implementation of these instruments. The recent attention to sexual violence in the agenda of the Security

Council (see Text Box 3.1) has dramatically improved awareness of the problem and established new mechanisms of reporting and accountability. But it remains to be seen what impact this will have on the lives of those being victimized every day throughout the world.

Seeking to explain the prevalence of sexual violence in armed conflicts

Both prevention of conflict-related sexual violence (CRSV) and the provision of appropriate care to its survivors require a solid understanding of CRSV's causes and consequences. In any conflict, it will be impossible to fully understand CRSV without close attention to the specific political, economic, social, and gendered history of the context from which the conflict arose. At the same time, the sheer scale and prevalence of sexual violence across conflicts seems to cry out for some broader theoretical analysis of its underpinnings, and in recent years a wide range of scholars and researchers have sought explanations for wartime sexual violence. Some have sought universal explanations; others have focused on specific types of conflict settings. In some cases, their analyses overlap with or are complementary to each other's and sometimes they contradict and compete, partly because they derive from different disciplines and use very different methodologies. In an attempt to simplify a sometimes confusing set of theories, we summarize below a few schools of thought, with the caveat that, in most conflicts, there are many factors at play and no one explanation fits all.

Biologically driven sexual aggression

The long-held popular notion of rape as an inevitable by-product of war most probably reflects the theory that sexual aggression is biological – something hardwired into the male of the species – and that only social control and cultural taboos restrain this impulse in peacetime.[9] According to this perspective, the breakdown of social controls in a chaotic conflict situation results in greater numbers of rapes. While the simplicity and biological determinism of this conceptualization may be appealing to some, it fails to adequately explain the phenomenon. It does nothing to help us understand the organized, purposive employment of rape as a weapon in war. Nor can it explain why levels of sexual violence vary so widely across different times, places, and types of conflict; why, for instance, did insurgent groups in Sri Lanka, Eritrea, Guatemala, and El Salvador not engage in sexual violence while state militaries in those same conflicts did? It also does not help us understand why rape becomes targeted toward one group rather than another. Nor why the great majority of men, even in situations where there would be no sanctions, do not rape. In short, this explanation is not very useful for understanding the complexities of the issue.

Patriarchy

Some analysts focus on patriarchal gender relations in explaining sexual violence in war.[10] Patriarchal cultures are characterized by misogyny, women being considered as the property of men, and women's overall subordination within the family; in exchange for this subordination, women are supposed to receive protection from their male family members. In this analysis, the belief that women are lesser than and should be subordinate to men leads men to feel entitled to rape women. Additionally, the patriarchal view of women as men's property underwrites the notion that rape is simply part of the legitimate bounty of war: the winners would be seen as entitled to "take" their opponents' women, just as they would loot other property.

While both of those explanations might shed light on opportunistic rape, the organized use of rape as a tactic of war can also be seen to draw its power from patriarchal gender arrangements. Because a critical aspect of patriarchal male roles is men's protection of "their" women, attacks against enemy women can be employed as "proxy" attacks against enemy men, graphic proof of the men's powerlessness, humiliating and demasculinizing. In other words, rape of women assumes this particular meaning (as a weapon against men) only within the context of patriarchal gender relations. While in this sense patriarchy seems like a useful contribution to understanding some kinds of rape in wars, it cannot explain variation; since patriarchy is by far the dominant mode of gender relations in the world, including in most conflict situations, it cannot, by itself, explain widely differing prevalence and patterns of wartime rape.

Militarization

Another school of thought relates sexual violence to militarization itself. In all cultures, people are socialized to get along with others and resolve daily conflicts nonviolently, and there are strong taboos on excessive violence, especially on the taking of life. Yet these values and behaviors are at cross-purposes with the goals of an army or rebel group at war, where wounding and killing is considered not only acceptable, but also sometimes admirable. Thus, most armed groups resocialize their members, purposefully breaking down civilian attitudes and behavior and inculcating the values, beliefs, and attitudes required for combat. Old ideas about acceptable levels of violence must be changed; combatants must not only be willing to risk their lives but also to kill. Old identities must be diminished and a new soldier/fighter identity must be created. Across time and throughout the world, combatants have predominantly been male and the resocialization process has been accomplished, in part, by creating new "hyper-masculine" identities, foregrounding attributes of aggressiveness, competitiveness, misogyny, violence, and dominance.

Another common strategy for getting combatants to risk their own lives, and to be willing to take someone else's, is the persistent portrayal of the enemy as both less than human and a danger to the community, culture, religion, and/or nation. Portraying the enemy as a danger enables combatants to justify violence as an act of self-defense or protection, and the dehumanization of the enemy helps soldiers to overcome any qualms about such violence.

Another important aspect of military training is the building of group solidarity and loyalty. Combatants are led to bond strongly with each other and taught that their highest allegiance must be to their unit; this reinforces the power of peer pressure and group solidarity, as well as the willingness to kill to protect one's buddies. The group solidarity so valued in military culture can play a problematic role. Peer pressure can have a whole group following the lead of a few members, especially when refusal gets translated into "not being a real man," the bad impulses of a few individuals can lead to collective rape and violence. Even where there are sanctions against such behavior, group loyalty can result in failure to report peers who break the rules.

All of these aspects of militarization – the redefinition of violence as acceptable or even desirable, the dehumanization of the enemy, the development of strong group bonds – take place through gendered processes, and all of them can manifest in sexual violence given the right circumstances. This combination of factors seems powerful in understanding wartime sexual violence, and may well be the best explanation, for example, for the collective attacks on women in East Timor after the vote for independence in 1999; the departing Indonesian militias were furious at the humiliation of defeat, and the rapes were a last effort to act out their anger and show their disdain for the Timorese (Powell 2006).

Yet the militarization explanation also has limitations. While militarization has many aspects that might be conducive to sexual violence and to impunity, there are also militaries and rebel groups which do not engage in or tolerate such behavior, which punish violators, and for whom respect for civilians is a driving value – or at least a strategy for mobilizing political support from the community. Clearly, militarization cannot, by itself, account for the variation in levels of sexual violence in armed conflicts; for that, other historical, social, and cultural dynamics must be explored.

Rape as a strategy of war

Thus far, we have mostly focused on the impulses, attitudes, constructed identities, and processes of militarization which may result in sexual violence. But these individual or group motivations are generally not what turn rape into an actual strategy of war. What happened in the Balkans and in Rwanda were not individual or collective impulsive actions, but was the premeditated and purposeful use of collective sexual violence as a strategy of war (Allen 1996). In these and other conflicts, rape is purposively used to terrorize and

demoralize civilian communities in an attempt to pressure them to stop supporting competing groups or to force them to leave an area. Widespread and
public rape can be a remarkably effective way to clear out a population when
the goal is to claim territory. This seems to be one of the driving factors in
the rampant sexual violence in eastern Congo and was evidently part of the
strategy of Libyan military forces against Libyan rebels as well.

But there is an even greater association of collective rape with conflicts that
are highly "communalized" or ethnically based – where the war is no longer
between groups of armed combatants but waged specifically on the hated
enemy group's civilian population.[11] In such cases, rape becomes not just violence against a particular individual but also highly symbolic action against
a whole group, planned and condoned within groups of armed forces, rather
than the action of an individual or a small group of combatants. Such situations are conducive to gang rapes and to rape as a purposeful public spectacle.
The rape of thousands of Indian and Pakistani women during the partition in
1947 was carried out as just such a tactic of war – to demoralize, punish and
humiliate a whole people – and also to ensure that those fleeing the territory
would never return. That the same thing happened in 1971 when Bangladesh
split from Pakistan reinforces one theory that rape may be particularly prevalent in ethnic conflicts involving actual partition of territory; it is a type of
violence meant to ensure that the separation is irreversible (Hayden 2000).

Rape as "ethnic cleansing"

In situations of highly charged ethnic competition and animosity, rape takes
on yet another dimension – as a tool of "ethnic cleansing." During the Balkans
War, Serbs repeatedly raped captive Bosnian women in notorious "rape
camps" until they were pregnant, holding them until it was too late for an
abortion. The goal was to force them to bear children with mixed ethnicity,
thus diluting bloodlines and destroying Bosnian ethnic identity. Systematic
rape simultaneously accomplished two military goals: humiliation of the
enemy and ethnic destruction (see, for example, Allen 1996; Fisher 1996;
Salzman 1998; Lentin 1999). The Rwandan genocide undoubtedly represents
this strategy at its most vicious. Thousands of Tutsi women were raped by
Hutu attackers, many times in gangs and sometimes by HIV-infected men
seeking to infect their victims, all as part of an explicit goal of exterminating
a whole people. The use of widespread rape as a strategy for ethnic cleansing
has now been considered in international law as possible evidence of genocide (see previous discussion of the ICTR).

This use of rape as a strategy for ethnic cleansing clearly relates back to our
discussion of patriarchal culture. Rape as part of ethnic cleansing happens in
societies where women's value is seen primarily in their reproductive roles as
the carriers of the culture, and where men's control of the reproductive power
in their families is central to upholding the honor of the family and larger

community. In such societies, "enemy" women are attacked precisely *because* they represent the honor of the group and reproduce the culture. Further, because in a patrilineal society the ethnic identity of a child is determined by the ethnicity of the father, a child fathered by an attacker from another group will belong to the attacker's group, not the mother's, so that pregnancy creates a social and cultural crisis for her whole community. In such cultural systems, any child born of rape by the enemy is not only a constant reminder of the humiliation of the community, but is also, by paternity, "an enemy in the house." It is no wonder that women in such circumstances often attempt to end their pregnancies. If a raped woman does give birth, it is not uncommon for the baby to be abandoned or neglected after it is born, and for both the mother and child to be stigmatized and ostracized by her community.[12]

Domestic violence

The purposeful use of rape and other forms of sexual violence as tactics in warfare is particularly appalling and has rightfully garnered much public attention. However, it is also important to remember that the most prevalent form of violence against women throughout the world, both in times of peace and war, is domestic violence, and war has been shown to have some specific influences on domestic violence.[13] First, it seems that the economic and social pressures of conflict, especially in cases of displacement and loss of livelihood, can increase the likelihood of domestic violence of all types. In Palestine, for instance, there have been marked increases in incidents of domestic violence during times of heightened tension in the Occupied Territories (UNFPA 2005b, pp. 1, 10; UNESCO 2010; *The Electronic Intifada* 2010). Similar patterns have been documented in many other parts of the world.

In many armed conflicts, when men are away fighting, gender roles change. Women begin to take on more economic and social responsibilities, sometimes including roles that are taboo for women under normal circumstances. Indeed, in many countries, women have been empowered by the absence of the men in their communities. This can have many positive benefits for all in the long run. But it can also become a problem for relations between men and women when men return to their communities after the conflict ends or when they complete their military service. In postwar East Timor, for example, domestic violence increased dramatically when men returned to find no jobs and their wives or sisters now making decisions for the family. The frustrating employment situation, combined with the violent responses men developed during their many years as independence fighters, had negative consequences for women (UNFPA 2005c; AusAID 2008). The newly independent country quickly had to establish special training for police forces to deal with domestic violence, including rape (Report of the Secretary-General 2002; VPU of East Timor Police et al. 2002). The levels of domestic violence in the families of American servicemen returning from Iraq and Afghanistan have also become a serious issue for the US military (Marshall, Panuzio, and Taft 2005).

While domestic violence can include sexual violence, there is yet another, perhaps surprising, motivation for rape in marriage within the context of war – and that is to force pregnancy on unwilling wives/partners. One study in South Sudan refers to women who "fear rape by militia, rape by men who distribute aid in exchange for sex and rape by husbands who demand that they replace dying children . . ." (Macklin 2004). The "replacement" factor is particularly important in post-conflict settings where groups may be motivated to increase their numbers either for security reasons or for the survival of the ethnic group or nationality. The ideology of replacement is not only at the family or community level; it is very common for newly independent countries or for countries at war to adopt formal pro-natalist policies, including restrictions on contraception.

Consequences of sexual violence

Physical health

Sexual violence, particularly rape, has serious physical and mental health consequences for survivors. Physical consequences include injury, infection, unwanted pregnancy, and HIV. Mental health effects can also be serious. They include anxiety, post-traumatic stress disorders, depression, and even suicide. Although awareness of sexual violence in many conflict situations is increasing, and there are now standard protocols for care of survivors,[14] only a small minority actually get the immediate medical care that they need. Rape can involve serious damage to a girl's or woman's body, including abrasions and tears which may require suturing. Antibiotics are required to prevent infection. Emergency contraception provided within 72 hours can prevent pregnancy. Post-exposure HIV prevention, a 28-day treatment with antiretroviral drugs, can prevent HIV infection. But all of these treatments require that the survivor have access to a functioning health clinic with the necessary equipment and supplies and trained personnel. The chances of this in isolated areas of poor war-torn countries are slim. Even wealthier countries such as Bosnia have suffered near complete collapse of health services during war. Consequently, many survivors go without treatment, suffering physically on top of the psychological stress they bear (Jansen 2006). Even where services are available, some survivors are ashamed to seek care or cannot get their family to support them in getting care. They may realistically believe that their future life options could be severely limited if others knew they were raped.

In the most horrible cases of gang rape and sexual torture, a woman or girl can require specialized surgery to repair the damage to her body (see Text Box 3.3). Panzi Hospital in Bukavu in the DRC and the HEAL Africa Hospital

Box 3.3 Obstetric and traumatic fistula

One of the saddest consequences of lack of health care during delivery is the development of *obstetric fistula*, a fissure between the bladder and the vagina or the rectum and vagina caused by prolonged obstructed labor without appropriate emergency obstetric care. In such cases, the baby almost never survives and the woman is left injured and incontinent for the rest of her life if surgical repair is not available. Such women usually end up isolated and stigmatized, many even rejected from their families due to their smell and inability to carry out their normal roles. In South Sudan, immediately after the peace agreement with the North, the Red Cross and UNFPA set up a surgical program for fistula repair. Women who heard about the program on the radio came from all over the region, some walking for days, in hopes of being able to have a normal life again. They had been living in misery for years without any chance for treatment. The surgery was life-changing – they could now be fully part of their communities again. But they at least had survived; in a place without emergency obstetric care, obstructed labor most often means death for both baby and mother.

Rape or penetration of the vagina with foreign objects can also cause a *traumatic fistula*. Such fistulas are normally much rarer than obstetric fistulas but can be significant in situations where rape and sexual torture is prevalent, such as in eastern DRC.

in Goma are hospitals that once specialized in emergency obstetric care and other gynecological surgery but are now famous for their care for victims of the most violent forms of rape and torture, having treated thousands of women and girls who have been raped in the long war in that region (Longombe, Claude and Ruminjo 2008). Such damage is so prevalent in the region that these hospitals have trained hundreds of medical staff to respond to the needs of rape survivors in smaller clinics throughout the area.

Psychological health

The mental health consequences of sexual violence can also be debilitating, particularly if rape is accompanied by extreme violence or torture or if the rape is done in front of or by family members or neighbors, as happens in some conflicts. In Sierra Leone, for example, a common pattern of attack involved forcing parents or children to watch or even participate in the rape of women and girls in their own families or villages. This was carried out as a way to terrorize the community and to impart maximum trauma on family members (HRW 2003). In Darfur, as well, village attacks included the public raping of women and girls, with the goal of humiliation and stigmatization (Leaning & Gingerich 2004). If rape is public and accompanied by severe humiliation, the trauma is particularly difficult to cope with. In addition to being a severe and prolonged trauma to the individual, it also affects that person's relationship with the community, which is critical for recovery (Hagen & Yohani 2010). If the trauma of the sexual violence is accompanied by an unwanted pregnancy or fear of HIV infection, it is even more difficult for victims to recover and deal with day-to-day life. It must also be remembered that some rape survivors may be the *only* survivors of an attack, with other victims involved having been killed. In such cases, the violence they experienced may actually be of lesser concern to them than the horror of watching loved ones suffer and die.

What is considered most helpful in terms of psychological support for victims of sexual violence varies across cultures. In western cultures, it is commonly believed that individual victims benefit from counseling, and that talking about their experience can help them to work through the trauma. In other cultures, this type of therapy would be totally inappropriate and probably harmful. There has recently been more commitment to supporting indigenous modes of healing which have been shown to be more effective than western style therapy in many contexts. In Liberia, some traditional women's societies provided ritual purification ceremonies which both seemed to help survivors and also smoothed their re-entry into their communities.[15] Spiritual support can also be a significant source of healing, and faith-based groups are becoming important actors in the response to sexual violence. One thing that seems to help rape survivors in any culture is the opportunity to receive social support from other women, whether or not that support specifically focuses on the experience of sexual violence. The opportunity to engage in productive activities and having a future orientation also seem to facilitate healing. Indeed, many trauma specialists have highlighted the critical importance for victims of having something to do, someone to look after; this provides victims something to focus on other than the past, and it seems to be the most significant determinant of recovery (Hobfoll et al. 2007). This understanding has begun to influence humanitarian assistance programs in ways that emphasize empowering aid recipients and supporting livelihoods in addition to simply providing basic supplies and services.

The impact of denial, victim-blaming and stigmatization

When some of us escaped from the rebels and went back to find our families, we got disappointed. They called us names. They said we were defiled and they didn't want us anymore. So what could we do? We had to live so we went to Freetown and sold ourselves just to survive. Didn't we already go through enough? Why do we have to do this now? What did we do wrong? Only God can help us now.[16]

Young woman who had been abducted by the Revolutionary United Front (RUF) in the war in Sierra Leone

Many long-term impacts of wartime sexual violence stem from the ways in which families and communities respond to the victims. In wartime as in peacetime, women are often accused of being complicit in their rape, and survivors of sexual violence stigmatized, blamed for bringing shame to their families and communities, and mistreated or cast out (Salzman 1998; Josse 2010; Mackenzie 2010). In societies all over the world, many men cannot bear either the thought of another man having intimate knowledge of their partner or the humiliation of being unable to protect her or prevent this shame on his family. Common responses are to deny the event or to blame the victim. In such cases, rape becomes much more than a traumatic incident in the life of a woman; it becomes a defining variable, determining the course of her life from then on.

If victims of trauma are stigmatized by their families or communities, they may not be able to access medical and psychological care even where it is available and will thus suffer doubly. When raped women or girls are marginalized or rejected by their families and communities, they not only lack the social support they need for healing, but they also may lose economic support, the chance to complete an education, or even ever to marry. In all too many cases, they become destitute, with very few options for survival other than prostitution or other forms of exploitative sexual relationships which expose them to further violence or to HIV. Those who seek to relocate to a place where no one knows their history become prime targets for trafficking. If the woman has a child from the rape, she may be forced to make a tragic choice between keeping her child and staying with her family.

Unsurprisingly, in some cases the level of stigma attached to rape inhibits survivors from telling anyone that the rape occurred; in others, it is the family members who ignore or deny it. As the husband of a Kosovar woman who had been abused by Serbian militia said to a reporter when asked about rape, "No, my wife was absolutely not raped while she was being held. If she had been raped, then I would not be able to let her come home and take care of the children and be my wife."[17] In this case, the husband's care for his family required a denial of the facts, accommodating a culture in which raped women brought shame onto the family. In a situation like this, the wife will have to forgo or hide any efforts she makes to get medical treatment or counseling, and she will have to pretend that the rape never happened for the rest of her life. The availability of social support, including faith-based support, seems to help destigmatize rape, as seen in Liberia and Sierra Leone, as well as some parts of the DRC (see Text Box 9.3). But we still need to understand much more about questions such as why the experience of rape is so stigmatized in some situations and less so in others, and why some men, families, and communities seem to be able to accept and support those who have suffered, yet others cannot. Overall, the stigmatization of rape survivors is an area that needs much more investigation.

Challenging traditional mores and changing social and cultural attitudes requires a long-term process of education, awareness-raising and the mobilization of community and religious leaders. This type of social change is difficult to bring about even in the best of circumstances. In conflict situations, where social chaos may make people cling ever more firmly to their traditions, such change in attitudes may prove impossible, but times of crisis may also present opportunities for new social dynamics.

Responses to sexual violence

Over the last twenty years, both local women's organizations and the international humanitarian community have mobilized around the problem of sexual violence. Nowadays, much more support for survivors is available, and attempts to prevent such violence and to punish those who are responsible for it have increased. In this section, we look at some of those responses.

Documentation and research

In addition to academic research on causes of sexual violence in conflict, there have also been many efforts to document experiences in specific conflicts and to record patterns and trends, with an eye toward developing appropriate response programs. Human rights organizations have sought to document sexual violence as a human rights violation and for use in prosecutions. Recent Security Council resolutions made it mandatory for all peacekeeping missions to report regularly on patterns and trends of sexual violence, leading to an upsurge in efforts to collect data on incidence and prevalence in the mission area. Because of the major difficulties in collecting and analyzing data on this very sensitive issue (in part because usually only a small proportion of rapes are reported), most quantitative reports are simply not reliable indicators. However, new methodologies for data collection are rapidly emerging, combining health service statistics, police records, survey data, and other sources to estimate trends and patterns. Still, this remains an extremely inexact science for many reasons, and some activists have questioned the use of scarce resources for developing documentation methodologies, arguing that resources could better be used for treatment of survivors. The use of data on sexual violence in conflict is also fraught with politics – as noted by some legal scholars, parties on all sides will always have different interests in distorting the data (Aranburu 2010).

Care and treatment – what can be done for survivors?

For some years there has been consensus on the health needs of survivors. Health workers all over the world have been trained in the medical protocols of care, and there has been a concerted effort to ensure that necessary supplies are available in humanitarian situations caused by conflict.[18] Many local and international organizations, as well as government health services, now provide medical care, counseling, and safe shelter for survivors. But financial support for setting up such services is extremely limited, and accessing them requires that survivors have sufficient resources and safety to get there. Even where resources and security allow, ensuring confidentiality for those undergoing treatment is sometimes a challenge, as seen in Darfur where Sudanese law required medical workers to file police reports on cases. Health workers also need specific training to deal with this sensitive issue; they require not only new healthcare skills but also better sensitivity toward survivors. This is a challenge for health workers who may have their own deeply entrenched attitudes and sensitivities about sexual issues.

Protection and prevention

There are many ways in which women and girls can be protected in conflicts and humanitarian situations. Focused security sector attention, such as neighborhood policing, can improve safety and make it easier for women and girls to carry out their daily activities with confidence. Humanitarian agencies' provision of fuelwood and water can relieve women of the risk of leaving a camp or community and walking long distances in unsafe environments to gather these supplies. In areas where cooking is done on woodstoves, the provision of more fuel-efficient stoves can reduce the requirements for wood, meaning less need for women and girls to gather wood in dangerous places. Alternately, women who do go out to gather supplies can be provided with security escorts, such as those the peacekeeping forces of the African Union/ United Nations Hybrid operation in Darfur (UNAMID) have been providing in some sites in Darfur. The design of camps for refugees or internally displaced persons now almost always includes safety considerations such as ensuring that latrines are not in isolated places and that camps are well lit (WCRWC 2006). Community sensitization to the risks for women and girls can also improve safety and security, and campaigns to raise awareness can help to reduce stigma. When wars end, protection and prevention of sexual violence depend very much on the rapid re-establishment of security services such as trained and functional police forces. And these security services must be responsive to the specific threats of sexual violence and exploitation. In Sierra Leone, for example, the police established Family Protection Units, special police stations with personnel trained to deal with mediation of domestic disputes, crimes against children, and sexual violence.

Legal redress and ending impunity

One of the most important means of preventing sexual violence is ensuring that possible perpetrators know that they will be punished. The capture and punishment of perpetrators is more challenging than it might at first seem; it requires having the right laws criminalizing sexual violence, a functioning security sector (police and prisons) and a judicial system that can manage prosecution. Unfortunately, in many places it was the lack of these things in the first place that contributed to the outbreak of war. In other conflict sites, war has destroyed these institutions and their infrastructures. In DRC, for example, most provinces do not even have a prison. In many countries, even after a war ends, and even if a survivor has the financial and social support to take a case through the legal system, there is very little chance of pursuing justice for victims of sexual violence. In response to this, the international community has started to ensure that prosecution for such crimes is included in support for national reconstruction programs.

Corruption can also be an obstacle to prosecution: if police, judges or prison guards are not paid a living wage, as is the case in many poor post-conflict countries, then it is easy for perpetrators to derail the case for relatively little money.[19] In one case in Kivu in eastern Congo, for example, the training of police and judges and the reform of the laws, combined with community sensitization, made it possible for the authorities and a rape survivor to pursue, arrest, and try her attacker. The perpetrator was found guilty, received a long prison sentence and was sent off to the only prison facility in the country. Unfortunately, the guards in that facility are not paid a living wage and thus regularly depend on bribes. The man bribed his way out of prison for a pittance and soon returned to the community.[20] This is a graphic example of how multiple components of the overall justice system must be restored after a war in order for rule of law to prevail. Every piece of the puzzle must be in place, yet restoring all the components may require a massive investment of financial and technical resources that most countries have trouble mobilizing. The rebuilding of security, justice and rule of law in a post-conflict society is a long-term task; short-term humanitarian assistance cannot do the job and most international donors lack systems that support long-term recovery.

Unintended consequences of well-meaning action: some special considerations around sexual violence in conflict

As public awareness of the horrible effects of widespread sexual violence in conflicts has grown, pressures from human rights and women's groups to respond to it have also grown. Unfortunately, sometimes the resulting responses have not only been ineffective but also, in some cases, harmful. Sexual violence in war is such a complicated social, cultural, and psychological issue that responding to it is fraught with possibilities for making policy and program mistakes. Over the last decade, many lessons have been learned about what *not* to do to help survivors; for example, we now know that well-meaning programs to treat survivors that have not respected privacy and confidentiality have actually resulted in deaths, due to retribution by the accused perpetrators.

Also, evidence is mounting on what is and is not effective for ending impunity. While "naming and shaming" perpetrators may seem appealing, it can also result in community or individual retaliation. In contexts where draconian punishment of rape has been established on the assumption that it would deter violators, there are some concerns that rapists are then more likely to kill their victims to avoid identification. Clearly, many questions and dilemmas remain in terms of how to design the most effective policy and program responses to the issue. It is important for those working in this area to keep an eye open for unintended consequences of good intentions, especially where programs are developed without sufficient attention to local culture and social and political dynamics.

The most important lesson is that generalizing about the issue is dangerous; every situation is different, with different combinations of causes and consequences, so every response must be fine-tuned to the specific situation. This seems only logical, but in a world of limited resources there is a strong tendency to find a formula and stick to it, both on the part of humanitarians and human rights activists, and by donors. Yet dealing with the consequences of rape as ethnic cleansing, for example, clearly demands a different strategy than dealing with frequent opportunistic rape. In the first case, precisely because of the stigma dynamics, maintaining privacy and protecting the confidentiality of survivors (even from their families) must be paramount.

There are other special challenges for establishing policies and programs to cope with sexual violence in conflicts. These include:

- Sexual violence is only one component of a larger repertoire of violence in an armed conflict. Treating it separately from the other types of violence that men and women face risks contributing to stigmatization and also to defining survivors by just one aspect of their life experience.
- As horrific as some forms of sexual violence can be, other forms of violence may be just as or even more important to deal with in a conflict. Focusing on one form of violence risks discounting the significance of others and can even result in a backlash by those who see their own suffering ignored.
- Programs designed specifically for sexual violence survivors have been created for good reason – the overall negligence of CRSV survivors' needs in broader health or social programs. But this sort of targeted programming may not be the most effective way to support survivors or to prevent further violence. If programs give special privileges to victims of sexual violence, such as free medical care or free legal assistance, this can create resentment among others in the community. In extreme cases, it can also lead to people claiming to be have been rape victims when they were not, just because they are desperate for services. When possible, any social and health services should be available to all war-affected persons.
- The experience of war likely includes many traumas – deaths or separations from loved ones, the loss of home and community, the shock of seeing or suffering atrocities, illness and injury, and the total loss of control over one's life. To a woman who has been raped, finding a livelihood so she can support her children may provide much greater peace of mind than any rape counseling ever could. To define her, for purposes of humanitarian response, primarily as a survivor of sexual violence, risks putting her in a category in which she does not define herself. And this, in itself, is a

fundamental denial of her own agency and her own priorities and can be a cultural imposition.

- Data on rape and sexual violence is notoriously unreliable, even in peacetime and in rich countries with easy access to care and well-developed legal and social systems. In a resource-poor environment with ongoing conflict and displacement and few services, it is nearly impossible to get anywhere near an accurate picture of the numbers and patterns of sexual violence incidents. Many survivors will not report information to their own family members, much less authorities. And the data collected in clinics where survivors are treated is valid only for those few who seek or get treatment. In isolated regions, with no services, there may be no information at all. Moreover, data on rape is frequently extremely politicized, with some actors (groups accused of perpetrating or covering up such violence) having a strong interest in minimizing the numbers, and others (such as affected political or ethnic groups or even human rights activists) seeking to dramatize the situation. In such situations, reliable numbers are impossible to establish. Even in unusual cases where there are decent data, numbers simply do not tell the whole story. Just as with the data on HIV prevalence (another sensitive issue), an increase in reported cases may mean that there is greater incidence of violence – but it could also mean just that the programs to respond are stronger and the reporting system is improving.

- Research on sexual violence is fraught with both ethical and methodological complications. Gathering information on such intimate and sensitive issues requires great delicacy, and it is generally accepted that investigators should not question a suspected victim unless there are services available. But what if there are not? The global attention to the issue and the increasing possibilities of international war crime prosecution of leaders have also led some authorities to deny the incidents and to put pressure on communities and survivors not to talk about sexual violence. Sometimes asking questions about sexual violence can put both the researcher and the respondents at risk of harm. Yet understanding the patterns is critical to designing effective prevention and response.

- There is a tension between the right to confidentiality and peace of mind of a survivor and the pressure on survivors to seek justice by those pursuing the larger goal of ending impunity. Legal assistance workers must make tough decisions about the ethics of encouraging the pursuit of a legal case against a perpetrator when the case may not succeed for any number of reasons and the survivor could then suffer stigma, or even be in further danger.

- There are similar dilemmas regarding the use of traditional means of settlement. In some societies, it has been the tradition to deal with rape through negotiation between families of the perpetrator and the victim for payment of restitution, or, if the rape is of an unmarried woman, even through arrangement of marriage to the perpetrator. While these methods may seem shocking to many people, it must be recognized that use of the modern legal system may also have drawbacks for some survivors (Henry 2010). And again, attempted fixes can have unintended consequences. In Darfur, when health workers treating rape survivors were required to file reports with police who were suspected of then harassing those women, human rights activists and the Save Darfur campaign soundly condemned the requirement for the now famous "Form 8," accusing the government of persecuting rape victims. Yet, in fact, the Sudanese women's movement had lobbied for this requirement for years, seeing it as the way to criminalize rape and force it into the formal justice system, instead of allowing families to marry off their already traumatized daughters in a traditional settlement.

• There is a very fine line between raising awareness of sexual violence in conflict in a responsible way and sensationalizing it. Some media coverage borders on morbid fascination with the topic and violates the privacy and dignity of survivors and their families without providing proper analysis of the situation or the responses needed. Some organizations also sensationalize it for purposes of fundraising for programs of dubious value. Even very responsible organizations often struggle with finding the right balance between the dignity of survivors and the need to shock by showing the terrible consequences so that donors will respond.

In summary, when responding to sexual violence, a good rule of thumb is that old adage "do no harm." But figuring out how to accomplish that is often a tough and complex task.

War's other health effects on women and girls

Wars, by definition, have casualties – among armed combatants on the battlefield and civilians who are targets or who just get in the way. People are killed, injured, and wounded as a direct result of armed violence; men, who make up the larger proportion of combatants, tend to have more of the direct arms-related injuries of war, while women also suffer wounds and injuries from small arms as well as from landmines (during and after conflicts) since they are often the ones farming or collecting fuelwood or water in mined areas. But the indirect consequences of war often also result in death and suffering. It is estimated that in conflicts in Africa over the past decade, there have been nine indirect deaths for every direct death.[21] And the number of actual deaths does not compare to the numbers who suffer illness and injury due to the conflict. Epidemics are common when large numbers of people are displaced and, while everyone is affected, women are at higher risk of many contagious diseases such as measles and pneumonia because they are most often the ones caring for children.

General health effects

In almost any major conflict, people lose access to health services due to the damage or destruction of health facilities, the lack of health workers, or because of their own displacement. In places such as Rwanda and East Timor, almost all health facilities were destroyed. In other wars, such as in El Salvador, health workers have been targeted, kidnapped and killed. In Liberia and Sierra Leone, almost all trained health staff fled the country during the war, leaving any remaining clinics unstaffed. The loss of basic health care has both immediate and long-term consequences: wounds and injuries cannot be properly treated; there is no immunization for disease prevention; contagious diseases go untreated and spread more quickly; and people suffering from chronic conditions such as diabetes or heart disease go without care. Even where facilities are not damaged, the sheer diversion of resources away from a health system can also cause decline in availability and quality of services, with serious consequences for the health of the population. And these consequences may remain long after peace has come.

Implications for reproductive health

Women face particular reproductive health-related risks. For example, anemia resulting from malnutrition has serious implications for the health of girls and women. Trauma and stress may result in miscarriages, which require treatment to prevent sepsis. Pregnancy and delivery, which can be dangerous even in the best of circumstances, become much more risky. Given that almost one-fifth of pregnancies (in any setting) will have complications which require emergency obstetric care to protect the life and health of mother and baby, losing access to health services can be a death sentence. Indeed, the risk of maternal death in countries with ongoing or recent armed conflicts is almost twice as high as the risks in peaceful countries. The highest rates of maternal death are in countries such as Afghanistan, Sierra Leone, and the Republic of South Sudan, all places with long conflicts which have impeded development and where communities continue to face severe difficulties in accessing basic health care.

When wars disrupt health services or leave women without access to health care, there are a variety of reproductive health consequences besides the complications of pregnancy. The inability to get family planning supplies or services leaves women and girls at risk of an unwanted pregnancy at a time when they can least manage the pregnancy or care for a new child. Because abortion is often inaccessible, unaffordable, or illegal, many resort to traditional and unsafe means to end the pregnancy. Unsafe abortion is a major contributor to maternal mortality throughout the world, even in peaceful settings. In the midst of conflict, or in a refugee situation, the desperation to end a badly timed pregnancy has led women to all sorts of life-threatening procedures (Lehmann 2002). The documentation of maternal deaths from unsafe abortion in a large refugee camp in Kenya in the 1980s was a major factor in the initiative by a group of humanitarian agencies to advocate for and develop standards of reproductive care for refugees, including family planning. Reproductive health services are now an integral part of the widely accepted standards for humanitarian response (IAWG 2010).

The provision of safe abortion services for victims of rape remains a very difficult issue within the humanitarian community. Although some legal rulings have found that denial of abortion for rape victims constitutes torture and cruel and inhuman treatment under the International Covenant on Civil and Political Rights, it remains true that many women and girls who would seek to end a forced pregnancy do not have the access or means to do so. The major humanitarian agencies providing health care in conflicts do not include abortion in their services. In some cases, abortion is illegal in the host country (although most countries allow for legal abortion in cases of rape). Some humanitarian organizations are faith-based and do not condone abortion for any reason (Lehmann 2002). In other cases, even where it is legal, many non-faith-based humanitarian organizations cannot provide or even refer patients for abortions due to the restrictions placed on them by major donors, such as the USA. The USA is the largest humanitarian donor worldwide and all foreign assistance, including emergency assistance, is governed by the Helms Amendment (sponsored by Jesse Helms, a conservative senator from North Carolina) which restricts recipients of funds from engaging even in "information, education, training or communication programmes . . . about abortion" (Global Justice Center 2010).

Sexually transmitted infections, including HIV/AIDS

An important component of reproductive health is prevention and treatment of sexually transmitted infections (STIs), including HIV/AIDS. Most common STIs are easily treated if basic health services are available. But untreated they can cause not only severe discomfort but also more serious health problems, including infertility. Prior infection with certain STIs also increases the risk of infection if the woman or girl is exposed to HIV. Risks increase in situations of social disruption where sexual behavior may change for any number of reasons. Young people may engage in sex earlier than they normally would have, either because of lack of adult role models or supervision or, as in some refugee or IDP camps, sheer boredom and lack of education or recreational activities. Girls and women may become involved in new relationships for security, for financial reasons, or even to gain access to food and shelter. Forced sex is common in such situations – whether it is rape by militias or fellow displaced persons, or coercion by security personnel, other authorities, or humanitarian workers. Conflicts and displacement inevitably bring greater exposure to STIs. The treatment of STIs is one of the minimum accepted standards for reproductive health care in emergencies but, in too many cases, resources and personnel are not sufficient to carry out such treatment.

Where HIV is prevalent in the displaced population or in the places they flee to, there is also increased risk of infection through exposure to infected blood or contaminated medical instruments in areas of battle, or to sexual transmission from an infected person. Women are biologically more susceptible to HIV than men. Women and girls generally find it difficult to negotiate safe sex even in consensual relationships when means of infection prevention, such as condoms, are available. In war situations, they often have no access to HIV prevention information and services, including condoms, and are also at greater risk of forced sex, thus greatly increasing the risk. For victims of rape, risks of infection multiply if there is trauma to the genital tissues which allows more efficient viral transmission (Klot & DeLargy 2007). In protracted conflict situations, where there is little access to HIV testing, those who are already infected may not know that they are infected and may continue to unwittingly transmit the infection. Contrary to previously held beliefs, there seems to be no clear, universal association between conflict and HIV transmission; some types of conflicts seem to have slowed the epidemic by isolating geographic areas and others seem to have exacerbated the epidemic (De Waal et al. 2009). But one thing is clear – in almost every part of the world, women are at greater risk than men for both biological and social reasons, which remains true in wars as well.

For those who are HIV-positive, regular monitoring and consistent treatment with antiretroviral drugs is critical for preventing the progression to AIDS and for preventing the other infections which so often accompany HIV infection, such as tuberculosis. Proper nutrition is also a very important factor in maintaining health for HIV-positive people. Damage to health services and the displacement of war can interrupt treatment and also result in malnutrition, and thus can be life threatening. Women who are HIV-positive often want to avoid pregnancy and need family planning services; those who get pregnant need special monitoring and care during pregnancy and also special attention at delivery to prevent transmission to the baby. All of these may be unavailable during conflicts.

In regard to the impact of war on health, there is real progress in the growing recognition of women's specific health needs and the improved access to appropriate health services within humanitarian programs. This is very much due to more than a decade of steady effort by a group of activists, humanitarian and donor agencies, and researchers who first came together in 1994 to advocate for reproductive health for refugees and who have worked together ever since to develop standards for reproductive health care in humanitarian situations, to document the impact of displacement on health, and to push the humanitarian and human rights agendas to include women's health. Their efforts have ensured that reproductive health for women and men is now firmly part of the accepted standards for humanitarian response.[22]

Conclusion

In this chapter, we have reviewed a number of ways in which war presents special risks to the health and safety of women and girls, deriving both from social and biological factors. It is clear that sexual violence, particularly rape, is not only a bodily trauma with possible physical and mental health consequences, but also, due to social constructions of gender, can be a radically life-altering event. Sexual violence inflicts multiple types of harm, not only on individuals but also on those around them, sometimes for a very long time. While there has been progress in global recognition of the problem, attention within international law, and methods of treatment and care, there seems to be much less success in preventing or ending sexual violence in conflicts in many parts of the world. There is also a long way to go to end the stigma that most survivors face. We have also looked at some of the challenges that policy makers, researchers, and health and human rights workers face as they attempt to design and implement prevention and care policies and programs. Without better understanding of the specific context of sexual violence in a conflict – why and how it happens – efforts to respond to the problem are bound to remain less effective than they could be. Worse, misinformed and misguided efforts can do real harm to those they were intended to help.

The good news is that most serious humanitarian responses now include attention to women's health, especially their reproductive health. But a recent study has shown that donor funding for reproductive health in the poorest conflict-affected countries, where it is needed most, is dismally low (Guy et al. 2008). And it is not a coincidence that the worst rates of maternal deaths are in places with long histories of conflict and poor governance, such as Afghanistan, Sierra Leone, and the Republic of South Sudan. War both directly damages health services and also diverts national resources (both human and financial) which could be used to improve health. Even when conflicts end, recovery requires a greater investment of money, skills, and energy than is available in most postwar settings. In the case of sexual violence and for women's health, the cost of war is both devastating and very long-lasting.

QUESTIONS FOR DISCUSSION

1 Why has sexual violence been dealt with separately from other types of violence in conflicts? Should it be? Why or why not?

2 How are peacetime gender roles and attitudes reflected in conflict situations? How can post-conflict recovery situations be opportunities for changing constructions of gender, especially in regard to sexual violence?

3 Should programs supporting survivors and assisting with legal redress be

based on universal human rights concepts or on local cultural values? If these are different, what are some ways in which they could be combined?

4   How could thorough analysis of the patterns and types of sexual violence in a conflict be used in the design of programs for prevention or response?

SUGGESTIONS FOR FURTHER READING

Baaz, Maria Eriksson, and Stern, Maria (2009) "Why do Soldiers Rape? Gender, Violence and Sexuality in the Armed Forces in the Congo (DRC)." *International Studies Quarterly* 53(2): 495–518.

Bartels, Susan, VanRooyen, Michael, Leaning, Jennifer, Scott, Jennifer, and Kelly, Jocelyn (2010) *"Now, The World is Without Me": An Investigation of Sexual Violence in Eastern Democratic Republic of Congo.* Cambridge, MA: Harvard Humanitarian Initiative and Oxfam International.

Leaning, Jennifer, and Gingerich, Tara (2004) *The Use of Rape as a Weapon of War in the Conflict in Darfur, Sudan.* Prepared for the Program on Humanitarian Crises and Human Rights. Cambridge, MA: Harvard School of Public Health.

Moore, Jina (2010) "Confronting Rape as a War Crime: Will a New UN Campaign Have Any Impact?" *Congressional Quarterly Global Researcher* 4(5): 105–30.

Sivakumaran, Sandesh (2007) "Sexual Violence against Men in Armed Conflict." *European Journal of International Law* 18(2): 253–76.

Wood, Elisabeth Jean (2009) "Armed Groups and Sexual Violence: When is Wartime Rape Rare?" *Politics and Society* 37(1): 131–61.

CHAPTER 4

Women Forced to Flee: Refugees and Internally Displaced Persons

Wenona Giles

Displacement from a woman's home, neighborhood or country can happen as a result of war, environmental or development-induced disaster, or as a result of being trafficked. At times, some or all of these four catastrophic events overlap and the challenges of displacement are compounded, as we see in Halima's story:

> Halima, 20, belongs to the Dajo tribe, one of the black African tribes being slaughtered by Sudanese-sponsored Arab militias called the janjaweed. The attacks began three years ago. . . . This March, Darfur's slaughter crossed the border and reached Halima's home-town in Chad. The janjaweed killed many men and seized 10 women and girls, including Halima and her little sister, Sadia. Halima says that the janjaweed, many of them wearing Sudanese military uniforms, mocked the women with racial epithets against blacks, beat them with sticks, and gang-raped them all. Halima, who was then four months pregnant, says she was raped by three men and saw two rape Sadia – who was just 10 years old. After two days of torment, the janjaweed released them. "But Sadia refused to give up her donkey, and so they shot her," Halima recalled. "I was with her. She died right away." The survivors trekked to a shantytown outside Goz Beida. At first they were safe, and Halima gave birth to a baby daughter. But a couple of months ago the janjaweed began to attack them when they left the camp to get firewood . . . (Kristof 2006)[1]

Women may find themselves internally displaced within their own country or they may be forced into crossing national borders. Either way, they are labeled with a new generic identity as *displaced women*. This is not just a descriptor – instead, it is a label that becomes an identity in the eyes of others, and a set of conditions that are imbued with gendered power relations. Halima has seen and experienced violence and tragedy beyond the imagining of most of us. Like many women from war-affected regions, she has been forced to flee her home, her village, and her family and is now in exile in her own country. As such, she is one of 27.5 million internally displaced persons (IDPs) in the world today (IDMC 2010) – and approximately 80 percent of IDPs are women and children (Buscher & Makinson 2006, p. 15). In addition, there were (as of 2009) another 16.2 million people, Convention refugees and asylum seekers, who have fled outside the borders of their own countries (USCRI 2009, p. 32), about half of whom are women (UNHCR 2009, p. 3).

In this chapter, we will examine the plight of this staggering number of IDPs and refugees. The chapter begins with a look at the sometimes confusing vocabulary of displacement, followed by a discussion of who is forced to flee their homelands and why. These questions take us to the causal roots of and the reasons for displacement, reaching back into history and up to the present day for answers. The specific gendered causes and experiences of displacement and exile for women and girls are examined, and this leads to an exploration of four gendered spaces of displacement: (1) long-term displacement; (2) internal displacement; (3) resettlement; and (4) repatriation. Having established some methodological tools for understanding the gender relations of displacement, we then explore feminist approaches to the development of the refugee protection regime from the 1970s to the present.

A vocabulary of displacement

The language of displacement can be confusing, in part because different people use the terms in different ways. In colloquial usage, the terms "refugees," "forced migrants," or "displaced populations" are often used interchangeably to refer to people who have been forced to leave their homes to seek refuge elsewhere. But in the international legal and humanitarian sphere, there are critical distinctions between forcibly displaced people who seek refuge elsewhere *in their own country*, known as **internally displaced persons** (IDPs), and those who *cross internationally recognized state borders*, known as **refugees**.

Moreover, while people such as politicians and journalists may use "refugee" to refer to anyone who crosses a border to seek refuge in another country – indeed, this is the way the term is most often used in this book – **refugee** has a specific, narrower meaning within international law. According to the 1951 United Nations Convention relating to the Status of Refugees, and its Additional Protocol, a refugee is:

> A person who owing to a well-founded fear of being persecuted for reasons of race, religion, nationality, membership of a particular social group or political opinion, is outside the country of his[2] nationality and is unable or, owing to such fear, is unwilling to avail himself of the protection of that country; or who, not having a nationality and being outside the country of his former habitual residence as a result of such events, is unable or, owing to such fear, is unwilling to return to it. (UNHCR 2007)

In other words, the Convention specifies a particular subgroup of cross-border migrants who are considered qualified for formal refugee status – i.e., people who are forced to migrate because their lives or freedom are threatened if they remain in their country of origin, rather than, for example, people who migrate for economic survival. Parties to the Convention are then obligated to protect anyone who is deemed to qualify for formal refugee status and not to force them to return home. Status as a refugee under the Convention gives a refugee access to humanitarian emergency resources, including food, housing, health services, some education, an identity card, and the right to protection. To distinguish the refugees who have attained this legal status and its protections from the people more generically referred to as refugees, this category of people is referred to as **Convention refugees**.

The term **asylum seekers** refers to individuals outside their countries of origin seeking Convention refugee status, but whose status has not yet been officially granted. In order to have Convention refugee status conferred, many asylum seekers must participate in a legal procedure through which the host country determines if she or he meets the criteria to be called a refugee under the 1951 Convention and its Additional Protocol (USCRI 2010). It is important to note, though, that most people who flee across state borders are never recognized with formal refugee status under the Convention.

Internally displaced persons, or IDPs, are people who have fled from their homes to seek sanctuary, but who, unlike refugees, have not crossed an international border. Even if they have fled for similar reasons as refugees (armed conflict, generalized violence, human rights violations), IDPs remain within their home countries. Thus, they are not covered by the UN Refugee Convention and legally they remain under the protection of their own government – even though that government's own actions (or failures or inability to act) are often the impetus for their flight – so they lack access to the humanitarian emergency resources and the legal protections accorded Convention refugees.[3] Currently, there are millions more internally displaced people than externally displaced refugees, and the number of IDPs continues to increase at twice the rate of Convention refugees (IDMC 2006b).

Trafficked persons include men, women, and children who are either forced or deceived into migrating to a place where they work in indentured conditions as sex workers, domestic workers, or in otherwise oppressive employment. Women, girls, and boys are among the most trafficked human beings in the world. War, ethnic conflict, and gender inequality contribute to trafficking. Refugee women are often victims of human trafficking; the process of the forced migration frequently leaves women and girls vulnerable to enslavement in the sex trade or being forced to become "mail order brides." Armed conflict also heightens the vulnerability of both girls and boys who are enslaved, violated, and forced into becoming soldiers, far from home and under terrible living conditions. The numbers of people who are trafficked are large, but the clandestine nature of this type of forced migration makes it impossible to compile accurate statistics.

Stateless people, who may or may not also be displaced, are not considered to be citizens by any state. As "[p]ossession of nationality is essential for full participation in society and a prerequisite for the enjoyment of the full range of human rights," the estimated 12 million stateless people worldwide exist in a kind of limbo, unable to obtain travel documents, access to basic health, education, and welfare services or exercise basic political rights (UNHCR, undated).

As we work through this vocabulary of displacement, it is important to remember that these categories derive from legal and political analytic frameworks – frameworks which attempt to define and manage refugee, IDP, and other displaced men and women, but which have yet to address the root

> **Box 4.1 Additional Human Rights Conventions that pertain to the rights of forced migrants**
>
> - The International Covenant on Economic, Social and Cultural Rights (ICESCR)
> - The International Covenant on Civil and Political Rights (ICCPR)
> - The International Convention on the Elimination of All Forms of Racial Discrimination (ICERD)
> - The Convention on the Elimination of All Forms of Discrimination against Women (CEDAW)
> - The Convention against Torture and Other Cruel, Inhuman or Degrading Treatment or Punishment
> - The Convention on the Rights of the Child (CRC)
> - The International Convention on the Protection of the Rights of All Migrant Workers and Members of Their Families (MWC)

causes of displacement. It is also critical to remember that, while it is easy to seemingly encompass people's identities when referring to them as refugees or IDPs, these terms do not refer to inherent characteristics of people; rather, they are legal descriptors that are imbued with specific social and political relations, which have a tremendous impact on the kinds of assistance and protection people might be able to access. Finally, though, even for those categories of forced migrants who are best protected by international agreements, rights are difficult to access. A very large number of forced migrants are restricted to camps or segregated settlements, and deprived of rights to food and health security, freedom of movement, and access to livelihoods and education. While there are, in addition to the 1951 Convention, a number of other Human Rights Conventions that can be used to argue for the protection and rights of forced migrants, they are underused by international actors, displaced populations lack the power to activate them, and many countries have not ratified all of them (see Text Box 4.1).

Who is forced to flee and why?

Today, the battlefields of war permeate cities, towns, and villages, and 60–90 percent of injuries and deaths are of civilian men, women, and children, as opposed to soldiers. These conflicts may be related to the rise of ethnic nationalisms, struggles over land and mineral wealth, or global power contestations. In these situations, not only are political activists targeted, but their families and friends may also be at risk. Homes and workplaces may be burned as those who are identified with a particular ethnic, religious, or regional group are rounded up by others who have the firepower or military might to oppose and terrify them. Women and men experience the violence of war differently, as other chapters in this book describe. Women are usually the main caregivers in the home, especially if their husbands are soldiers, or have been killed or captured by their enemies, or have fled to survive.

Sometimes, the only way to escape the horrors of war is to run from one's home, and women's responsibility for dependent children and the elderly often creates a special urgency to flee as quickly as possible, even while it hampers that flight.

The need to escape is caused not only by wars, but also by environmental disasters such as hurricanes, floods, earthquakes, or tsunamis. Development-induced disasters, such as the flooding of land related to the construction of large dams, or the loss of farms and arable land due to the building of oil pipelines and the development of mining, also force people to flee, and often lead to militarized conflict between those who have instigated the development projects (e.g., the state and/or corporations) and the local populations. When the infrastructure is destroyed by war, environmental, or development-induced disasters, when trade in markets, shops and banks is gone, and when people's lives are at risk as they venture out to find food, to attend school, or visit friends, the only alternative – risky as it may be – is to flee. Further, all of these causes of displacement can lead to the trafficking of people as indentured workers in the global sex industry, in factories, and as soldiers. And because women and children are especially vulnerable to trafficking, trafficking becomes another reason for flight to safety.

In practice, the different kinds of catastrophic events which cause displacement often overlap and the challenges are compounded. Halima, for example, finds herself displaced as a result of overlapping catastrophes in her home country, Chad, and neighboring Sudan. She was first abducted and forced to cross into the Darfur region of Sudan where a civil war concerning control over resources has merged with ethnic conflict; she later managed to return to a camp in Chad, where she is now an IDP. Another example can be seen in Sri Lanka, where populations already internally displaced by war were further traumatized when the 2004 Indian Ocean tsunami destroyed their sites of refuge (Hyndman 2011).

Roots of the displacement problem

In addition to the fact that forced migrants lose their homes and communities and sometimes family members, they also share one further characteristic: for the most part, their countries of origin are located in "the global South" (also referred to as "developing regions" or the "Third World"). The countries from which most of the refugees in the world flee are very poor countries in comparison to the countries of "the global North" (e.g., Canada, Western Europe, Australia, and the United States). And those countries to which they turn are neighboring countries that are also economically deprived. Consequently, the economic effect of hosting refugees is felt mostly by countries in the global South. In 2008, the group of nations with per capita gross domestic products (GDPs) of less than $2,000 hosted one half of all refugees in the world (USCRI 2009, p. 31). These countries can barely support their

> **Box 4.2 Key terms: humanitarian assistance versus development aid**
>
> **Humanitarian assistance or relief aid** is aid geared toward meeting the needs of people in emergency situations. It is given by foreign governments and international relief agencies, such as the Office of the United Nations High Commissioner for Refugees (UNHCR), the International Committee of the Red Cross (ICRC), and the World Food Program (WFP).
> **Long-term development aid** refers to the transfer of money and resources from wealthy regions of the world, via international agencies such as the United Nations Development Programme (UNDP), to poor regions for long-term sustainable development. These programs are geared toward making people, communities, and countries independent and self-reliant.

own citizens, so an influx of refugees is a heavy burden and these "host" countries often want refugees to return to their home country as soon as possible. Refugees may be *tolerated* in these economically deprived host countries (with the support of humanitarian aid from the international community), but are *not welcome* to settle permanently.

In order to understand why such large numbers of displaced populations exist in the world today, we must turn to a study of the structural problems that exist between wealthy and poor regions of the world. Most contemporary wars in the global South are historically preceded by nineteenth- and twentieth-century violent struggles for independence from imperialist powers. Colonial wars have transmuted to present-day conflicts and to massive human displacements caused by ethnic violence, armed struggles over scarce resources, and environmental disasters made worse by extreme poverty. Most of the military assaults of the global and regional wars transpire in the regions of the global South, and it is mostly civilian men, women, and children who are affected (see Text Box 4.2).

Northern decisions about the kind of aid to give have also had an impact. During the 1990s, **humanitarian emergency assistance** for regions in conflict increased fivefold to a high of five billion dollars a year. But, during the same period, **long-term development aid** dropped overall, and this pattern continues to the present day.

This emphasis on "band-aid" treatment has meant that forced migration situations that are meant to be temporary (for example, the existence of large numbers of stateless refugees inside and outside of camps) have now become permanent lifestyles that are lived as long-term emergencies by millions of people. In other words, a person like Halima, who has to flee her home and neighborhood into exile in another region, may be an IDP for decades to come, raising her child on WFP rations, unable and often forbidden to make a living of her own in exile, and unable to access more than the elementary education provided by international agencies and nongovernmental organizations (NGOs) in her IDP camp for her child or herself.

The scale of the long-term displacement problem has been exacerbated by possible countries of resettlement in the global North having all but closed their doors to most IDPs and refugees, even though many of these countries are engaged in militarized conflicts that result in massive forced displacements. Canadian and American involvement in the war in Afghanistan, for example, has contributed to over 900,000 Afghan refugees in Iran; the American involvement in Iraq has contributed to 1.6 million Iraqi refugees in Jordan and Syria (USCRI 2009, p. 33). For countries of the global North, 9/11 intensified an already growing fear and disparagement of foreigners, and they have fortressed themselves against the entry of all but a very few of the global number of refugees. In 2008, for example, the world total of refugees was 13,599,900 persons (including both refugees and asylum seekers). Of this number, Canada resettled 10,804 (0.08% of the total), the United States resettled 60,191 (0.44% of the total), Australia resettled 8,742 (0.06% of the total) and the top three Western European resettlement countries combined (Sweden, Norway, and Finland) resettled 3,868 (0.02% of the total) (USCRI 2009, p. 29). All told, wealthy countries of Western Europe, North America, and Australia resettled a combined figure of only 0.6% of the total number of refugees in the world by the end of 2008.

Roots of women's and girls' vulnerability as forced migrants

The gendered experiences of women and girls prior to war or other disasters that warrant flight will affect what happens to them during and afterwards. Prior to escape, women the world over are generally less mobile and monied than men. Their gendered responsibilities of caring for children and other dependents tend to hamper their ability to flee. Their access to resources that they can carry, such as cash, depends on their exposure to and involvement in the market and whether they have the same access as men to any household finances. Depending on the specific sociocultural situation, they may experience little control over their mobility, especially if they are considered to be the repositories of a community's culture and honor. For example, women in purdah (the practice of concealing or secluding women from men or strangers through the use of clothing or various degrees of isolation) are very limited in their mobility and completely dependent on the protection of men to move beyond their household. Exile poses special dangers for these women if their spouses or other male family members have been killed, jailed, or have taken refuge in other regions.

The process of escape itself poses gender-specific challenges for women. Crossing a border (whether it is a country border or an ethnic boundary within one's own country) is often more complicated and dangerous for a woman than a man. Especially if she is without financial resources, she may have to engage in "survival sex" or prostitution in return for food, shelter, and/or protection and this may lead to her being further trafficked for sex or as an indentured worker.

Gender relations in the household may change during and after this emergency period, especially if men are absent due to soldiering duties or for other reasons. For example, prior to flight, women may have to replace men as workers on the family farm, or they may have to take up marketing activities to support their families. When they find themselves in exile, they may need to supplement emergency household food rations by engaging in marketing, agricultural, or other types of resource gathering (for example, food and firewood) activities whenever possible. While such changes may, temporarily, at least, raise women's status in their household and community, they also challenge traditional gendered expectations and place women at risk of gendered forms of violence when they leave an IDP or refugee camp to work in isolated farmlands, bushlands, or in the marketplace. There is no doubt that the gender relations of displaced women's and girls' lives prior to war or other emergencies is at the root of their hyper-vulnerability during war and that this condition is intertwined with their role as providers and family mainstays.

There is also another danger that women confront in exile and that is their invisibility to humanitarian workers (NGOs and international agencies) due to the gendered assumptions of these workers. When women are perceived as only dependents, the result, too often, is that they effectively become invisible; a lack of gender-sensitive attitudes and skills among many agency workers means that women's and girls' presence and needs may be ignored (El-Bushra 1995, p. 84). The case of the "Lost Girls" of Sudan is a prime example.

In South Sudan in the late 1980s, both girls and boys had been forced into becoming child soldiers. The story of the "Lost Boys" of Sudan is better known than that of the girls who were also part of the journey from South Sudan. The escape by these boys and girls and their multi-year trek across Eastern Africa in search of protection led them to the Kakuma refugee camp in northwestern Kenya. There, while the boys were located in group homes with minimal adult supervision, the girls were dispersed and "hidden" in households around the refugee camp for their "protection." This gendered policy decision left the boys in more independent identifiable groups, and resulted in the boys' much greater visibility to resettlement humanitarian workers. So, for example, when the USA resettled 3,700 Sudanese children through the "Lost Boys" program, only 89 were girls (McKelvey 2003 as cited in Newland 2004, p. 10). For the "Lost Girls," the perception of females as dependent and reliant on families rendered them doubly lost, eclipsing them from view and foreclosing their opportunities for resettlement.

This case study is indicative of the different treatment that male and female refugees receive, which is based on gendered assumptions about women and girls as "helpless" and in need of protection. These types of presumptions assume that women and girls should not control their own fates, that young men can be dangerous unless counseled and attended to, and that young women are best housed in strange families, rather than with their well-known friends. But a question remains. By the late 1980s, feminist research on unequal gender relations and on the experiences of women forced migrants was readily available – so why *did* the UNHCR and NGO staff fail to search out the "Lost Girls" who had been allocated to foster families and other less visible gendered sites? It is not only the gender relations of refugee and other forced migration movements that we need to understand, but we also need to challenge the gendered relations of humanitarianism that make women and girls less likely to receive the protection and assistance that they need and that is their right.

Gendered experiences and spaces of forced migration

We now turn to four gendered experiences and spaces of displacement. These are: (1) long-term displacement/protracted refugee situations; (2) internal displacement; (3) resettlement; and (4) repatriation. But before addressing each separately, there are two important points to keep in mind. First, different kinds of forced displacements are very often interrelated. For example, the effects of the 2004 tsunami (an environmental disaster) on people in Sri Lanka cannot be isolated from the effects of the Sri Lankan ethnic-nationalist conflict (which has led to *both* internal and external displacements). The tsunami and the civil war affected many of the same people – one form of displacement exacerbating the effects of the other displacement and resulting in many of the same experiences of extreme poverty and isolation from one's home community. Also, internal and external displacements are often not cleanly separated. People who are internally displaced within their homeland may have to flee across borders to another country. They may move back and forth clandestinely across a border in order to support members of their household in both places, or engage in economic activities in both countries. Refugees who repatriate may need to return to exile in another country if fighting and violence continues or resumes in their homeland. This has been the case, for example, for many Afghan refugees who have returned to Afghanistan from Iran and Pakistan, only to find that their homeland is still fraught by war and extreme insecurity.

Second, it is well known and well documented that, when the tensions of war increase, sexual violence also increases. Similarly, in times of disasters, such as the 2004 Indian Ocean tsunami or Hurricane Katrina, masculinities often become violent or militarized. In this regard, Cynthia Cockburn (2004) refers to "a connectedness between kinds and occasions of violence" wherein "one seems to flow into the next, as if they were a continuum" (p. 43). Trafficking is a point on this violent continuum. As you will see below, trafficking and the sexual exploitation of women and girls commonly accompany wars, disasters and exile. Sexual violence and trafficking of women and girls are strategies of war used to destabilize, threaten, and dominate a community of refugees or an enemy, and to force communities off their land. Displaced women and girls are at a high risk of being "abducted and used as combatants, laborers, spies, trainers, or sex slaves" (Martin & Callaway 2008, p. 27) because they are more likely than men to be without economic resources and more vulnerable to gender violence without the protection of their traditional social networks.

While keeping in mind these two key points – the interrelatedness of different forms and spaces of displacement and the common increase in sexual violence that accompanies displacement – we will now explore specific experiences and sites of displacement in more depth.

(1) Long-term displacement/protracted refugee situations

Sexual and gender-based violence is endemic in the camps. Women and girls as young as nine years old are routinely abducted by local villagers and forced into so-called marriages only to be returned to the camps when they become pregnant. There were reports of young girls and young women being abducted and trafficked into the sex market in nearby Cox's Bazar and Chittagong and of organized child prostitution within the camp. Women described their fear of going to the latrines and having to collect firewood or green leaves for food in the local forest

> Eileen Pittaway, "The Rohingya Refugees in Bangladesh: A Failure of the International Protection Regime" (Pittaway 2008, p. 91)

Since 1991, large numbers of Rohingya refugees have lived in Bangladesh. Denied citizenship, land, and confronting persecution in Burma, Rohingya refugees have experienced forced migration within Burma and beyond. They are victims of colonial and postcolonial politics and are now a stateless people – unable to return to Burma and unwanted in Bangladesh (Pittaway 2008, p. 86). There are about 28,000 Rohingya refugees who are under the protection of the UNHCR and located in two camps, and another 150,000–200,000 who have no legal status and live in villages outside the camps (Radio Free Asia 2010).

The Rohingya are among the 6 million people (excluding the case of 4 million Palestinian refugees) in the world today who are living outside their homelands in what are called "protracted refugee situations." These refugees have been living in exile inside and outside of camps for at least five years or more. According to the UNHCR, there are more than thirty of these situations around the world, mostly located in poor regions of Africa and Asia. Although the UNHCR has articulated what they refer to as "durable solutions" for refugees, many refugees are "stuck" in long-term exile because none of these "durable solutions" are available to them: they cannot go home when home is not a secure place; they cannot settle in the host country of exile because that country is too poor to support them as new citizens or for other political reasons; and they cannot move to wealthier countries because they are not considered to be acceptable citizens by those countries. They are living on humanitarian or emergency assistance, mainly provided through refugee camps, for years and sometimes decades.

Most refugees either end up living in camps set up by the UNHCR or other international agencies, or they live anonymously in towns and cities where they find it is easier to access employment, but where they lack the protection and support of international agencies. The organization of and support for camps varies greatly. Some have the appearance of prisons, some resemble ramshackle shanty towns, while others look like villages or small towns. They are often located in the most inhospitable and isolated areas of the host country, where arable land is scarce and services beyond those provided by humanitarian agencies are nonexistent. The WFP works with the UNHCR and other agencies to distribute food, housing materials, and provide health services, education, and identity cards. However, most refugees in camps will tell you that many of these services are inadequate and that they are not allowed to work to supplement their own and their family's requirements, even for food. And it is generally agreed by refugee scholars and the UNHCR that camps and isolated settlements are not a preferred solution for those who are in exile.

Refugee camps are spaces where social relations take a particular form, depending upon the culture and history of the women and men located therein, but also upon the effects of war in the region (e.g., the location of different, possibly warring ethnic groups in a camp), and the impact of humanitarian assistance on the social relations of the refugee households and communities. Humanitarian assistance often works to define women, girls, and gender relations in a camp in homogeneous ways as vulnerable and as victims. For example, women may be defined as the sole caregivers in a household to the exclusion of men, and traditional gender roles may be assumed, thus contributing to and/or entrenching gender inequalities in refugee camps. But refugee women are not always or only caregivers, vulnerable, or "at risk." While it is true that women and men may have many new and gendered responsibilities in a camp, it is not helpful to assume that refugee women cannot speak for themselves about their own needs and desires.

Long-term dependency on humanitarian assistance has particular implications for women and the gender relations of refugee households. The stress on households and families in these situations is enormous as refugees try to cope over many years with restrictions to their employment and mobility, while trying to survive on inadequate humanitarian handouts. Men's frustration, anger, and loss of self-esteem increases women's exposure to domestic and sexual violence during long-term refugee situations. Women are also the targets of the resentment and violence of the host community when they leave a camp to gather firewood and other survival resources for themselves and their families (Loescher & Milner 2008, p. 31).

Even those in positions of authority who are meant to protect and support refugees have sometimes proven to be a grave danger for women and girls. As Ferris (2008) points out, when parents have little or no possibility to access education for their children, and no income, then the only "currency" that girls have in long-term and hopeless refugee situations is their bodies. Aid workers, peacekeepers, and community leaders recognize the power they have over these refugees and many have sexually exploited young refugee women and girls in camps around the world (Ferris 2008, p. 89).

(2) Internal displacement

Internally displaced populations oblige policy makers and researchers to think "beyond the box" of UN Conventions and policies. They are women, girls, boys, and men who have fled from conflicts or human rights violations but, unlike legally defined refugees who are protected by the UNHCR, they have not crossed international borders and therefore are not able to seek international protection under the 1951 Refugee Convention and the 1967 Protocol. Thus they have even less access to food, education, health care and other social services than legally defined refugees do. Often they are caught in the cross fire of civil war in isolated regions of their country, or are escaping from disaster zones. Millions of people in the global South have been internally displaced from their residences, environments, and livelihoods as a result of the large infrastructural development projects that began displacing people from their farms and villages in the 1960s and 1970s, and continue to the present day (Vandergeest, Idahosa and Bose 2007, p. 3). In fact, they may become *personae non gratae* in their own country because they are seen as belonging to a particular ethnic or regional group that is out of favor with the state or with other groups. They may be stripped of their citizenship rights and confront extremely dangerous situations with little or no humanitarian protection.

Although IDPs outnumber Convention refugees two to one, their plight receives far less international attention. In 2010, there were 27.5 million people who had been internally displaced due to conflict in at least 52 countries (IDMC 2010) and these situations are escalating in number and severity (IDMC 2008). Sudan, the Republic of South Sudan, the Democratic Republic of the Congo, Uganda, Colombia, and Iraq have been recent sites of intense internal displacement. Like refugees, IDPs are often separated from their regular livelihood or employment; they have to flee their homes, which may be destroyed; they may be separated from other family members; they may live in camps or try to merge into the anonymity of urban areas, where it may be easier to find work. Unlike Convention refugees, they have less access to humanitarian support and protection, and without the latter, they face great risks of exposure to their enemies (state or ethnic). While "on the run" in their own home country, schooling, and health care may be disrupted and inaccessible from any source.

As in other forced migration situations, poverty has impelled many IDP women into prostitution, trafficking, and "survival sex" or "transactional sex" to access humanitarian aid, including for food (IDMC 2006b, p. 68). According to the Geneva-based Internal Displacement Monitoring Centre (IDMC), the leading international body monitoring conflict-induced internal displacement worldwide, sexual and gender-based violence is one of the most pervasive violations of the rights of women and girls during armed conflict and displacement (IDMC 2006a).

(3) Resettlement

The median length of civil war conflicts is now eight years; the average duration of a protracted refugee situation has increased from nine years in 1993 to more than twenty years in 2010 (Milner & Loescher 2011, p. 3). There are dozens of long-term refugee and IDP situations across the world, including those in Kenya, Tanzania, Thailand, Pakistan, Iran, Bangladesh, Sudan, India, and Israel/Palestine.[4] For many displaced populations, resettlement to a new country is the only prospect of a way out.

Here, too, the experience of forced migration is gendered. Third-country resettlement to the global North has been even less available to women than to men because women do not have the money needed for transportation; they may not be perceived as having the right academic or employment credentials; and/or they are responsible for dependents in a household. They are thus less attractive than men who are perceived as lone, unencumbered, mobile migrants. When they do manage to resettle in the global North, refugee women report that the many bureaucratic demands they experience are often reminiscent of the dehumanizing violence they experienced in their home country prior to their flight. There is a kind of transnational connection between their experiences during flight and exile that is transposed onto the local, institutional bureaucratic culture that women have to understand and negotiate in their new home (Chambon 2008, pp. 106–7).

Identity transformation in exile has been much discussed in the literature on refugee women and relates to a woman's personal history, her experience of trauma, her resilience, her level of family and community support, and the site of resettlement. In their research on Sudanese refugee women who resettled in Canada, Hayward et al. (2008) identified four experiences that affected the identity and mental well-being of these refugee women: loss, life in limbo, economic hardship, and raising children in Canada (p. 200).

- **Loss**: Refugee women who arrive in countries of the global North have invariably lost children, spouses, parents, and friends, often under violent circumstances. They may also have been required by the resettlement country to leave certain family members in refugee camps, and have often lost the possibilities of locating family and friends left behind. They have also lost livelihoods and employment, homes, and belongings. It is hard to overcome such dispossession.

- **Life in limbo**: Refugee women live lives of waiting: first in camps or other stateless situations and then in resettlement as their cases move through the bureaucracy. Resettled refugee women interviewed by Adrienne Chambon described the Canadian bureaucratic demands in their lives as "torture" because these are "reminiscent of routine acts used in military regimes and dictatorships that consist in individuals being constantly checked, documented and observed" (Chambon 2008, p. 106).

- **Economic hardship**: Difficulties in accessing employment commensurate with their abilities and educational qualifications and the high cost of a university or college education in the global North leave many refugee women scrambling for low-paid and insecure jobs to support their families. Their gendered experience of exile persists into resettlement where they may be classified as "dependents" of men and therefore not "destined for the labor force." In some resettlement countries, such as Canada, this hinders their access to language training and skills upgrading/training programs that are designed for those who are regarded as household wage earners and workers.

- **Raising children**: A new and unfamiliar school system, cultural differences in child rearing practices, combined with a harried work life and lack of easy access to transportation leave many refugee women feeling overwhelmed. Misunderstandings by school officials, the police and Children's Aid workers exacerbate sensitive situations. Hayward et al. (2008) describe the case of a young mother who had recently arrived from exile in a series of refugee camps. Her newborn and other children were removed by social workers who misunderstood different child-rearing practices. The children were eventually returned, but not before the desperate mother, who had little or no experience of the legal system, had to negotiate the court system. As she later said, "In our country, it is the army that kidnaps our children. We came here hoping to find safety for them, but here they are kidnapped by the organization that is supposed to protect them" (Hayward et al. 2008, p. 203).

(4) Repatriation

Repatriation refers to return to one's homeland. The UNHCR states that return must not be forced – in other words, those who wish to return to their home community should only do so if the conditions in the homeland are hospitable, acceptable, and they are returning of their own volition. (Involuntary or forced repatriation is commonly referred to as *refoulement*.)

The extent to which women are able to freely choose to repatriate is a gendered issue. On the one hand, women who do not wish to repatriate because they feel more secure and fulfilled in their country of exile may have to return if the decision rests with their spouse. On the other hand, women who are threatened by exploitation and abuse in the first country of asylum may not be able to repatriate alone as easily as men can, especially if they are widows or otherwise without a male spouse and thus are targets for violence.

While danger awaits refugee and IDP women and girls who try to return home, or indeed travel anywhere alone, many feel a simultaneous urgency to escape life in a camp. A story in the *Toronto Star* by Michelle Shephard about the attempted return of a 13-year-old Somali refugee girl to Somalia describes just how deadly the journey home can be for women and girls. Asho, born and raised in the Dadaab refugee camp in northeastern Kenya, told her school friends that she very much wanted to visit her grandmother in her homeland of Somalia, a country she had never been able to visit. One day, she disappeared, apparently on foot, and her worried parents were told that she had somehow found her way to the Somali border – 80 kilometers from the camp. They assumed that she had been abducted somewhere on the road to the Somali border. As it turned out, Asho had not only been abducted, but also brutally attacked and raped, then dragged by the al-Shabaab militia before a Sharia court in the Somali town of Kismayo, where she was "convicted" of adultery and stoned to death before a crowd of onlookers, some of whom tried unsuccessfully to intervene, and were themselves injured or killed. As David Copeman, Amnesty International's Somalia campaigner, wrote, "This was not justice, nor was it an execution . . . . This child suffered a horrendous death at the behest of the armed opposition groups who currently control Kismayo [Somalia] . . ." (Shephard 2008). It is in the retelling of Asho's experience that we still hear and honor her voice about the dangers that await refugee women and girls who try to return home, or indeed travel anywhere alone, but also, the simultaneous urgency that they feel to escape life in a camp. It also reminds us of the horrors of ethnic and religious fundamentalism, and the need that all of us should feel to confront and address gendered violence in whatever ways that we can.

Feminists' responses to protection and assistance approaches

Feminists have been defining, redefining, and addressing issues related to the gender relations of exile and displacement since the 1980s. This work has had some important direct and indirect impacts on how international agencies, host governments and resettlement countries have awakened to and addressed the gender relations of forced migration.

Prior to the 1980s, refugees were discussed and analyzed as "genderless stereotypes"; this is evident in the 1951 UN Convention and the 1967 Protocol relating to the Status of Refugees which make no mention of women and give no attention to gendered forms of violence or persecution. Interest in the gender relations of forced migration can be traced to the early 1980s, a decade after research had begun on the gender relations of development. In fact, many feminists who became interested in this topic came from a gender and development background, where they were already examining the gendered relations of poverty between the global South and the global North. And approaches to the study of Women in Forced Migration (WIFM) and Gender and Forced Migration (GAFM) paralleled, with some delay, the earlier Women in Development (WID), Women and Development (WAD), and Gender and Development (GAD) approaches that originated in the 1970–80s.

From women in forced migration to gender and forced migration in the 1980s

WIFM is concerned with refugee women conceived of as in need of protection, and as attached to their households and their children: *womenandchildren*.[5] Grounded in a modernization framework[6] that does not challenge existing structures or root causes of oppression, conflict, and flight into exile, WIFM eschewed long-term development in the late 1970s and early 1980s, prioritizing humanitarian aid in the form of food provision and basic protection. It did not address the gendered subordination that many refugee and/or IDP women experience in their home countries or countries of exile, inside and outside of their households and beyond their family attachments.

One of the early impetuses to feminist attention and action at this time came from the experiences of women in Indo-China. Six to seven percent of refugee women between 11 and 40 years of age who arrived in Thailand in the late 1980s reported being raped (Kelley 1989). Their traumatic stories of sexual violence and torture opened the door to discussions about the gendered forms of violence against women in war at the UN Second World Conference on Women in Copenhagen in 1980 and again at a UNHCR workshop on Indo-Chinese refugees in 1981. Protection of refugee women was uppermost in the minds of the conference participants in these two gatherings, rather than the identification of the root causes of forced displacement. Several other international conferences and events in the early 1980s also highlighted the protection of refugee women and addressed gender-related violence.[7]

The UN Third World Conference on Women in Nairobi in 1985 saw the increasing importance of NGO participation in an NGO Forum, which ran parallel to the official UN conference. NGO delegates in Nairobi and the NGO Subcommittee on Refugee and Migrant Women led the way in making links between a critique of a separation of the "public" and "private" in women's lives. They argued that there was a relationship between gendered forms of violence that women experienced in their households and homes (in the so-called "private sphere") and state complicity (in the so-called "public sphere"). For example, it is well known that when there is an intensification of militarized war violence in a country or region, there is also an increase in domestic violence in the so-called private sphere of the home; and in such a situation,

---

Box 4.3 UNHCR Conclusion No. 39 (XXXVI) Concerning Refugee Women and International Protection

"States, in the exercise of their sovereignty, are free to adopt the interpretation that women asylum-seekers who face harsh or inhuman treatment to their having transgressed the social mores of the society in which they live may be considered as a 'particular social group' within the meaning of Article 1A(2) of the 1951 United Nations Refugee Convention." (UNHCR 1985)

---

domestic violence is usually ignored by the state authorities and by leaders in the refugee communities. NGOs at the Nairobi conference argued that women's rights in international law, including in refugee law, were being ignored and transgressed by their governments. And they determined to change this.

Clearly influenced by and benefiting from the GAD discourse of this era that characterized the Nairobi conference, these NGO delegates were extending the debates on the gender relations of forced migration from WIFM into a more progressive Gender and Forced Migration discourse. This period saw the first arguments for the inclusion of gendered forms of persecution in the 1951 Refugee Convention, which resulted in the 1985 Conclusion No. 39 (XXXVI) Concerning Refugee Women and International Protection (see Text Box 4.3). Importantly, this resolution reflects NGO critiques of cultural relativism (which says that local culture should take precedence over rights), and promulgates the idea that women must be protected from gendered forms of violence even where the cultural norms of a country condone violence against women.

Lagging behind the politics of the NGO Forum, the official UN Nairobi Conference sustained an approach that focused on refugee women's vulnerability, need for protection and location in the family household (private) sphere (Baines 2004, p. 27). However, the momentum from the NGO Forum propelled the International Working Group on Refugee Women (IWGRW), founded at the Nairobi NGO Forum, to organize the first international Consultation on Refugee Women in Geneva in November 1988. But once again, root causes received little mention in the conference, and humanitarianism (i.e., protection and emergency approaches) was the overarching focus. The conference outcomes reflected a neoliberal approach[8] that "appealed to the economic sensibilities of Western decision-makers and humanitarian workers" (Baines 2004, p. 31). The more critical and progressive feminist GAD discourse that had begun to emerge from the Nairobi NGO Forum was toned down in this joint post-Nairobi NGO–UNHCR endeavor. Thus a pattern was developing in which feminist NGOs would take a lead position on women and forced migration issues, only to be argued back to a "softer" position by the more powerful UNHCR organization.

Add "assistance" to "protection" in the 1990s . . . and stir

In the 1990s, many resettlement countries developed special categories that could be specifically used to address emergency cases for particularly vulnerable refugees, one category of which was called "women at risk." Internally displaced populations were not yet considered, nor were their needs addressed through these legal protection tools. During this period, a continuing WIFM approach concerned with protection was mixed with some attempts to move beyond more "traditional" approaches that considered women as linked only to the "private" sphere of the household. The Canadian Working Group on Refugee Women, formed in the mid-1980s, played an important role in encouraging the Canadian government to adopt and implement the UNHCR Women at Risk program (see Text Box 4.4). This program incorporated both *protection* of a vulnerable population (i.e., women in need of immediate removal from a dangerous situation) and also *assistance* through integration into a country of the global North (i.e., where they would be assisted toward achieving an independent livelihood). Canada was the first country to institute the "women at risk" category of refugees in 1988, followed by a number of other countries, including the USA, Sweden, Australia, Benin, Burkina Faso, Chile, Iceland, and New Zealand. It is worth noting, however, that in order to be eligible for this refugee status, a woman has to be identified as "in need" and therefore dependent on others, for her survival. Women who had lost spouses, families, and/or a community network, for example, and were without male or other family/community protection would fit the profile of a "woman at risk." But as Newland (2004) rightly notes, the identification of women as dependents in this program ignores the fact that in many cases women may be at risk *because of* their families or communities. She argues that "[w]omen should be considered for resettlement on the basis of their vulnerability for any reason" (Newland 2004, p. 9).

Gradually, into the 1990s, feminist researchers began to break down and

---

Box 4.4 UNHCR definition of "women at risk"

According to the UNHCR, "women at risk" are:

"[t]hose women who have protection problems, and are single heads of families or are accompanied by an adult male who is unable to support and assume the role of the head of the family. They may suffer from a wide range of problems including expulsion, refoulement and other security threats, sexual harassment, violence, abuse, torture and different forms of exploitation. Additional problems such women face could derive from persecution as well as from particular hardships sustained either in their country of origin, during their flight or in their country of asylum. The trauma of having been uprooted, deprived of normal family and community support or cultural ties, the abrupt change in roles and status, in addition to the absence of an adult male head of family, renders some women, under certain circumstances, more vulnerable than others." (UNHCR 2002, p. 13) address separately (but without losing sight of the connections) the various postwar stages of a refugee woman's life: the catastrophic events leading to flight; the traumatic experiences of the flight itself; and the way that gender and age identities are reorganized as men, women, and children adjust to life in refugee camps or elsewhere in exile. It was recognized that the particular effects of forced resettlement on women had been ignored and more research was needed on the gender relations of resettlement.

Also at this time, legal definitions regarding refugee status were challenged from gender perspectives. Feminists pointed out that the legal definitions of persecution were based on men's, not women's, lives, and they interceded by producing the *Gender Persecution Guidelines* (IRB 1996). This is particularly important because Convention refugee status hinges on persecution. Feminists have never been satisfied with the "genderless" stereotyping of the UN Convention on Refugees and its Protocol. However, for better or worse, feminists were discouraged from opening up a debate about it by those who argued that opening up a forum to change the Convention might result in a much more exclusionary refugee convention than already exists.

The *Gender Persecution Guidelines* are the result of bringing a feminist lens to the Refugee Convention definition that was originally developed as an instrument of universal protection for refugees following the Second World War. The *Guidelines*, built on Conclusion No. 39 which pertains to membership of a particular social group (see Text Box 4.3), make the following points: (i) legal definitions of persecution are primarily based on the experiences of men, and the Refugee Convention definition of persecution has not, until recent times, been widely applied to women's experiences such as female infanticide, genital mutilation, bride burning, forced marriage, forced abortion, compulsory sterilization, or domestic violence; and (ii) the fact that certain forms of harm, such as sexual and domestic violence, may be acceptable in specific cultures is irrelevant when determining whether these gender-specific crimes constitute forms of persecution. The *Guidelines* argue against cultural relativism in definitions of what constitutes violence against women.

The process by which the *Guidelines* came into being can be traced to Dutch feminists and their supporters in the Dutch Refugee Council who were, in 1988, the first to officially recognize that gender-related violence was a form of persecution. The UNHCR followed the Dutch lead in 1991 and developed its own *Guidelines on the Protection of Refugee Women*[9] to draw attention to the specificities of the gender relations of forced migration.

Two years later, in 1993, the Canadian government, under pressure from national and international NGOs and Canadian feminist policy makers, was the first national government to develop and approve the *Gender Persecution Guidelines*. Other countries followed suit: the USA, Australia, Sweden, and the UK. They are meant to assist those who are considering the cases of women refugee claimants who are fleeing a country where violence against women is tolerated by the government and the police.

However, to the present day, the *Guidelines* or related legislation or jurisprudence are mainly applied in those cases of refugee claimants who are able to reach a Canadian, American, Australian, Swedish, or British border and, for the gendered reasons discussed above, many fewer women than men are able to do so. The extent to which the *Guidelines* are applied in overseas selection (in the first country of asylum) – where refugee women may have more ease of access to an asylum claim (though still much less than men) for refugee status and resettlement to a third country, such as Canada, the USA, or Australia – is unknown. Access to asylum procedures in the first country of asylum (usually in the global South) is also less likely for women than men, because of the familiar gendered distribution of resources and responsibilities we have seen before. For example, women find it more difficult than men to travel to the relevant offices, both because they lack the resources and because they are often responsible for children and the elderly. And they are more likely to be illiterate than men (depending on their home country) and thus they will have less (or no) access to information about the *Guidelines*. As well, they may be unable to interact with strangers due to cultural restrictions. And as mentioned above, women are commonly ignored as *primary* asylum seekers, but rather are regarded as dependents of a spouse or male relative. So it is a minority of women refugees who are able to seek protection in third countries of resettlement, such as Canada, the USA, the European Union (EU), and Australia.

Losing gendered ground in the twenty-first century?

Following on from the 1995 Beijing Fourth World Conference on Women and into the late 1990s and 2000s, the UNHCR was compelled to move beyond a discourse of "women" and/or "*womenandchildren*," toward the use of "gender" and "gender mainstreaming."[10] However, attempts to change gendered practices and politics within the UNHCR have met with some resistance and the agency has been slow to accept that complex, on-the-ground humanitarian emergencies are gendered and responses should therefore take this into account.

Indra (1999) argues that a GAFM approach could lead to a better gendered understanding and constructive critique of cultural relativist arguments, as well as of international agency discourse (p. 19). This kind of approach includes attentiveness to gendered and other power structures among those engaged in relief agencies and those who are the recipients of humanitarian assistance. It is also, therefore, a very challenging framework to these parties (Indra 1999, p. 20) and to the ways they have historically essentialized refugee women's roles and the gender relations of refugee and forced migrations. This kind of relationship requires that both agencies and beneficiaries interact and negotiate equitably. Is this possible?

GAFM approaches have been criticized by those who argue that survival comes first and gender second. What they argue is that, while gender is a key issue, the most important and first thing to deal with is the emergency, and only after that should we think about issues of gender inequality. This has been referred to as the "emergency excuse" by feminists working in situations that have been defined as humanitarian crises where, over and over again, gender is put on the back burner while "emergencies" are addressed (Hyndman & de Alwis 2003, p. 214). How do we define emergencies from a feminist and gendered perspective?

Hyndman and de Alwis (2003) urge us to go further than a GAFM approach. They counter with an argument for a Feminist Approach to Development (FAD) or humanitarian crises in which gender is not prioritized but is only one part of *an intersectional analysis* in which history, location, and politics are analyzed and integrated (Hyndman & de Alwis 2003, p. 219). We need more than a "particular explanation" of the gender, class, and race dimensions of each disaster (Hyndman & de Alwis 2003); instead, we need to understand the intersectionality of the multiplicity of identities and differences that comprise the population in a humanitarian disaster, including race, class, gender, caste, ethnicity, age, religion. Can this type of analysis make a difference to the lives of refugee women? In the face of the inability of humanitarian organizations and states to solve an ever-expanding refugee situation, where the total population of refugees and IDPs is now a little more than the population of the states of California and Oregon combined, and about the same as the total populations of Sweden, Denmark, Norway, Finland, and the Netherlands combined, perhaps it is time to give feminism a chance? Perhaps it is time to take a feminist approach to so-called "emergencies."

Conclusion

Women forced migrants have everything to lose. Indeed, while there may be a few gains for women during the process of displacement and exile (e.g., education and health services that refugee women could not access in their homeland, particularly if they are poor), for the great majority of women, these will be far outweighed by huge losses. The "empowering" experiences some researchers argue that women gain in refugee camps are generally far outweighed by the desolation and deprivation experienced in these spaces. It seems that for tens of millions of women in the global South, their entry into the modern experiment of the market economy and capitalism is through the infernos of war, death, loss, rape, violence, homelessness, and statelessness. The wars that the global North and South impose and engage in lead to the demise and destruction of the lives and livelihoods of massive numbers of men and women in the global South, who are subsequently forced into long-term displacement. The gender relations that accompany refugees from their homelands interact with the gender relations of humanitarian organizations, conventions, and legal instruments of the international community. Today, where a displaced woman ends up depends greatly upon where she begins her journey, the life tools and survival skills she has managed to accumulate prior to and along the road to exile, and unfortunately, but perhaps most tellingly, her luck. What happens tomorrow is still up to her . . . but now, with your increased knowledge of her plight, it is also, more than ever, up to you.

QUESTIONS FOR DISCUSSION

1 Why and how is mobility a gendered issue for forced migrants? Give two examples from this chapter and/or from your personal experience to support your response.

2 Imagine that you have the job of redesigning the approach that a humanitarian agency should take to help displaced populations as they arrive in a refugee camp. Describe three or four steps that your humanitarian worker employees should take to address the gendered concerns of the families who are arriving after several days of walking from a disaster: (a) name four gendered concerns that the families may have; (b) imagine three or four innovative ways to address these concerns.

3 What are the three "durable solutions" for refugees according to the UNHCR? What are the possibilities for women to achieve any one of these solutions? Describe the gender relations of each of the solutions with examples.

4 What are some "root causes" of displacement? How have women been affected by these causes of displacement?

SUGGESTIONS FOR FURTHER READING

Giles, Wenona, and Hyndman, Jennifer (2004) *Sites of Violence: Gender and Conflict Zones.* Berkeley: University of California Press.

Giles, Wenona, Moussa, Helene, and Van Esterik, Penny (eds.) (1996) *Development and Diaspora: Gender and the Refugee Experience.* Dundas: Artemis Enterprises. ON, CAN. http://site.ebrary.com/lib/celpublicpolicy/docDetail.action?docID=10 360646&p00=wenona%20giles

Hajdukowski-Ahmed, Maroussia, Khanlou, Nazilla, and Moussa, Helene (eds.) (2008) *Not Born a Refugee Woman: Contesting Identities, Rethinking Practices.* New York: Berghahn Books.

Indra, Doreen (ed.) (1999) *Engendering Forced Migration: Theory and Practice.* New York: Berghahn Books.

Korac, Maja (2009) *Remaking Home: Reconstructing Life, Place and Identity in Rome and Amsterdam.* New York: Berghahn Books.

Martin, Susan Forbes (2004) *Refugee Women,* 2nd edn. Lanham, MD: Lexington Books.

CHAPTER 5

Women and Political Activism in the Face of War and Militarization

Carol Cohn and Ruth Jacobson

Introduction

How do women figure in the *politics* of war? What images come to mind? Perhaps, very few, if your store of images comes mostly from the mass media or conventional political science classes. But perhaps, depending on your location, you think of images such as US Secretary of State Hillary Clinton announcing US military action in Libya, or Prime Minister Margaret Thatcher taking Britain to war against Argentina in the Falklands/Malvinas? Perhaps you think of Afghan women in blue burqas holding up fingertips inked purple after casting their votes in the 2009 presidential election? Or of American women tying yellow ribbons to trees in their front yards as a symbol of support for US troops? Perhaps it is Argentinean mothers in the Plaza de Mayo protesting against the Argentine government's "dirty war" against its own people? Or Liberian market women, lining the road taken to work each day by the murderous dictator Charles Taylor, shouting "We want peace; no more war!" Or perhaps, before the 2011 Nobel Peace Prize was awarded to Liberians Leymah Gbowee and Ellen Johnson Sirleaf and to Yemeni activist Tawakkol Karman, you were unaware of women's political activism in Liberia and in the "Arab Spring" – and throughout the world wherever wars are taking place?

Women engage in many different forms of political action related to war. Some of them are quite overt, as in the examples above. Other actions that would conventionally be recognized as "political" include women choosing to join state militaries or non-state armed groups in order to support a particular political ideology or cause (see chapters 6 and 7 in this volume), or women participating in peace processes (see chapter 8). Other forms may not always "look" like political action, even to the women themselves. In a world in which constructions of identity – e.g., gendered, religious, ethnic, national – are both mobilized for the purposes of war and constructed through processes of militarization, everyday acts can functionally be either complicit with or resistant to war and militarization (Enloe 2000, 2004). A US mother buying toy guns or the latest violent video game for her son, or the latest "camo" fashions for her daughter, for example, may see herself as simply responding to her child's wants, rather than helping reproduce the gendered social arrangements that make wars possible. Or a Rwandan widow who adopted a child orphaned by the 1994 genocide, and did so *across* ethnic lines, may have done so for the most personal of reasons, but her action is also a form of resistance which undermines the power of those who would use constructed ethnicized identities to fuel political violence.

As these examples begin to suggest, feminist theorists and activists have, over the last several decades, contested conventional notions of "the political" and "political action," complicating and expanding our notions of what these might mean. Refusing to accept the western liberal tradition's construction of social life as divided into two spheres – the public, masculinized, "political" realm of governance and the "private," domestic, feminized, "nonpolitical" sphere of home and family – feminists have since the late 1960s insisted that "the personal is political": that even our most intimate, personal experiences and relationships are imbued with systemic power relations, shaped by the multiple ways power is ordered in a society as well as by the actions of governmental, economic, cultural, and religious ("public sphere") institutions. Where, then, does "political action" lie? In coming to understand and expose those power relations within what was formerly seen as simply personal experience? In making what feel like seemingly "private" choices? In individually or collectively trying to influence "public sphere" institutions on and within their own terms? Or in contesting those terms? In insisting that so-called "feminine" concerns and values which have been relegated to the "private" sphere actually have a legitimate place in determining governmental values and actions? In destabilizing and transforming not only political structures but also our own identities, which have been constructed as part of the systemic power relations within which we live? In understanding "personal" suffering as political and as the basis for a kind of political movement? These are among the questions suggested by feminist interrogation of "the political,"[1] and by looking at women's actions in relation to war. They open the way to seeing that, in a sense, women's political action vis-à-vis war is evident throughout the whole of this book.

These questions are also evident throughout this chapter, which focuses primarily on women's organized collective political action in response to war and militarization. As emphasized throughout this volume, this investigation will need to discard comfortable generalizations such as "women are more peaceful than men," and to look instead at the ways in which differences among wars and among women shape women's varying political stances and actions. So our examples reflect a range of wars, from inter- and intra-state conflicts, to situations where, in effect, regimes are "waging war" on their own populations (e.g., the oppressive regimes of Latin America in relatively recent decades). And the women we look at will reflect a range of the positions women take: some women organize to support armed violence; some accept what they see as the necessity of war and militarization in general, and believe in the possibility of "just wars," but oppose a particular war – either on their own soil, or violence that their country's military visits upon foreign lands; some are steadfastly pacifist, opposed to *all* wars; some oppose not only the physical and political violence of war, but also what they see as the social and economic violence required to create a society in which war is materi- ally and politically possible, and in which gendered ideals and identities support militarization itself. Unfortunately, a single chapter cannot begin to adequately represent all of the locations around the world in which women organize for and against militarized violence, nor the full range of political positions women take. Instead, our examples, a small taste of the rich range of conceptual and field-based material available, are meant to be illustrative of particular themes and analytic questions that can be carried forward when you later read about women's political actions in other contexts.

The discursive context

"Men are naturally aggressive, violent and warlike, while women are naturally peaceful."

"Men must risk their lives in battle to protect the women and children back home."

"Women are not as interested as men in amassing political power; they just want to be able to create a peaceful, nurturing environment for their families."

Statements such as these are more than simply a set of beliefs about the gendered politics of war, and about women's and men's "natural" and mor- ally appropriate place within them; they need to be understood as part of the discursive context within which women's political action takes place. In other words, women's actions vis-à-vis war never exist somehow in and of themselves as the political acts of (gender-neutral) citizens; rather, they are always perceived and represented through a pervasive set of meanings about gender and war, seen against its prescriptions. Some women fully subscribe to their society's dominant narratives about gender and war; others attempt to resist or subvert those narratives. Some women self-consciously employ those narratives as a resource, fitting them to their own purposes; many do some combination of the above. Although there is some variation in gendered war narratives cross-culturally, what remains true in every context we know of is that the symbolic and material inextricability of gender and war is an ines- capable presence shaping the meanings of women's political actions – and inactions – in the face of war.

Or, to think about it slightly differently, the inextricable connections of gender and war create a situation in which the relation of women to war is, in a sense, *always already inherently political* – whether or not individual women consciously see themselves as political actors. Women are politically posi- tioned by war discourses, and their actions politicized – e.g., by war narratives glorifying patriotic mothers who willingly sacrifice their sons to the nation; by military planners promulgating and relying on specific standards of what it means to be a "good" military wife; by politicians who invoke the need to protect women and children as a way to justify military buildups, or specific wars, or authoritarian security states. So before (or whether) any individual woman makes the conscious decision to "take political action," women are already political factors in war, and in the ideologies, institutions, and processes of militarization which make war possible.

The association of men with war and women with peace

The themes which form the context of meanings for women's political actions, although not entirely uniform across time and place, seem to have some core elements which are at least pervasive enough to be thought of as themes with variations. The key dominant theme is the idea that men are "naturally" aggressive, violent, and warlike, while women are "naturally" peaceful, valuing the nurturance and preservation of life (see chapter 1, p. 12). This theme is so hegemonic that it seems not to require confirmation in the form of actual men's and women's behaviors – indeed, it almost seems immune to counter-evidence. The association of men and masculinity with war seems untouched, for example, by our own experience of the wide variety of masculinities enacted by different men in their daily lives, only a small number of which might fit the stereotype of masculinity which is seen as linked to war.[2] The association of women with peace is equally problematic, as Sara Ruddick argues:

> Women's peacefulness is at least as mythical as men's violence. Women have never absented themselves from war. Wherever battles are fought and justified, whether in the vilest or noblest of causes, women on both sides of the battle lines support the military engagements of their sons, lovers, friends, and mates. Increasingly, women are proud to fight alongside their brothers and as fiercely, in whatever battles their state or cause enlists them. . . . War is exciting; women, like men, are prey to the excitements of violence and community sacrifice it promises. War offers personal adventure and economic advantage to men and women. It may be, however, that women are especially enlivened by war's opportunities just because they are traditionally confined by domestic expectations in peacetime. Nonetheless, women usually justify their militarism as men do, in terms of loyalty, patriotism and the right. Even peace-loving women . . . support organized violence, at least in "emergencies." Like some men, some women are fierce and enthusiastic militarists; others, also like some men, see war as a natural catastrophe but collude with it, delegating to leaders political and military judgments they do not intend to understand. Most women, like most men, believe that violence must be met by violence and that the virtue of a cause justifies the horrors done in its name (Ruddick 1989, p. 154).

No matter how problematic the symbolic association of men and manliness with war and women with peace may be when we look at real men's and women's actions, it nonetheless has significant political effects. How does it affect the perceptions of women as political actors in the face of war? For one thing, at the level of state politics, perceptions of the (lack of) desirability of having women as state leaders have been shaped by the presumption that a head of state must be willing and able to lead (his) country into war, a quality which is equated with manliness. This framing appears in the vernacular everywhere from political cartoons to journalists' headlines to the discourse of both military and national security elites (Cohn 1993). It is also an implicit assumption in the arguments of many political scientists, although only occasionally made explicit, as in Francis Fukuyama's assertion that women are naturally more peaceful than men, which, in turn, he argues, makes them unfit to hold political power in an international context filled with aggressive male leaders (Fukuyama 1998; Tickner 1999). This framing puts great pressure on women who wish to ascend to public office to prove that they can be just as tough, aggressive, and bellicose as men, so it should be no surprise that among the relatively few modern women heads of state, several have presided over wars, including Margaret Thatcher, Indira Gandhi, and Golda Meir. Their actions, though, rather than functioning as disruption of the association of men with war and women with peace, are generally taken as proving that a few exceptional women can be as tough as men.

In the arenas of women's grassroots political action, women's transnational civil society, and feminist scholarship, the men–war/women–peace association has varied effects. Donna Pankhurst (2004) reflected that:

> [t]here has been a surge of international interest in "peaceful women," also featured in much of the writing on war-torn societies . . . . This seems to have occurred partly as a revulsion against the violence of war, and in the hope that a focus of attention on women might reveal the way towards a more peaceful, less violent world. (pp. 20–1)

There are certainly also many women antiwar activists around the world for whom the belief that women are more peaceful than men has a kind of "felt-truthfulness" and who find in it an energizing and effective basis for organizing against war. In many cases, they locate this desire for peace *not* in women's biology, but in a combination of factors, including the ways war makes "women's work" – of tending children, the elderly, gardens, fields, animals, homes, communities, and marketplaces – impossible. At the same time, they see powerful men, far removed from the challenges of daily caring labor, as having little motivation to end wars, especially because of the political and economic rewards these men reap from the continued violence. So, for example, when women from Liberia, Sierra Leone, and Guinea came together in 2000 to form the Mano River Women's Peace Network (MARWOPNET), they decided to focus their initial efforts on pushing male leaders to become more serious about ending the violence; they launched successful initiatives to convince the leaders of their respective countries to negotiate and cooperate with each other, and to get the Liberian government and rebel factions to come to a peace agreement (see chapter 8).[3]

War, motherhood and women's claims for a public voice

Although women base their antiwar activity in many different dimensions of both their identities and their political analyses, the attribution of greater peacefulness to women is so often linked to motherhood – both the capacity to give birth, and a social life of nurture – that it is worth examining this theme in some greater depth. It is a theme that goes back in global history, whether in Western Europe (Elshtain 1987) or South Asia (Jeffery & Basu 1998). It is also a theme that appears frequently in the course of women's antiwar and antiviolence organizing, and many women activists have themselves identified motherhood as the reason for their willingness to take political action, and/or the identity around which it is easiest to mobilize other women, or to legitimate their demands to be part of peace processes (see chapter 8). Critically, women have also found that framing their actions as based in their concerns as mothers has been an (at least partially) acceptable way for women to take oppositional political action. Additionally, in highly authoritarian, oppressive regimes, acting under the banner of motherhood may provide a slightly less dangerous way to voice dissent.

The case of the *Madres* of the Plaza de Mayo is illustrative. During what is known as "The Dirty War" in Argentina (1976–1983), the military government kidnapped, tortured, and murdered some 30,000 people whom they labeled as subversives. In the majority of the cases, these people were "disappeared," with no trace or record of their fate. And people who dared protest this terrorist behavior of the state put their own lives in danger. But in 1977, after desperately seeking information from the military officials about the whereabouts of their children without success, a group of mothers of the "disappeared" came together in the Plaza de Mayo, the central public space in Buenos Aires, to demand the return of their children. They walked around the square every Thursday afternoon for a decade, with the names of their disappeared children embroidered on their headscarves (when carrying photos or placards had been prohibited by the government). The protests were women-only, but not in fact restricted to actual mothers, since there were other female family members such as aunts.

There can be no doubt about the degree of courage required to initiate and maintain a movement of this kind; indeed, at least a dozen of the *Madres* were "disappeared" by paramilitaries in 1977 and never seen again, but the *Madres* persisted. Their protests were the first, and for a long time the only, public demonstration against the military regime's brutality. What we see here is the power of basing political organizing in maternal identity, particularly when in a repressive political space where no form of political opposition is safe. This power is in part due to the acknowledgment of and moral authority accorded to mothers' bonds with their children. But at the same time, it is in part due to the lack of gravity or respect accorded mothers in patriarchal social and political life. While on one level mothers are honored, on another, in the (masculinized) world of realpolitik, mothers are seen as not legitimately belonging in the public, political sphere at all – and thus they don't warrant being taken seriously as a political threat. Indeed, within Argentina, the response of the regime was at first dismissive – these were, at best, just over-emotional women or *madres locas* (mad mothers); only later did the regime comprehend the power of their protests. A specialist in Latin American women's movements, Georgina Waylen (2000), notes that the *Madres* were "an important force in bringing about the 'end of fear' under the dictatorship and delegitimizing the military government internationally through their campaign demanding the return of their disappeared children. The symbolic, ethical, and non-negotiable nature of the *Madres*' demands was effective in a political environment in which bargaining was impossible" (p. 772). It is important to remember, however, that different kinds of wars in different kinds of contexts will produce very different results: for example, the violent repression of the "Mothers' Movement" in the former Yugoslavia stands in stark contrast to the relative protection maternal identity afforded the *Madres* in Argentina (Korac 2003).

Within feminist writings on peace, militarism, and war, motherhood constitutes a central but highly contested topic. One concern is that an emphasis on maternity as the grounds for women's opposition to war seems to leave little basis for antiwar political agency among women who are not mothers, or who base their own antiwar positions in a different kind of political analysis, as we will see below. A second concern is that maternalist politics may be seen to rely on a notion of motherhood which is both biologically reductionist and universalizing. Although one of the pioneering feminist theorists in this field, Sara Ruddick (1989) argues that "motherhood" is not necessarily confined to biological mothers or even to women, and that anyone who takes on the task, male or female, can adopt this position, a more biologistic notion of motherhood has wide cultural currency and is subscribed to by some activists and some feminist writers (e.g., Caldicott 1985). This tends to lead to universalizing claims about mothers which don't easily accommodate an awareness of the differences among women across class, race/ethnicity, religion, culture, or location. In fact, some feminists stress that the image of (a supposedly universal) "maternal peacefulness" should more accurately be understood as reflecting a historically specific western ideal of motherhood (e.g., Mukta 2000; Scheper-Hughes 1992, 1996).

A third issue concerns the scope of political change that an antiwar politics grounded in a universalized maternal identity is capable of producing. Waylen (2000), for example, argues that the *Madres* succeeded in putting some pressures on the post-military regime, but that their activities have not confronted the wider gendered underpinnings of injustice, particularly in terms of class. Another example is the Mothers' Front in Sri Lanka, an initiative which tried to bring together Sinhalese and Tamil women but which ultimately collapsed because it could not really confront ethnicity (de Alwis 1998).

A fourth issue concerns the question of whether maternalist politics can actually undermine the systems which create war. For feminists who see conventional constructions of femininity and masculinity as essential underpinnings of militarism and war, the degree to which maternalist politics are rooted in traditional gender roles is of concern: if mothers' movements do not challenge those conventional gender constructions, how can they possibly undermine the underlying structures of war itself? Of course, the question of just how conventional a gender role is embodied in maternalist politics is a complicated one; while there is little transgressive about mothers asserting their love and right to protect their children, the very act of asserting that concern in the *public* sphere, and claiming it is a relevant counterweight to the highly valorized, masculinized realm of national security, *is* highly transgressive of "women's place," and may serve to transform it. However, even a somewhat transformed conception of motherhood is not necessarily inherently anti-militarist. But there are some instances where maternalist groups have evolved over time, moving from a politics stressing maternal protection of children in a specific war to a broader anti-militarist analysis. The Committee of Soldiers' Mothers of Russia is one example (see Text Box 5.1).

One other area of feminist contention about maternalist politics concerns the claim of "maternal peacefulness" itself. Sara Ruddick (1989) argues that mothers are not necessarily nonviolent or peaceful. Rather, she sees maternal practices as the basis for developing *ways of thinking* that *could* be resources for peace politics, but she does not claim that mothers necessarily apply those ways of thinking to their political commitments or actions – e.g., "even if only some mothers in some practices are effectively governed by [ideals of non-violence] . . . , there is no evidence that mothers more or less automatically express domestic ideals of non-violence publicly" (p. 176).

As Ruddick stresses, there are characteristic undersides to maternal practice which can lead to the support of militarized violence. To choose but three: first, mothers' investments in assuring the social acceptability of their children (Ruddick 1989, ch. 5), combined with the carefully produced social equation of military service with manhood, lead many mothers to encourage their sons to enlist. Second, as Nancy Sheper-Hughes (1996) found in her research in a Brazilian shantytown, there are many contexts in which mothering is predictably filled with loss, as poverty, malnutrition, preventable disease, the lack of clean water and/or pervasive violence defeat and even inhibit anything that might be called maternal "preservative love";[4] in these contexts, many mothers cultivate "the notion of inevitable, acceptable, and meaningful death," (p. 354), which fits well with militarists' constructions of patriotic motherhood. Indeed, it is not only in contexts of great poverty that political leaders have been able to channel maternal grief and anger about the loss of their sons and daughters in combat into support for the continuation of war, so that their children's deaths "would not be in vain," as Lorraine Bayard de Volo (1998, 2004) shows in her study of mother's organizations in both the USA and Nicaragua. Third, mothers' desires to protect their own children can be linked to "distinctive and virulent forms of self-righteous hatred and fear of the outsider, sometimes issuing in a racism that fuels and is fueled

Box 5.1 The Committee of Soldiers' Mothers of Russia: from "maternalism" to anti-militarism?

The Committee of Soldiers' Mothers of Russia (CSMR) was founded in 1989 by 300 mothers of soldiers. Their initial aim was to campaign for their sons to return home early from military service in order to resume their studies, and they succeeded in bringing home nearly 180,000 young men. Through their work, these mothers came face to face with the appalling conditions in the armed forces, which included beatings, abuse and humiliation of conscripts, lack of food, and widespread corruption (Right Livelihood Award 1996). This led them to broaden their goals, beyond what might be seen as the "private," maternal aim of improving the lives of their own sons, to the "public" goals of reforming military structures on a democratic basis, establishing effective civilian control over the military, and passing legislation to provide for alternatives to military service. In November 1994, another phase of the war in Chechnya broke out and "the peaceful time for the Committee was over" (CSMR 2011). They opposed the state's rationale for the war, seeing (then) President Putin's militaristic stance as a threat to still-fragile Russian democracy (Liborakina 1996). While continuing to campaign for changes in the legal and political systems, they instigated more dramatic antiwar activities. Hundreds of mothers organized by CSMR actually went to Chechnya to take their sons away from the war. They negotiated with the Chechen army and obtained the release of captured conscripts. At the same time, they started a campaign encouraging mothers to support the right of their sons to refuse military service – something highly controversial in the context of Soviet (and Russian) history (Right Livelihood Award 1996). They also publicized the impact of human rights abuses by the Russian forces, and their effects on Chechen women (Liborakina 1996).

In 1996, Marina Liborakina, then head of the Feminist Research Department at the Russian Institute for Cultural Research concluded that:

> "[a]ltogether, the women's antiwar movement has challenged not only the authorities, but the entire 'Hero's Mother' myth so popular in Soviet culture. Mothers of soldiers killed in Afghanistan [in the 1970s] were encouraged to deliver speeches on international solidarity, and not be seen in tears in public. The 'hero's mother' rhetoric did not leave space for natural human feelings of sorrow, grief, or anger. Now that women are free to publicly express these emotions, they have used this power to push the antiwar movement from its early narrow focus on maternal rights to a broad call for human rights".
> (Liborakina 1996)

by violence" (Ruddick 1989, p. 177). Given that ethno-nationalist, religious fundamentalist, and communalist movements, as well as the mobilization for *any* war, all rely on the construction of the dangerous "other," it should hardly be surprising then that maternal identity can be enlisted in pro-war sentiment and activism.[5] Returning to the "Mothers' Movement" in the former Yugoslavia, for example, although Croatian and Serb women organized across ethnic lines to protest their sons' mobilization during the buildup to war, shortly after the fighting started, their alliance fell apart under the weight of competing nationalisms (Nikolić-Restanović 1998).

Thus, while the identity of mother has unquestionably been one that women have used in organizing against war and violence, it is also an identity which has been drawn upon in support of militaristic ideologies and par-

Box 5.2 Maternal practice as a *potential* resource for peace politics

"Although mothers are not intrinsically peaceful, maternal practice is a 'natural resource' for peace politics. For reasons both deep and banal, it matters what mothers say and do. Women, and perhaps especially mothers, have serviced and blessed the violent while denying the character of the violence they serve. A peacemaker's hope is a militarist's fear: that the rhetoric and passion of maternity can turn against the military cause that depends on it. . . . The question peacemakers face is how the 'peacefulness' latent in maternal practice can be realized and then expressed in public action so that a commitment to treasure bodies and minds at risk can be transformed into resistance to the violence that threatens them." (Ruddick 1989, p. 157).

ticular wars. So "maternal peacefulness" needs to be understood as a "truth in the making" (Ruddick 1989, p. 160), a specific political choice, engaging and transforming ideas about both maternity and militarism, rather than as an inevitable product of giving birth to and raising children (see Text Box 5.2).

Some political implications of the association of men with war and women with peace

Even though an often widely shared sense that women are more peaceful than men can be a rich source of power in women's organizing, it can also, paradoxically, have a disempowering effect on women. To the extent that women's peacefulness is posited to be "natural," women's antiwar action is in danger of being dismissed as "not really political," or not something that needs to be reckoned with politically. That is, whether or not women themselves see and articulate their politics as arising from their identities as women, the trope of "women's peacefulness" positions women's war/peace politics as rooted in their identities. And if women are positioned as taking a particular stance *because* they are women or mothers, i.e., only as a reflexive product of their biological or social status (and its associated emotions), the rational thought and analysis which led to their political positions is obscured, discounted.

This depoliticization of women's politics, beyond simply being insulting, has pernicious political effects. First, it makes it easier for those in power not to take women's political action particularly seriously – e.g., to discount it as "just women's natural reaction to war; they are so involved in caring about their family members that they cannot see the larger political issues." Second, it makes it easier for those in power to exclude women from both peace processes and state power structures when the war is over. That is, to the extent that women's activism has been seen as rooted in their particularistic identities, rather than in their political thought, analysis, and interests, it is easy to imagine that they should – and will want to – return to their "proper place" of family, home, and hearth, the so-called "private sphere," when the war ends. So, for example, male leaders might find it easy to rationalize their exclusion of women from peace processes with the idea that: "If these market women wanted us to come to a peace agreement because they were tired of the killing and of the ways war made their work of caring for family and community impossible, then a cessation of the shooting should send them home; there is no reason to think they would have any interest in defining the terms of the constitution or the form of postwar governance, nor in the negotiations around the postwar division of power, or any other 'public sphere' role."

To point out the potentially depoliticizing effect of this trope is not to deny that many women – and men – ardently desire nothing more than being able to return to a peaceful family life when war is over. However, as is evident throughout the chapters of this book, it is no more than a comfortable illusion to assume that women simply and happily return to a cozy domestic sphere. Many cannot return to the home and family they knew: their loved ones have been killed or left wounded, traumatized, unstable, violent; they are rejected by their own families and communities because they have been raped, have borne children of "the other," or have committed atrocities themselves; their homes and means of livelihood have been destroyed; or perhaps their homes and fields may even be unharmed, but as widows they have no rights of ownership and so no way to go on living there. Many other women, even if their former lives could be returned to, do not wish to: their wartime experiences have likely included more fluid gender roles, and may have left them feeling empowered in new ways, and/or with new thoughts about the meaning of fairness, equality, and justice – so a return to the way things were becomes a dreaded, rather than desired, future. Some will return to those lives anyway, encumbered by the responsibilities of caring for others or by lack of resources and options. But some of them will forge new lives, and some will see political participation in the reconstruction of their countries as crucial for creating the more just, democratic, peaceful, and gender-equitable society in which they wish to live. However, for the men who hold power and do not wish to share it, the trope of women's "natural peacefulness" can make it easy to discount the political work women did during the war, and to justify their exclusion from the political process during and after war's end.

At this point, one might reasonably stop to wonder whether the association of men with war and women with peace has a similarly depoliticizing effect on men's political actions. After all, if we are arguing that this trope ends up positioning women as taking a particular stance *because* they are women, a product of their "nature" rather than their informed reflection on political issues, wouldn't the trope do the same thing to men? The answer is complicated. To the extent that anyone, man or woman, feminist or not, attributes a man's bellicosity or willingness to fight simply to his biological and/or social status as a man, to his "naturally greater" aggression, this trope could be seen as similarly depoliticizing men's actions. But at the same time, it seems that men's political stances on war are reduced to their gendered identities far less frequently than women's are. Although in the USA during the Cold War, for example, it was not uncommon to hear comments like, "Do you really want a woman's finger on the [nuclear] button? What if she had PMS?", there was never a parallel popular political discourse suggesting that men shouldn't be trusted with their fingers on the button because "their judgment is distorted by aggression-inducing testosterone." Why would there be this difference? Why do assumptions about women's biology play a bigger role here than those about men's biology? In part, it goes back to the idea of "gendered organizations" described in chapter 1. In our gendered political institutions, men are the default assumption; masculinity is embedded in the (supposedly objective) models of what makes a good leader, so it is the *absence* of sufficient masculinity, rather than the *presence* of masculinity itself, which will perceived to be a problem. In that case, the question becomes, "is he man enough to go to war?" not, "does the fact that he is a man make him too likely to go to war?" In part, the answer can also be found in classic gender stereotypes which reduce women to their bodies and emotions, while seeing men as less bound by theirs. In many societies, women are seen to be governed by their bodies, hormones, emotions, and particularistic attachments to others in a way that men are not. In contrast, men are seen to be more able to be dispassionate and rational and to make decisions based in abstract universal principles (such as honor or patriotism) rather than in the bonds of personal relationships – e.g., "I love my son, but I am ready to sacrifice him for the defense of my country, or the glory of God, if necessary." So to the extent that men's purported rationality and dispassion are seen to enable them to transcend the emotional entanglements of the physical body, most prevailing gendered belief systems do not reduce men's politics to their embodied identities; thus, even a belief that men are "by nature" warlike and women are "by nature" peaceful would not lead to the discounting and depoliticizing of men's actions in the way it does for women's.

The protector, the protected, and the justification of war

Traditionally, in most cultures, it has been men's lot to fight while women watch, suffer, applaud, ameliorate, and forgive . . . Her admiring tears make his fighting possible; her danger from his enemy makes his fighting necessary (Ruddick 1989, p. 143).

The embedded corollary to the idea that men are naturally violent, aggressive warriors is the idea that women need protection – from (some) men by (other) men. So the masculinity of the warrior both requires and constitutes an additional masculinity – that of the protector. In some senses, these may appear to be opposites; as Iris Marion Young frames it:

The logic of masculinist protection, then, includes the image of the selfish aggressor who wishes to invade the lord's property and sexually conquer his women. These are the bad men. Good men can only appear in their goodness if we assume that lurking outside the warm familial walls are aggressors who wish to attack them. The dominative masculinity in this way constitutes protective masculinity as its other. (Young 2003, p. 5)

But it is also important to see that violent masculinities and protective masculinities do not divide neatly along lines of "bad men" versus "good men." In fact, it may be more useful to see these two masculinities as twinned aspects of militarized masculinity, conjoined in the same person. That is, rather than the appeal *of* aggression, it is often the appeal *to* protection (of women, children, and the nation) that is used to mobilize men to join militaries and armed groups; then, their ensuing training in violence and aggression is framed as the tool that will enable them to be protectors. And their later use of violence, as they wound, torture, murder, or rape, can, paradoxically, be celebrated not (or not only) as acts of violence, but as acts of protection.

Feminist theorists, such as Cynthia Enloe (1990b, 2007), Judith Stiehm (1982), Ann Tickner (1992, 2001), and Iris Marion Young (2003), have explored the use of the gendered trope of "the protector and the protected" as a justification for war, and also for a state's repression of its own people. For centuries, military and political leaders have found it expedient and effective to solicit public support for wars, and men's loyalty to fighting forces, by appealing to the need to protect women, children, and the nation – made easier by the symbolic elision of women and nation, as discussed in previous chapters. This is arguably an easier "sell" than arguments such as "we should fight a war to gain access to resources," or "to install a political regime friendly to the economic interests of our corporations." Sometimes the protection of women is publicly framed as the overt reason for the war. More often, it is somewhat less direct – e.g., we must fight to protect our way of life, our freedoms, our nation from the infidels, our tribe from their tribe, the world from communism, "us" from whomever is defined as "them" – but it is always implicit, and sometimes explicit, that it is the defenseless women and children back home whom soldiers must protect from these scourges. There is also a variation on this theme. Although usually it is "our" women who are to be protected, wars of colonial or imperial conquest have sometimes been framed as "white men saving brown women from brown men," in Gayatri Spivak's memorable phrase (Spivak 1988, p. 297) – a framing which also resonates with much of the current rhetoric about the "global war on terror" (see Text Box 5.3).

When a war is cast as a matter of protecting women, it can be a way of appealing both to fear and to some of the more gallant and honorable motives that men and women hold. In the case of the US invasion of Afghanistan, the Bush administration's couching it as the rescue of Afghan women from the Taliban did, in fact, appeal to many US women and led some American women's organizations, notably the Feminist Majority Foundation, to support the war. Many other US women and women's organizations, however, joined women in many other countries in actively opposing the war. They saw this framing as little more than cynical opportunism, noting the USA's long

Box 5.3 Laura Bush on the US war in Afghanistan

The George W. Bush administration, in an effort to strengthen popular support for its war on Afghanistan, employed a variety of rhetorical strategies, one of which was to invoke the "protector and protected" trope, casting US military intervention as a way of protecting Afghan women. Laura Bush delivered this message in a November 17, 2001 radio address:

"Good morning. I'm Laura Bush, and I'm delivering this week's radio address to kick off a worldwide effort to focus on the brutality against women and children by the al-Qaida terrorist network and the regime it supports in Afghanistan, the Taliban. . . . The brutal oppression of women is a central goal of the terrorists. Long before the current war began, the Taliban and its terrorist allies were making the lives of children and women in Afghanistan miserable. . . . Only the terrorists and the Taliban forbid education to women. Only the terrorists and the Taliban threaten to pull out women's fingernails for wearing nail polish. The plight of women and children in Afghanistan is a matter of deliberate human cruelty, carried out by those who seek to intimidate and control. . . .

Civilized people throughout the world are speaking out in horror – not only because our hearts break for the women and children in Afghanistan, but also because in Afghanistan we see the world the terrorists would like to impose on the rest of us. . . . And they must be stopped. The fight against terrorism is also a fight for the rights and dignity of women." (Bush 2001)

history of subordinating women's rights to other political agendas, and, in particular, the billions of dollars the CIA poured into creating and supporting Islamist groups in Afghanistan, including the Taliban, during the Soviet occupation (Weaver 2000; Roy 2001), and the fact that the Taliban's oppression of women, as exposed by the clandestine organization Revolutionary Women of Afghanistan (RAWA), had for years been completely ignored by US administrations. RAWA itself rejected the idea that this war was fought to, or would in any way, protect Afghan women, and split with the Feminist Majority over their support of the invasion (Russo 2006).

Indeed, the so-called "global war on terror" has erased women's diverse political histories in favor of a racialized narrative of Islamic oppression and of "rescue" by the forces of modernity represented by the West (Bhattacharyya 2008). In countries far beyond Afghanistan and Iraq, oppressive regimes have found it convenient to reclassify long-standing resistance movements as "Islamic terrorists," thereby justifying greater repression and garnering increased US military aid. One example is the insurgency in the region of Mindanao in the Philippines. Philippine feminist organizations, such as Gabriela, have campaigned against the state's abuse of human rights of women and men in this area for a long period. However, since 2002, the USA has deployed military forces to "assist" the Filipino army, with numerous reports of continuing abuses (HRW 2010).[6]

Recent nationalist and ethno-nationalist conflicts have also been sites where "the need to protect women" has figured prominently not only in the justification for war, but in strategies used to mobilize both men and women to support war; when women are represented as the embodiment of the nation and the nation is represented as a woman under threat, women acquire political meanings as targets, and "protection of the nation" reso-nates as a deeply personal motivation in specifically gendered ways. There is now a substantial body of evidence and analysis of how deeply gendered meanings inhere in discourses of nationalism and in nationalist and ethno-nationalist conflicts.[7] Within this literature, there is a growing exploration of the extent to which women support violent ethno-nationalist, communalist, and sectarian movements, often participating in violence themselves, as well as urging their men to greater violence, including sexual violence against other women.[8]

The opposite of protection: highlighting the harms of war and militarization

The trope of the "protector and the protected," while providing a powerfully resonant justification for supporting war, also opens up a powerful avenue for resisting war. That is, to the extent that women's and men's political support for war can be mobilized by evoking the desire to protect women, showing that war has the opposite effect can be a powerful way of mobiliz-ing opposition to it. And indeed there is a wide range of women's antiwar organizing that works to do just that. Women's antiwar organizations and networks, from the local women's groups that oppose the ongoing wars in their own countries, to the international advocacy network that has coa-lesced around passing and implementing UN Security Council Resolutions on women, peace, and security (see Text Boxes 3.1 and 8.3), have made showing the ways war victimizes women one of their major strategies. It is a strategy that arises directly out of the experiences of women in war-affected areas; it is also a strategy that serves to undercut the justificatory protection narrative of war itself.

Almost always, when women antiwar activists point to the excruciating harms done to women in war, they do so in the context of demands for justice, for the end of impunity, and for women's right to participate in formal peace processes, postwar governance and reconstruction, and the prevention of armed conflicts. As the women of MARWOPNET, for example, put it: "a group of African women decided to come together to promote their participation in the process of preventing and managing conflicts and restoring peace in Africa. They realized that, being the principal victims of conflicts along with their children, they should have a say in the decisions made regarding these conflicts" (MARWOPNET 2005). So, rather than women's victimization stand-ing alone, it is linked to women's political agency and the transformation of existing gendered power structures. Unfortunately, to date, in international forums such as the UN Security Council, there has been more attention paid to the women-as-victim element, and less to the demand for women's greater decision-making power in political institutions (Cohn 2008). This is perhaps a good illustration of a point made by feminist theorists about the trope of "the protector and the protected": both in the family and in politics, the role of the masculine protector puts those protected – women, children, citizens of other states – in a subordinate position; in return for protection, they are expected to obey their protector and cede their own agency.

Taking apart war's promise of protection is not only a strategy of women activists who oppose a particular war; some women activists focus more widely on the harms inflicted by militarization itself, and on the gendered social, economic, political, and symbolic processes and structures that make war possible. These activists insist that we look not only at *war*, and the wrenching depth and complexity of its costs to women, but at the costs of living within a *war system*. Although they may or may not choose to describe themselves with the word "feminist," many of these activists are motivated not only by the direct human, economic, and environmental costs of militarization, but also, and especially, by the ways militarization both relies on and constructs pernicious gender relations. The Turkish organization Amargi Kadın Akademisi is one example of a group which dissociates itself from the idea that "women suffer the most from war" in order to focus more directly on the inextricable links between militarization and gender subordination. "They direct their feminist activism against the military because, 'like nationalism and heterosexism, it's a mechanism through which masculinity is produced.'"[9]

Several far-reaching transnational women's networks also explicitly link their opposition to militarization and war systems with a systemic critique of gender relations. The Women's International League for Peace and Freedom (WILPF), founded in 1915 by 1,300 women from Europe and North America, now has sections in Africa, the Asia-Pacific region, South Asia, the Middle East, the Americas, and Europe; its UN office played a key role in the passage of Security Council Resolution 1325.[10] Women in Black, which started in Israel in 1987 as a group of women protesting Israel's military occupation of the West Bank, has become a worldwide network of women who engage in nonviolent direct action to protest militarism, nationalism, war, and violence against women.[11] The International Women's Network against Militarism (IWNAM) is "a network of individuals and organizations from South Korea, Philippines, Okinawa, Japan, Puerto Rico, Hawai'i, Guam and the continental United States who are organizing against the harmful effects of US bases, military budgets, and military operations,"[12] including the USA's support for right-wing, repressive regimes, increasing economic inequality, environmental pollution, military prostitution, and the large numbers of children left behind by American soldiers. They are explicit in their critique of militarized conceptions of gender: "Masculinity in many countries, including the United States, is defined in military terms. We need a redefinition of masculinity, strength, power and adventure; an end to war toys and the glorification of war and warriors" (Network 2002 as cited in Cockburn 2007, p. 68). Their multidimensional, gendered analysis of the impacts of living with the physical, institutional, and political manifestations of the war system is in many ways echoed by feminist antinuclear activists, as we shall see in the next section.

Refusing the promise of "protection": women's antinuclear protest

Feminist antinuclear activists have also focused on the contrast between the militarized promise of protection and the realities of daily harm. In the case of nuclear weapons, the purported protection is supposed to come in the form of "deterrence," the theory that if a state has nuclear weapons, its opponents will be deterred from attacking it with nuclear, and in many cases, conventional, weapons. Feminist antinuclear activists have tended not to focus on the (largely theological) question of whether or not deterrence works. While many have focused on the literally incomprehensible destruction caused by the use of the weapons themselves, what has united feminist antinuclear activists across continents has been attention to the gendered physical, social, political, environmental, and ethical costs of developing and possessing nuclear weapons, *even if* they are never again used in an attack (Cohn 1987, 1993; Cohn & Ruddick 2004; Cohn et al. 2005).

Indian antinuclear feminists, for example, have focused on economic and social costs:

> The social costs of nuclear weaponisation in a country where the basic needs of shelter, food and water, electricity, health and education have not been met are obvious. . . . [S]ince patriarchal family norms place the task of looking after the daily needs of the family mainly upon women, scarcity of resources always hits women the hardest. Less food for the family inevitably means an even smaller share for women and female children just as water shortages mean an increase in women's labour who have to spend more time and energy in fetching water from distant places at odd hours of the day. (Sangari et al. 2001, p. 48)

They also point out that India's possession of nuclear weapons has been taken as conferring a national "virility" which has produced social consent for increasing levels of violence (Sangari et al. 2001, p. 48). And they examine the effect of nuclear weapons on the gendering of moral thought, and, consequently, political life:

> [T]he strange character of nuclear policy-making not only sidelines moral and ethical questions, but genders them. This elite gets to be represented as rational, scientific, modern, and of course masculine, while ethical questions, questions about the social and environmental costs, are made to seem emotional, effeminate, regressive, and not modern. This rather dangerous way of thinking, which suggests that questions about human life and welfare are somehow neither modern nor properly masculine questions, or that men have no capacity and concern for peace and morality, can have disastrous consequences for both men and women. (Sangari et al. 2001, p. 48)

Box 5.4 The Women's Peace Camp at Greenham Common

In 1981, preparations had started for the arrival of 96 American Tomahawk Cruise missiles at the Greenham Common Airbase in southern England. Each nuclear missile carried the destructive power equivalent to 50,000 tons of TNT, four times that of the atomic bomb that obliterated Hiroshima. Concurrently, in Wales, a few women had begun to worry about nuclear waste disposal sites planned for near their homes and, more broadly, about the doctrine of "national security" through nuclear weapons. The idea of a women's peace camp grew from very small beginnings – 36 women, and a few men and children, who walked the 120 miles from Cardiff to Greenham Common. Although not originally envisaged as a women-only protest, according to most records it became one when disputes broke out between men present at the camp over nonviolent tactics – and who was doing the washing up! Although this caused some friction, there was always some support from male partners and other men.[13]

Some 35,000 women were mobilized to surround the nine miles of wire around the camp by linking arms and hands – the largest women's demonstration in modern history, and an image that went round the world. Women also scaled the fence on several occasions, and managed to climb atop one of the missile silos. Much of the women's resistance was expressed in forms that emphasized concern for the well-being of children and families; for example, the protestors encircling the base's fence attached items like children's toys. However, they also constantly emphasized the economic costs of the UK and US nuclear arsenals, the effects on workers in the nuclear industry, and related issues. Although the protestors ultimately failed to prevent the deployment of the Cruise missiles to and from the base, there is a general consensus amongst defense experts, such as Dan Plesch, the founder of the British American Security Council (BASIC), that "The Greenham protestors came to symbolize a much broader international mass movement" and that this movement "had a decisive impact in preventing nuclear war, and helping ease the tensions so that the Cold War ended peacefully."[14]

Activists in the USA and UK have similarly refused the idea of "protection" through nuclear weapons and highlighted their many destructive costs. In the 1960s, members of Women Strike for Peace (WSP) brought baby carriages into the US Congress as part of their campaign against above-ground nuclear weapons testing, highlighting that the tests resulted in radioactive Strontium-90 being found in mothers' breast milk, as well as cow's milk. Amy Swerdlow, a historian as well as a member of WSP, sees WSP as an example of women's movements which self-consciously employ and invoke traditional gender roles for the purpose of undermining the same militarized patriarchal culture that produces and relies on those roles. A similar employing/undermining strategy was used in the 1980s, during the height of Cold War rhetoric about fighting and "winning" nuclear wars, by women antinuclear activists who created peace camps at nuclear installations (see Text Box 5.4).

Feminist transversal politics in the face of violent ethno-nationalism

Women have had diverse political relations to different kinds of nationalist projects. There is a long history of women's support for nationalist anticolonial liberation movements, perhaps particularly because the ideologies of national liberation movements have often included support for women's rights and the transformation of some of the more egregious patriarchal practices. Kumari Jayawardena (1986), looking at late nineteenth- and early twentieth-century anti-imperialist struggles in Turkey, Egypt, Iran, Afghanistan, India, Sri Lanka, Indonesia, the Philippines, China, Vietnam, Korea, and Japan, finds that nationalist struggles have long been seen by some women as a vehicle for advancing women's rights, and in some cases, for more thorough-going feminist transformations of gender relations. (For more recent examples from Latin American and African anticolonial wars, see chapter 7.) However, when independence movements succeed, too often these feminist gains fail to materialize in the newly independent state, and feminist analysis and critiques of recent decades have turned their focus to the genderings of nationalism itself, as well as the ways that both state-building processes and the political and economic relations between states rely on particular constructions of masculinity and femininity. Nationalist discourses which portray women as the biological and social reproducers of the nation, the embodiment of national identity and communal honor, have proved toxic for women, serving to legitimize control of women's lives and bodies, to make rape and forced impregnation into weapons of ethno-nationalist conflicts, and to construct woman and nation as passive victims rather than political agents in the masculinized state – even while women have supported a wide range of nationalist projects, from anticolonial to genocidal.[15]

It is in the context of violent ethno-nationalist, communal, and sectarian conflicts which build powerful identifications along lines of ethnicity, religion, caste, race, tribe that we find a form of activism that is explicitly informed by feminist antiwar thinking – a form that can be summarized as transversal antiwar politics. This approach also takes the wartime suffering experienced by women as its starting point, but locates this within a broader analysis of the gendered nature of violent ethno-nationalism, and integrates the need for intersectional analysis (Crenshaw 1991; Yuval-Davis 2006), the examination of the way in which the different forms of identification and discrimination interact on multiple, often simultaneous, levels and how they contribute to an outcome of systematic social inequality. Transversal antiwar politics aims to enable "dialogues which give recognition to the specific positionings of those who participate in them as well as to the 'unfinished knowledge' that each such situated positioning can offer" (Yuval-Davis 1997, p. 130), and it has been put into practice by a section of the women's antiwar movement in order to enable dialogue with conflict-affected women across the divides of religion, ethnicity, or political ideology.

Cynthia Cockburn has written about women's organizations that take this approach in three contexts: Northern Ireland, Bosnia-Herzegovina and Israel/Palestine. In the case of Bosnia-Hercegovina, the work was associated with the Medica Women's Therapy Centre which was established in the town of Zenica in 1992, during the worst phases of the Serb nationalist project, to offer a refuge to women (Cockburn 1998, p. 174). As a result of their activities, it was possible for the supporting international political network to use the news of Bosnian women's experience "not to institutionalize women as victims, not to incite men to more carnage, but to explain anew how war makers rely on peculiar ideas about masculinity" (Enloe 1994, p. 220 as cited in Cockburn 1998, p. 223). Feminist activists in Belgrade (Serbia) were also able to draw on this form of activism in their vision of an alternative future. This kind of feminist analysis and activism in turn contributed to the landmark shifts in international humanitarian law represented by the International Criminal Tribunal for the former Yugoslavia (ICTY).

Turning to Northern Ireland, the work of the Women's Support Network in Belfast made it possible for women to physically and figuratively cross the dividing lines (Catholic/Protestant; Republican/Loyalist) without feeling that they were surrendering their own identities. Combined with numerous other initiatives, including the Northern Ireland Women's Coalition, this kind of activity played a significant role in dismantling the "politics of fear" and was a definite element in the political atmosphere that led to the historic Good Friday Agreement of 1998 (Jacobson 2000). In both countries, the women involved were "not on the whole, pacifists. What they are looking for is an opening to justice so that words can replace weapons sooner than might otherwise be the case" (Cockburn 1998, p. 8).

Conclusion

As we have seen, women take a wide range of political stances in relation to war. They can be found anywhere and everywhere on a continuum from militant inciters and supporters of war's violence to steadfast pacifist opponents of the use of armed force in any circumstance. Among those who take an anti-war position, some are motivated by the desire to prevent or end a particular war, either in their own country or beyond its borders; others extend their analysis and activism to the society-wide militarization underlying international war systems, and to the gendered processes and inequalities they rely upon and create.

This chapter has argued that both the "men/war women/peace" trope and the "protector/protected" trope need to be understood as politically potent themes employed in the mobilization of societies to support both war and militarization. They also shape the political space within which women act and the ways in which their actions are perceived. While some women find these tropes resonate with their own perceptions and draw on them as a resource in their own political organizing, others purposefully attempt to subvert these tropes, and still others do both. However, no matter the degree to which any specific woman or women's organization accepts or rejects the idea of women as more peaceful and/or in need of armed men's protection, the tropes can act as a filter through which women's actions are perceived, and as a means to discount their political actions.

Those women's antiwar politics that rest comfortably in received gender roles and dichotomies exist in a kind of tension: although the roles and binaries themselves are a critical part of the structures underlying patriarchal war systems and processes of militarization, these women, by virtue of their taking political action, also resist and undermine some of the very conceptions of their roles that are embedded in the trope of "women's peacefulness" – at least to a degree. Antiwar feminists, who tend to take a broader anti-militarization stance, view war as the outcome of multiple interlocking layers of gendered, militarized processes which are themselves deeply destructive – to economies, democratic processes, the environment, human rights, social justice and ideas about masculinities, femininities and power relations between men and women – and thus they believe that a challenge to the entire militarization/gender nexus is central to the prevention of war. Whatever their specific politics, though, when women take political action against war, the costs of their activism can be tremendous; many have been beaten, jailed, tortured, cast out by their husbands, ostracized by their communities, disappeared and murdered because they dared to analyze, write, organize, protest, and speak out. But increasingly, transnational women's and feminist antiwar networks of activists, practitioners, and scholars have worked to make their struggles more visible, helped provide moral and financial support, and fostered the kinds of cross-regional exchange of experience, ideas, and analysis that invigorate and strengthen women's political action in the face of war.

QUESTIONS FOR DISCUSSION

1 In your own experience, what kind of statements are most commonly used to support the argument that women are "naturally" more pro-peace than men (include sources from the media)? Do you consider that these statements constitute sound evidence?

2 There are many differences in the ways women organize in response to war, including: some choose to work in mixed-sex groups while others work in women-only groups; and some choose to act "as women," or "as mothers," or "as feminists," while others downplay gender and prefer to act "as citizens." What do you see as the strengths and weaknesses of each of these choices?

3 Do you think a feminist gender analysis is critical to antiwar politics? Why or why not?

SUGGESTIONS FOR FURTHER READING

Bayard de Volo, Lorraine (1998) "Drafting Motherhood: Maternal Imagery and Organizations in the United States and Nicaragua," in Lois Ann Lorentzen and

Jennifer Turpin (eds.) *The Women and War Reader*. New York: New York University, pp. 140–253.

Cockburn, Cynthia (2007) *From Where We Stand: War, Women's Activism and Feminist Analysis*. London: Zed Books.

Cohn, Carol (2008) "Mainstreaming Gender in UN Security Policy: A Path to Political Transformation?" in Shirin M. Rai and Georgina Waylen (eds.), *Global Governance: Feminist Perspectives*. London: Palgrave Macmillan, pp. 185–206.

Enloe, Cynthia (2007) *Globalization and Militarism: Feminists Make the Link*. Lanham, MD: Rowman & Littlefield Publishers.

Gbowee, Leymah, and Gautam, Shobha (2006) *A Conversation with Women Peacebuilders*. Talk given at The Boston Consortium on Gender, Security and Human Rights. The Fletcher School of Law and Diplomacy, Tufts University, March 8, 2006. www.genderandsecurity.umb.edu/Leymah%20Gbowee%20and%20Shobha%20Gautam%203-8-06.pdf (accessed December 24, 2011).

Jayawardena, Kumari (1986) *Feminism and Nationalism in the Third World*. London: Zed Books.

Ruddick, Sara (1989) *Maternal Thinking: Towards a Politics of Peace*. Boston: Beacon Press.

CHAPTER 6

Women and State Military Forces

Jennifer G. Mathers

Introduction

According to the eminent military historian John Keegan:

> Warfare is . . . the one human activity from which women, with the most insignificant
> exceptions, have always and everywhere stood apart. . . . Women . . . do not fight . . . and
> they never, in any military sense, fight men. If warfare is as old as history and as universal
> as mankind, we must now enter the supremely important limitation that it is an entirely
> masculine activity (Keegan 1993, p. 76).

Keegan is but one among the many scholars who have ignored or dismissed
the possibility that women can have important relationships with wars and
militaries. On those occasions when the presence of women in war *is* acknowledged, women are usually depicted exclusively as opponents or victims of
war. However, while many women do oppose war and suffer as a result of the
destruction that wars inflict, women do not "stand apart" from war in other
respects. On the contrary, research done by feminist scholars has revealed
that militaries depend on women for every aspect of their existence. Women's
work, both paid and unpaid, sustains armed forces around the world, and has
done so for generations.

But militaries do not only depend on women; they also depend on gender.
They construct, rely on, and perpetuate beliefs about gender, and they depend
on women and men to accept, internalize, and act on those beliefs. This
means that both women and men must not only believe that women and men
"naturally" have different characteristics and behaviors; they also must see
military organizations and war itself as inherently gendered and "naturally"
masculine, so that women are seen as fundamentally *not* suited to soldiering
and warfare.

The reluctance to acknowledge the many ways in which women and militaries are inextricably linked extends to those women who join state militaries. Women soldiers are often dismissed as an insignificant, token element. It
is true that women soldiers are completely absent from some militaries and
that they tend to comprise a very small part of those armed forces in which
they are present. And the restrictions militaries place on the posts in which
women can serve would appear to provide further justification for regarding
women soldiers as insignificant. But the low proportions of women serving

and the narrow range of jobs they perform are not accidents. The very fact that states devote so much attention to defining and policing the boundaries of women's service suggests that women soldiers are far more important than their numbers would indicate.

The presence of women in state militaries is unsettling, raising uncomfortable questions for militaries, politicians, governments, and societies. It challenges assumptions about appropriate roles for men and women within a society and about the nature of masculinity and femininity. As Annica Kronsell (2005) argues, the presence of even a few women in a military "challenges hegemonic masculine norms and puts the entire military to the test" (p. 286). This level of challenge helps explain why women's military service has overwhelmingly been depicted as exceptional and, often, as a measure which may be necessary in wartime but which should be reversed as quickly as possible once the immediate crisis has passed. For societies to believe that it is normal or natural for women's actions and beliefs to shape and be shaped by militaries would risk destabilizing the very basis on which those militaries operate, and that would, in turn, have serious implications for the ways in which we think about what it means to be a woman or a man.

This chapter draws on historical and contemporary examples in order to explore some of the complex connections between women, men, militaries, societies and gender. It is important to start with the awareness that state militaries differ from each other, and women's relationships with militaries will vary depending on the nature of the military. An all-volunteer force that must appeal to women as well as to men as potential recruits will form a wider range of links with women than a military that is staffed entirely through male conscription. A military that is under civilian control is more likely to be required to conform to social norms and legislation, for example concerning equal opportunities for men and women, than an armed force whose leaders control or have replaced the civilian political elites in their country. A military that is the source of high-paying jobs or where military service is a passport to political power may be more reluctant to accept women as soldiers or to allow them to achieve high-ranking positions than an armed force that occupies a more marginal position in its country's society. Much of the research that explores the links between women and state militaries focuses on North America and Europe but, by combining these sources with the growing number of publications that examine this dynamic in other parts of the world, it is possible to build up a picture of the ways that militaries operate as gendered institutions, which often requires them simultaneously to exclude and co-opt women and to both draw on and reshape prevailing ideas about gender.

The military, gender, and society

As noted in chapter 1, militaries are gendered institutions. They make use of, rely on and perpetuate the assumptions that women and men not only can but must occupy different roles, and that the place which is right and proper for men to occupy is privileged above that of women. This notion of a hierarchy or a privileging of (what is construed as) the masculine over (what is construed as) the feminine is very important because it helps to explain why militaries need to preserve their status as distinctively masculine institutions – that is, as places where the most important people (men) engage in the most important (most manly) activities. But in order for a military to preserve its exalted position, this privileging of the masculine over the feminine must also occur in civilian society. This means that there is a complicated relationship between the construction and maintenance of beliefs about masculinity in the military and the civilian spheres – each one actively shapes, depends upon, and supports the other (Enloe 1988, p. 212).

It is striking that the military, which has such a close association with masculinity, is often the most powerful of all the departments of the state. The military is powerful in the obvious sense that it has the ability and indeed the responsibility to use destructive and deadly force in support of state policies. But the military is also powerful in comparison with other departments, for example those that are responsible for more "feminized" sectors such as education or health care. The power of the military is also reflected in economic terms. Most states place a high priority on their military forces when it comes to setting budgets and allocating state revenue among various competing interests. Finally, the power of the military is visible in political terms. In some states, such as Burma, the power of the military is overt and senior members of the military are formally in charge of politics and the government. Elsewhere – for example, in Pakistan – the military exercises so much influence over policy-making that it is difficult to speak of meaningful civilian control over the armed forces. Even in those states where the military is clearly under civilian control, such as the United States, military leaders tend to be treated with great respect by the political leaders, and their opinions on matters of foreign policy and national security are likely to carry greater weight than the opinions of civilian advisors. Militaries and their leaders therefore are usually able to exercise considerable influence over the policies and priorities of the state.

The interdependence between masculinity and the military is not only visible at the societal and political level, but also at the level of the individual (male) soldier. In some cases, for example in wartime or in those societies which rely on conscription to staff their armed forces, every male of a certain age is required to serve in the military unless he is deemed unfit. (Very few societies conscript women for military service.) Even where military service is performed by a minority of men, it is nevertheless usually perceived as an activity which is natural for men to engage in and also as the ultimate test of masculinity, as the rite of passage from boyhood into manhood. The positive characteristics that are associated with soldiers, such as physical strength, self-sacrifice, courage, and honor, are also characteristics that are typically associated with an ideal type of masculinity that all male members of the society should aspire to achieve and against which all men are measured.

It should be noted, however, that masculinity operates slightly differently within the military than it does in civilian society in that a male soldier is expected to behave in some ways that are associated more with women than with men. For example, soldiers are required to be obedient in following orders from their superiors and to demonstrate concern for the well-being of their fellow soldiers, especially those who serve in the same unit. Although a male civilian behaving in a subservient and nurturing manner might risk having his masculinity (and his sexuality) questioned, a male soldier can perform these tasks without raising an eyebrow because his own hegemonic masculinity is secured by virtue of his membership in the military – an institution which is culturally seen as a guarantor and producer of masculinity (Cohn 1998, p. 130).

The links between masculinity and military service are very strong even in those societies that place a high value on gender equality. Sweden, for example, has long traditions both of women's political activism and of neutrality in times of war. These factors might be expected to weaken the bonds between military service and the construction of masculinity, but research by Swedish feminists reveals that this is not the case. Instead, Swedish men who serve in their country's armed forces place a high value on the masculine character of their military and have resisted the integration of women in order to protect it. In the words of one male Swedish soldier, "Everything would fall apart if women joined . . . . It would be enough to see a woman, to destroy the masculine games going on around here" (Kronsell & Svedberg 2001, p. 163).

Central to these links between men, hegemonic masculinity, and the military is the ideological construction of the military (staffed by masculine men) as the protector of society and especially of those who are too weak and vulnerable to protect themselves (primarily women and children). In an influential essay published in 1982, Judith Hicks Stiehm (1982) drew attention to this dynamic and to the gendered character of state militaries, in which only men are regarded as legitimately occupying the role of the protector, positioning women in a subordinate role as the protected (p. 367). The idea of this mutually reinforcing gendered binary was further developed by Jean Bethke Elshtain (1987), who used the terms "Just Warriors" and "Beautiful Souls" to describe these roles, and has frequently been invoked by other feminist scholars since (e.g., Young 2003; Kronsell 2005). The use of images of women in military recruiting campaigns, which was widespread during the First World War, evoked the notion of men going to war to protect women. In Britain, a famous poster pictured a woman and children waving to a group of soldiers marching away under the words "Women of Britain Say Go!" while in the United States women were often depicted as victims in need of rescue from a brutal and inhuman enemy (Grayzel 2002, pp. 9–21).

That the military not only valorizes but also privileges men and masculinity can also be seen in the linking of citizenship with the obligation for military service to the state, a long tradition, going back to ancient Greece (Hartsock 1984). It was the willingness to fight and die to protect the state that earned one the full rights and privileges of citizenship. By this standard, women, who until recently were rarely allowed to be soldiers in state militaries – and then temporarily and in limited roles – could only be seen as second-class citizens, not entitled to the same privileges or political authority as men. In the last several decades, there has been much discussion about this link between military service and citizenship among feminist scholars and activists. Some have seen it as grounds for supporting not only women's right to serve in the armed forces but also universal conscription, reasoning that it is only when women are subject to the same military obligations as men that they will be recognized as equal citizens (Snyder 1999; Solaro 2006). Most feminists who write about this topic, however, are critical of the assumption that citizenship – male or female – should be based on or justified by military service. They critique the militarization of citizenship, challenging the idea that military service should be valued above other kinds of service to the state. A notion of citizenship that is based on performing activities traditionally associated with men (such as fighting) invites a perpetuation of the sharp distinction between the public and private spheres which makes it difficult for women to be regarded as full citizens (Enloe 1992; Feinman 2000; Jaggar 2005, pp. 4–7).

The militarization of women's lives

The image of state militaries as quintessentially masculine organizations has long required obscuring an important fact: in addition to depending on and promulgating certain ideas about masculinity and femininity, militaries are also dependent on women – even if they have no women soldiers. So in a chapter on women and state militaries, it is important to look not only at women in uniform, but also at civilian women whose lives are also shaped, to varying degrees, by this gendered institution.

It is not necessary for a woman to be a soldier or even to be acquainted with a soldier in order for her actions and beliefs to contribute to the functioning of a military – in other words, for her to become militarized. According to feminist political scientist Cynthia Enloe (2000), the term "militarization" refers to "a step-by-step process by which a person or a thing gradually comes to be controlled by the military or comes to depend for its well-being on militaristic ideas" (p. 3). The process of militarization is often subtle and it occurs through many, often seemingly unimportant, decisions taken by ordinary civilians as well as by political leaders and members of the armed forces. Enloe's research has been crucial in drawing attention to the many ways in which militaries depend on women and, as a result, seek to control their beliefs and behavior. If we fail to take seriously the relationships between state militaries and civilian women, then we cannot fully appreciate the extent of militaries' reliance on beliefs about gender or the extent to which militaries affect the everyday lives of ordinary people.

At the most basic level, militaries depend on the willingness of women to permit (or encourage) their husbands, brothers, and sons to become soldiers, and this in turn depends on women as well as men regarding military service as a necessary or even desirable activity for men to engage in. We can see the importance to the military of getting women to support men's military service when we consider what can happen when women refuse to cooperate. In Russia, for example, groups of women organized themselves into a loose network known as the Committee of Soldiers' Mothers in 1989, initially to lobby the Soviet political leadership to end the war it was then fighting in Afghanistan and bring their sons back home. The organization quickly developed and expanded its activities to include helping young men find legal ways to avoid compulsory military service and the actions of the Committee were among the key factors in the breakdown of Russia's system of conscription. During post-Soviet Russia's first war against Chechnya in the mid-1990s, the Committee organized several trips of Russian mothers to Chechnya to look for their missing soldier sons and to meet with Chechen mothers to discuss their mutual desire for peace. The publicity that accompanied these trips helped to draw attention to the savagery of the conflict and contributed to the hostility of Russian society toward that war (Zawilski 2006, pp. 228–40).

Soldiers' wives are crucial to the functioning of state militaries in multiple ways. They not only provide the soldier with emotional and practical support, but are also expected to create and sustain a stable home life for the family and to accept with good grace the soldier's absence when his unit deploys. This in turn enables the soldier to devote his full attention to his military duties without being distracted by domestic concerns. A "good" wife puts the needs of her husband's job ahead of her own (if she has one) and participates in the community of other military wives and families that she belongs to. The wives of officers, in particular, are often expected to devote considerable time and attention to doing voluntary work within the military community, organizing social events and mentoring the wives of lower-ranking staff. In many cases the behavior of a soldier's or officer's wife can have an impact on the progression of the husband's career, even if her behavior is not formally part of the criteria for promotion (Weinstein & Mederer 1997, pp. 8–14), and the "good" military wife is rewarded for her sacrifices by an increase in her own status when her husband advances in his career. Militaries know that wives who refuse to conform to the model of the good military wife can create significant problems for the armed forces by, for example, questioning the way that things are done, complaining about the additional requirements placed on them, and even by encouraging their husbands to abandon their military careers.

Another way that the wives, mothers, sisters, and girlfriends of soldiers are drawn into shoring up state militaries can be seen when a male soldier is physically or emotionally injured in the performance of his duties. His closest female relatives are expected to play a key role in his recovery and in his care through long-term disability. This is an experience that is very familiar to the female relatives of American soldiers (both male and female) who have been seriously injured in the post-9/11 conflicts in Afghanistan and Iraq. The speed with which these soldiers can be transported to medical care, combined with advances in medical techniques, mean that many soldiers survive horrific injuries but need extensive support and care for years after – in some cases, for the rest of their lives.

Another category of women whose presence is integral to the functioning of most state militaries is sex workers. Although the association between armies and prostitutes has a long history, few non-feminist scholars have exhibited much curiosity about it. Instead, they usually dismiss the women concerned as being a drain on the military, spreading disease among the men and undermining discipline. For many years, the term "camp follower" has been used as a derogatory term and as a synonym for prostitute, but research by historian John Lynn (2008) has revealed that the roles performed by camp women encompassed far more than having sexual relations with the soldiers. Large numbers of women routinely accompanied military campaigns in Europe before the mid-seventeenth century because they performed a key economic role; at a time when rulers hired mercenaries to fight their wars but were unable to provide them with regular wages, it was the women who were responsible for converting the goods they or their soldiers pillaged into food, clothing, and money. Later, when states began to consolidate their power, raise their own armies, and take on the responsibilities that had previously been carried out by the women of the camp, the numbers of women who were permitted to accompany armies to war in Europe fell drastically (Lynn 2008, pp. 215–31).

Feminists have played a key role in revealing that the relationship between state militaries and prostitution is not accidental, somehow "natural," or merely tolerated by militaries; instead, militaries actively encourage, arrange, and seek to control prostitution. As described in Text Box 3.2, the Japanese armed forces organized military prostitution on a large scale during the Second World War, forcing women from China, Korea, and the Philippines into servitude. Euphemistically known as "comfort women," many were, in fact, teenage girls who were kept in conditions of slavery and subjected to repeated and brutal rape (Enloe 2000, pp. 79–89). During and after the Korean War, the US and South Korean governments engaged in negotiations to ensure a supply of women as prostitutes for US soldiers (Moon 1997). In other research into prostitution in the bars that surround US military bases in South Asia, Hughes, Chon, and Ellerman (2007) have shown that, under these negotiated arrangements, US soldiers have, over the past six decades, not only used over a million Korean women as prostitutes; they have also been actively involved in trafficking Korean women to the USA.

Women in state militaries

Considering the efforts that militaries expend on constructing and perpetuating beliefs about the masculine character of armies and the soldiers who serve in them, it is reasonable to ask why state militaries permit women to enter the armed forces at all. The short answer is that there are occasions when state militaries do need women serving in uniform, sometimes as a result of a shortage of men who are able or willing to become soldiers or due to a commitment on the part of the ruling elite to greater gender equality in society. But, as we will see, militaries nearly always preserve some aspect of their activity – usually the activity labeled "combat" – for men only in order to protect the identification of the military with men and masculinity (see Table 6.1).

It is rare for a state to extend compulsory military service to women, even in times of war and national emergency when women might be encouraged or required to undertake other types of war work, such as making weapons or nursing wounded soldiers. In those cases where women are conscripted into the state's armed forces, the motivating factor is either dire necessity (a severe shortage of suitable men to fill the ranks) or an ideological position

Table 6.1 Proportion of women serving in state militaries around the world[1]

Afghanistan**	0.3%
Australia**	15.7%
Bangladesh*	0.4%
Brazil*	3.5%
Canada**	14.5%
Germany**	8.9%
Ghana*	8.7%
Nepal*	3.8%
New Zealand**	16.5%
Peru*	4.7%
Poland**	1.8%
Switzerland*	0.5%
United Kingdom**	13.6%

* statistics from 2008
** statistics from 2010

on the part of the state's political leadership. In the case of Libya, which has had compulsory military training for girls, both factors are relevant; following the 1969 military coup which brought him to power, Colonel Muammar Gaddafi presented military service for young women as a necessary step in the modernization of society, as well as an element in the mobilization of the citizenry to defend the country against hostile powers, such as the USA and Israel (Graeff-Wassink 1994, pp. 137–40). In Eritrea, which gained independence from Ethiopia in 1993, many women participated in the national liberation forces, and the new state's armed forces continue to conscript women as well as men; this decision would appear to be based on a combination of practicality (providing sufficient military personnel in a small country engaged in nearly continuous conflict) and some commitment to the principle of gender equality. The conscription of women into the Israeli Defense Force (IDF) is a policy which links military service with citizenship and is often referred to as an example of genuine equality between men and women although, as we will discover later in the chapter, it is misleading to regard it in this light. Other states which conscript women into military service, such as North Korea, appear to be motivated primarily by the need to fill the ranks in the absence of sufficient numbers of men.

During the Second World War, only a few combatant states conscripted women but, even in these cases where state militaries had urgent personnel needs to fill, great care was taken to restrict the terms and conditions of women's service. Britain introduced the conscription of women reluctantly in December 1941, after the country had been at war for more than two years, but even then women were only permitted to serve in the rear, not the front lines. The closest that British women could come to participating in combat was service on anti-aircraft batteries, but they were not permitted to fire the guns. Instead, every anti-aircraft crew had to include at least one man, whose job was to pull the trigger (Noakes 2006, pp. 115–20).

Although few states compel women to join the military, it is more common for a state to permit women to enter as soldiers, especially during wartime. Even during periods of national emergency, however, states and societies often resist the large-scale entry of women into the ranks. During the First World War, which was certainly a period of national emergency for many of the combatant countries, there are records of a handful of individual women who fought as members of national armies, such as Flora Sandes in Serbia, Ecaterina Teodoroiu in Romania, and Wanda Gertzowna in Poland, but only a few combatant states actively recruited women into military service. In Russia, the Provisional Government, which had come to power as a result of the February 1917 revolution, authorized the formation of women's battalions, partly in an attempt to shame the male soldiers – who were deserting the military in large numbers – into greater feats of bravery. The most famous of the women's battalions was led by the formidable Maria Bochkareva. The accounts of Bochkareva's battalion in action praise the women for the performance of their duties, but the presence of women in the ranks provoked derision and contempt from their male counterparts, who concluded that Russia's chances of winning the war must be hopeless if it was now sending women to fight. Britain also recruited women into military service during the First World War but, while women wore military uniforms, they did not serve in the regular armed forces. Instead, special services were created for them, such as the Women's Army Auxiliary Corps, which were explicitly designed to enable women to perform support roles that would release men to fight in the front lines (Grayzel 2002, pp.54–6). The Ottoman empire, which later became the modern state of Turkey, formed a special women's unit in 1917 which carried out tasks such as road building, agriculture, and sewing. As in the case of Britain, Ottoman women were permitted to join the military but were restricted to roles that would support male soldiers and keep the women away from combat (Altinay 2004, p. 49).

A shortage of male recruits in peacetime can also lead to the introduction of women into the armed forces (or a substantial increase in their numbers in those states where some women are already in the military). This situation often occurs when a state decides to replace or supplement compulsory military service with a volunteer force, as happened in the United States in the early 1970s, when the unpopularity of the war in Vietnam contributed to the US government's decision to end conscription. The American military leadership realized that military service would need to be presented as an attractive option for women if it were to recruit enough volunteers, and so it launched a separate advertising campaign which emphasized the opportunities for women to gain training and employment through service in the armed forces (Brown 2006). In post-Soviet Russia, an element of voluntary or "contract" service was introduced in the early 1990s once it was clear that large numbers of young men were prepared to use any legal (and some illegal) means to avoid serving in the armed forces. In the Russian case, however, the recruitment of women into the military was not part of a calculated plan by the Ministry of Defense, which was apparently taken by surprise when tens of thousands of young women applied for contract service. Russian military officials did subsequently begin to make efforts to make military service more appealing to women, mainly by sponsoring an annual beauty competition among its female recruits (Mathers 2006, pp. 216–17).

The expansion of military recruitment to include women can serve an ideological as well as a practical purpose. The recruitment of white women into the apartheid-era South African Defense Force (SADF) is a good example of this phenomenon. Although white women served in the SADF during the Second World War, they were all demobilized after the war and formed no part of the state's armed forces until the 1970s, when military service again opened up to them. This was a time when the government felt that its policy of racial separation and white supremacy was coming under threat from protests and activism within the country, as well as from the rise of national liberation movements in neighboring states such as Angola (Unterhalter 1988, pp. 101–17). But while the recruitment of white women was undertaken in order to support the ruling regime by providing a demonstration of white political unity, the government stopped short of extending compulsory military service to women out of concern that it would be bad for morale and a sign of desperation. Great care was taken, also, to delineate those positions and types of behavior that were appropriate for the new female recruits. Women soldiers were banned from active service, and concentrated in subordinate positions in areas such as administration, communications, logistics, medicine, and education. Their training, which was conducted entirely separately from the training of male soldiers, included instruction in the use of cosmetics (Cock 1994, pp.155–7).

In addition to considering the reasons why militaries recruit women to be soldiers, we need to ask why women choose to become soldiers rather than to do some other type of job. It is important to recognize that the motivations of women for joining militaries are as varied as the women themselves, and indeed as varied as those of the men who serve beside them. Some women soldiers join state militaries because they feel a strong sense of patriotism and loyalty to their country and wish to defend it against its enemies, particularly in times of war or when war threatens. For some women, military service is a family tradition and they wish to follow in the footsteps of their fathers and grandfathers (or mothers and grandmothers). Some women are attracted by the opportunity to gain experiences or training not readily available or affordable in civilian life, such as travel abroad or learning to fly an airplane or helicopter. For some, the attraction is the chance to escape the conventional gendered expectations of women's lives. In many instances, in both rich and poor nations, women's primary motivation is economic. In war-torn societies where the means of livelihood have been destroyed, or where women have few economic options, military service offers pay and status – and sometimes food and clothing – that are not otherwise available. During the 1983–2009 war in Sri Lanka, for example, some Sinhalese women saw joining the military as the only path to economic reward and social mobility that was open to them (Soysa 2011). Even in countries which are not at war, for women whose options are limited by factors such as their class and racial or ethnic background, military membership may seem to offer the best chance to gain training, skills, and employment. In China, for example, military service has been a popular career choice for young women, who saw the People's Liberation Army (PLA) as providing opportunities for education, training, and better jobs than they might be able to get in the civilian economy (Li 1993, pp. 70–4). In the United States, many African American women have seen military service as a means of gaining education, training, job opportunities, and economic security which have not been readily available to them in a civilian society where African Americans have been twice as likely as Euro-Americans to experience unemployment (Moore 1996, pp. 118, 124, 127–8).

The entry of women into state militaries has created mixed reactions among feminists. Some feminists argue that women's military service is a necessary step toward achieving full equality in society, and that, by their presence in the armed forces (especially in the higher ranks), women can alter the military for the better (Barkalow 1990; Katzenstein 1990). Other feminists, while supporting women's equal opportunities throughout society, see an inherent contradiction between militarism and feminist values. They argue that when women join the armed forces, they become co-opted and perpetuate rather than undermine the dominant military culture, and that their presence legitimates and contributes to militarization (D'Amico 1998; Enloe 2000; Feinman 2000). The US creation of "Female Engagement Teams" in an attempt to improve relations with civilians in Afghanistan and Iraq, for example, is seen as an example of this process. The women soldiers are instructed to visit local women in their homes, to gain their trust by distributing food and talking with them about their families, and in so doing present a less threatening, more human face for the occupation of their country (Ricks 2009). But this "kinder, gentler" face does not alter the character or effects of US military presence in these countries (for example, it continues to use deadly force).

Negotiating conflicting identities

All new entrants into state militaries undergo a process of resocialization; the aim of the process is to break down the individual civilian identities of new recruits, and to build up new identities as soldiers. Crucially, the deployment of ideas about masculinity and femininity is often a key part of this process. While part of the initial training for new recruits involves being fitted with uniforms, put through physical training, and learning to obey orders unquestioningly, an important element is also the creation of a sense of unity and camaraderie among the troops, instilling a sense of loyalty within each soldier to fellow soldiers, the unit, and the military. Among the methods used to promote this sort of bonding are ones that place emphasis on the differences between soldiers and others. But in many cases the "other" that the new soldiers are encouraged to see themselves in opposition to is not civilian society in general or some notion of an enemy, but women. In her study of US military culture, for example, folklorist Carol Burke documents the use in basic training of marching chants that belittle women and describe their rape, violent injury, or death at the hands of soldiers. Burke also found extensive use of synonyms for the word "girl" applied in a derogatory way to male soldiers who fail to meet the standard required in performing a task (Burke 2004, pp. 28–30, 45). The use of these sorts of woman-hating techniques in training are reported also in Turkey (Altinay 2004), Britain,[2] and in South Africa under the apartheid regime (Cock 1994), but relatively little research has been done on this topic and this practice is likely much more widespread than these few examples suggest.

The repeated use of negative comments about women during training further emphasizes to new recruits that the ideal soldier is male. Any sign of weakness or failure is associated with girls, women, and femininity and is to be ruthlessly eliminated if the apprentice soldier is to successfully complete the initial training and be accepted as a full member of the military. A woman who joins the military is therefore presented with an impossible dilemma. In order to be a "real soldier," she must suppress those aspects of her appearance and behavior that mark her as female; she must become as close an imitation of a man as possible. In other words, she must strive to become the "modal worker" referred to in chapter 1, which is based on the physical and social characteristics of a (heterosexual) man. But at the same time, she also must be a "real woman"; the very military institution which insists that every soldier must be male also insists in other ways that a female soldier cannot be regarded in the same way as a male soldier. In fact female soldiers are expected to conform to a type of militarized femininity which, in the words of Laura Sjoberg (2007), "expects a woman soldier to be as capable as a male soldier, but as vulnerable as a civilian woman" (p. 93). This creates a tension between the conflicting identities simultaneously demanded of a woman soldier that she must constantly negotiate and renegotiate.

Perhaps the only military role that women are permitted to perform which does not require them to simultaneously behave "like a man" while continuing to "be a woman" is in military medicine, especially nursing. But while nursing is widely regarded in militaries as being legitimately gendered female, military nurses do not necessarily have an easy time of it. In addition to doing a job that is highly skilled, complex, and very demanding, nurses are often required to perform their duties near the front lines and are therefore exposed to significant dangers. Although female nurses may be subject to fewer gender-negotiation challenges than women in other military specialties, when their military service is over they may find that they are regarded as not having been "real soldiers." This was the experience of Lynda Van Devanter, a nurse who served in Vietnam. After she returned to the United States, she was prevented from joining a march organized by Vietnam Veterans Against the War on the grounds that she did not "look like a vet" (Van Devanter 1984, p. 272).

Women and the masculine preserve of combat

Women who enter military service and are accepted, even in a qualified way, as soldiers, almost always find that they are limited to a relatively narrow range of positions in areas such as administration, communications, logistics, and medicine. Not coincidentally, these are the roles within militaries that most closely resemble the roles that women play in families and in civilian employment. As the presence of women soldiers becomes more established in a state military, there is a tendency for a wider variety of positions to gradually open up to them, although it is rare for all restrictions on women's roles to be removed (or indeed for there to have been no such restrictions imposed in the first place). There is almost always a category of roles that are retained as the sole preserve of male soldiers, and those roles tend to be most closely associated with combat.

Combat is regarded as the central activity of militaries, the place where real war happens and the core of a soldier's duty. This view underlies the practice, which is widespread among state militaries, of restricting promotion to the highest ranks to those who have served in a combat role; it also effectively prevents women from occupying the top leadership positions in many state militaries. The protection of a special area of the military's work from the presence of women is very important in helping to preserve the link between military service and masculinity. If women were permitted to engage in combat and acknowledged to have performed well *as women* rather than as exceptional (or perhaps freakish) individuals, it would undermine an important basis for the argument that men and militaries are entitled to their privileged positions in states and societies.

The importance of retaining a place in state militaries that is distinctively male explains the creativity employed in ensuring that "combat is where women are not," i.e., in defining and redefining combat so that the actions and presence of women soldiers continue to fall outside that definition. It also explains the contradictions that emerge between official definitions of combat and the messier realities of war. We can see an example of these kinds of contradictions when we consider the experiences of American military women serving in the post-9/11 wars in Afghanistan and Iraq. Although US women soldiers are not permitted to serve in units which have ground combat as their primary mission, many have been exposed to the risks of injury and death traditionally associated with combat by the circumstances of those conflicts and many have also responded to enemy attacks on themselves and their fellow soldiers by returning fire, thus behaving as combat soldiers in all but name. In fact, two women serving in these conflicts (Sergeant Leigh Ann Hester and Army Specialist Monica Lin Brown) have received the Silver Star, which is the third highest military decoration given for service in the US armed forces, and is given for "valor" which is defined as extraordinary heroism in the face of the enemy.

The official definition of a combat role can vary considerably from one society to another, often depending upon the state's geography and the proximity and capabilities of its likely opponents. In practice, this can mean that roles that are open to women in one state's military are firmly closed to them in another. The Singapore Armed Forces, for example, began a trial in 2004 in which women were permitted to lead motor platoons in infantry units. This piece of information may suggest that the Singapore Armed Forces are far in advance of their counterparts in the United States in opening up nontraditional military roles for women, but this is not the case. In all other respects, the extent and nature of women's participation in the Singapore Armed Forces conforms to the usual pattern of a relatively small number of women soldiers, confined primarily to support roles, with very few attaining senior positions in the military command structure. The explanation can be found, instead, in Singapore's specific situation; it occupies a relatively small land mass surrounded by water and separated from its most likely opponents by considerable distances. Any combat engaged in by the Singapore Armed Forces is likely to be carried out by the Air Force or the Navy, which are, not coincidentally, the services which enjoy the highest status and which impose the most restrictions on women's roles. The infantry, by contrast, is regarded as a less prestigious service and struggles to recruit suitably qualified men into officer positions (Walsh 2007, pp. 265–85).

The debate about whether women should be permitted to serve in combat roles is a particularly fierce one in the United States, where some arguments against this course of action tend to be based on claims about differences between women and men which are represented as "natural" and therefore presumably unchangeable. For example, it has been argued that women lack the upper body strength and the stamina to undergo the rigors of long marches carrying heavy packs and the physical and emotional capabilities to cope in situations where they might be required to fight and kill enemy soldiers at close quarters. Another argument relies on hypothetical situations and assumes that the behavior of women and men in combat conditions will be dictated by the social norms of civilian society rather than by their military training. An example of this type is the argument that the presence of women in combat units would disrupt the cohesion and bonding of the fighting force and would distract the male soldiers from the performance of their duties – either because the women would require the men's help to carry out essential tasks, or because in the heat of battle the men would seek to shield and protect their female comrades rather than fight the enemy. It has also been suggested that the healthy, young male soldiers would be sexually aroused by the close proximity of women's bodies; this last argument assumes, of course, that the ideal type of male combat soldier is heterosexual and would therefore be attracted to women but not to fellow male soldiers (Skaine 2011, pp. 56–66).

An experiment with mixed-gender units conducted by the United States Army during the Second World War suggests that the decision to keep women out of "combat positions" (if not out of actual combat itself) is based less on women's capacities and more on gendered belief systems. This experiment, which sought to determine whether anti-artillery units which combined women and men could perform combat roles effectively, revealed that the mixed-gender units actually outperformed those which contained only male soldiers. Although a number of senior army officials were enthusiastic about the prospect of introducing these more efficient units into the field, the War Department argued that women's service would be more useful in

Table 6.2 Examples of countries where women may serve in at least some combat roles[3]

Some countries in which women can fly military aircraft	Australia, Belgium, Brazil, Canada, Chile, China, Denmark, France, Germany, India, Israel, Japan, Kenya, Morocco, the Netherlands, New Zealand, Pakistan, Portugal, Russia, Singapore, South Africa, South Korea, Spain, Sri Lanka, Taiwan, Turkey, United Kingdom
Some countries in which women can serve on combat ships	Australia, Belgium, Canada, Chile, Denmark, France, Germany, Israel, Italy, the Netherlands, New Zealand, Norway, Portugal, Singapore, South Africa, Spain, Sweden, Tunisia, Turkey, United Kingdom
Some countries in which women can serve in ground combat operations	Belgium, Canada, Denmark, France, Germany, Hungary, Israel, the Netherlands (except the marines), New Zealand, Norway, Portugal (except marines and combat divers), South Africa, South Korea, Spain, Sweden
Some countries in which women can serve aboard submarines	Australia, Canada, Norway, Spain, Sweden

other, chiefly clerical and administrative, positions and that American public opinion was not ready to accept women serving in combat. Army Chief of Staff General George C. Marshall brought the experiment to a speedy conclusion and ordered that the results be kept secret (Campbell 1993, pp. 302–6).

Even the instances where women have been allowed in some combat roles have done little to transform the idea of combat as the defining, masculine core of militaries, with the valorizing and privileging of masculinity that entails. There are now a number of countries around the world that permit women to serve in at least some combat positions, whether as a result of legal challenges, as in Canada, or a commitment to equal opportunities for women and men, as in Norway, or for other reasons, such as a shortage of men (see Table 6.2). Detailed information about the proportion of women serving in such roles is not always available, but the research that has been done on women's military service in some of these countries makes it clear that very few women actually do serve in combat positions. For although a woman may *in theory* be permitted to serve in any military role, the culture of the military in which she serves or the society in which she lives may discourage her from even considering exercising her legal right to do so. Women in Norway, for example, have had the same opportunities for military service as men since 1984, but very few Norwegian women choose to join the armed forces, and research by Skjelsbæk and Tryggestad (2009) suggests that the country's military culture continues to be defined by Norway's practice of male conscription. In Canada, all military occupations have been open to women since 1989 (apart from service on submarines, open to women since 2000) and approximately 13 percent of Canadian military personnel are women, but women comprise only 2 percent of Canada's regular force combat troops (Skaine 2011, p. 95). The Canadian military also has a high rate of attrition among its women soldiers, a point which may be connected to the persistent allegations of sexual harassment within the armed forces (Zeigler & Gunderson 2005, pp. 84–9).

Israel is an example of a country where women continue to face formal and informal barriers to full equality in the armed forces, in spite of having an obligation to perform military service and the opening up of some combat roles to women in recent years. Universal military service was established by the Defense Service Law of 1949, which was influenced by Prime Minister David Ben-Gurion's idea that the military should be an instrument of nation-building (Sasson-Levy 2007, pp. 484–5). But from the earliest years of conscription, men and women were treated very differently. Married women and mothers were exempted from compulsory military service on the grounds that the chief duty of a woman citizen of Israel was to bear children. It is also relatively easy for unmarried women to obtain exemptions from military service, for example on the basis of religious objections. Until 1995, all women soldiers served in a separate Women's Corps, known as "Chen" (the Hebrew word meaning charm) and were barred from combat roles. Since 1995, the IDF has begun to integrate women into some combat roles, but they are still barred from those areas which are considered to be the core of combat (infantry, armor, and reconnaissance units) and from positions which have traditionally provided pathways to promotion to high ranks in the military (Sasson-Levy & Amram-Katz 2007, pp. 106–14).

Discrimination and abuse

Some of the most powerful and effective barriers which women face in state militaries are the ones that are informal and invisible. These range from the gendered assumptions that can prevent soldiers and officers from even perceiving (much less rewarding) the competencies demonstrated by women, to undermining slander and innuendo, to violent sexual assault and abuse by fellow soldiers.

Gendered assumptions about a woman's ability or attitude toward her professional responsibilities can make people perceive that she is less suitable for some or all military jobs than her male colleagues – and obscure the evidence to the contrary. For example, a study of the Texas A&M University Corps of Cadets found that both women and men cadets rated men higher for qualities necessary for military performance and leadership, even though there was no distinction between the results of the female and male cadets in objective tests which were designed to measure those very qualities (Boldry, Wood & Kashy 2001, pp. 689–705). Those women who are among the first to fill positions that were previously held only by men also often find that their abilities and qualifications are questioned. In 1994, one of the first women to qualify as a fighter pilot in the US Navy, Lieutenant Kara Hultgreen, died while attempting to land her plane on an aircraft carrier. Despite the results of an official investigation which found that the crash was caused by an engine malfunction, rumors, apparently originating from within the military, began to be reported in the media suggesting that Hultgreen had not been fully qualified and that she had been promoted above her abilities because the Navy wanted to demonstrate that it was opening up more positions to women (Spears 1998, pp. 273–91). Reluctance to accept women as competent professionals in this competitive and male-dominated world of fighter pilots can also be seen in India, where Vice Chief Air Marshal P. K. Barbora has described training women as fighter pilots as a poor return on the state's investment of time and money (Singh 2010).

Women soldiers are also often subjected to slander and innuendo concerning their personal morals and sexuality simply because they are women soldiers. Civilians as well as fellow male soldiers frequently assume that any woman who chooses to join such a male-dominated institution must have done so in order to catch a man (or many men). There were persistent rumors during the First World War that members of Britain's Women's Army Auxiliary Corps exhibited immoral behavior. A public investigation not only confirmed that the rumors were unfounded but traced them to letters written by male soldiers who resented being transferred from non-combat duties into the trenches as a result of the arrival of the women (Noakes 2006, pp. 75–81). Similar rumors (with very similar origins) circulated about American military women during the Second World War (Campbell 1990, p. 115).

More recently, as sociologist Melissa Herbert reports, American military women describe being caught in what she calls the "dykes or whores" conundrum. If a female soldier chooses to have sexual relations with one or more of her male colleagues, she may be seen as a woman of loose morals who will sleep with any man. If, on the other hand, she refuses male sexual overtures, she may find herself labeled a lesbian, regardless of her sexual orientation. Herbert points out that these labels are also used as a form of punishment for military women who are perceived by male soldiers to violate gender norms and therefore may bear no relationship to the sexual behavior of the women concerned (Herbert 1998, pp. 55–80). This treatment of military women can be seen in part as a logical consequence of the woman-hating techniques used in the training of new recruits to the military. When male soldiers are taught to dismiss women in general as insignificant or unworthy, it is much easier for them to relate to female soldiers exclusively as sexual objects rather than as fellow human beings.

The kind of verbal harassment described above can be very difficult to deal with day in and day out. Even more damaging, though, is the continuum of sexual abuse military women experience from their fellow male soldiers,

Box 6.1 The "double whammy" for US military women

A 2003 report financed by the Department of Defense revealed that nearly one-third of a nationwide sample of female veterans seeking health care through the V. A. [US Department of Veterans Affairs] said they experienced rape or attempted rape during their service. Of that group, 37 percent said they were raped multiple times, and 14 percent reported they were gang-raped. Perhaps even more tellingly, a small study financed by the V. A. following the Gulf War suggests that rates of both sexual harassment and assault rise during wartime. The researchers who carried out this study also looked at the prevalence of PTSD symptoms – including flashbacks, nightmares, emotional numbing and round-the-clock anxiety – and found that women who endured sexual assault were more likely to develop PTSD than those who were exposed to combat.

Patricia Resick, director of the Women's Health Sciences Division of the National Center for PTSD at the Boston V. A. facility, says she worries that the conflict in Iraq is leaving large numbers of women potentially vulnerable to this "double whammy" of military sexual trauma and combat exposure. "Many of these women," she says, "will have both."

> "Being sexually assaulted by a fellow soldier may prove extra-traumatic, as it represents a breach in the hallowed code of military cohesion – a concept that most enlistees have drilled into them from the first day of boot camp. 'It's very disconcerting to have somebody who is supposed to save your life, who has your back, turn on you and do something like that,' says Susan Avila-Smith, the director of Women Organizing Women, an advocacy program designed to help traumatized women navigate the vast V.A. healthcare and benefits system. 'You don't want to believe it's real. You don't want to have to deal with it. The family doesn't want to deal with it. Society doesn't want to deal with it.'" (Corbett 2007)

ranging from repeated unwanted sexual advances to violent sexual assault. The results can include severe physical and psychological trauma, including post-traumatic stress disorder (PTSD), early termination of a woman's military career, and undermining of trust and cohesion in the military unit itself.

The United States military has been shaken by a succession of scandals involving the systematic sexual harassment and rape of women soldiers. These include the 1991 Tailhook Convention, where male naval aviators abused female officers at a Las Vegas hotel, and the Aberdeen Proving Ground Ordinance Center scandal of 1997, where male instructors raped women trainees. More recently, substantial numbers of US military women deployed to Afghanistan and Iraq have reported that they have been the victims of rape and other sexual assaults committed by their fellow soldiers, often with extremely traumatic effects (see Text Box 6.1).

Such abuse within the US armed forces has received a great deal of publicity since the establishment of the Miles Foundation, an organization dedicated to researching, publicizing, and opposing these offenses (Jeffreys 2007, p. 20). In 2010, the US Department of Defense (USDOD) released statistics showing an 11 percent increase in reports of sexual assault in the military over the previous year, representing more than three thousand individual incidents, with a 16 percent increase in reported assaults in combat areas (mainly Iraq and Afghanistan) (Bumiller 2010). While more than three thousand incidents of sexual assault occurring in one year in one military is a staggering statistic, even the USDOD acknowledges that most sexual assaults in the US military are not reported, and those that are represent only a very small portion of the phenomenon (Bumiller 2010).

The reasons for the failure to report sexual assaults in the military are not difficult to understand. Military women who have been assaulted are aware that if they accuse their attacker, they are likely to face the same kinds of responses that rape victims receive in civilian society; depending on *which* society she is in, this can range from "blaming the victim," to the difficulty of proving assault in a legal proceeding, to being so stigmatized as to become unmarriageable (see Text Box 6.2). But military women also face additional pressures specific to the armed forces. The military environment, with its strict hierarchies and chain of command, can make it more difficult for a woman to file a complaint and get the medical and psychological help that she needs because she has few other avenues to pursue if her superiors refuse to take her accusations seriously (or indeed if it was her commanding officer who assaulted her). Women who do report abuse are often pressured by other soldiers to withdraw the accusation to avoid damaging the reputation and career of "a good soldier," while those who persist in filing a complaint are likely to find themselves ostracized by their colleagues and passed up for promotion, and that their careers are effectively over.

An example of the hurdles that a woman soldier can face in these circumstances is provided by the experience of Jacqueline Ortiz, a US Army Reserve engineering specialist deployed in Operations "Desert Shield" and "Desert Storm" in the early 1990s, whose sergeant forced her to perform oral sex in his tent. When Ortiz attempted to report the assault, she was refused medical treatment and her supervisors accused her of making a false accusation. After an appeal to her Congressman and a three-year delay, Ortiz's attacker finally pled guilty and was discharged from the military. Ortiz's experience was unusual only in the publicity that it received and the fact that her attacker was eventually punished. During the post-9/11 wars in Afghanistan and Iraq, American military women who have attempted to report sexual assault have often found that they are themselves threatened with punishment – for example when Sergeant Marti Ribeiro reported that a fellow serviceman raped her while she was on guard duty in Afghanistan, she was threatened with court martial proceedings for leaving her weapon behind during the sexual assault (Benedict 2009).

The USA is among the few countries where the military does collect and publicize statistics about sexual assault within the armed forces. For most other countries, we must rely on scattered information available through occasional news stories and reports by human rights groups to gain some insights into this aspect of the lives of military women. Such reports have

Box 6.2 Sexual assault and abuse in the North Korean military

"An investigation by the South Korean human rights group NKHR has revealed that both civilian and military women in North Korea are subjected to sexual violence from male soldiers. Women traders in the country's private markets are often put under pressure to provide sexual services for soldiers to avoid being arrested for engaging in illegal activities. Women who join the military, many in the hope of gaining respect and social status, are at great risk of sexual abuse. At the same time, virginity in women is so prized that a woman who reports rape will lose her reputation, her chance of promotion as well as the opportunity to marry and have a family. As former North Korean soldier Kim Young-Ok testified, 'When young female soldiers get raped, they cannot report it anywhere . . . Victims of sexual or physical violence are forced to try to hide what happened to them because of the general perception that any sexual violence a woman faces was promoted by her.'" (Jong-Hean 2011)

revealed sexual assault within the armed forces of countries including Eritrea (UNHCR 2009), Canada (Davis 1997, pp. 186–91), India (Singh 2010), Israel (Jacoby 2010), South Africa (PeaceWomen 2010), North Korea (Jong-Hean 2011) and Russia (Mathers 2006, pp. 211–12) (see Text Box 6.2).

Although there are enormous barriers to using legal remedies where they exist, it is important to note that in many militaries these procedures are absent. A state which is able to enforce a rule of law on all of its citizens and which maintains civilian control of the armed forces is more likely to have legal and procedural mechanisms for dealing with these kinds of abuses within the military; it is also more likely to include some kind of gender awareness in its training of soldiers and officers and finally is more likely to collect and publish information about those abuses which are reported through official channels. Women serving in the militaries of less democratic states will have few, if any, of these structures to support them. Male soldiers subjecting their female colleagues to sexual abuse or assault may not even be recognized as a problem which needs to be solved, but instead regarded as falling within the normal range of behavior that is exhibited by a male soldier. But while there are clear benefits to having access to formal means of redress, the experience of American women soldiers demonstrates that, in spite of a wide range of mechanisms intended to prevent sexual abuse or deal with it when it occurs, widespread abuse continues to take place and the perpetrators are rarely brought to justice.

Conclusion

This chapter began with a quotation from John Keegan, in which he argues that women have nothing to do with the "real" business of fighting wars. Keegan's claim often goes unchallenged by non-feminist scholars precisely because of the way that the dependence of militaries both on women and on beliefs about what it means to be a woman or a man are usually hidden from public view. Notions of masculinity and femininity are created and reinforced by states, societies and militaries in a wide variety of subtle and reciprocal ways. Accepting the ideas that militaries are distinctively male entities which have nothing to do with women and that it is natural for men to become soldiers makes it easier to accept the privileging of masculinity and men over femininity and women in society at large. States and militaries devote considerable attention and effort to militarizing civilian women while simultaneously limiting the numbers of women who do serve in militaries and the professional roles that they are permitted to fill. Even if women soldiers do match the performance of their male colleagues in physical fitness tests, in training exercises, or when confronting an enemy in combat conditions, those experiences may be dismissed, ignored, or explained away, but they are almost never acknowledged as evidence that women can be "real" soldiers. As Cynthia Enloe (1988) put it, "Women may serve the military, but they can never be permitted to *be* the military" (p. 15).

QUESTIONS FOR DISCUSSION

1 What is it about military service which makes it such an important site for the construction of masculinity?

2 How widespread is the militarization of civilian women? Can you identify any examples of this process in your own community?

3 Some feminists argue that if women join the armed forces in sufficient numbers and achieve enough high-ranking positions, then the character of the military institution will be changed by their presence and their actions, making it less masculine. Other feminists argue that when women join the armed forces it is the women soldiers who become changed by the institution. Which position do you find most persuasive, and why?

SUGGESTIONS FOR FURTHER READING

Altinay, Ayşe Gül (2004) *The Myth of the Military-Nation: Militarism, Gender, and Education in Turkey*. New York: Palgrave Macmillan.

Benedict, Helen (2009) *The Lonely Soldier: The Private War of Women Serving in Iraq*. Boston: Beacon Press.

Cock, Jacklyn (1994) "Women and the Military: Implications for Demilitarization in the 1990s in South Africa." *Gender & Society* 8(2): 152–69.

De Groot, Gerard J., and Peniston-Bird, Corinna (1999) (eds.) *A Soldier and a Woman: Sexual Integration in the Military*. London: Longman.

Enloe, Cynthia (2000) *Maneuvers: The International Politics of Militarizing Women's Lives*. Berkeley and Los Angeles: University of California Press.

Herbert, Melissa S. (1998) *Camouflage Isn't Only for Combat: Gender, Sexuality, and Women in the Military*. New York: New York University Press.

CHAPTER 7

Women, Girls, and Non-State Armed Opposition Groups

Dyan Mazurana

A young man in worn street clothes defiantly holding an automatic weapon – that is the image often conjured up by the words "insurgent," "armed rebel," "terrorist," or "freedom fighter." When images of women and girls appear in such a scenario, it may be as the grieving mother or sister, or as the victim of men's violent actions. These images, however, belie the fact that women and girls have themselves operated inside of most armed opposition groups, as they are essential to enabling and sustaining insurgencies.

Drawing on current and recent armed conflicts, this chapter uses a feminist gender analysis to understand how armed groups draw on, manipulate, and attempt to militarize masculinities, femininities, and patriarchies in order to carry out their armed insurgencies. To do this, we will pay close attention to the role of women and girls inside insurgent movements. On one level, this chapter serves to introduce the reader to the reality of women's and girls' presence and participation in non-state armed groups (NSAGs). On another level, the analytic purpose of this chapter is for the reader to begin to understand the amount of concerted effort it takes, and how power is wielded in those efforts, to construct and mobilize the militarized and gendered identities, consciousness, and actions needed to create and maintain an insurgency movement. Furthermore, we use a feminist analysis of women and girls inside armed opposition groups to reveal where power is at play inside the groups and among the communities those groups rely on for support. What we learn is that none of these manipulations or constructions of identities, ideologies, and actions that are so essential to maintaining insurgencies happen without the groups paying attention to gender identities, both inside and outside of their group. We also learn that none of this goes on without being contested (perhaps especially within the armed groups themselves) and shifting over time.

By way of introduction, in this chapter we review how and why women and girls join NSAGs, their roles and experiences inside those groups, and how their presence changes the tactics and ideologies of the groups. We then investigate how women's and girls' experiences vary within different NSAGs. Next, a series of case studies helps us to track how and why insurgencies use women and girls and how this shifts over time; to make gendered sense of their recruitment strategies; to make sense of the increase in public acts of violence by women and girls in insurgent groups over the last decade; and to investigate armed groups in which women and girls are purposefully kept out of the public eye. Throughout, we use case studies to help bring to light the gendered reasons for and struggle around NSAGs using or not using women and girls in particular ways.

A brief note on some of the terms we employ in this chapter. We use the terms "armed opposition groups" or "armed insurgencies" or "NSAGs" to refer to organized non-state groups that have taken up arms to challenge the state or another armed group over control – or the state's or another armed group's attempt to hold a monopoly of control – of political, economic, natural, territorial, and/or human resources. We refrain from using the term "terrorist" to identify any of the groups we discuss. We do so because such designations are always highly political and are increasingly used as a way to dull rigorous thinking and curiosity about a group, its history and demands. Not surprisingly, armed opposition groups themselves strongly disagree with being labeled "terrorists," as many members have joined insurgent movements as a result of state violence against themselves, their families and communities and as a means to liberate themselves and others from such violence.

In discussing armed opposition groups, we also specifically refer to both women *and girls*. This distinction is important because armed opposition groups often recruit, value, and use girls differently than they do women – or boys and men (McKay & Mazurana 2004). For example, when insurgent groups abduct females, it is girls, not women, who are the main target of abductions. Girls are targeted in part due to their younger age and mental and physical development, which often enables the insurgents to more easily influence their thinking and behavior (see, for example, Annan et al. 2008). For those groups that give abducted females as rewards to commanders and use them to provide support functions to the group, girls are also preferred over adult women, due to their hoped-for virginity and lower risk of being infected with sexual diseases.

Overview of women and girls inside armed opposition groups

Some of the earliest evidence of women's participation in armed conflict comes from the Celts and the ancient Romans, and historic accounts of girls' active participation goes back at least as far as the fifth century (Mazurana et al. 2002). As noted in chapter 1, there have been important shifts in how and why conflicts have been fought over the past decades, including how women and girls have been mobilized to participate in and support wars. Insurgent groups rise up for many different reasons. Though all wars have their specific contexts and historicity, in general many of the wars fought in Latin America from the 1960s to today began as grassroots, popular uprisings against rightist politicians (and their politics) and the militaries that helped keep them in power and quash civil rights. In all of the wars in Latin America during this time period, women and girls played crucial roles within groups that took up arms to challenge the rightist states' violence (Luciak 2001). In Africa from the 1960s to the 1990s, populations fought wars of independence against colonial powers and their local proxies, and in all of them women and girls were heavily involved. With the end of the Cold War, some insurgent groups that had relied on the support of the superpowers found their funding sources running out. Instead of abandoning their conflicts, they shifted their focus to extracting natural resources and used shadow economies to generate the support they needed to continue (even expand) their fights and to build and maintain new forms of wealth and patron systems (Duffield 2001; Nordstrom 2004), as seen throughout the wars in Africa, Central Asia, and Colombia in the 1990s and into the twenty-first century. The recent wars in Iraq and, to a much lesser extent, Afghanistan have seen women and girls mobilize to fight what they perceived as occupying forces. In Africa, Asia, and the Middle East, armed groups mobilized to attempt to overthrow state systems and replace them with their own forms of governance and government. In all of these cases, women and girls were central to the mobilization, maintenance, and abilities of the armed opposition groups.

Over the last two decades, tens of thousands of women and girls have been members of armed opposition groups participating in armed struggles in 59 countries (see Table 7.1). While insurgencies have their own overall goals and agendas (as noted above), women and girls participate in armed conflict for many reasons; some join willingly, others join when they believe no other options are available to protect and provide for themselves, others are tricked and forced. In many instances, women and girls decide to join for a combination of reasons, including protection, revenge, or political ideology. Interviews with women commanders from 18 different armed opposition groups around the world found that, before actually joining the armed opposition group, some of the women reported that, as girls, they were detained under accusation by government forces that they or their family members were part of the opposition. While in detention, they were beaten, sexually assaulted, and tortured by government police, military, or militia forces. Detention lasted from days to months. In some cases, the women said they or others were carved or tattooed as a means to identify them to their families and communities as victims of sexual assault. Some of these women were then rejected and divorced by their husbands. Some women claimed that governments intentionally used troops known to have HIV/AIDS to rape women to infect them. Others witnessed the execution of their brothers, sisters, or parents by government forces and were told while in detention they would be executed next. In most of these cases, when the women were released from detention, they went immediately in search of the armed opposition group, seeking to join them; they reasoned that this was now their only means of self-preservation (Mazurana 2004, p. 28). Joining an armed opposition group is not a decision taken lightly; once a woman or girl joins one, it is extremely unlikely she will be allowed to leave while the conflict is ongoing.

Table 7.1 Women and girls inside armed opposition groups 1990–2011

Africa	Americas	Asia	Europe	Middle East
Algeria	Colombia	Afghanistan	France	Iran
Angola	El Salvador	Cambodia	Ireland (Northern)	Iraq
Burundi	Guatemala	India	Macedonia	Israel
CAR	Haiti	Indonesia	Montenegro	Jordan
Chad	Honduras	Myanmar	Russia	Lebanon
Côte d'Ivoire	Mexico	Nepal	Serbia	Syria
DRC	Nicaragua	Pakistan	Spain	Turkey
Eritrea	Peru	Papua New Guinea	Former Yugoslavia	Yemen
Ethiopia		Philippines		
Liberia		Sri Lanka		
Libya		Thailand		
Mauritania		East Timor		
Morocco		Uzbekistan		
Mozambique				
Rwanda				
Sierra Leone				
Somalia				
South Africa				
Sudan				
Uganda				
Zimbabwe				

Many women and girls who join NSAGs on their own accord do so for ideological and political reasons, as seen throughout armed insurgencies in the 1980s in Latin America and Africa, and today most notably in the conflicts in Chechnya, Colombia, Iraq, Nepal, Turkey, Sri Lanka, and the Arab–Israeli conflict. According to a woman commander from the (then) insurgent Sudanese People's Liberation Army (SPLA): "One reason people go to war is because of social difficulties in the patriarchal systems. The [SPLA] movement talked of justice for all and that joining them in their fight was a way to abolish unequal systems . . . Women are fighting for justice. This is where women felt they could get their rights."[1]

Violence and injustice at the hands of state forces and dominant elites, as well as lack of security and fear for their lives, are also among the primary reasons women and girls join armed groups. A female commander from the (then) insurgent National Council for the Defense of Democracy/Forces of Defense of Democracy (CNDD-FDD) in Burundi described her own process of joining the insurgent group after the assassination of the elected president and the hunting down and murder of his supporters. She explained:

> I had voted for the president that was killed after his victory . . . I was staying in Burundi, but ran away with my husband and my baby after the destruction of our house [by army forces]. Fifteen of my relatives were killed. The army was following us. There was a massacre in the village in which we were hiding and we decided we could not stay there. In 1996, I took the decision to join the armed group.[2]

Sexual violence perpetrated by state forces is another common reason. The woman commander of the Widow's Battalion of the Free Aceh Movement (GAM), for example, said that the majority of the women and girls who joined her group were victims of rape at the hands of the Indonesian military – against whom they were fighting – and were there in part to exact revenge.[3] Economic and social factors, including access to food, shelter, education, revenge, escape from forced marriage, or abusive family relations, may also contribute to women and girls joining armed groups.

While some join willingly, in other instances women's and girls' entry into insurgencies is not a choice. In recent and current armed conflicts, some women and girls have been abducted or forced to participate in armed groups. Such was the case in Angola, Burundi, Colombia, DRC, Liberia, Mozambique, Nepal, Rwanda, Sierra Leone, and Somalia. Abductions of women and girls take place for several reasons; the most important is that some armed opposition groups lack popular support, and abducted women and girls serve roles that are vital to keeping those armed groups operational (Mazurana et al. 2002).

The majority of women and girls in armed groups carry out labor such as cooking, looting, washing clothes, serving as porters, collecting water and firewood. Other roles include but are not limited to commanders, frontline fighters, spies, intelligence officers, weapons dealers, messengers, recruiters, and political strategists. For women and girls inside armed opposition groups, there is rarely a clear division between roles and one individual may perform several functions, though most receive some military training and many participate in combat (Mazurana et al. 2002; Mazurana 2004; McKay & Mazurana 2004; Mazurana 2005a). For example, in Nepal, during the armed conflict between the Maoists and the state, all members of the Maoists received military training, and regardless of which wing of the party a woman or girl entered (e.g., student wing, women's wing, cultural wing), she could be called to fight or provide support to the group at any time.

Though there is much talk of women and girls inside armed groups as "sex slaves," such classification only applies to some females within a handful of insurgent groups over the last 20 years. All insurgent groups have rules (with varying degrees of rigidity) around sexual access to women and girls inside the insurgent group. In the rebel Lord's Resistance Army (LRA), Uganda, known for its widespread abductions and brutality, sexual access is tightly regulated by the senior LRA leadership, and those who violate it risk death. In other cases, there may be mass abduction and rape of women and girls, such as with the notorious rebel Revolutionary United Front (RUF) of Sierra Leone, although even within this group there were still clear hierarchies of access to those females. For others, such as the Maoists in Nepal, most sexual interactions are at the will of the females, and couples must petition (in writing) a senior level Maoist panel for permission to be together as a couple. Among leftist and some nationalist armed opposition groups, women's and girls' sexuality is often off-limits inside the group, in part because of the groups' proclaimed beliefs in women's rights. The point here is to be wary of media and other reports that often make blanket statements on the ubiquitous use of females inside armed opposition groups as "sex slaves."

When cease-fires and peace accords are reached, women and girls associated with armed groups are repeatedly excluded from official state disarmament, demobilization, and reintegration (DDR) programs. Many other women and girls do not want it known they were involved with insurgent forces, for fear of being stigmatized and ostracized by their families and communities. In most situations, women and girls "self-demobilize" back into civilian communities where they face numerous challenges, as discussed in chapter 9.

The above overview highlights some of the common patterns among women and girls associated with armed opposition groups. However, it is imperative to keep in mind that the context of the conflict always matters; the ways in which notions and practices of masculinities, femininities, and patriarchies, as well as ethnicity, class, and caste, are experienced and lived by women and girls in NSAGs and the resulting outcomes vary tremendously. To illustrate how important it is to historically and contextually locate any understanding of an NSAG, we take an in-depth look at women's and girls' participation in one opposition group, the Liberation Tigers of Tamil Eelam (LTTE) of Sri Lanka.[4] This case study is intended to help the reader better recognize and understand the different roles that militarized masculinity, femininity, and patriarchy play in shaping the ideologies and practices of the armed groups, as well as the motivations, roles, experiences, and positioning of women and girls within the group.

The Liberation Tigers of Tamil Eelam and the Birds of Freedom

In 1976, the LTTE's initial central political platform emphasized traditional Tamil values, which did not allow women and girls to serve in nontraditional roles, such as combat. A decade later, the LTTE began to include women and girls in nontraditional roles, and started to borrow ideas from leftist and feminist ideology to create its own rules and mythologies to justify this action.

In 1986, the LTTE created an all-female military wing known as the "Birds of Freedom," and began integrating women and girls into all aspects of the group (Stack-O'Conner 2007).

The LTTE leadership's decision to expand women's and girls' roles was likely motivated by several practical considerations. First, Tamil and Sinhalese constructions of gender – both ideas about women themselves and ideas about appropriate relations between men and women – made women and girls particularly effective for the LTTE's purposes. Tamil women and girls could travel easily throughout Sri Lanka because they were not seen as threatening by security forces. Moreover, cultural sensitivities about men touching females reduced the likelihood that they would be searched at checkpoints. Consequently, it was easier for women and girls to get close to political figures, which was essential to the LTTE's ability to carry out armed operations.

Demographic pressures in the 1980s provided the LTTE with another incentive to allow women and girls to serve in combat roles. Some estimates suggest that between 1982 and 1987 the LTTE lost 8 percent of its membership due to the Tamil population becoming disillusioned with the group's practices and political claims. The supply of men willing and able to join the LTTE was also decreasing due to emigration, detention, and death. Women and girls, on the other hand, were eager to join the movement. Thus, allowing women and girls to join enabled the LTTE to increase its numbers and strengthen its force.

The involvement of women and girls also served as a powerful public relations tool, particularly in the competition for legitimacy among Tamil groups, as the LTTE was competing with other militant Tamil groups to be the sole representative of the movement for a Tamil state. Publicly including women and women's issues in the fight strengthened the LTTE's ability to argue that it was representative of the Tamil nation and that it offered a progressive vision for the future. Their use of women was also essential to the LTTE's ability to attract sympathetic outside media coverage. When interviewing women, reporters generally emphasized the individual women's stories, which often included personal suffering, victimization, and the absence of opportunity outside of the LTTE (Alison 2003; Stack-O'Conner 2007).

Women's and girls' motivations for joining the LTTE

In the mid-1980s the LTTE started to aggressively recruit females. Women and girls joined the LTTE both for reasons common to men and boys, and for reasons unique to women and girls. Like men and boys, female LTTE members cited their nationalist desires for a free Tamil state and self-determination as a significant reason for joining the movement. In some cases, these feelings related to personal experience, while in others they were part of the greater communal narrative of suffering and injustice. Women and girls said that they joined because of their anger over deaths of loved ones who were killed by the Sri Lankan police or military, and the displacement of their families and communities. Several women who were interviewed by the authors also identified the disruption of their education as a result of displacement as a reason for their decision to join the LTTE.

While all the above reasons for joining would be influenced by and experienced through gender, some motivators were specifically tied to being female. Women and girls discussed their fear of and anger about sexual violence as one of the motivating factors that led them to join the LTTE. Some women and girls saw fighting for Tamil freedom as the only way to redeem themselves after rape (Cutter 1998; Jansz 1998). Ideas related to the emancipation of women and increasing women's life opportunities also motivated women and girls to join. The LTTE ideology asserts that females can only gain equality through the nationalist movement. Adele Ann, a former leader of the female contingent of the LTTE, put it this way: "The emergence of the Liberation Tigers on the Tamil national political scene has provided Tamil women with opportunities and horizons that would never have entered the minds of Tamil women a decade ago. Normally, young women remain under the control of the father and brother" (Ann 1993, pp. 16–17). Thus, some women and girls joined the movement to simultaneously advance both nationalist and feminist goals. In short, joining the LTTE was also appealing to women and girls because they saw it as a way to break cultural taboos and they believed that their participation would advantage them in the future (Schalk 1994; Alison 2010).

Women's and girls' roles in the LTTE and the effect of their participation

Initially, women and girls served in supporting roles in propaganda work, administration, medical care, information collection, fundraising, and recruitment. But within two years, women and girls had been trained to participate in combat; they fought their first battle against the Sri Lankan military in July 1986. The female force continued to grow, as the LTTE's naval force, the Sea Tigers, became primarily female, and the suicide squad known as the Black Tigers included a significant number of females. The female Black Tigers have perpetrated about 30 percent of the Black Tigers' suicide bombings, becoming notorious for their assassination of Indian leader Rajiv Gandhi and 16 others at a rally in Tamil Nadu, India (Alison 2003; Stack-O'Conner 2007). Estimates suggest that women comprised anywhere between 15–30 percent of the LTTE's core combat force in a variety of roles. While women and girls inside the LTTE were not prevented from serving in any roles, there were certain roles such as nursing and social work that were still considered "women's work" and were not open to men (Stack-O'Conner 2007).

Female LTTE members have noted that through their membership in the LTTE they were able to achieve independence from the traditional lifestyles that confine Tamil women and girls to the home. They also have reported feeling empowered by their contributions to women's liberation and the Tamil cause (Jordan & Denov 2007). Yet it is unclear to what extent women and girls have been able to achieve any permanent gains. The LTTE's fundamental goal is the independent state of Eelam; it is assumed that emancipation of women will automatically be achieved through nationalist victory. Evidence from other armed liberation movements, however, shows that once wars ended, women in armed forces and groups were expected to resume their traditional roles or were restricted to supportive positions in the public sphere. Given the crushing military defeat of the LTTE (at least presently), and the increased militarization of Sri Lanka in the aftermath, we see no indication of the government fundamentally addressing Tamil women's social concerns, and it is extremely unlikely that any gains that women and girls made inside the LTTE during wartime can be consolidated in the present post-conflict period.

As the LTTE example illustrates, there is significant effort undertaken by armed opposition groups to militarize gender, ethnicity, and nationalism, make use of women and girls, and help shape how women and girls understand and experience their participation. The LTTE case study also makes clear that in these contested situations (contested even within the group and societies themselves), these factors will shift and change over time.

When NSAGs think about gendered power dynamics, gender-based violence and recruitment

NSAGs are savvy about the societies they live in, receive support from, and fight against. And this means that they must be savvy about the gender dynamics in those societies. Why? Because no NSAG can survive without the support of local communities, although the degree to which they rely on support freely given by the community versus on coercion varies over time. Even when NSAGs can draw in foreign fighters to their cause, their main forces are usually drawn from local communities in the territories where they seek to establish bases or to hold land or resources. In some cases, they walk a fine line, trying to appeal to those communities to test their ideological tenets, while also relying on them for essential material support and as bases for recruitment. Obtaining, maintaining, and trying to ensure community support is no easy task and a lot of power is at play in these maneuvers. Hence, NSAGs pay attention to, at the least, gendered divisions of labor, gender relations, gender violence, gender disparities, and gender-based grievances to help win support from crucial portions of local populations. The long-standing rebel force Fuerzas Armadas Revolucionarias de Colombia-Ejército del Pueblo (FARC) offers a rich case study of what some of these dynamics look like and what they reveal about the armed group itself.

The Fuerzas Armadas Revolucionarias de Colombia – Ejército del Pueblo (FARC)

FARC was founded in 1964 with a goal of establishing a state that ensured social and economic equality for all Colombians. Although it apparently did not figure expressly in the founders' objectives, the FARC evolved to include gender equality in its platform for social and political change (Stanski 2006). This evolution appears to have begun in the mid-1980s as the guerrilla group faced increased difficulty in recruiting, sustaining public support, and resisting military opposition by the expanding government-backed paramilitary forces. Although women had played a role in the FARC's struggle since its founding in 1964, they mostly provided support functions such as cooking and cleaning, and were restricted from direct combat and leadership positions (Ortiz 2006). It was not until 1985, when an internal statute ensured females equality with their male comrades, that the FARC began to recruit women and girls specifically for combat (Herrera & Porch 2008). The trend in female recruitment continued to grow in the face of increased military opposition by state and non-state forces, and estimates suggest that female composition expanded from approximately 20 percent of FARC ranks in the 1970s and 1980s, to 40–50 percent in the 2000s (Brittain 2010).

The FARC is highly dependent on support and cooperation from local populations in its mostly rural areas of operation. Thus, the FARC uses an array of positive and coercive means to help ensure its appeal to the local population, the local implementation of its ideological priorities, and the maintenance of its military capacity and security. One way to understand how the group attempts to coexist with and draw recruits from local populations is to pay attention to how gender norms and ideologies are used, manipulated, and incorporated into the FARC's strategies. We look at an example of how the FARC pays attention to gender-based violence and grievances in its recruitment strategies.

Intra-family physical and sexual violence against boys, girls, and women is common in Colombia and is symptomatic of a larger, culturally ingrained sense of male superiority and domination, or "machismo," that permeates social relations. In regions under its control, the FARC endeavors to promote and enforce gender equity, and to prohibit physical and sexual abuse. Soon after arriving and establishing control in a territory, the FARC informs the population of their rules, their processes for dealing with allegations of wrongdoing, and corresponding punishments. In cases of intra-family violence, there is usually a three-tiered system of punishment, with the third level being execution. In cases where sexual violence is proven, the consequence is immediate execution of the guilty party by FARC members. Not surprisingly, depending on the level and regularity of FARC control in a local territory, it may not be able to enforce these rules consistently. Nonetheless, its rules and authority are made known by public example when it is present, and frequently upon return for acts committed in its absence.[5] In this way, the FARC seeks to establish itself among segments of the population as an ideological leader, a social mediator, and a responsible authority; in the case of condoning intra-family violence, including sexual violence, the FARC attempts to sway the opinion of particular portions of the population through its "gender-sensitive" manner.

In some situations, the FARC takes an instructive approach, such as conducting public workshops on gender equity in social and economic realms (Brittain 2010). More consistently, however, the FARC's efforts to ensure gender equity are manifested in its prohibition and punishment of intra-family and intra-community physical abuse and sexual violence. The FARC considers sexual abuse of minors among the worst of crimes.

The FARC is aware of the high levels of physical abuse of boys and girls in their homes, and there appears to be a distinct FARC practice of appealing to girls and boys who suffer physical and sexual abuse to join their ranks. Their approaches take gender into account. In the case of girls, guerrilla members spend time convincing them that they will be safer and better off in the armed group. There may be elements of courtship, as older male guerrilla members develop relationships with young girls, with the ultimate agenda of recruitment. To a girl facing abuse and minimal opportunity, a kind, attentive, and encouraging male – perhaps the only one in her daily life – may be particularly convincing. This tactic is employed in spite of the fact that the girl will not ultimately join the group as a partner of the guerrilla member who recruited her, but as one more fighter; new members will be subject to FARC rules on relationships just like other females and males. The ultimate departure of the girl into the FARC may be in violation of her parents' will. This reveals that the group has crafted this recruitment strategy to target minor females, and that risking the disapproval or anger of an adult male in the household is an outcome the FARC is willing to accept, since they apparently need minors more than adults to maintain and build their fighting base. In other cases, as in circumstances of poverty or intra-family abuse, the recruitment of a girl may be with the family's approval, as the recruitment signifies the girl coming under the financial and rearing charge of the FARC. Other approaches strongly link sexual abuse and recruitment. In one example, the FARC reportedly responded to sexual abuse allegations by killing the alleged male perpetrator (the father) and taking the girl into the group.[6]

There appears to be a fine line between FARC efforts to eliminate physical and sexual abuse in communities it seeks to control and its capitalizing on these realities for recruitment efforts. While the FARC uses forced conscription (despite its public commitment to eliminate this practice), the majority of its recruitment is voluntary and of minors (both forced conscription and recruitment of minors are illegal in Colombia). To illustrate, a 2005 study of demobilized minors showed an average age of recruitment of 12.6, and that 85.4 percent had joined voluntarily (Defensoría del Pueblo de Colombia 2006);

an earlier study of FARC minors in 2001 found a slightly higher average age of recruitment at 13.8 years of age (Defensoría del Pueblo de Colombia 2001). Significantly, in the 2005 study, 20.8 percent declared that their motivation for joining was to escape from physical abuse in their homes.

It is unclear whether the FARC's limited effectiveness in controlling and prohibiting intra-community physical and sexual abuse reflects the limits of their own power, or if it is a conscious decision to strategically allow certain levels of abuse and discontent to strengthen their recruiting pool. By recruiting youths who have been victims of physical and sexual abuse, the FARC not only exercises its ideological and military authority, but also continues to replenish its ranks with able-bodied individuals who will have a strong ideological allegiance to FARC, based on its stance against physical and sexual abuse.

Yet the FARC's need to coexist with local populations, combined with their push for gender equity and freeing females from sexual violence as a means to recruit, can also put them in a tenuous situation when communities rise up against their actions. In regions that are particularly strategic for the FARC, the group may be especially sensitive to demands of the population, and here too gender comes into play. Whether in recognition of ideological wrongdoing or for practical relations, in some situations the FARC may correct for its mistakes or reverse its decisions in response to strong protest by local populations. One example is in the enforcement of FARC rules prohibiting rape by its members. In a case where a guerrilla member commits an unauthorized rape[7] of a member of the community, an individual or the entire community may report this incident to the local FARC commander. If proven true, following an internal FARC "war trial," the FARC will execute the responsible member publicly and in front of the victim, thus reinforcing their ideology, their "respect" for the community, and their absolute and final authority. On the other hand, even acts which fall within the FARC's normal, internally accepted realm of activities, such as the forcible conscription of a minor, may be reversed if met by strong protests from a significant portion of the community, and the boy or girl returned.[8] Such reversals appear to be a rare occurrence, however, and most likely occur in well-organized communities such as on indigenous reservations, which can easily mobilize groups of individuals to stand up to the FARC. While communities employ different tactics according to their local context and previous relations with the guerrilla group, significantly, in some situations these efforts appear to be most effective when the women of the community initiate actions in defiance of the FARC. This is because in contexts of particularly tried and sensitive relationships between the FARC and the community, women are less likely than men to be perceived by the FARC as ideological or political opponents. Additionally, women may gain leverage by couching their demands within their (honored) status as mothers within Colombian society.[9]

This case study shows that in situations of armed conflict, NSAGs are paying attention to gender dynamics within their societies and looking at how they can use or modify those dynamics to meet their needs. Yet NSAGs cannot always afford to follow a straight line in their efforts to further an ideological cause. Just as one element of the group's action may directly support a goal such as achieving gender equity, other priorities may explicitly seek to take advantage of gender inequity to serve other essential operational functions (e.g., recruitment, as our case study illustrates). The FARC case study also makes clear that even within the ranks of a NSAG, leaders and members may not be able to model the social equality that they seek to achieve with their platform for society. Finally, as seen in instances where women rise up to demand the return of conscripted children, the FARC case study shows that even powerful NSAGs are subject to gendered power dynamics in the societies in which they live and interact, and that communities themselves can at times leverage those dynamics to resist FARC demands.

Female suicide bombers

In this section, we examine the role of female suicide bombers in armed opposition groups. Suicide bombing by females is often sensationalized by the media, and this practice is both rare and not representative of women's typical role in NSAGs. However, we include it in this chapter as a site for further analysis of the often contested and never stable workings of militarization, gender, and patriarchy within some NSAGs.

Suicide bombing places women and girls in what are usually public spaces of "combat," tasking them with killing particular "high value" targets or as many people as possible – i.e., it places them in spaces and roles typically reserved for males and identified with masculinized valor. Transgressing gender norms in this way, female suicide bombing can heighten the tensions within and between insurgent groups, their fighters and members, and the communities within which they operate, destabilizing the group if the leadership does not carefully handle how this role comes into being and is manipulated and understood. In other words, cultures, communities, families, and individuals – both inside and outside of insurgencies – are not particularly challenged or destabilized when a female serves as a cook, courier, intelligence agent, or supporter of an armed insurgent movement. But the same cannot be said for females' violent and radical acts of bombing, in which one kills oneself and others. And because all insurgent movements depend on the support of the communities in which they are based, they cannot afford to alienate either those communities or the male fighters they have brought into the movement. Hence, the role of females in suicide positions is one in which leaders of armed opposition groups must tread carefully and, as such, it provides a window into which we as analysts can look to learn more about the gendered internal dynamics of these groups.

In 1985, when Sana'a Mehaydali blew herself up near an Israeli military convoy in Lebanon on behalf of the Syrian Socialist National Party (SSNP), she became the modern world's first female suicide bomber (Bloom 2005). The other women bombers who followed Mehaydali over the next two years were secular members of the communist SSNP. The next wave of female suicide operatives began on May 21, 1991, when a female member of the LTTE assassinated former Indian Prime Minister Rajiv Gandhi. Since then, the LTTE have used more female suicide bombers than any other militant group (Burton & Stewart 2007). Over the next 20 years, an increasing number of women have acted as suicide bombers, and by one count made up 25 percent of all such attackers (Bloom 2005). Some armed opposition groups have used female suicide bombers only recently and sparingly, some not at all, while others have trained and deployed dozens.

The LTTE and the Kurdistan Workers' Party (PKK) incorporated large numbers of women (40 percent and 65 percent respectively) into their bombing attacks throughout the 1990s (Forest 2006). In Chechnya, women have carried out a number of deadly attacks against the Russians since 2000 (Sjoberg & Gentry 2007). The al-Aqsa Martyrs' Brigade (AMB) became the first modern armed opposition group to employ a female suicide bomber in January 2002 in an attack inside Israel (Zedalis 2004). Though the more religiously configured armed opposition groups operating in Israel were hesitant to use women in suicide attacks, the AMB's successful operations using women soon led the Palestinian Islamic Jihad (PIJ) and Hamas to follow suit and send out their own female bombers (Forest 2006). Similarly, where once al-Qaeda had refrained from sending in female suicide bombers, they did not hesitate to do so in Iraq against Coalition forces after the 2003 invasion (Bloom 2005); in 2008 alone, there were 39 attacks by female suicide bombers (Pessin 2009), the youngest being 13 years of age (Hider 2008).

Why women and girl bombers?

We need a feminist curiosity about both the traditional resistance to using women and girls as suicide bombers, and the reasons for their increased use in these roles by some NSAGs. There are a number of reasons why armed opposition groups may choose to use female suicide bombers, most of which relate to improving the chances of mission success by relying on ideas about gender. As Debra Zedalis (2004) writes, "The success of suicide bombers considerably depends upon surprise and accessibility to targets. Both of these requirements have been met by using women" (p. 1). Female bombers, for example, can and frequently have concealed an explosive device underneath their clothes, at times disguised as a pregnancy. Because of the traditional sensitivities about the female body and restrictions upon which males have access and can touch individual females, there is usually a lesser chance that a female will be searched (or searched thoroughly) or otherwise subjected to invasive security measures, a fact that the PKK has long exploited (Shay 2004).

Religious armed opposition groups have historically and today been less receptive to the use of female suicide bombers than more secular NSAGs. Indeed, Hamas at first refused to use women as bombers on religious grounds. In January 2002, Hamas founder Sheikh Ahmed Ismail Yassin categorically denounced such a role for women because he viewed their proper role in jihad as providing support to the male fighters and raising their children as the next generation of militants. Yet two years later, his organization had apparently rationalized the direct involvement of women for the purpose of ease of operations, and Hamas sent out its first female suicide bomber (Bloom 2005).

The power of gender works here in multiple ways. Ideas about women, including that they are less likely to take violent action, as well as ideas about female modesty and proper relations between men and women, make it less likely that women will be suspected or searched. Ideas about gender also enable militant groups to use a woman's action as a suicide bomber as a way to increase the visibility of the armed group in the press, and to motivate male fighters. By using females in suicide bombings, some NSAGs can mobilize the image of women desperately fighting because the men have failed to bravely step forward – and so, by playing upon notions of the urgent need for male valor, incite men to join (Hadid 2008).

Information about the motivations of female suicide bombers is limited, but some research suggests that, in several ways, the characteristics of women and girl bombers are not all that different from those of male bombers; they are young, have experienced the painful loss of loved ones because of conflict, and are susceptible to recruitment appeals aimed at their gender, age, enthusiasm, nationalism, religion, or desire for vengeance. Some of the women fighters and suicide bombers in Chechnya, for example, reportedly are avenging the deaths of their husbands or other male relatives (Charny 2007), as well as violently protesting the practice by which Russian security forces ransom the bodies of loved ones back to their families (Bloom 2005). Militarized religious and anti-imperialist ideologies are two additional factors causing women and girls, like men and boys, to join suicide missions.

Another important motivating factor for some women and girls apparently is the desire to prove their capabilities, or to achieve equal status with the men within their society, and leaders of some armed opposition groups recognize and manipulate this appeal, as in the case of the LTTE. In traditional Kurdish society, women and girls hold subservient positions and are treated as the property of men, but, in the PKK infantry, they complete the same training and fight alongside men, which some female PKK recruits say is an exciting escape from repressive village life (Reuter 2004). Those females in the PKK who become suicide bombers can use the patriarchal conservative Turkish values against the state, as their gender gives them an advantage in carrying out their suicide missions (Shay 2004).

Connected to this desire for recognition of her own abilities and worth is the expectation of admiration for herself and her family. Perhaps paradoxically, suicide bombing may be seen as a path to gender equality and being valued as a woman. Just as male suicide bombers are exalted and hailed for their heroic contributions to the cause, so too are women and girls rewarded. LTTE female suicide bombers, like the males, were regarded as heroes and treated to triumphant funeral processions and elaborate shrines (Reuter 2004). The PKK purports to express its admiration and honor for its female suicide attackers by having them escorted to their target location by men (Shay 2004). In some cases, a woman's suicide attack is even seen as more impressive than a man's, precisely because of the traditional view of females as marginalized and subordinate (Berko & Erez 2007).

Some women and girls who join an armed opposition group may feel alienated from their society – outcast or socially stigmatized – or may not feel as though they have a family or community to return to, as noted among some female PKK members (Shay 2004). In other instances, women and girls from the armed opposition group's communities have suffered rape or other abuse at the hands of their targets, and are seeking revenge. In many cultures, rape and other sexual activities that are unsanctioned by the family (e.g., through marriage) are seen not only to damage the female, but to bring terrible shame on her family's honor and standing. In such cases, the glory and respect that is bestowed upon them via their martyrdom may seem much more appealing than the alternative (Bloom 2005).

Although ideological, emotional, and economic circumstances may motivate women and girls to become suicide bombers, their involvement is by no means always voluntary. At times, women and girls are forcibly recruited and trained by husbands, relatives, or local "emirs," another name used by leaders of the organization al-Qaeda in Mesopotamia (BBC Monitoring International Reports 2008; Zavis 2008). That process may include, for example, younger women's repeated sexual and physical abuse at the hands of their older husbands, who eventually force them to undertake suicide missions (Fried 2008). In some rarer instances, women are forced to wear explosive belts or transport bombs without knowing that the bomb will detonate by remote control (Fried 2008; Kingsbury 2008).

What we learn from female suicide bombers

There are several important lessons we learn from our discussion of female suicide bombers. First, the perceived role of female suicide bombers varies among armed opposition groups, and within those groups it varies over time. Second, religiously constructed armed groups have reinforced the militarized traditional supportive role of the jihadist woman, even as they accede to the deployment of female suicide bombers. Third, the identity of any suicide bomber is deeply gendered. Violent self-sacrifice in armed conflict is, in most cultures, located clearly in the masculine domain. As women and girls engage in suicide bombings, they are deeply engaged in gendered, militarized acts that in large part seek respectability in the eyes of the communities that support the armed group. Yet including women and girls as suicide bombers can also make the ways in which the armed group has militarized its own brand of masculinity more problematic, indeed more fragile. At times, some groups seek to counter this: by sacrificing women and girls who have stepped outside the ideal feminine terrain (e.g., that their actions have shamed their family's honor); by maintaining the dominant role of male protector (e.g., males escorting women bombers to their destinations); and by making the women's sacrifice of their lives akin to idealized virtues of women (e.g., where suicide bombing is framed as akin to the sacrifices of being a wife or mother). Finally, what our analysis brings to light is the complexity of the militarized and gendered processes by which men's relationships to their male commanders, women's relationships to their male counterparts, and communities' relationships to the armed group are challenged, shaped, and reshaped.

When armed groups struggle internally over excluding women and girls from public roles and joining the ranks

There are important things we can learn not only by paying attention to where women and girls are highly visible inside armed opposition groups, but also where they are kept out of the public eye. In this section, we use a series of short case examples to explore why females are kept invisible in some NSAGs.

Cynthia Enloe's writings over the last thirty years have clearly shown how state militaries and armed groups rely on females to maintain their forces and fight their wars (see, for example, Enloe 2000). Thus, we know that the exclusion of women and girls from *directly and publicly* participating in armed opposition groups is also a conscious decision based on the underlying militarized gendered values, motives, and goals of the group. So when we see an NSAG whose public face is completely male and we cannot easily "find" the women and girls that we know must in some ways be supporting them, we should immediately become curious. What does the apparent lack of females in a group tell us about how the group positions itself, how it makes decisions about who is seen (males) and who is rendered less visible (females)? How does it position itself within the communities it seeks to represent *and* those that it occupies? Who does it want to attract and recruit? Although some of the groups examined in the case studies below draw on similar religious interpretations to oppose the presence of females within their visible ranks, and all are avowedly patriarchal, these movements are not monolithic; distinct social, political, and historical factors inform how groups approach the involvement of women and girls.

Given the closed and secretive nature of many NSAGs, much of the information about their decisions on how visibly they use and rely on women and girls comes from statements the groups themselves disseminate. Common threads within these statements and apparent changes in women's and girls' participation reveal important shifts. Groups that previously had banned women and girls from publicly joining their ranks but are now increasingly including them are often doing so out of tactical necessity; the changing nature of armed resistance requires techniques that can overcome increased security and exploit gendered "terrorist" profiles. For example, groups such as Hamas, al-Qaeda, and the Taliban have found ways to reconcile militarized patriarchal beliefs with the use of females to carry out their armed struggles, with the Taliban making the least visible use of females, and al-Qaeda using them more frequently. Importantly, when females are included, the way in which this occurs often continues to reflect and support patriarchal control.

We look briefly at three different armed groups (Harakat Al-Shabaab Al-Mujahideen, Hamas, and the United Self-Defense Forces of Colombia) to understand the drivers behind women and girls being excluded from visibly joining their ranks and the factors behind their inclusion in public roles when (if ever) it occurs. The first two groups in our case study are Islamist groups, though they vary in their public use of females. We hypothesize that these groups are actually restricted from using women and girls more publicly and more often by their own cultures' constructs around femininity, the private space to which women are relegated (which limits their movements in public or among men to whom they are not related), and the role of males as the dominant provider and protector. We believe that while these groups observe other NSAGs successfully using female operatives, they cannot risk putting females into more public spaces for violent activities, as it would likely undermine some of the central gendered ideologies of their group and threaten the support they receive from the communities that house them and from which they recruit male fighters. At the same time, Hamas (like al-Qaeda) has had internal and external debates about the use of females for combat operations, and has tried to justify using female combatants to its constituents, in an interesting example of how NSAGs attempt to manipulate and militarize gender relations and roles. The third group we look at comes from Colombia, and represents a highly masculinist and violent group. We include this example to illustrate that not all groups that keep their female members out of the public eye do so for religious or community support reasons. For some, the masculinist identity of its male fighters is so central to the group that it cannot withstand the presence of females on any equal level.

Harakat al-Shabaab al-Mujahideen (al-Shabaab)

The Islamist al-Shabaab youth movement in Somalia is believed to be led by a combination of Somali warlords and foreign fighters and is largely comprised of men between the ages of 20 and 30. Over the last five years, they have emerged as one of the most powerful armed groups in the war in Somalia.

The group claims to be waging jihad against the enemies of Islam (including the Transitional Government of Somalia, the African Union, and the United Nations' mission in Somalia, among others).

Women are accorded no public role in al-Shabaab, although women are recruited to raise funds, recruit new members, and provide support for the group. Women are also recruited to serve as wives to al-Shabaab recruits and fighters. According to one young wife of an al-Shabaab fighter, female recruiters approach the parents of a young woman and tell them, "Before a man is given a gun, he must be given a woman, so that he can leave something behind." To the young woman herself they say, "There is no need for you at home. Get married to the mujahideen who are fighting in the fields" (Baldauf & Mohamed 2010).

Any explanation which attributes al-Shabaab's rejection of public roles for women and girls to its Islamist ideology would be far too simple. As stressed throughout this chapter and this book, the specificity of a conflict's context is always crucial to understand. In this case, the exclusion of women from visible positions is in part a reaction to decades of internal warfare in Somalia which fundamentally altered the economic and social expectations placed upon women and girls, and consequently challenged patriarchal Somali notions of masculinity and manhood. As brutal conflict and famine seized Somalia in the early 1990s, most Somali men lost access to employment; in the absence of income, large numbers of women and older girls entered the workforce to support their families, including husbands, fathers, and male relatives. By 1998, the United Nations High Commissioner for Refugees (UNHCR) estimated that 90 percent of Somalia's workforce was female. These gendered changes in labor fundamentally revised household and community dynamics; in some cases, Somali men were increasingly forced to consult women on financial matters and as men "lost decision-making powers at the household level [they were] also excluded from community decision-making" (El-Bushra & Sahl 2005, p. 55). In re-establishing a social order that places women and girls within the home and under the control of men, al-Shabaab seeks to overturn women's power and agency. Al-Shabaab has in the past used violence against women they perceived to challenge males' domination over females (Hansen 2008).

Hamas

In its founding charter of 1988, Hamas emphasizes the significance of women's involvement in jihad, stating that Muslim men and women have an equal obligation to jihad. The definition of female jihad, however, differs significantly from its male counterpart. Women are supposed to wage jihad by imbuing their children with Islamic values, whereas jihad increasingly calls for men to take up arms (Zamkanei 2008). This interpretation values women's domestic abilities and relegates them to the private sphere, but it is by no means uncontested. The founder and former spiritual leader of Hamas was initially opposed to women taking part in violent jihad, arguing that there were more than enough men willing to carry out suicide bombings (Dickey 2005). His rationale does not discredit women's involvement, but rather asserts that men's participation takes precedence. Other Hamas leaders disagreed, claiming that women's and girls' involvement was the most important "strategic weapon" of Palestinian resistance and that suicide attacks should not be "monopolized by men" (Ness 2008, p. 27). Their views were the minority, as women's and girls' involvement in Hamas was limited to supporting men. However, Hamas would refer women to other organizations supportive of their goals if they expressed a strong desire to participate as suicide bombers (Ness 2008).

In January 2004, however, Hamas employed its first female suicide bomber. After this occurred, some religious leaders supporting the Palestinian struggle amended their earlier positions, stating that female suicide bombers are allowed if they are accompanied by a male chaperone (Bloom 2005). Hamas has since continued to publicly legitimize women carrying out suicide missions, citing historical examples of female militants and arguing that the current war against Israel demands innovative methods. Leaders of Hamas seem to have decided that the tactical advantage of using females is necessary and therefore they must find creative ways to reinterpret cultural or religious prohibitions against female involvement in a more violent jihad.

The United Self-Defense Forces of Colombia (AUC)

The United Self-Defense Forces of Colombia (AUC – Autodefensas Unidas de Colombia)[10] was an umbrella organization of regional right-wing paramilitary groups operating in Colombia. The various paramilitaries were originally intended to protect different local economic, social and political powers and their interests by repressing insurgents in their regions. At its height, it was believed these militias had over 20,000 militants. The AUC recruited women and girls for support roles but excluded them from active fighting or political discourse. The rigid gender roles within the AUC mirror Colombia's traditionally gendered institutions which have an extreme bifurcation of the roles of males and females, with strong elements of female subservience. In Colombia, *machismo*, or the cult of virility, embraces "an exaggerated aggressiveness and intransience in male-to-male personal relationships and arrogance and sexual aggression in male-to-female relationships" (Stevens 1973, p. 91 as cited in Bunster 1993, p. 100). *Machismo* by definition cannot exist without reference to women (e.g., *Marianismo*), but its exercise is threatened by any action that would undermine men's patriarchal authority or actions that would assert equality between men and women.

The re-creation of a militarized, masculinized, patriarchal system within the AUC was essential to the group's underlying mission and encouraged a culture of *machismo* within the AUC itself (Schmidt 2007). Women and girls were excluded from more visible public roles (and all combat roles) because the AUC believes their presence might make the group appear less *machista* and intimidating (Schmidt 2007). Beyond excluding women from fighting, the AUC consistently reinforced *machista* notions of masculinity, carried out gender-based violence, and imposed dress codes, mandatory birth control and forced termination of any pregnancy for those women inside the AUC (Schmidt 2007).

As these three short case studies seek to make clear, some armed opposition groups' religious, cultural, and social identities are so militarized and masculinized that the existence of females inside their ranks has to be handled in ways that do not destabilize a central component of their ideology, recruitment, organization and identity – that of the male fighter/warrior/martyr, the male who is powerful and in control. Where women and girls move out of support roles to carry out armed violence in the public eye, their numbers are few and, even within the training and preparation for their roles, their gendered identities, (enforced) dependence on men, and subservient status to men is reinforced. Finally, it is important to note that even when women's and girls' presence is highly contained, it is still not without influence; indeed, their limited roles and visibility (i.e., containment) remains a crucial factor in defining, recruiting, and motivating the male fighters within.

Conclusion

We tend to underestimate how much concerted effort it takes, and how power is wielded in those efforts, to construct and mobilize the identities and consciousness needed to create and maintain an insurgency movement.[11] A feminist gendered analysis of women and girls inside armed opposition groups can help reveal where power is at play inside the groups and among the communities those groups rely on for support. It is important to understand that if women and girls (both inside the group and in the communities) cannot be effectively controlled to play the roles needed by the armed group, it is questionable whether men's participation in the group can be assured.

Militarization is highly gendered. The militarization of any insurgency and the communities that support it occurs in large part through the gendered workings of power. And it is in part through these gendered workings of power that insurgent groups create new forms of authority, wealth, protection, and legitimacy. In some armed groups, women and, to a lesser extent, older girls play significant roles not only in providing material and labor support to the group, but *as females* they symbolize the depth of power and determination of some armed opposition groups (e.g., when women "leave" their traditional roles and families and join armed movements). Females may also be particularly important in sustaining the groups' claims on legitimacy, and hence, power.

Male leaders of NSAGs count on the fact that certain sectors of a society from which new male recruits are drawn are militarized in ways that help spur those males to believe they are brave protectors of their families and cultures. Those leaders then carefully shape their male recruits' service in a way that affirms their desire to appear manly in the eyes of other insurgents, their families, lovers, and communities. War reinforces masculine conceptions of trustworthiness, suffering, hardship, strength, determination, and fearlessness; particular notions of female identity and male/female relations are essential for reasserting these concepts and strengthening their value within the armed group and the communities that support them. Additionally, some groups may believe that males considering joining an armed group may be further motivated to show their courage if they see their sisters joining, as their sisters' actions may challenge their own notions of what it means to be a real man in their society.

Militarization also has to be appealing to the women and girls that armed opposition groups rely on, and so it offers promises of equality, worth, of being taken seriously, of operating within an elite, respected force, of redeeming oneself for past (usually gendered) transgressions, and liberation. Thus, armed groups' relationship to masculinity and femininity is never a simple matter. Adding women and girls to an armed group means that male leaders have to tread carefully so as not to unbalance the fragile masculinity they have helped to create among their predominately male force.

Efforts by armed groups to militarize the communities they rely on for support and recruits can be strengthened or undermined by how masculinities and femininities are constructed inside the armed group. In order for armed opposition groups to continue their struggle, gender must be militarized within these communities. All kinds of experiences need to be militarized to encourage male and female recruits to join – danger, frustration, boredom, liberation, despair, and determination. Perhaps two of the most important experiences that armed groups need to engender and militarize in ways that draw young people to them are young women's and men's experiences of humiliation and injustice at the hands of state forces.

It takes a lot of power and effort to militarize any section of a society. Male leaders of armed opposition groups walk a fine line as they incorporate women and girls into the mix, especially as women and girls take public roles in combat, which is perhaps the quintessentially masculinized (and thus idealized) role. How women and girls should appear and in what roles are sites of power struggles and debates within and among armed opposition groups.

The post-conflict period is ripe with both risk and possibility for women, men, girls and boys coming out of armed struggle, imagining that maybe this time they will be treated with more dignity, have better chances to improve their lives and the lives of their families, and more opportunities to reach their goals. There is a very real risk that power will be re-inscribed into the hands of the "winners" and that the group of "winners" that claims the largest share of power will be small and predominately male. Yet this is not a given, and what may seem like prescribed futures can be re-imagined, even challenged (Enloe 2000).

QUESTIONS FOR DISCUSSION

1 What are the most important ways in which armed opposition groups need women and girls to support their movements and insurgencies?

2 Which experiences of women and girls do armed opposition groups need to tap into to help mobilize those females to join and support the insurgency? How do those experiences and roles differ for those women and girls that the insurgency hopes to recruit as members to carry out violence, as compared to those women and girls it hopes will remain in the communities and support its activities?

3 What are the tensions that leaders of armed opposition groups face from within their own groups, as well as supporting communities, in recruiting women and girls to carry out violence in the name of their insurgencies? How do they seek to manage these tensions?

SUGGESTIONS FOR FURTHER READING

Enloe, Cynthia (2000) *Maneuvers: The International Politics of Militarizing Women's Lives.* Berkeley: University of California Press.

Luciak, Ilja A. (2001) *After the Revolution: Gender and Democracy in El Salvador, Nicaragua and Guatemala.* Baltimore: Johns Hopkins University Press.

McKay, Susan, and Mazurana, Dyan (2004) *Where are the Girls? Girls in Fighting Forces in Northern Uganda, Sierra Leone and Mozambique: Their Lives During and After War.* Montreal: Rights and Democracy.

Sjoberg, Laura, and Gentry, Caron E. (2007) *Mothers, Monsters, Whores: Women's Violence in Global Politics.* London: Zed Books.

CHAPTER 8

Women and Peace Processes

Malathi de Alwis, Julie Mertus, and Tazreena Sajjad

Because delegates to the 1998 peace talks in Northern Ireland were chosen through public elections, Monica McWilliams, a Catholic feminist academic from South Belfast, and Pearl Sagar, a Protestant social worker from East Belfast, formed the Northern Ireland Women's Coalition (NIWC) to lobby political parties to include women in their candidate lists. When ignored, they decided to form their own political party and contest the elections. The NIWC only received 1.03 percent of the popular vote but it managed to secure two seats (out of 110) under the quota set aside for minority parties. McWilliams and Sagar were thus able to participate in multi-party negotiations resulting in the intergovernmental Good Friday Agreement which devolved legislative powers to the Northern Ireland National Assembly and brought about a significant de-escalation of violence.

During the peace talks in Somalia in 2000, participation was restricted to Somalia's five clans. As clans were traditionally represented only by men, Somali women found themselves closed out of the negotiations. A cross-clan group of women peace activists, led by Asha Haji Elmi, declared themselves to be representatives of a "sixth clan," the clan of women, and camped outside the location of the talks, demanding that they be allowed to participate in the formal peace process. They were eventually accepted as participants, and negotiated, among other measures, a gender quota for Transitional Federal Parliament seats and the establishment of a Women's Ministry. The National Charter they helped draft is considered the best in the region.

These two examples offer a glimpse of how women, from both the global North and South, have struggled to be represented and to participate in peace negotiations. While the women of Northern Ireland fought their battle via formal political institutions and processes, the women of Somalia found an ingenious, informal way to circumvent a major sociopolitical obstacle. However, peace processes encompass much more than lobbying and negotiation and the drafting and signing of agreements; to understand them, we need to broaden our focus, both temporally and spatially, far beyond the peace table. Not only is it important to pay attention to both the formal and informal processes that take place among representatives of the state, militant groups and civil society over an extended length of time, but also to understand how the conflicts being negotiated have arisen, the kinds of political stakes involved, and the influence wielded by neighboring states, regional alliances, international bodies, and UN organizations.

   It is also crucial to be cognizant of the specific social, historical, political, economic, and cultural contexts within which women seeking greater representation and participation in peace processes and thereafter are situated so as to get a better sense of the challenges and obstacles they face. Who participates in peace talks, how peace agreements are drafted, what is contained in them, and how they are adhered to and implemented is largely dependent on these contexts, which are themselves always already gendered. Thus, peace processes can offer a crucial space within which gender relations in post-conflict societies can be restructured, or they can become spaces within which women could lose some of the gains they have made during wartime or what they fought for in the war. The viability of implementing UN Security Council Resolution (UNSCR) 1325, which seeks to enable gender-equitable restructuring of post-conflict societies, is dependent on such contingencies. This chapter will discuss some of the complexities and nuances highlighted above while also exploring what constitutes peace processes and analyzing some of the dilemmas of women's representation and effectiveness they raise.

Overview of peace processes

The most common image that comes to mind when we think of a peace process is that of various warring parties meeting in a neutral country, sitting around a table and, with the help of an external actor who facilitates the negotiation, hammering out an agreement that would end the conflict in which they are involved. You may be familiar, for example, with the high profile talks which took place between the United States of America and North and South Vietnam in 1973, resulting in the Paris Peace Accords, or the 1993 talks between Israel and Palestine, facilitated by Norway, resulting in the Oslo Peace Accords. The key signatories of both peace accords went on to win the Nobel Peace Prize (though Vietnamese politburo member Le Duc Tho refused to accept it). However, this is a very limited view of a peace process, as peace processes involve much more than peace talks and agreements; it is also a very gendered one, as most warring parties and facilitators at the peace table are represented by men. Unfortunately, this is frequently the only segment of the process which is covered by the media.

Several crucial factors need to be kept in mind as we probe the complicated nature of peace processes. First, a peace process does not merely begin when warring parties sit down to peace talks nor does it end with the signing of a peace agreement.

Second, it does not only involve the warring parties and facilitating parties but also encompasses a wide swathe of local, national, regional, and international institutions and actors, many of whom have been working behind the scenes to enable these talks to happen over an extended period of time, sometimes decades. Their continued involvement is needed once a peace agreement is signed in order to ensure that what is contained in the agreement is adhered to and implemented and the warring parties do not return to a state of war.

Third, while a key purpose of peace talks is to bring an end to armed conflict, a peace agreement is about more than cease-fires. It also lays the groundwork for how the post-conflict society will be structured once a political settlement is achieved. An agreement would usually address immediate issues such as restoration of law and order, demobilization and reintegration of combatants, and resettlement/relocation of displaced populations, as well as set out longer term agendas regarding how political power should be devolved among warring parties, constitutional changes that are needed, and social, economic, and political inequalities and exclusions which need to be redressed. It thus provides a crucial opportunity for more equitable gender relations and power sharing to be introduced with regard to short-term as well as longer-term issues.

What is a peace process?

If we begin with a basic definition that a peace process refers to political processes and strategies for resolving conflict through peaceful means, we can now also add, based on the three key premises set out above, that a peace process involves years of groundwork being laid before peace talks, and sustaining work after talks; that it includes a variety of both local and international institutions and actors; and that it provides a unique opportunity to restructure post-conflict societies.

Peace processes, like all other social processes, are deeply gendered and often reiterate gendered and other power hierarchies and inequalities, even while simultaneously offering opportunities for change. It is therefore important to probe how peace processes are conceptualized. Who gets to participate in them, i.e., who gets included and who gets excluded, and why? Who gets to make such choices? What issues get prioritized and by whom? Scrutinizing the language used in peace processes is a useful place to start as terminology, names, and labels play a central role in constituting our social reality. This means that if we can figure out the consequences of particular terms and usages, then we can also try to change our social reality by changing those terms and what they have come to signify. We are particularly interested here in illuminating underlying gendered, neocolonial assumptions that buttress the language of peace processes as they are often the most invisible. We offer below a brief discussion of some key terms which are mobilized in peace processes.

- **Conflict resolution** refers to the resolving of conflicts through mediation, negotiation, and diplomacy. It has spawned a significant population of conflict resolution "experts," the majority of them men, who "parachute" into war-torn countries to "fix" conflicts. This has resulted in a certain "cowboy" attitude toward mediation with a concern to notch up successfully signed cease-fire agreements rather than a longer-term commitment toward establishing a sustainable peace.[1] The notion that there is one set of strategies or a foolproof model that can be applied to the mediation of conflict in any part of the world has resulted in such "experts" not taking the time to understand the history of the country in question, the reasons for the conflict, the pressure and interference from national constituencies and neighboring states, who has been excluded from peace talks, and whether the agreement reached can be viably sustained given the political stakes involved.

- **Conflict transformation** is also concerned with resolving conflicts but takes a more broad-based approach in seeking to support a more sustainable peace by repairing the social fabric and reconciling estranged communities, designing new political institutions, supporting democratic processes, and enabling the implementation of human rights guarantees. Terms such as accountability, transparency, good governance, and rule of law are very much part of the vocabulary of conflict transformation. The restructuring of state institutions, as well as the encouragement and funding of civil society organizations, especially women's initiatives, are a key focus. Certain bilateral and multilateral donors, the UN, and other international institutions discussed below (see "International Actors and UN Security Council Resolution 1325") have been involved in supporting conflict transformation; some critiques of their involvement will be discussed in greater depth in that section. The key point we wish to raise here is the danger of neocolonial relationships being reinforced when former colonial powers and international agencies seek to impose a framework of democracy and governance that may not be organic to that country and thus not sustainable. Indeed, it may even lead to increased nationalism and resistance.

- **Road map** delineates the trajectory of a peace process. It requires passing several key signposts which mark different phases of the journey: (1) the pre-negotiation phase which involves secret meetings and backroom maneuvering to get all the warring parties to agree to talks; (2) the cease-fire phase when warring parties call a truce to stop fighting; (3) the negotiation phase to reach a political agreement and the drafting of a peace accord; and (4) the post-conflict phase where the peace accord is implemented and rehabilitation begins.

- **Road blocks** are the obstacles such a process encounters, such as walkouts and withdrawals from peace talks, disagreements, and impasses over agreements, and return to warfare.

- **Track I** refers to the key stakeholders involved in the peace talks, usually including: the warring parties; the facilitating country, organization, or individual; and maybe a few representatives of neighboring and donor states and/or the UN and other international and regional bodies. The latter representatives usually have only observer status, but are nevertheless able to wield great influence through backroom negotiations and deals. The common perception is that the "real" work of political negotiation takes place in this formal, masculinized domain where all the "hard" issues are discussed and debated.

- **Track II** refers to secondary stakeholders who seek to influence the outcome of Track I talks through lobbying, advocacy, and the issuing of statements and recommendations. Track II meetings often parallel the Track I meetings in order to closely monitor and respond to what is taking place at the Track I level. Several Track II stakeholders might also be allowed to attend Track I talks, as observers. Track II is perceived as the feminized space of civil society which is concerned with "soft" social issues and operates at a more informal level.

Drawing an analogy between a peace process and a road map that has two parallel tracks narrows what is clearly a very complex process into a linear, schematic narrative; it also obscures the longer time frame within which peace processes take place. The gendering of Tracks I and II gives center stage to the masculinized, formal political negotiations linked with Track I while marginalizing and devaluing the less publicized Track II and other informal work of civil society, including women's groups, where often the more innovative and substantive work of peace-building is conducted. In the sections that follow, we will explore the kinds of struggles waged by women's groups to participate in both Track I and II processes as well as beyond, while also exploring why it is important for women to be part of peace processes.

Overview of women's participation in peace processes

When considering women's participation in peace processes, it is crucial to understand their status within their respective countries and the kinds of social, economic, and political structures with which they coexist. In most parts of the world, not only do women have to struggle against patriarchal structures in their homes, neighborhoods, places of worship, schools, and offices, but they are barely represented in the political arena as well. For example, in Sri Lanka, which produced the world's first woman head of state way back in 1960 and was ruled by another woman head of state for much of the 1990s, women's representation in parliament has never exceeded 6% and remains at around 4% at provincial and local government levels, despite women having a literacy rate of 98%, propping up the national economy with their labor, and being well represented in all other arenas of national life (Kodikara 2010, p. 12). This is due to the fact that political patronage structures are very patriarchal, dynastic, and classist as well as corrupt and violent, all major deterrents for women. A group of multi-ethnic women who contested as a women's party only received a minuscule number of votes, as the general trend in the country is to vote either for the two major mainstream parties or for ethnicity-based parties. This political configuration was echoed in the various peace talks which took place during the three-decade war which finally ended through a military defeat of the Liberation Tigers of Tamil Eelam (LTTE) in 2009. Peace talks which took place in 1985, 1990, and 1994 only had one woman present, Adele Balasingham, the Australian wife of the chief negotiator for the LTTE; she was there as an observer and in her capacity as a nurse since Mr Balasingham was a diabetic. The exception was the talks which began in 2002 (see "Women at the Peace Table," below).

Why should women be part of peace processes?

One could argue that since women do not play a significant role in politics in most countries, it shouldn't really matter if they are not part of peace processes either. Indeed, such an argument is often used by negotiating parties to exclude women from peace talks. During the 2002 Democratic Republic of the Congo (DRC) peace talks in Sun City, South Africa, for example, the Congolese government, as well as other warring parties, sought to keep women out by insisting that "war and peace are exclusively the business of men" (Mpoumou 2004, p. 122). "Women did not have any right to participate," they further argued, "because they were not fighters nor had they enjoyed meaningful representation in local or national decision-making bodies before the war" (Mpoumou 2004, p. 122). One women's group which was mobilizing to send representatives to the talks in Sun City, Réseau des Femmes pour la Defense des Droits et la Paix, located in the Kivu region of DRC, received threats from the rebel group, Rassemblement Congolais pour la Démocratie (RCD), had their offices repeatedly ransacked and their peaceful marches interrupted (Mpoumou 2004, p. 122).

At the beginning of the peace process in Burundi, Burundian men engaged in negotiations were adamant that they could represent women's interests so there was no necessity for any women to be present (Puechguirbal 2005, p. 5). Indeed, they went one step further and suggested, like their Cypriot counterparts, that the women should go home and take care of their children (Sorensen 1998; Puechguirbal 2005, p. 6). In Guatemala, both the left- and right-wing factions questioned the need to include a separate women's voice in the 1994 peace negotiations. Both sides were in agreement that the women's movement was a "foreign import"; the right questioned the relevance of the movement to "Guatemalan culture" while the left argued that gender issues would divide their supporters at a critical historical moment (Berger 2003, p. 202).

Women's groups are also frequently accused of being too bourgeois and elitist, thus not representing the majority of their countrywomen. This assumption is often linked to the argument that women's movements are a "foreign import" or a "western concept." However, in some cases, a diametrically opposite charge is leveled at women's groups – that their views and interests are no different from those of men, so it is unnecessary to accord them a special seat at the peace table.

Local peace organizations may also be resistant to the involvement of women. Male-dominated groups – even those devoted to peace – can reproduce assumptions about appropriate and inappropriate roles for women in society. As such, even though women can be involved in mixed-sex peace groups, they may be denied access to decision-making positions within the organizations and relegated to "housekeeping" functions (Anderlini 2000). In this regard, women peace activists and women combatants face similar treatment. In the case of women combatants, this bitter reality comes in the form of their not being allowed to participate as leaders in their communities for nation- and state-building processes; rather, in many cases, they are treated as pariahs and shunned from society for their activities during the war.[2]

Some policy makers have argued that gender equality or "women's issues" are "irrelevant" or "not suitable" topics for discussion at the peace table (Anderlini 2000; Potter 2005, 2008). Certain international organizations have cautioned that the presence of women's groups, perceived as not being directly involved in conflicts, could be viewed with mistrust, seen as disruptive and even capable of jeopardizing peace talks (Villellas Ariño 2010, pp. 34–5).

Because they are innately peaceful? If women are tolerated at peace talks, even only as observers, it is often on the assumption that they have a "natural" propensity to be more empathic and peaceful than men. As Boru Raba, a male leader of a peace committee of elders in Ethiopia commented: "Women are better than men . . . [they] can play both a fuelling role and cooling role in conflict [and] if men get initiated for conflict and women interject, the men might change their minds" (as quoted in McCabe 2007). This kind of feminization of peace, in turn, reinforces the masculinity of war. As Cynthia Enloe (2002) has warned, "militarized masculinity is a model of masculinity that is especially likely to be imagined as requiring a feminine complement that excludes women from full and assertive participation in postwar public life" (p. 23).

However, women's groups themselves have sometimes mobilized such patriarchal assumptions to their advantage in order to call for an end to violence, to gain moral authority, and to seek inclusion in peace processes. But such a positioning ignores the myriad instances where women, by virtue of choice or coercion, have participated as combatants, torturers and destroyers in the front lines of war, as detailed in chapters 6 and 7 of this volume.[3]

Because they have moral legitimacy as mothers? In 2003, when the Moro Islamic Revolutionary Front's (MIRF) main camp was bombed by the Philippine government and they withdrew from peace talks, Mothers for Peace (M4P) launched a campaign to urge the militants to return to the negotiating table. An emotive TV advertisement aired repeatedly by M4P generated a great deal of national interest and sympathy and is believed to have spurred the MIRF's

return to the negotiating table. A plaintive song comments on three successive images, a young man, a teenager and a boy: "First our husbands," "Next
our brothers," and "Now our sons," and ends with the query, "Who else will
stand up for peace in Mindanao?"[4]

Such forms of maternalism, i.e., the political mobilization of motherhood,
are not a new phenomenon. It has been resorted to in different parts of the
globe at different moments in history with, for example: Women Strike for
Peace in the United States, pushing their babies in strollers into city halls
and federal buildings to protest nuclear arms tests in the 1960s; the *Madres*
of Argentina silently and continuously circling the Plaza de Mayo wearing
white headscarves evocative of diapers and holding photographs of their
"disappeared" sons and daughters since the late 1970s; the Relatives' Action
Committee in Northern Ireland observing fasting vigils, wrapping themselves
in blankets and shackling themselves with chains to call attention to the
harsh prison conditions in which their sons were being kept in the early
1980s; the Committee of Soldiers' Mothers of Russia braving artillery fire in
Grozny, Chechnya to stop their sons from fighting what they perceived to be
a pointless war in the 1990s; and, in the 2000s, members of the All-Manipur
Social Reformation and Development Samaj, responding to the rape of a
young Manipuri girl by the Indian army, by baring their aged bodies in front
of the army headquarters and demanding that they all be raped because they
were all mothers of the raped girl.[5]

As Seth Koven and Sonya Michel (1993) have argued, "maternalism always
operates on two levels: Extol[ling] the virtues of domesticity while simultaneously legitimating women's public relationships to politics and the state, to
community, workplace and marketplace" (p. 6). Because maternalism seeks
to "evok[e] traditional images of womanliness, [it] implicitly challenge[s] the
boundaries between public and private, women and men, state and civil society" (Koven & Michel 1993, p. 6). Indeed, while previously feminist critiques
saw maternalism as producing either victims or agents, or as either essentializing women or empowering them, more recent feminist engagements with
maternalism have recognized its resiliency and malleability and its complicated and contingent unfoldings (de Alwis 2004 and 2012).

Because they are victims of war?   While women's groups have mobilized maternalism in innovative and radical ways, they have rarely succeeded in destabilizing
dominant perceptions – held by the state and other warring parties as well as
international NGOs, UN organizations, and human rights groups – of women's
vulnerability and victimhood.[6] They are frequently referred to as being weak
and vulnerable, as victims, in need of protection, dependent on men, always
associated with children and sometimes other "vulnerable groups" such as
the elderly, the disabled, and the mentally disturbed, unable to articulate
their own needs and having no control over their lives. This kind of thinking
is reflected in UNSCR 1470, adopted on March 28, 2003 to extend the security

---

Box 8.1 (Where) have women appeared in peace agreements?

The Lomé Peace Accord signed in July 1999 to end the conflict in Sierra Leone contains only one reference to women in the body of the text:

> "Given that women have been particularly victimized during the war, special attention shall be accorded to their needs and potentials in formulating and implementing national rehabilitation, reconstruction, and development programmes, to enable them to play a central role in the moral, social and physical reconstruction of Sierra Leone." (as quoted with added emphasis in Puechguirbal 2005, pp. 2–3)

Note that there is no reference to the possibility of women having a role to play in the political or economic reconstruction of the country. Most importantly, special attention is being accorded to them because they have been "victimized during the war."

Women were essentially invisible in the peace agreements of Bougainville (2001), Angola (2002), Eritrea and Ethiopia (2000), Aceh (2005), and Côte d'Ivoire (2003 and 2007).

Since peace accords will frame the society that will be built in a post-conflict environment it is crucial that the language used in such documents should be chosen with care and that women are involved in drafting such agreements or at least have access to the drafters of the document.

---

mandate in Sierra Leone, which emphasizes the need to "pay special attention to the needs of women and children," and UNSCR1509, adopted on September 19, 2003 to extend the security mandate in Liberia, which stresses that the mission's mandate should pay "particular attention to vulnerable groups including refugees, returning refugees, and internally displaced persons, women, children and demobilized child soldiers" (as quoted in Puechguirbal 2005, p. 3) (see Text Box 8.1). It is critical not to downplay the importance of protecting women – from sexual as well as other forms of violence, social discrimination, and economic exploitation – but as Puechguirbal points out, the repeated portrayal of women as vulnerable victims obscures women's agency and the fact that women should "be involved in the definition of protection and should be part of the solution in the reinforcement of protection mechanisms as well as in the fight against impunity" (Puechguirbal 2005, p. 3).

Because . . . ?

> The question that is frequently asked is "Why an All-Women Contingent of the Mindanao Peoples Caucus in the Civilian Protection Component (CPC) of the International Monitoring Team (IMT)? Why women?" The knee-jerk reaction, albeit a nasty one, is: Why not? Why is women's participation in any formal peace and security structure always put into question?
>
> After explaining the long litany of reasons why women should be part of the formal cease-fire mechanisms as mandated by UN Security Council Resolution (UNSCR) 1325, which has been there for more than 10 years already, the follow-up questions thrown to MPC [Mindanao Peoples Caucus] are, "Are these women trained? Can they possibly do it? Will they be effective? Can they make a difference?"

> Why is it that women should bear the burden of proof of showing that they could make a difference while the men have long been making a total mess of our security situation? Again, the naughty answer can be, "Well, we don't even have to make a difference. Like you, we have the right to be here. Period."
>
> Mary Ann Arnado, Secretary-General, Mindanao Peoples Caucus (Arnado 2011)

So far, we have discussed a variety of arguments which are used to exclude women from peace talks, as well as several arguments offered by women's groups and other organizations and institutions for why they should be included. Instrumentalist arguments, such as women should be included in peace talks because they are better at peacemaking, have been countered with several feminist arguments which reflect subtly different ideological stances. Some feminists have argued that women should be included in peace talks because they constitute half the population and because it is their right as political subjects. Indeed, women do not have to be better than or more peaceful than men to exercise their democratic right. Others have argued that women should participate in peace talks because if women are not present their interests will not be represented. An assumption linked to this argument is that women's concerns and perspectives are different because their experiences are different from men's. Yet other feminists have argued that the kinds of gender transformations women can introduce to post-conflict societies are not only crucial for women but for society as a whole.

These feminist arguments also return us to the perennial conundrum – faced in struggles for women's franchise as well – that if women seek representation at the talks *as women*, albeit women as political subjects, they have to bear the burden of all the negative characteristics and stereotypes that are assigned to women. "This paradox – the need to both accept and refuse 'sexual difference' – is a constitutive condition of feminism as a political movement" (Scott 1996, pp. 3–4). Given that it is in the nature of paradoxes to be irresolvable (Scott 1996, p. 174), we shall explore how different women's groups, in several different parts of the world, have struggled with such a conundrum as well as other obstacles, both while involved in peace-building work ("Women and Peace-building") and while seeking a place at the peace table ("Women at the Peace Table").

Women and peace-building

As noted above, women's participation in peace processes, in most contexts, has been restricted to the feminized, less valued, informal level where they are unable to participate meaningfully in decision making. As a result, "the majority of [women's] voices go unheard during formal processes, including: peace negotiations, disarmament, demobilization and reintegration (DDR), constitution-creation, elections, reconstruction, rehabilitation, truth and reconciliation, and establishing a judicial system" (Dyfan and Piccirilli 2004). In other words, women's concentration within the sphere of informal peace-

Box 8.2 Sudanese women in the processes of building peace

"Sudanese women have worked very hard to keep families and communities together during conflicts through singing peace songs, persuading their husbands, sons and brothers to stop fighting, risking dangerous peace missions across enemy territories, or marrying across enemy lines to unite or reconcile warring communities. There were times when women stopped conflict from escalating by defying or opposing decisions by male members of the community to go to war. In one case women from a community in southern Sudan were reported to have threatened not to comply with their conjugal obligations until their husbands stopped killing each other, while in some areas of the south women threatened to expose their nakedness (a curse in most Sudanese customary beliefs) to protest ethnic conflict.

Women have also taken a leading role in creating links and forums for resolving inter-ethnic conflict, leading to many grassroots peace accords. Examples include the people-to-people processes, such as the Wunlit Covenant between the Nuer and the Dinka and the Lilir Covenant between Nuer groups. . . . Women stood together in solidarity against their husband's political position . . . following the split in the SPLM/A [Sudanese People's Liberation Movement/Army]. Women from both sides of the split continued to visit one another, maintain communication and provide a forum to discuss issues that affected their communities, something no man was capable of.

In order to effectively address social, economic and general problems of war facing women, many women organized themselves into groups, networks and NGOs on both sides of the political divide. These activist networks (including the Sudanese Women's Voice for Peace, New Sudan Women's Federation, and New Sudan Women's Association) went all over the world advocating peace and drawing attention to what was then referred to as 'the forgotten war.'

It is clear that the absence of women at the negotiating table in Naivasha or Abuja was not due to lack of experience and capacity, but to the perceptions of their role." (Dr Ann Itto, member of the SPLM's delegation to the Naivasha peace talks (2002–2005) and Minister of State, Ministry of Forestry and Agriculture of the Government of National Unity, 2006)

building does not simply reflect their harnessing of their social roles to adapt to informal processes of building peace – it has just as much been a product of their systemic and systematic marginalization from the formal sphere (see Text Box 8.2).

However, this glaring under/nonrepresentation of women in all formal aspects of peace processes is being challenged more and more through women's effective and innovative leadership, in a variety of Track II efforts, across the globe. In Nagaland (Northeastern India), a fifty-year-old independence struggle has failed to negotiate a permanent peace despite two cease-fire agreements that remain in place. Naga women have played a critical role in sustaining the cease-fire by mediating among factions and encouraging communities, tribes, and neighboring states to form a broad constituency in support of peace. For example, the Naga Mothers' Association (NMA) and the Naga Women's Union of Manipur (NWUM) have worked together to protect communities, mobilize for reconciliation, sustain the cease-fire, and promote an inclusive peace process (Chenoy 2002). M4P in Mindanao have played a similar role along with many other women's/feminist/peace groups located in Mindanao and elsewhere in the Philippines (Santiago 2011).

In Liberia, women perfected the art of "corridor lobbying," literally waiting in corridors to talk to negotiators as they entered and exited the rooms during breaks in the 1994 Accra conference. They issued statements and formulated resolutions that they presented to mediators from the Economic Community of West African States (ECOWAS). Through their contacts with regional media, they also ensured that their exclusion from the official talks was made public.[7]

However, even the most persistent lobbying at the Track II level can come to naught if women are not present at the Track I level to push a recommendation through the final stage. Dr Ann Itto, member of the Sudanese People's Liberation Movement's (SPLM) delegation to the Naivasha peace talks in 2002, recalls what happened when women in her delegation sought to propose that a minimum quota of 25% for the representation of women in the civil service, legislative, and executive at all levels of government (as provided for by the SPLM/A constitution) be submitted for Track I negotiations, through the SPLM/A:

> One senior male member of the SPLM/A delegation laughed and asked me where the women would be found to fill these positions. The 25% quota was eventually accepted in the larger group, where there were at least three women, but then the all-male SPLM/A drafting committee reduced this figure to 5%. The SPLM/A Chairman raised this to 10% as a compromise. Later on we learned that it had been dropped altogether when government negotiators refused a quota for women in power sharing on the grounds that they had not been "fighting women." (Itto 2006)

While women's Track II work is slowly gaining recognition due to their indefatigable lobbying of the local and international media during peace talks, and the support they have received from international as well as UN organizations and resolutions (see "International Actors and UN Security Council Resolution 1325"), the less visible, longer-term and often more effective work they do – as grassroots organizers, community catalysts, and cross-community interactors, even while a conflict is ongoing – needs to be recognized and engaged with as well.

Even women's groups which have "progressed" onto Track I talks or pushed for the implementation of gender-sensitive provisions in peace agreements have been able to do so because of their involvement in peace-building efforts over the long term. The innovative creation of the "Sixth Clan" which enabled Somalian women to participate in peace talks in 2000, mentioned at the beginning of this chapter, would not have been possible if not for the existence of Save Somali Women and Children (SSWC), which provided the foundation for the "Sixth Clan." Shunned from her clan for marrying a man from another clan, Asha Hagi Elmi formed this group at the height of the civil war in 1992 in order to provide support to other women and their progeny who had to face a similar experience. Since its inception, SSWC had played a crucial role in uniting women across entrenched clan and ethnic divides. Similarly, the creation of the Northern Ireland Women's Coalition would not have been possible if women had not formed and fostered links between Protestants and Catholics, radicals and liberals, middle classes and working classes from the inception of "the Troubles."

In Sri Lanka, women's groups drew upon long-established national, regional (i.e., South Asian), and international feminist networks to pull together a high-profile women's mission to the war-affected regions of the north and east of the island to document the situation of women in those regions. The report, based on these findings, was submitted to the government of Sri Lanka, the LTTE, the Norwegian facilitators, and Sri Lanka's major bilateral donors as part of local women's groups' demands to be included in the peace talks which were due to take place in 2002, as well as to have women's issues and concerns made an integral part of the peace agenda (International Women's Mission to the North East of Sri Lanka 2003).

In Guatemala, women's groups have struggled long and hard with a very repressive state to push for progressive reforms which were agreed to in the 1996 peace accords. One such struggle came to fruition only 13 years later, in 2009, when the National Congress passed a law censuring violence against women and requiring all judges to receive training on how to hear such court cases (Godoy 2010). In order to continue pressuring the government for further reforms, a coalition of women's groups organized a "Tribunal of Consciousness," inspired by the International War Crimes Tribunal for Japanese "Comfort Women" (Godoy 2010). This tribunal focused primarily "on sexual crimes committed during the civil war by the Guatemalan army especially against Mayan women" (Godoy 2010).[8] During the tribunal, in March 2010, hundreds of Mayan women spoke publicly, for the first time, about the crimes that had been committed against them, insisted that the offenders be brought to justice and demanded that reparations be paid (Godoy 2010).

A very important and significant feature of women's peace-building work – be it at Track I, Track II or grassroots/community level – has been women's ability to build bridges across political, ethnic, religious, clan, caste, and class barriers as well as across battle lines and national borders. The innovative and inspiring alliances that have been formed between Israeli and Palestinian women, Protestant and Catholic women in Northern Ireland, or among Bosnian, Serbian and Croatian women often come to mind, but there are many lesser-known examples as well. Hands Across the Divide integrates women from Greek and Turkish communities in Cyprus in order to incorporate a gender perspective in the analysis of the Cypriot conflict as well as the peace process (Hadjipavlou 2006). The women's network, Ahotsak (Voices), has created a unique space for Basque women belonging to a variety of political parties (often holding opposing views), trade unions, and feminist groups to debate each other and share opinions as they struggle to find a political solution to the violence that has besieged that region (Villellas Ariño 2010, p. 27). The Women's Peace Coalition, comprised of Women in Black (Serbia) and the Kosova Women's Network (involving 80 organizations throughout Kosovo) linked women across ethnic and religious lines as well as state borders in order to promote the participation of women in Kosovo's peace process, including the status negotiations (Villellas Ariño & Redondo de la Morena 2008) (see also Text Box 8.3).

Although some people see such bridge-building as somehow easier for women to accomplish because they impute to women a more muted nationalism, "natural" reconciliatory manner, and ability to empathize with the "other" based on shared experiences as women, this explanation has problems. It not only overgeneralizes, as demonstrated by the diversity of women's relations to war illustrated in this book, but it also, assuming these characteristics and actions are "natural" to women, effectively erases the extensive, hard, *political* work that is involved in both initiating and sustaining such alliances – often at the cost of being labeled a betrayer/traitor/infidel/terrorist (Cockburn 1998). Nira Yuval-Davis (1997) distinguishes these kinds of coalition politics, in which "the differences among women are recognized and given a voice" as "transversal politics"; boundaries are set "not in terms of 'who' we are but what we want to achieve" (p. 126).

International actors and UN Security Council Resolution 1325

As noted in previous sections, peace processes have rarely taken place without the involvement of myriad international actors and institutions. It would be naive to assume that such interventions are the result of purely altruistic concern or goodwill, given the missionizing, imperialist, capitalist, and patriarchal framing of global networks of power: access to natural resources, markets and trade routes and the control of spaces, peoples, beliefs, and ideas have long animated both wars and peace processes. The "war for peace" in Iraq or international concerns regarding conflicts and concomitant abuses in countries such as the DRC or Syria cannot be de-linked from a variety of interests, be it accessing oil or diamonds, controlling the spread of communism or religious fundamentalism or pandering to local constituencies or international allies.

Humanitarian and development aid, often employed in pursuit of conflict transformation, and even some international feminist campaigns (often with no links to locally based organizations) against specifically cultural forms of violence, such as *sati*, female-genital cutting, and honor killings, have been criticized by postcolonial scholars and activists for their ethnocentric, Christian, and civilizational biases which assume the West to be intellectually enlightened and morally superior seeking to create civil society in its own image (see, for example, Mohanty 1988; Mamdani 1996, 2009; Henkel &

Stirrat 2001; Jenkins 2001; Manji & O'Coill 2002). It is in light of such critiques that we earlier cautioned against blanket impositions of what are seemingly perceived as democratic "universals" – civil society, good governance, accountability, and transparency – which may manifest in very different forms in different societies; for example, *ubuntu* philosophy, which aspires to interconnectedness rather than individual freedoms, is being revived in post-Apartheid South Africa (Ramose 1999; Krog 2009).

Even the UN is not beyond reproach, given that veto powers are vested in only five permanent Security Council member states – the United States, the United Kingdom, Russia, France, and China – and the production of "subalterns" within the UN system (Spivak 2003).[9] However, the fact that all recognized nation-states do have representation in this body, that most decisions are arrived at through consensus, and that the UN's mandate is binding on all nation-states continues to make it a powerful institution that can effect change globally, regionally, and nationally. In such a context, the adoption of UNSCR 1325 has been considered a landmark achievement by feminists located in various parts of the world.

UNSCR 1325, adopted in October 2000, mandates women's inclusion in all stages of peace-building processes, including peace negotiations. For the first time in the history of the UN, Resolution 1325 acknowledged the contribution of women as agents of change for peace, rather than mere victims of armed conflicts, and enabled women's organizations to gain leverage in accessing official peace negotiations. This breakthrough did not appear out of nowhere. Rather, it was the result of intense advocacy efforts of war-affected women for several decades, culminating in the 1995 UN World Conference on Women in Beijing and the 1998 UN Commission on the Status of Women in New York City. These women, in turn, have been supported and strengthened by a global network of women's movements, organizations, and groups, as well as a handful of courageous and indefatigable feminists who work within UN bodies.

Resolution 1325 concentrates on four thematic areas: gender-based violence, access to decision making, peacekeeping operations, and disarmament, demobilization, and reintegration processes (see Text Box 8.3). Although nation-states are the central focus of the text, UN bodies are addressed as well. Significantly, Resolution 1325 provides that "the Security Council should ensure Security Council missions consult with local and international women's groups on their perspectives on gender considerations and women's human rights in their areas."

Three additional developments in the ten years since the passing of Resolution 1325 underscore the dire need for greater recognition and engagement with the realities of women's experiences in conflict and peacemaking. UNSCR 1820, adopted in June 2008, establishes a strong link between sexual violence and sustainable peace and security. UNSCR 1888, adopted in September 2009, provides concrete building blocks to advance the

---

Box 8.3 Issues addressed by UN Security Council Resolution 1325

Displacement: stresses the protection of settlements and camps and consideration of the special needs of women and girls during displacement (Para. 12).

Repatriation and resettlement: provides that all actors involved should take into account the specific needs of women and girls during repatriation and resettlement and for rehabilitation, reintegration, and post-conflict reconstruction (Para. 8(a)).

Disarmament, Demobilization and Reintegration: mandates that all those planning DDR programs should consider the different needs of female and male ex-combatants and take into account the needs of their dependents (Para. 13).

Post-conflict institution building: requires the incorporation of gender perspective, including measures for the protection of and respect for women's human rights concerning the electoral system in the implementation of peace agreements (Para. 8 (c)).

Peacekeeping: addresses the need for the expansion of the role and contribution of women, especially among military observers, civilian police, human rights, and humanitarian personnel in field-based peacekeeping operations (Para. 4). Requires the incorporation of a gender perspective into peacekeeping operations and, where appropriate, the inclusion of a gender component (Para. 5).

Training of peacekeepers: recognizes the need for the development of training materials and guidelines on women's human rights and gender mainstreaming, as well as the need for HIV/AIDS awareness for military and police personnel, and civilian personnel of peacekeeping operations (Para. 6).

Rape and sexual abuse in armed conflict: calls on states and UN bodies to fully respect international law applicable to the rights and protection of women and girls and to bear in mind the relevant provisions of the Rome Statute of the International Criminal Court (Para. 9). Asserts the need for special measures to protect women and girls from gender-based violence, particularly rape and other forms of sexual abuse, and all other forms of violence in situations of armed conflict (Para. 10).

---

implementation of Resolution 1820 and signals a robust political commitment to addressing conflict-related sexual violence as a peace and security issue. UNSCR 1889, adopted in October 2009, pays particular attention to the implementation of UNSCR 1325 in the immediate post-conflict peace-building period. It focuses greater attention on the continuing absence and exclusion of women in peace-building planning and the consequent lack of prioritization or adequate funding for responding to women's needs, including their safety and access to services. Even more significant, perhaps, UNSCR 1889 commits the Security Council to developing an agreed set of global indicators to track and monitor the implementation of UNSCR 1325, calling for recommendations in 2010, on how the Council will receive, analyze, and act upon information relating to UNSCR 1325. Finally, the resolution calls for a report on gender and peace-building, and makes specific reference to the need for input from the UN Peacebuilding Commission on this report.

UNSCR 1325 and the more recent UN resolutions have contributed to a new, normative framework not only by integrating gender perspectives in all critical aspects of transition and post-conflict reconstruction but by bringing greater visibility to women in spheres that have thus far been accepted

Box 8.4 1325 in practice: the case of Afghanistan[10]

During the peace negotiations in Afghanistan, the United Nations pressured all parties to include women delegates. Women were full delegates in two of the four parties and advisors in the other two parties. The resulting Bonn Agreement, in 2001, paved the way for institutional changes by eliminating restrictions on women's public participation and creating a Ministry of Women's Affairs. This resulted in 100 women delegates participating in the subsequent Constitutional Loya Jirga. Twenty-eight percent of parliamentary seats are now allocated to women and they also have reserved seats in the provincial councils. A woman can even run for president now!

Ten years after the Bonn Agreement, it remains moot whether such drastic, external interventions regarding women's rights can be sustained without adequate, organic support from among those in power or from within a devastated society, most of whose intellectuals and liberal leaders have long fled that country. Women demonstrating leadership abilities and espousing women's rights continue to be deemed un-Islamic and as aping western values and mores. Shukria Barakzai, one of a handful of women MPs in the National Assembly who supports women's rights, is under death threat for articulating such views.

The treatment of Malalai Joya – an articulate, young, female parliamentarian who has consistently criticized the presence of war lords, drug lords and criminals in the National Assembly and the US government for supporting them – is another case in point. Now known as "the bravest woman in Afghanistan," Joya was thrown out of the 2003 Loya Jirga and physically and verbally attacked for criticizing its members and then expelled from the Lower House of the National Assembly in 2007, despite having received the second highest number of votes from her home constituency of Farah Province. She has now gone underground and only ventures out with a battalion of bodyguards.

as unproblematically masculinized spheres, particularly at formal levels of peacemaking. For example, the resolutions challenge common assumptions about who should be at the negotiating table deliberating over the shape and direction of the transition process. In other words, the resolutions clearly outline the importance of paying attention to the need for women negotiators, mediators, and signatories at the negotiating table for peace agreements, to involve more women in decision-making processes within the UN system, and to create provisions for women to be involved in all aspects of governance, such as in the drafting of the constitution and electoral laws, in parliaments, in security sector apparatuses, and in regional and national bodies (see Text Box 8.4).

Since its adoption, UNSCR 1325 has been used by many local and transnational women's groups and international organizations to make the case for women's inclusion in peace negotiations and post-conflict decision making across the world, including the Philippines, Sri Lanka, Afghanistan, Kosovo, Burundi, and Colombia. The Indian all-woman formed police units that the UN sent to Liberia in 2007, in accordance with this mandate, not only managed to reduce incidences of rape and sexual harassment in Liberia, but also inspired the launch of a women's corps in the peacekeeping contingent in the Civil Protection Component (CPC) of the Malaysia-led International

Monitoring Team (IMT) in Mindanao, Philippines (Arnado 2011). This women's corps is also providing an important space where Bangsamoro and Lumad women as well as Christian settlers can work together.[11]

However, as we have noted at the outset, the implementation of UNSCR 1325, as well as those resolutions which build on it, is dependent on a variety of factors, including the social and political status of women, cultural and religious beliefs, the kinds of warring parties and political stakes involved, and the forms of support/pressure offered by international organizations. As noted in previous sections, most warring parties are not interested in including women in the formal aspects of peace processes for a variety of reasons. Similarly, international donors, aid workers, and conflict resolution experts, a vast majority of them men, also may not be particularly supportive, given patriarchal and imperialist stereotypes they may harbor about women in general, and Third World women in particular, as subservient, passive, and weak. Some international organizations and actors who may be supportive of implementing UN resolutions often do not have the legitimacy to push for such measures as their own countries may not uphold UNSCR 1325. In the following section, we shall focus on some of the ways in which women have sought to influence peace negotiations and ponder the resultant consequences in order to better understand some of the complexities and conundrums which are faced in the implementation of UNSCR 1325 (see also Text Box 8.4).

Women at the peace table

It must be clear to you by now that, in order to bring women to the peace table as active participants, a range of prior activities are necessary – awareness raising, mobilization, alliance building, lobbying, and calling for the implementation of international instruments such as UNSCR 1325. Sometimes women are given a place at the table only as a gesture to showcase democracy and inclusiveness; even if they are present, their perspectives and their experiences in peace-building and negotiation may not be recognized or fully utilized. Sometimes they are not even given a chance to speak and are thus present at the peace table as mere tokens.

A real danger exists that, once women make it to the table, the most salient and important issues will have already been discussed in backroom, male-only, negotiations. In several cases, women have been misinformed about meetings and where they were taking place, refused visas, locked out of negotiations and had their proposals ignored. As Christine Bell (2005) aptly observes, "to impact on the negotiation process, and on the resulting peace agreement and its implementation, women must simultaneously find ways of accessing the process as conceived of without them, while reframing the issues that are at the heart of the process" (p. 99).

Throughout this chapter, we have stressed the importance of having women at the peace table but we have not as yet discussed *which* women, i.e., who do they represent? A political party? The state? Autonomous women's organizations? What kinds of ideological positions do they inhabit about women's place in that society, as well as about the various issues which have fuelled the conflict? At the beginning of this chapter, we mentioned the presence at the Sri Lankan peace talks of the wife and nurse of the key negotiator of the LTTE. Several wives of army colonels were part of the select group of Burundian women who were allowed to participate in the 1998 Arusha III talks (see pp. 189–91). Of whom are they representative? How effective can they be?

Women nominated by the state or from political parties or rebel movements often have to "toe the party line." For example, Edita Tahiri, the only woman involved in the failed negotiations with Serbia that preceded the NATO bombardments, has noted that her role in the Albanian delegation at that time was driven by her Albanian nationalist agenda, rather than a feminist one, which she developed much later (Villellas Ariño 2010, p. 35). Indeed, her contributions at the negotiating table would have been quite different had she been more gender aware, she has confessed (Villellas Ariño 2010, p. 35).[12] However, autonomous women's groups can face various kinds of constraints as well. In order to better understand the complicated sociopolitical scenarios within which they have to operate, we shall consider examples from three different countries in slightly greater detail (see also Text Box 8.4).

Guatemala

The Guatemalan peace process "is considered one of the most inclusive, participatory, and human rights-oriented negotiation processes, in which women contributed to both the official and civil society-led parallel negotiations" (Nakaya 2003, p. 463). The Framework Accord, signed in 1994, established the Assembly of Civil Society (ASC) which allowed civil society organizations to submit recommendations to the talks between the Guatemalan government and the Guatemalan National Revolutionary Unity (URNG), comprised primarily of Mayan peasants (Nakaya 2003, p. 463). Many of the gender-specific provisions were endorsed by the URNG owing in large part to the involvement of Luz Méndez, who participated in the peace negotiations as a member of the URNG's delegation – the only woman in the delegation during the first four years. Méndez herself notes that it was her membership in the National Union of Guatemalan Women which equipped her with the feminist consciousness to defend women's rights at the table.[13]

The Guatemalan Peace Accord, signed in 1996, pioneered the protection and empowerment of women and their participation in peace negotiations and in the political process in general, four years before the UN Security Council's adoption of Resolution 1325.[14] It called for gender equality in the receipt of education, land, credit and development aid, the elimination of discrimination against indigenous women, and support for gender equality in the home and workplace (Berger 2003, p. 203). It also required the creation of the Defensoría de la Mujer Indígena (Office for the Defence of Indigenous Women), as well as the Foro Nacional de la Mujeres (National Women's Forum, commonly known as FORO) in which women, indigenous groups, and state authorities would work toward the implementation of the accord. The tussle between women's groups and the state regarding the control of the FORO is a lesson in perseverance, patience, and courage on the part of indigenous and ladino women's groups: "The unity gained by the women's movement during the peace negotiations," notes Berger, "helped sustain it through these arduous debates and numerous political manoeuvrings" (Berger 2003, p. 204).

Fifteen years after the signing of the peace accords, the picture for women is a complex one. The peace processes opened spaces for women's social and political participation, especially at the local level. However, during the four electoral processes held after the peace accords, the proportion of women elected to the parliament has gone down. Among the main factors that constrain women's political representation are continuing gender discrimination, high levels of poverty, racism against indigenous women and violence against women, as well as the structure of the political and electoral system itself. But the women's organizations are campaigning to change the electoral law in order to include an affirmative action system. They also continue their activism in other arenas: for women's access to land, health, and education; for their ability to exert their sexual and reproductive rights; to end violence against women, especially femicide; and against impunity for sexual violence against women which was committed during the armed conflict.

Sri Lanka

As noted earlier in this chapter, Sri Lankan women's groups successfully lobbied all major parties involved in peace negotiations, begun in 2002, to be included in the talks. This was the first time, during a prolonged war with intermittent peacemaking overtures, that women's contributions to peace-building were recognized by both warring parties. A formal space for engagement was created through the Sub-Committee on Gender Issues (SGI) which would meet separately but report directly to the plenary of the peace talks. This format would be followed by several other subcommittees which were created, including the Sub-Committee on Immediate Humanitarian and Rehabilitation Needs (SIHRN), on De-escalation and Normalization (SDN) and on Political Matters (SPM), none of which had women appointed to them.

The government delegation of five women (three Sinhala and two Muslim) was comprised primarily of feminist scholars and activists from within the nongovernmental sector with a long history of peace-building, while the five delegates from the LTTE included senior (Tamil) women cadres.[15] The SGI's meetings were facilitated by a Norwegian academic, Dr Astrid Heiberg. It was the only mechanism associated with the negotiating process which was given the freedom to formulate its own terms of reference, which ranged from sus-

taining the peace process, to resettlement, livelihood and employment, political representation and decision making, and reconciliation (Royal Norwegian
Ministry of Foreign Affairs 2003).

Unfortunately, the SGI was rather short-lived due to the breakdown of peace
talks in 2003, but it raised several provocative issues for Sri Lankan feminists
to ponder. Firstly, conversations which took place outside the confines of the
formal talks were crucial for building trust and enabling warmer interactions
during the formal talks: "We had fascinating conversations about marriage,
caste, dowry and even how it was like to survive in the jungle, during our tea
breaks," recalls Dr Kumari Jayawardena, who headed the government delegation.[16] Secondly, the existence of the SGI enabled all the other subcommittees
to avoid discussing the gendered aspects of reconstruction, de-escalation and
political restructuring, thus leading to an unfortunate ghettoization of wom-
en's concerns and issues, as well as of gender analysis. Thirdly, the formal
constitution of the SGI was both its strength and its weakness. Due to its
formal constitution, the negotiating parties had to take its recommendations
seriously (this was not fully tested due to the breakdown of talks). However,
because its existence and relevance was dependent on the political will of the
government and the LTTE, the SGI could not continue without their mandate
after the formal peace talks broke down. Feminists in the government delegation did try to continue meeting with the women in the LTTE delegation, at an
informal level, but the latter were forbidden to do so by the LTTE hierarchy.

Burundi

The Burundi peace process was one of the first that was spearheaded by an
African regional initiative, spurred by concerns regarding the protracted
nature of the conflict and its destabilizing impact on the region. Led by
Tanzania, the regional overseers also included Uganda, Kenya, DRC, and later
South Africa. It was mediated by Julius Nyerere from April 1996 to October
1999, and, after his death, by Nelson Mandela from 1999 to 2000. Financial
support for the talks came from international donors such as the UN, EU,
USA, and Canada. The former colonial power in the region, Belgium, and
other francophone states such as France and Switzerland, took a keen interest
in the proceedings, as did international NGOs such as International Alert and
Search for Common Ground (Daley 2007, p. 340).

Burundian women's participation in the long drawn-out peace process,
ably supported by regional women's groups as well as international actors,
has been lauded by feminists (Burke et al. 2001). In 1998, a delegation of
women from Uganda, Rwanda, and Tanzania had meetings with the chief
negotiating parties in Burundi, demanding an explanation for the exclusion of Burundian women's organizations from the talks. This intervention
led to three women being appointed to represent the government at the
negotiations and another three being appointed to represent le Front pour la

Démocratie au Burundi (FRODEBU) (the main political party participating in the talks). Representatives of women's organizations were allowed to attend as observers in October and December 1998 during the Arusha III talks, but this was always a tenuous inclusion as it was never clear whether they were appearing as representatives of political parties or as token women. Some delegates at the talks also accused some women of being wives of military officers and of not contributing anything specific or unique to the talks (Burke, Klot & Bunting 2001, p. 343).

When Burundian negotiators "categorically refused" to include women in the peace negotiations in 2000, the peace facilitation team headed by Nelson Mandela requested that a panel of gender activists from South Africa, Uganda, Eritrea, and Guatemala should brief the parties involved in the Burundi peace talks (Africa Recovery 2000). The briefing, organized by the UN Development Fund for Women (UNIFEM), enabled the panelists to draw upon their experience in resolving conflicts in their home countries and to emphasize the important role women can play in fashioning a durable peace.

Burundian women, supported by UNIFEM and the Mwalimu Nyerere Foundation, sought to further strengthen their case by holding an All-Party Women's Peace Conference in Arusha, a month prior to the signing of the peace agreement. "The fifty Burundian women who participated came from all social groups, including the diaspora and refugee camps" (Daley 2007, p. 343), and were able to unite across ethnic, political, and class lines to draw up the wording for specific gender-related clauses to include in the peace agreement.

The confluence of a complicated set of vested interests in the Burundian peace process has led Patricia Daley to describe the 2000 Arusha peace agreement, signed without a cessation of hostilities, as "not necessarily consensual or reflective of a compromise for the sake of peace" but rather, "a temporary stalemate in the power play between international, regional and local actors and their competing visions of peace" (Daley 2007, p. 334). Daley thus describes it as a "liberal" or "negative" peace because it merely consolidates the sovereignty of the state while continuing to jeopardize the security of the people (Daley 2007, p. 333). The contradictory nature of this peace is exemplified in the opening up of political spaces for women and marginalized ethnic elites while simultaneously closing off space for public participation by "institutionalizing violence as [a] mode of political contestation" (Daley 2007, p. 337). Additionally, "the absence of a gendered understanding of the state and of the nature of violence has contributed to the proliferation of sexual violence even in areas considered peaceful and 'safe'" (Daley 2007, p. 349).

However, there do seem to be some signs of hope. Since the approval of the new constitution by an overwhelming majority in February 2005, women have been at the forefront of reconciliation and dialogue at the community level. Fifty women from ten provinces formed the network *Dushirehamwe*, meaning "Let's reconcile" (WCRWC 2001). Through a variety of trust building activities and inter-ethnic dialogue, *Dushirehamwe* leaders have worked

Box 8.5 After the peace agreement: women building peace in Aceh

"Signing the peace agreement is only the beginning; the next great task for all of Aceh's people is to undertake reconciliation, reconstruction and rehabilitation…Acehnese women have not been sitting idly, but have responded with new determination. The Women's Policy Network (JPuK) (established 2004) has been monitoring the development and implementation of the Law on the Governing of Aceh (LoGA) and of *qanun* (local laws) that will detail provisions of the LoGA to promote the equitable inclusion of women's interests. The Women's Peace Network (JPuD) (established December 2005) comprises 26 organizations and seeks to socialize the MoU [Memorandum of Understanding] and strengthen women's participation in peace-building strategies. A Gender Working Group (GWG) has been established as the hub for monitoring the policies of all parties involved in the reconciliation, reconstruction, and rehabilitation processes to ensure that they take into account the gender perspective in policy making and application and budget development. At the grassroots level, women's groups perform political education and strengthen individual and organizational capacity through various training, workshops and seminars." (Suraiya Kamaruzzaman, Executive Director, Flower Aceh, 2008)

with approximately 7,500 women at the community and provincial levels. International Alert (2006) notes that the broader impact of their activities is increasingly gaining recognition and members are often requested to intervene to help defuse tensions within different communities.

We trust these detailed examples will have given you a better sense of the arduous terrain which has to be traversed by women to be represented, to be heard, and to effect change during peace processes and beyond. As with representation for all marginalized groups, the mere presence of a few individual women at the peace table does not by itself ensure that women's concerns will be taken seriously. They need the support of a well-organized national women's network to buttress their claims as well as to sustain them throughout the process. They also require a change in perception and attitude on the part of male negotiators. It is also clear that such endeavors would not be possible without the funding and support provided by regional, international, and transnational organizations and networks, as well as UN institutions. While women seek to influence formal peace processes and demand to play a more engaged role at this level, they also have to struggle continuously not to lose their autonomy and purpose. The greatest challenge, however, is for women to effect structural transformations within social, political, and economic spheres, through peace processes, a task they have not yet been able to accomplish very successfully.

Conclusion

Feminist analyses are crucial for the problematization of how peace is conceptualized, constituted, and institutionalized and the mechanisms through which women can participate in these processes. As we have noted above, peace processes are as gendered as wars. If peace agreements are written, accorded, and implemented solely by men, the gender dynamics that were present throughout the armed conflict will remain unquestioned and intact. It is also important to question liberal formulas such as "add women and stir," which are often offered as a response to arguments that women should be equal partners in peace processes, as this offers an extremely simplified approach to a very complex situation constituted by historical norms, social expectations, and assumptions about women, their potential, and their limitations. Women should participate in peace processes not because they are innately peaceful or they have been victimized by wars, but because they are themselves political subjects with rights. Women don't need to be better than, or more peaceful than, men to exercise those rights. Including women also implies bringing in many other social segments to the peace table as gender intersects with ethnicity, religion, class, caste, and clan.

Our exploration of the indefatigable peace-building work of women, spanning many regions of the globe, should serve to highlight how women's peace activism never ends. It has to continue whether a formal peace process is ongoing or not, and it has to continue long after a peace agreement has been signed. However, no matter what women do, they are always acting within an already gendered terrain of power which itself requires transformation. This remains women's greatest challenge.

QUESTIONS FOR DISCUSSION

1 What are the problems with arguing that "peace and security depends on the inclusion of women"?

- How do you decide which women to include?
- Which issues do you address?
- If women's involvement does not lead to peace, do we need to include them?

2 Consider the implications of the contention that women are "naturally" more peaceful than men and that women "naturally choose" to work on peace processes in the informal sector.

3 What are the advantages and disadvantages of international actors being involved in peace processes?

4 Can UNSCR 1325 and the resolutions that build on it be considered a breakthrough?

5 When women do arrive at the formal peace negotiations, what kind of issues might they face?

- Which women? How did they get there, and who do they come as

(members of a party, representative of women's organizations or a constituency of women, sisters or girlfriends, etc.)?

- Do they have a voice? Literally, do they get to speak? If so, can they represent women's issues and concerns, or will they only be taken seriously
when they speak "like a man" about men's concerns? Are women's issues
viewed as irrelevant and soft?

- Is their priority to get the men to finally reach an agreement, or do they
focus on ensuring women's rights in the constitution and post-conflict
government? Which takes priority, the agreement or women's needs?

SUGGESTIONS FOR FURTHER READING

Chinkin, Christine (2003) *Peace Agreements as a Means for Promoting Gender Equality
and Ensuring Participation of Women: A Framework of Model Provisions*. EGM/PEACE/
REPORT/2003. Report of the Expert Group Meeting, November 10–13, 2003,
Ottawa, Canada. United Nations Division for the Advancement of Women: Office
of the Special Adviser on Gender Issues and Advancement of Women and the
Department of Political Affairs, New York. www.un.org/womenwatch/daw/egm/
peace2003/reports/Finalreport.PDF (accessed November 20, 2010).

Cockburn, Cynthia (1998) *The Space between Us: Negotiating Gender and National
Identities in Conflict*. London: Zed Books.

Godoy, Julio (2010) "Guatemala: Crude Awakening in the Cradle of Resolution
1325: Interview with Luz Méndez," *Visionews*. www.visionews.net/guatemala-
crude-awakening-in-the-cradle-of-resolution-1325/ (accessed on April 16, 2011).

Itto, Ann (2006) "Guests at the Table? The Role of Women in Peace Processes." *Accord*
18. www.c-r.org/our-work/accord/sudan/women.php (accessed April 12, 2011).

UNIFEM (2005) *Securing the Peace: Guiding the International Community towards
Women's Effective Participation throughout Peace Processes*. New York: United Nations
Development Fund for Women. www.unifem.org/attachments/products/
Securing_the_Peace.pdf (accessed May 3, 2011).

Villellas Ariño, María (2010) *The Participation of Women in Peace Processes: The Other
Tables*. ICIP Working Papers. Institut Català Internacional per la Pau, Barcelona.

CHAPTER 9

Women, Girls, and Disarmament, Demobilization and Reintegration (DDR)

Dyan Mazurana and Linda Eckerbom Cole

Introduction

By 1992, the brutal war in Mozambique that began in 1977 – between the newly established Frelimo (Frente de Libertação de Moçambique) government and its allies, and the Renamo (Resistência Nacional Moçambicana) rebels and their South African and subsequent United States backers – was drawing down. The Rome Peace Accord laid out the country's political framework for moving out of war, including making provisions for the disarmament, demobilization and reintegration (DDR) of tens of thousands of armed fighters and their "dependents" on both sides. Yet many of the international officers in charge of helping to plan and carry out the DDR of those fighters seemed to be completely unaware of what most people in Mozambique knew: that Renamo fighters were known for their abduction of females, many of whom had been held captive with their children at sites where the fighters were gathered and had not been released. The United Nations Development Programme (UNDP) officers charged with the logistics of decommissioning the fighters and transporting them back to their homes recounted harrowing scenes of fighters deciding which among their captives they would take back home as so-called family members. They witnessed the male fighters forcing captive women onto lorries to take back with them, while the women shouted, "But I want to go back to *my* home!" (Jacobson 2005, p. 140). At the same time, both the thousands of girls who had willingly joined and those who had been tricked and abducted into the Renamo and Frelimo forces somehow remained invisible to the international DDR planners and child protection agencies; the early efforts to assist child soldiers were only made on behalf of boys (McKay & Mazurana 2004). As the adult male fighters left the cantonments and went home with their meager stipends, the women, girls, and boys left behind fell into increased destitution. They received no monetary assistance once they were no longer attached to the adult male fighters, and church and welfare organizations working in the area reported increased poverty, hardship, and prostitution among them (Jacobson 2005). Despite this, the DDR efforts of Mozambique were heralded internationally as a success.

Though now more than 20 years old, Mozambique's story is still relevant today. While there have been important advances in how DDR programs are designed and implemented, the invisibility and marginalization of women and girls within DDR processes continue. At the heart of this chapter, we seek to understand why DDR has traditionally focused on the needs and security of adult male ex-combatants and overlooked the presence of women and girls who have filled diverse roles in armed forces and groups. We also explore the challenges facing women and girls during economic and social reintegration. In trying to understand reintegration of women and girls who have been with armed groups, what we are really trying to understand, in large part, is how gendered, militarized, organized violence reshapes relations among individual women and girls, their families, communities, and societies, and what this means for the present and near future of all those involved.

We begin with introducing the reader to the sociopolitical context in which many DDR programs occur, and we then describe what official DDR processes entail and the actors who carry out the various DDR functions. We next examine when, where, and why women and girls are so often excluded and/or choose not to participate in DDR programs. We investigate what happens to women and girls formerly associated with armed forces and groups during peace negotiations, official DDR processes, and as they attempt to move back into civilian life, whether in their home communities or new locations. We look at some of the gendered assumptions held by DDR planners and programmers and the ways those affect women's and girls' involvement in actual programs. We pay attention to the shifts in power that are occurring around the DDR process for members of armed opposition groups, and how that plays out in their experiences of DDR and beyond. Finally, we offer some concluding thoughts about what DDR planners and programmers should consider in designing and carrying out their programs.

DDR: setting the stage

While large-scale, organized, armed violence may stop at the end of a war, societies still must address many challenges in order to avoid reigniting the violence and to create more secure conditions for their populations. Among these challenges are dealing with both the large numbers of armed fighters who took part in the war, either in state military forces or in non-state armed groups, and the large numbers of weapons that have poured into the country during the conflict. Fighters need to be demobilized so that armed groups cannot readily start up the fighting again – and so that they can have a postwar livelihood that is not dependent on armed violence. These fighters will need to move out of the social structure of their armed groups and reintegrate into civilian society, at times into the very communities in which they may have committed serious acts of violence. Since their livelihoods were derived from participation in militarized organizations, they will now need new means of meeting their basic needs and supporting themselves and their families. If they entered or were abducted into armed groups as children, chances are good that they have little or significantly reduced formal education. If they have spent years "living by the gun," they may have little practice in getting what they need without violence, and few skills which will help them in a postwar economy. And if they still possess and use guns, chances are good that their daily lives and those of everyone around them will be much more violent, as organized crime, street crime, and domestic violence are made more deadly by these weapons.

All of these challenges exist and unfold within larger, dynamic political contexts. During the time in which formal DDR processes are being negotiated, it is likely that peace talks will be under way, which have their own complexities and dynamics and may or may not involve all the armed groups. Indeed, most peace agreements since the First World War have included DDR programs. There may be active attempts to remobilize on the part of various armed groups and forces, or fighters may take their weapons and move into neighboring countries to join other armed conflicts in the region; for example, when the conflict in Sierra Leone reached a point where fighters were disarming and demobilizing, a significant number decided it was more lucrative to take their weapons and travel to Liberia and/or Côte d'Ivoire to join fighting forces in those countries. Militias may be formally demobilized only to re-emerge as key players in criminal networks and other mafias; this is currently the case in Colombia, where government-backed militias that had been officially demobilized have now re-emerged as key armed actors within the narco-trafficking circuits. Most likely, there are many weapons in circulation during these times as a result of the war, and fighters may drift in and out of civilian populations. Where populations have been displaced, they may begin to make initial attempts to return to their homes, resulting in conflicts over land and access to resources.

The DDR period is a time in which insurgent forces, militias, and some members of the state armed forces will be in transition, which means their members will be in a period of questioning what their identity or role is to be in a postwar period. The militarized masculinities and femininities that were needed to sustain them during armed conflict will likely have to change as an armed group makes the transition into a political party, for example. Young men who felt (and were) highly valued during the fighting may find themselves rather suddenly on the perimeters of the group, as older and more established males (often from the supporting communities, including the diaspora) come in to fill the places of power, as we now see happening in Afghanistan, Iraq, and Nepal.

In this transition period, the political wings of the armed groups, i.e., insurgent groups, will almost certainly maintain a militarized patriarchal stance within the political arena, and the ones putting it forward will predominately be older, established men within the group. Given the shift to consolidating political and economic gains, the armed groups will encourage the majority of middle- to lower-ranking males, and most all the women and girls associated with the armed group, to return to civilian life in ways that support the authority, power, and legitimacy of the group. This may also move those people several steps away from access to any real power or wealth that may be possible in the post-conflict period. It is these populations, but particularly the males, that national DDR programs largely target. And it is important to remember that many of the females make conscious choices *not* to identify themselves as fighters or participate in any formal DDR programs, as part of their attempts to avoid stigma and try to reintegrate into civilian life (discussed below).

Outside the immediate influence of the armed groups, these young males and females find themselves once again subject to their societies' dominant notions of masculinity and femininity, and these notions may be not at all congruent with those that were desired and nurtured inside the armed group during the conflict (Hale 2001). This is an especially challenging time for women and girls known to have been in armed groups because their violations of traditional forms of female respectability, so often tied up with patriarchal constructions of chastity and virtue, will put them at odds with how traditional forms of femininity are often re-entrenched in the post-conflict. Their families and communities may stigmatize and ostracize them, particularly at first, when they do not meet expected gender norms and behaviors (Veale 2003; Mazurana 2004; McKay & Mazurana 2004; Verhey 2004; Coulter 2009).

DDR: what is it and who does what?

The United Nations defines DDR as "a process that contributes to security and stability in a post-conflict recovery context by removing weapons from the hands of combatants, taking the combatants out of military structures and helping them to integrate socially and economically into society by finding civilian livelihoods" (UNDDR 2006a, p. 6).[1] DDR processes can occur with or without the presence of peacekeeping or peace-building missions and with or without the United Nations taking the lead. Typically, establishing the general parameters of formal DDR processes is done as part of peace negotiations, and those parameters are then solidified in peace accords (UNDPKO 1999).

DDR consists of a number of multifaceted and interrelated elements. Decisions are made about disarming, demobilizing, and reintegrating fighters within negotiated settlements. There are efforts to collect and destroy weapons. Decisions must also be negotiated regarding the role of state and international militaries in administering disarmament and demobilization of ex-combatants. There will likely be attempts to integrate some ex-combatants into new armed forces or private security forces. There are numerous efforts to move many former fighters into civilian life, including building civilian support for demobilization and reintegration processes as fighters are coming back into local communities (UNECHA 2000).

The importance of DDR in peace-building is a matter of debate. While some authors claim that DDR is an essential cornerstone of post-conflict recovery, others note that:

> It should be clear that DDR programs are not *the* answer to post-conflict situations. They are only one small but critical part of peace consolidation. Basically, by breaking up armed groups and command and control structures, DDR buys time so that the root causes of the conflict can be addressed and peace strengthened. And DDR programs must be complemented by other recovery activities, which together can reinforce security and stability and pave the way for development (Correia 2009, p. 16, emphasis in original).

With this caveat against imagining that DDR programs are sufficient for meeting all of a society's complex needs in the transition from war to peace, we now turn to examining each of the key elements of formal DDR.

Disarmament

Disarmament is believed to be necessary to help decrease any possible resurgence in violence or an increase in banditry and criminal and interpersonal violence due to the ready availability of weapons. Formal disarmament is defined as the "collection, control and disposal of all weapons including small arms, explosives, light and heavy weapons of both combatants and civilians" (Report of the Secretary-General 2000, p. 15). Formal disarmament processes usually occur following peace accords. Importantly, fighters do not normally turn in the majority of weapons they possess; as a result, the importance of a disarmament process is often more symbolic than practical. Following the war in Kosovo, for example, it was estimated there were between 313,000 and 440,000 illegal weapons in the hands of civilians; efforts by the United Nations, the NATO force in Kosovo and Kosovo police forces to gather those weapons resulted only in approximately 4,000 weapons being confiscated (Perry 2004).

Disarmament planning involves clarifying which actors are responsible for oversight and coordination of the various aspects of the process, including laying out details of timing, methods, logistics, and funding. Another key requirement is to establish an accurate assessment of the populations to be disarmed and weapons to be collected. Where necessary, international arms embargoes need to be enforced and actors need to establish cooperative measures with neighboring countries and arms suppliers to ensure proper management of arms transfers. It is also important to monitor the armed forces and groups to ensure they comply with the parameters set for disarmament and demobilization. Throughout, it is necessary to develop public information programs, using radio and other means to inform and build confidence in the fighters regarding the DDR process, as well as the communities into which they return (Report of the Secretary-General 2000).

Disarmament programs seek to get fighters to surrender their weapons and ammunition, which are then registered and destroyed. Because fighters often would not choose to hand in their guns voluntarily, DDR programs sometimes offer incentives in the form of material goods or cash payments in return for each weapon handed in. For example, in Sierra Leone's DDR process, reception centers were established in numerous locations throughout the country, and combatants would voluntarily present themselves to disarm and surrender their weapons and ammunition. When people arrived, officials would assess whether they were eligible for the program (i.e., were they really combatants?) by asking a series of questions, and by seeing whether they could disassemble and reassemble a gun, usually an AK-47. (Officially, those under 18 years of age were not required to present a weapon to enter DDR, though this was inconsistently applied.) Persons who passed these tests were then sent to a demobilization center where they received a pre-discharge orientation, their benefits package, and a small amount of resettlement and transportation money. Then they were discharged. Children (17 years and under) were sent to interim reception centers and then could select either skills training or an educational program of their choice (McKay & Mazurana 2004).

While the primary responsibility for all DDR processes rests with the political and armed forces and groups that took direct part in the conflict, the international community provides important support. See Text Box 9.1 for a guide to some of the multiple actors involved in DDR processes.

Box 9.1 DDR processes: who does what?[2]

UN Department of Political Affairs (DPA):

- supplies political leadership during pre-negotiation and negotiation of peace accords;
- oversees the implementation of DDR political objectives;
- identifies combatants, their arms and disarmament provisions (with the UNDPKO);
- plays a principal role in carrying out demobilization functions.

UN Department of Peacekeeping Operations (UNDPKO):

- identifies combatants, their arms, and disarmament provisions;
- participates in the removal and destruction of arms;
- contributes to the establishment of secure armories;
- supports disarmament programs for paramilitaries and civilians;
- plays a principal role in carrying out demobilization functions;
- supports or carries out social and economic activities within DDR processes.

UN Children's Fund (UNICEF):

- provides technical and policy guidance in DDR designs relating to children and youth;
- plays a principal role in carrying out demobilization functions;
- supports or carries out social and economic activities within DDR processes.

UN Office for Disarmament Affairs (UNODA):

- advocates small arms disarmament;
- gives advice on design of weapons collection programs;
- participates in the removal and destruction of arms.

UN Development Programme (UNDP):

- participates in the removal and destruction of arms;
- supports disarmament programs for paramilitaries and civilians;
- plays a principal role in carrying out demobilization functions;
- supports or carries out social and economic activities within DDR processes.

World Bank:

- provides technical and financial support for disarmament programs;
- plays a lead role in carrying out demobilization functions;
- supports or carries out social and economic activities within DDR processes.

International and National NGOs:

- implement programs aimed at providing basic amenities and training, education, and support services to ex-combatants;
- support or carry out social and economic activities within DDR processes.

Other organizations which play a principal role in carrying out demobilization functions and support or carry out social and economic activities within DDR processes:

- UN Food and Agricultural Organization (FAO)
- UN Office for the Coordination of Humanitarian Affairs (OCHA)
- Office of the Special Representative of the Secretary-General for Children and Armed Conflict (OSRSG/CAC)
- World Health Organization (WHO)
- UN World Food Program (WFP)
- International Committee of the Red Cross (ICRC)
- International Organization for Migration (IOM)
- International Labor Organization (ILO)
- Various regional, sub-regional and bilateral organizations

Demobilization

Demobilization is the process by which government and/or opposition or factional armed forces and groups "either downsize or completely disband, as part of a broader transformation from war to peace" (UNDPKO 1999, p. 15). Demobilization involves identification and design preparation of cantonment sites – the sites where fighters are to gather. To attract fighters to cantonment sites, there may be the provision of demobilization incentives and assistance programs for them and their families. During cantonment, there is the need for provision of food, water and sanitation, and health screening and care, including reproductive care. Services are, at times, available to ex-combatants with disabilities or who have chronic or mental illness. There may be support for families of ex-combatants. There may also be the provision of special measures to women and child combatants. During cantonment, socioeconomic surveys and skills inventories are at times undertaken to help prepare ex-combatants to return to civilian life. Demobilization may also involve mine clearance for the sites and areas where ex-combatants will return. Importantly, families often accompany ex-combatants to assembly areas and establish temporary residences around cantonment sites, but, at present, there is no clear policy regarding DDR processes and these families. Issues that need to be addressed include the types of support the family will receive and eligibility criteria for services (UNDDR 2006b).

Reintegration

It is important that former combatants leave their roles as fighters and return to a civilian life. Reintegration programs are programs designed to try and increase the likelihood that former combatants will become socially and economically active in the communities they return to, and that they resist taking up arms again (UNDPKO 1999). Social reintegration includes efforts to help raise awareness among the communities to which fighters are returning and to prompt their role in helping to integrate ex-combatants back into the community. This community support is necessary to help build the ex-combatants' confidence in their decisions to disarm and demobilize and is an important step toward ensuring sustainable peace. Returning people to their families, called family reunification, can also play an important role in helping ex-combatants reintegrate. Key leaders within these processes include public officials, community elders and leaders, religious organizations and leaders, and local NGOs. Social reintegration also entails longer-term care of wounded, disabled, mentally ill and chronically ill ex-combatants, and special programs for high-risk groups, such as child soldiers and women and girls who have been subjected to sexual abuse or slavery (Report of the Secretary-General 2000; UNDDR 2006b).

Economic reintegration of ex-combatants is also critical and requires a multifaceted approach which includes skills assessment, training, education, job placement, and assistance in grants and loans, including land grants. National governments may be encouraged to create jobs for ex-combatants, often employing them in the reconstruction of damaged social and educational infrastructure and public works. The establishment of private security agencies is also often used to absorb large numbers of ex-combatants.

There are many short-term activities within social and economic reintegration. This includes family reunification services, such as locating the parents or caregivers of former child soldiers. Health, medical care, and counseling services are also important activities to aid in reintegration. There are activities that address general education, job counseling and referral, and vocational training. Some reintegration efforts focus on the distribution of departure packages, including tools, cash, clothing, food and food coupons, housing, and housing materials. Specific social and economic measures are often needed and put into place for vulnerable groups, including child combatants, former captives, and the disabled, among others.

Long-term initiatives for social and economic reintegration include efforts to integrate programs for ex-combatants and returning refugees and internally displaced persons. There are also a number of economic programs, including credit programs, land grants and land reform, professional and vocational training, public works job creation, income generation programs, hiring incentives, and efforts to assist in business development. Legal services and children's programs are also used in some longer-term initiatives.

Where are the women and girls in DDR?

As detailed in chapter 7, women and girls participate in numerous, and often multiple, roles both inside and in support of armed forces and groups. These include: cooking, looting, washing clothes, portering, and collecting water and firewood. Women and girls are also commanders, frontline fighters, spies, intelligence officers, weapons dealers, messengers, recruiters, and political strategists. Among non-state armed groups (NSAGs), most women and girls are trained in combat and are expected to fight or support fighters when called upon, and some groups, such as the Revolutionary Armed Forces of Colombia (FARC) and the Maoists in Nepal, make extensive use of females in combat and/or support functions.

If DDR programs are to be effective, they need to be responsive to the women and girls within these armed forces and groups. The Integrated DDR Standards (IDDRS) recognizes the shortfalls of many past DDR programs' treatment of women and girls, and calls for expanded eligibility criteria that would ensure all females associated with fighting forces are eligible. Yet the theory of IDDRS is a far cry from the practice of DDR programs in the recent past and today, as we explore in this section.

Despite their wide range of roles and responsibilities within fighting forces and groups, women and girls are too often excluded from participating in or contributing to peace talks. Instead, negotiation and conflict resolution specialists are brought in from the outside, and their focus is on securing a deal which is acceptable to both the belligerents and the national government. Typically, the disarmament and demobilization of male fighters is prioritized, and women's and girls' issues and rights sidelined (Barry 2005), as illustrated in Text Box 9.2.

Often it is during these negotiations that the parameters for DDR are set, including the definitions of combatants and eligibility requirements for entering the program. The invisibility of women and girls in formal DDR programs is often due to a narrow definition and understanding of what makes a person a "combatant" in fighting forces or groups. Most DDR programs focus on adult males who have participated in active combat, and this tends to exclude women, girls, and, to a lesser extent, boys who have primarily served in auxiliary positions that provided the backbone for the fighting forces. One should question whether those providing auxiliary positions can rightly be

Box 9.2 A woman commander speaks on DDR in Burundi

"The progress of the DDR process is doubtful, it is not moving as expected. . . . As time goes by, women and girls are feeling they have been abandoned. However, women are not involved in the DDR policy or process, and thus cannot represent women's needs. The result is that there are very poor conditions for women in the cantonment camp; there is no balanced nutrition, no clothes for women, no toiletries, no feminine hygiene supplies. So the women are treated like men. And although the women are treated as men, the women's contingent of the group is excluded from DDR. There were expectations that women would be integrated with the police force or the military, but this is not happening. The movement tried to put pressure on the relevant actors to integrate women, but the government refused. The army and the police have no principle of equality of the sexes. As a consequence, little space is given to woman fighters either during cantonment or in job options in the revised security sector." (A senior woman commander from one of the leading insurgent forces in Burundi (CNDD-FDD), Mazurana 2004, p. 63)

excluded from an understanding of what constitutes a fighting force. Looking at the United States military, for example, only 15–20% of military personnel actually engage in active combat, while the overwhelming majority serve in crucial backup and logistical roles in service and support units (USDOD 2005). Yet most people would find it shocking if the remaining 75–80% were not granted the recognition and status of being considered members of the US military. Likewise, we argue, it makes no sense to restrict DDR programs to only those fighters most closely engaged in combat.

In most non-state armed groups (NSAGs), women and girls are and have been present, and their percentage of the fighting group is usually higher than their counterparts in the government forces and militias (see chapter 7). However, their failure to participate in DDR programs is pronounced, particularly in Africa. Four examples of national DDR programs in Africa serve to illustrate our point. In Angola's DDR, of the estimated 30,000 people in the National Union for the Total Independence of Angola (UNITA) insurgent forces, only 60 females, or 0.2%, were identified for DDR, even though numerous media and human rights reports indicated a larger number of women and girls had been part of UNITA. In Burundi, of the over 85,000 combatants thought to exist, 55,000 were anticipated to pass through the national DDR program. Although no figures were given on women's overall participation in the national DDR, it was reported that in October 2005, out of 14,000 demobilized fighters, 438 (3%) were women. In the Republic of Congo, DDR consisted of three major programs. The first phase (July 2000 to November 2002) reintegrated 8,019 ex-combatants (but no one kept track of how many were male or how many female). A subsequent DDR project ran from October 2002 to February 2005 and enrolled 9,884 ex-combatants, 297 (3%) of whom were women. A smaller specific DDR project followed in March 2005 and served 442 ex-combatants, of whom seven (1.6%) were women. The Rwandan national DDR program occurred in two stages and, by 2005, 54,159 ex-combatants had taken part in the program, 334 (0.06%) of whom were female (MDRP & UNIFEM 2005). Given that women's and girls' presence in all of these conflicts is well documented, their absence from official DDR programs should be cause for concern.

Broadly speaking, the case of women and DDR in Latin America looks different from that of Africa for a variety of reasons. In Latin America, many armed groups contained a significant proportion of women and girls, up to 30% in some cases, and females within these armed groups primarily had joined voluntarily (as compared to being forcibly recruited) and were more visible. Women's rights and grievances were also given priority and voice in a number of the leftist movements in Latin America, especially in conflicts from the 1960s, 1970s, and 1980s, which motivated women and girls to join the armed groups. Many other women joined for survival and protection against government-sponsored violence. Importantly, in Latin America we see women and girls participating in DDR programs in proportions that reflect their actual proportion in the armed groups. This is often the direct result not only of women's and girls' visibility in the movements, but also of having women present at peace negotiations, who helped secure women's and girls' inclusion in programs established to benefit ex-fighters. These women at the peace negotiations also facilitated the recognition of the need to address females associated with fighting forces and groups that served in supportive functions (Luciak 2001; Conaway & Martinez 2004). In El Salvador, for example, 29% of the 8,552 Farabundo Martí National Liberation Front (FMLN) fighters who were demobilized were female. Women from the FMLN were present, along with other women as negotiators. According to one of those FMLN negotiators, Maria Marta Valladares:

> In negotiating when the time came to discuss the concept of beneficiaries, it was understood in our heads that women would participate, but that wasn't put down specifically. And we had problems because at the time the lists were being formulated with the names of the beneficiaries, members of the team did not specifically put down the names of women. It was a very serious problem that we had later on because only the men were thought of as beneficiaries and we had to redo the lists (as quoted in Conaway & Martinez 2004, pp. 15–16).

As the examples from Africa and Latin America show, it is essential to have political involvement in peace negotiations of people who are aware of the gender dimensions and gender composition of the fighting forces. It is also essential that those negotiating are clear about the reality of women's and girls' involvement in the fighting forces and groups, and that negotiations that set the parameters of DDR and reconstruction programs recognize and account for this reality.

Disarmament and demobilization: challenges for women and girls

The first two stages of DDR, disarmament and demobilization, have posed significant challenges for women and girls associated with armed opposition groups to even access a DDR program, and this is particularly the case in Africa. As discussed above, this is in part due to narrow definitions of combatants which have typically excluded women and girls and, to a lesser extent, boys (MDRP & UNIFEM 2005). Among DDR programs in various countries, there is no commonly accepted definition of "female combatant" or "female associated with fighting forces" which could make it easier to recognize women and girls eligible for entry.

The selection criteria for entry into DDR processes can also be gendered in less overt but equally discriminatory ways. While the criteria vary from country to country, previously a common strategy was "one person, one gun" (UNDPKO 1999; UNDDR 2006b). In Sierra Leone, for example, eligibility for DDR programs was initially determined according to possession of and ability to handle a gun, usually an AK-47. This meant that a large number of women and girls were excluded as they often did not have a weapon. This criterion was later changed to group disarmament, i.e., one weapon was used for several persons to gain entry. However, this change was not always enforced by disarmament administrators, nor was it properly announced amongst potential participants, leading to the continued implementation of the "one person, one gun" rule and the continued exclusion of the majority of women and girls (Mazurana & Carlson 2004).

Another major challenge that women and girls face during disarmament and demobilization lies in the logistics and communication of DDR processes. Most communication goes through the commanders of armed opposition groups, and DDR programs rely on these commanders for information about troop numbers and the composition of their forces, as well as about numbers of weapons and the best ways to collect them. This often results in commanders having significant control over who is deemed eligible, so corruption and deceit on their part can become particularly damaging (Mazurana 2004, 2005a). Women and girls have reported being left off lists to the benefit of commanders and their relatives. Additionally, in programs where weapons were traded for cash and used as evidence of participation in an armed opposition group, women and girls were often tricked into handing their weapons to commanders prematurely.

Gendered assumptions of DDR officials – both about who is a fighter and what those (presumed male) fighters need in a DDR program – can also work strongly against women and girls. If DDR officials believe that women and girls do not participate in fighting forces and groups, they simply turn them away from disarmament and demobilization efforts. To illustrate, the lead author, in interviews with officials during DDR in Sierra Leone, asked why the many women and girls who were part of the militia or Civil Defense Forces (CDF) were not taking part in the process. The officials proudly voiced a widely held (though inaccurate) international opinion at the time: "Yes, we saw hundreds of women and girls come in claiming they were CDFs, but we knew those forces only contained men, so we took their weapons and turned them all away."[3] Even when some women and girls are included, programs that require long periods of travel or long stays (sometimes up to several years) within the cantonment sites make it difficult for women to participate because of transportation and childcare issues. Furthermore, women and girls who want to enter demobilization sites and try to claim some of their benefits may leave shortly after arrival because those sites lack health care (particularly reproductive) and supplies for females, and provide no protection from sexual violence, exploitation, and harassment from other fighters gathered there (Mazurana 2004; Mazurana & Carlson 2004; UNDDR 2006b).

Reintegration realities and challenges

Whether due to exclusion or personal choice, the vast majority of women and girls who were active in armed forces and groups will not enter into nor receive benefits or support from national DDR programs. Most will self-reintegrate. The circumstances which form women's and girls' economic and social reintegration experiences are complex and context-specific. Analyses of their experiences show a variety of factors that influence women's and girls' ability to return to, and take part in, the societies in which they will live. These include, but are not limited to: how they entered the fighting forces (Rehn & Sirleaf 2002; Mazurana & Carlson 2004; Verhey 2004); whether the forces they were with were "winners" or "losers" within the conflict (Barth 2002; Farr 2002); how long they have been gone from the community (Verhey 2001; Veale 2003); and whether they entered the fighting forces as children (Veale & Stavrou 2003; Hobson 2005). It also matters whether they were sexually abused, and if so, by which force (Thompson 1999; Sewonet & Taouti-Cherif 2004; Verhey 2004; UNICEF 2005); if they return pregnant or with a child (Verhey 2004; McKay et al. 2006); levels of community acceptance when societal norms and taboos have been broken by the fighters (Brooks 2005; Hobson 2005; McKay et al. 2006). Levels of unemployment and poverty in the communities to which they return also play a key role, as do government attitudes regarding women's and girls' roles and participation during armed conflict and how that translates to their political and economic participation in post-conflict times (Schroeder 2003; Veale 2003). For example, women participants in the Eritrean war of liberation against Ethiopia had different reintegration experiences depending on their political identity and where they settled. In some communities, they were seen as liberators whose participation in the movement was greatly appreciated, which facilitated their integration. In other areas, where there was a dislike of the present government, they were viewed with suspicion (Veale 2003).

Many women and girls associated with fighting forces encounter serious economic difficulties as they seek to rebuild their lives. In most post-conflict societies, there is a lack of formal employment and, where it is available, men are often given priority both by governments and private employers. The inability of women and girls to earn an income may increase their vulnerability to additional shocks or unexpected expenses, furthering the risk of destitution. This may mean that access to health care and the ability to participate in training, education, or to send children to school may be severely affected. It may also result in an inability to participate in communal savings groups, or to enter into endeavors requiring an initial investment, such as farming, trading, or small business. For some women and girls, economic difficulties may lead to high-risk behavior such as living in abusive relationships or engaging in dangerous or demeaning work to try to meet their basic needs. Marginalization, an erosion of social capital, and economic constraints combine to leave few opportunities available to these women and girls to create sustainable livelihoods.

Women and girls may also be extremely reluctant to declare their involvement in fighting forces and groups for fear of being stigmatized and ostracized by their families and communities. It is thus important to understand the lived experience of stigmatization and its impacts in terms of livelihood and human security. Women and girls who are stigmatized are often cut out of the social networks of their communities; this is particularly significant in a post-conflict setting, where the state is often unable or unwilling to provide welfare and basic services, so community exclusion leaves women and girls without essential forms of support and protection. Exclusion may also mean not having access to child care, so a child may be left alone, abused, or blamed for anything that goes wrong. Exclusion may mean not being able to borrow food from a neighbor when the children are hungry, nor being able to borrow money or participate in community activities such as communal farming. Thus, an understanding of stigma's effects must inform the interpretation of women's and girls' vulnerability and the responses designed to address it. In all cases, their children need to be taken into account as well, since children's presence strongly affects their mother's ability to socially reintegrate and participate in education, skills training, and viable livelihoods options. The example from Sierra Leone in Text Box 9.3 illustrates some of these challenges and how women have sought to overcome them outside of formal DDR programs.

Social reintegration also means reintegration into a differently gendered world than the one the ex-combatants are leaving. In most situations, when women and girls "self-demobilize" back into civilian communities, they are under intense pressure to convert back into the gendered status quo, and assume their "proper" place within their family and community structure (Mazurana 2004, 2005b; Coulter 2009). While this so-called return to normalcy may be attractive to some, for others it is not. Although many women's and girls' experiences of armed conflict are profoundly negative, there are times, especially in national liberation movements, when women and girls can reach positions of power and gender equality which may be greater than previously realized in their pre-conflict societies (Barth 2002; UN 2002b;

Box 9.3 The Women in Crisis Movement: a response to the challenges of reintegration

During a decade of civil war, the people of Sierra Leone experienced the worst that war can bring. Vicious attacks on villages and towns caused the flight of tens of thousands to neighboring countries and the total dislocation of over half of the country's population. Tens of thousands were killed, and thousands who survived were tortured, including having limbs cut off. Others were traumatized by being forced to watch or even participate as their family members were tortured or killed. Rape and sexual torture was a common tactic of terror. The abduction of women and girls to serve as "bush wives" to the rebels meant that, throughout the war, many lost all contact with their families and became a part of rebel society in order to survive. Many bore children during those years. When peace came, and refugees returned and communities sought to recover, many of these women and girls were identified as having been with the rebels or having been "spoiled" for normal society and they faced rejection by their communities and even their families. They were, in effect, blamed for their plight. The children they had borne during captivity were doubly stigmatized. For many of the women, peace did not bring relief; they had no education, no skills, no families to return to.

Juliana Konteh, Director of the Women in Crisis Movement (WICM), began to notice these women in her neighborhood. She started helping them feed their children and then gathering them together to talk about HIV prevention. She negotiated with NGOs to get them free health care. And eventually she created a school and community center under a tarpaulin – a place where these women could come and have a meal, learn to read, receive child care, share their problems, and pray and sing together. With UN support over the years, what started under a tent has now grown into an institution which is serving the needs of thousands of women and children in Sierra Leone – there are three vocational training centers, a school for the children of the trainees, a clinic, and outreach into communities across the country. A credit program for graduates has helped hundreds to establish small businesses. By all the "measurable" indicators, the Women in Crisis Movement has succeeded – helping women find alternative livelihoods, helping them avoid HIV and keeping them healthy, improving literacy and life skills, and helping them care for their own children well, which will break the poverty chain. But the most important aspect of the Movement, according to the women involved, was less measurable.

"WICM gave me a family, a place to feel safe, a place where other girls had been through the same problems and so did not judge me," said Violet, an early student who has now become a teacher in the tailoring program. "We used to feel hopeless, like rubbish, surviving from day to day. Doing anything to get food to eat. Like we had no place in this whole world. Now we feel like tomorrow can be better, and we can take care of our children and they can learn and we can all look forward. Pastor reminds us that God is with us, Mama Juliana has shown us that we have a future, and together we have built something good for other girls who suffered. When we sing together, we forget the pain of the past. We just feel hope."

There are many lessons to be learned from the WICM program. It was not designed from outside by "experts" or DDR planners; it grew organically, out of the needs of the women and girls who had suffered during the war. It was holistic, combining skills training with health care and counseling and spiritual support. It created community and solidarity. For the traumatized women it served, and continues to serve, it provided the most important thing of all – hope.[4] Written for this book by Pamela DeLargy.

Bouta 2005). In cases where the armed group provides benefits and services to its members, such as the Maoists in Nepal, there is a strong potential for women to resist reintegration, favoring instead the status they attained as part of armed groups which have now successfully transformed themselves into political parties, or to continue their fight, as in Colombia.

Through their participation in armed struggles, women and girls may gain self-confidence and a sense of liberation as they challenge existing gender norms which would normally restrict their actions (Mazurana 2004); however, these experiences rarely translate to women's liberation once the war is over. For example, in the national liberation wars of both Mozambique and Eritrea, women and girls were encouraged by political and military leaders to join the fighting, and there was an implicit understanding that they would be part of creating a new society based on equality. In the Eritrean People's Liberation Front (EPLF), men and women shared tasks equally and women and girls were involved in combat and farming activities. They also took on community leadership roles, commanded regiments, and administered justice (Mehreteab 2002; Veale 2003). The post-conflict reality, however, was radically different: the new government made women's rights and priorities secondary as national reconstruction became its main priority. Women and girls who had been part of the fighting forces in Eritrea returned to a society that was not ready, nor being encouraged, to accept the kind of equality the women and girls had experienced while fighting. Thus, female EPLF members have had a difficult time adjusting to traditional gender norms and reintegrating into societies not ready to accept more liberated women, and gender equality that was realized during the war did not survive into peacetime (Hale 2001; Barth 2002).

Many of the women and girls returning from fighting forces and groups have difficulty getting married, which can have long-term social and economic consequences in societies where marriage is the expected norm and forms the basis of social networks and access to resources. Marriage prospects can be affected due to the women's own changed gender norms and expectations, but also due to stigmatization and pressure from the potential suitor's family. For women and girls who willingly joined fighting forces that were victorious, community perceptions of these women as having become masculinized and as no longer subscribing to cultural notions of femininity can lead to rejection by potential or existing in-laws (Veale 2003). Women fighters in Eritrea, for example, experienced difficulties getting married due both to the gender norms they came to identify with during the war, and the perception that they were too assertive and not "modest" (Mehreteab 2002). Woman and girl fighters who married male fighters during the war also experienced high levels of post-conflict divorce, as their husbands wanted to remarry civilian women they considered more feminine, more like "soft dolls" (Hale 2001; Mehreteab 2002).

Sexual abuse, or the perception that a woman or girl has been "used" sexually, radically shapes females' experiences of reintegration. For example, women and girls in the Democratic Republic of the Congo (DRC) are considered to be of no value if they have had sexual contact with a man outside of an officially sanctioned marriage, regardless of whether sex was voluntary or rape (Verhey 2004). In many societies, women and girls who have been raped are seen as "damaged goods," and are deemed worthless as they are perceived as having broken social and moral codes of conduct (Farr 2002; Verhey 2004). In some contexts, this problem is made worse by the actions of armed groups that tattoo, brand, or carve the flesh of women in order to permanently link them to the group. Some women and girls captured by the rebel Revolutionary United Front (RUF) in Sierra Leone, for example, were carved with the letters "RUF" to signify their ownership by the force. Upon leaving those forces, the tattoos and scarification come to signify past sexual abuse, often severely limiting the women's and girls' life options (Mazurana 2004; McKay 2005).

Overlooked skills: what women and girls can bring to reintegration

Women and girls associated with armed forces and groups have criticized formal reintegration processes for being too shallow and not addressing the needs of women, girls, and communities at large. These needs include psychosocial healing, health services, security, justice, educational and economic opportunities, and community development. Often, the reintegration processes are short-term and do not address or consider the root causes that lead many women and girls to enter armed opposition groups. However, given the scope of what is truly needed for reintegration, it is questionable what DDR programs could realistically hope to accomplish, even in best-case scenarios.

Even when they do manage to get into DDR programs, women and girls have priorities, needs, and concerns that are not addressed. Equally important, they also bring skills that are currently underutilized in their reintegration. African women from more than 11 countries[5] who had fought or were fighting inside armed opposition groups identified the following skills that women like themselves bring into their post-conflict societies (see Text Box 9.4).[6]

Within the armed groups, women in particular are often trusted insiders who can influence leaders and can be instrumental in resolving conflicts. After the conflict, women and girls may transfer many skills they gained during the conflict, such as leadership, organization, communications, networking, medical care, and literacy. For example, women members of the armed opposition group in El Salvador have been active in schools, emergency response efforts, and economic development (Anderlini 2007). Supporting women and girls in applying and further developing their skills in negotiating, networking, and collaborating could positively impact reconstruction and peace-building. But that would require that people implement-

Box 9.4 Skills developed by women members of armed opposition groups in Africa

- assessing infrastructure of cities
- calculated risk assessment and risk taking
- communication skills and the ability to build relationships under difficult conditions
- coordination skills
- decision-making skills
- handling weapons
- information searching and gathering, dissemination of information to members within groups, and acting on information in a timely manner
- management skills
- management of teams and team logistics
- map reading
- mediation and conflict resolution skills
- medical skills
- military intelligence work
- mobilizing people
- negotiation skills
- problem-solving skills
- protecting civilians by organizing their movement and access to food, water and shelter
- results-oriented approaches
- scarce-resource management
- searching for common ground and mobilizing as women
- solidarity, discipline, commitment and team work
- spying and disguising oneself
- survival strategies
- tolerance and perseverance under difficult conditions
- understanding city layouts

ing reintegration and reconstruction programs notice and acknowledge that women have these skills, instead of ignoring them.

Women inside armed opposition groups recommend that reintegration programs should provide education and job-building skills for women and girls, particularly for livelihoods that are not capital-intensive (Mazurana 2005a). But the skills-building programs offered by most DDR programs rarely account for the local market's ability to absorb new labor. They offer training at a very low level and for a short time; therefore, both females and males who go through these programs often cannot find work (Anderlini 2007). Women inside armed opposition groups stress the need for micro- and macro-credit programs that can bolster livelihood strategies. In addition to programs that target women and girls as individuals, women have identified the need to bolster community-wide development and sensitivity as part of the reintegration process, in part to help them overcome community resentment and stigma toward them (Mazurana 2004).

Conclusion: why DDR planners need to think about gender and militarization

Governments and donor institutions place high expectations and demands on DDR programs. Not only is DDR supposed to help facilitate peace processes, it is also expected to create developmental change through the reintegration process, a task which is much more complex than disarmament and demobilization. Further complicating the situation are donor expectations of long-term benefits from short-term involvement and planning.

Add into this mix the fact that there is a disconnect between the realities of the women and girls who participated in armed forces and groups and the ways in which many DDR programs are planned and executed. As demonstrated in chapters 6 and 7, militarized notions of masculinity and femininity are essential to creating, motivating, and maintaining an armed group. Women and girls play vital roles in helping to establish the identity of a group and in supporting its ability to project its authority, power, and protection, both within the group and among supporters. They may also hold crucial positions to carry out the work needed within an armed group.

National and international policy makers and programmers carrying out DDR consistently fail to understand the centrality of militarized gender relationships and the roles of women and girls to armed opposition groups. One of the results is that the vast majority of all women and girls associated with any armed group never pass through national DDR programs. This is more than just a technical dilemma. Rather, at its core, it is about the gendered notions of threats, violence, security, stability, and legitimacy that DDR planners bring to the table.

To understand why DDR programs routinely fail to address the realities of women and girls inside armed groups, it is necessary to recognize that DDR planners and programmers come with their own often militarized notions of masculinity and femininity and their own militarized gendered notions of who was involved in the conflict and in what capacity. This helps inform their understanding of who are the "real fighters" and who the "camp followers." Perhaps most importantly, these militarized gendered notions help inform their understanding of who is considered a threat and hence who has credibility and must be taken seriously, i.e., who will call the shots within negotiations for establishing the parameters of how the DDR program will interface with the armed groups. The result that we see consistently is that DDR processes have traditionally focused on the needs and perceived security threat of adult male ex-combatants and at times overlooked even the presence of women and girls in armed opposition groups, seeing them as auxiliary forces that have little to do with underpinning the functioning or identity of an armed group (MDRP & UNIFEM 2005).

Peace negotiators and planners and programmers of DDR routinely fail to be aware of or even be curious about the state of gender relations before, during, and after the conflict. They have little if any understanding of how gender identities have been militarized in the conflict, and hence they underestimate the effect of gender identity on mobilizing the insurgency and sustaining the conflict. They may be more aware that war may stress, rupture, and change gender relations in society, but for the most part they do not consider this relevant to their immediate work. They tend to view the violence that occurred as social breakdown, dislocation, and destruction, rather than seeing it as struggles – over meanings, power, and identities – that may actually be sites of dynamic forms of innovation and social reordering (Duffield 2001). Women and girls are active members of armed groups and many have acquired new understandings of themselves and their societies, as well as new goals, roles, and skills during the conflict. These realities must be reflected in the thinking and actions of peace negotiators and DDR planners (see, for example, Knight & Özerdem 2004; Mazurana 2005a; Anderlini 2007).

QUESTIONS FOR DISCUSSION

1 How do you account for the very different understandings of leaders of armed opposition groups, the women and girls involved in the armed opposition groups, and the peace negotiators, policy makers, planners, and donors of DDR processes regarding the presence, role, and importance of women and girls in armed insurgencies?

2 Why do so many women and girls choose not to enter DDR programs? What does this tell you about the limits of what DDR can accomplish for women and girls?

3 If you were tasked to help set up a DDR program, what would be the key areas you would focus on to ensure women and girls had access to your program?

SUGGESTIONS FOR FURTHER READING

Conaway, Camille Pampell, and Martinez, Salome (2004) *Adding Value: Women's Contribution to Reintegration and Reconstruction in El Salvador.* Washington, DC: Hunt Alternatives Fund: Women Waging Peace.

Coulter, Chris (2009) *Girl Soldiers and Bush Wives: Women's Lives through War and Peace in Sierra Leone.* Ithaca: Cornell University Press.

Mazurana, Dyan (2005) *Women in Armed Opposition Groups in Africa and the Promotion of International Humanitarian Law and Human Rights.* Report of a workshop organized in Addis Ababa by Geneva Call and the Program for the Study of International Organization(s), November 23–26, University of Geneva.

McKay, Susan (2004) "Reconstructing Fragile Lives: Girls' Social Reintegration in Northern Uganda and Sierra Leone." *Gender and Development* 12(3): 19–30.

MDRP and UNIFEM (2005) *Taking a Gender-Perspective to Strengthen the Multi-Country Demobilization and Reintegration Program (MDRP) in the Greater Great Lakes Region.*

Multi-Country Demobilization and Reintegration Program and United Nations Development Fund for Women, Rwanda. www.mdrp.org/PDFs/MDRP_UNIFEM_ Gender_DDR_010207_en.pdf (accessed October 5, 2011).

Schroeder, Emily (2003) "A Window of Opportunity in the Democratic Republic of the Congo: Incorporating a Gender Perspective in the Disarmament, Demobilization and Reintegration Process." *Peace, Conflict and Development* 5: 1–45.

CHAPTER 10

Women "After" Wars

Ruth Jacobson

When the horrors of war have come to an end or the appalling regime is over-thrown, there are enormous possibilities for political and social transforma-tion. This chapter is concerned with how women and girls experience these transformations. Overall, it will attempt to give an overview of concepts and arguments around gendered endings, beginnings, and continuities. The term "post-conflict" has come to be used as a shorthand in multiple contemporary contexts, but one of its historical reference points is the twentieth-century European experience of the First and Second World Wars. In this framework, it is assumed that when the guns fall silent, soldiers will return home to the bosom of their families, and economic and political life will return to normal. However, as made clear in the preceding chapters, the global scene in the second decade of the twenty-first century presents a much more complex pic-ture, not just of the characteristics of contemporary warfare, but also of how armed conflict comes to an end. On a positive note, the political shifts of the immediate post-Cold War period opened the way for settlements of decades-long conflicts, such as those in Angola and Eritrea. Processes of democratiza-tion in Central and Latin America have seen the overthrow of regimes that effectively waged war against entire sections of their own citizenry, as was the case in Argentina and Guatemala. In other contexts, such as Nepal and Northern Ireland, there have been negotiated settlements between long-standing antagonists. On a less positive note, there are conflicts such as Sri Lanka's, where it was only overwhelming military force, regardless of civilian suffering, that brought about an end to combat. In addition, recent years have seen the collapse of negotiated settlements, such as those in Côte d'Ivoire.

Moreover, it is unmistakable that, while not "technically" at war, several regions of the world are marked by levels of deaths and casualties that invoke the same terminology, for example, when regimes such as those in Brazil and Mexico send in their armed forces to urban *barrios* in an attempt to curb the killings associated with the drug trade. Taken in conjunction with the evidence of growing global inequalities and environmental destruction, this suggests that we must, at the least, be wary of claims that "conflict" is a thing of the past in any state. Instead, it is more constructive to examine the pro-cesses through which any particular society moves through the immediate "post-*combat*" phase, usually involving some form of political settlement, into a more sustainable phase of peace. Since all forms of war impact women and men differently, as the previous chapters demonstrate, it is logical to expect that these transitional processes will also manifest gendered characteristics. In addition, the institutions involved will *themselves* be gendered, as examined in chapter 1.

In attempting this overview, the chapter draws on a large range of work in international relations and security studies. The resolute androcentrism of this field has been demonstrated by a range of feminist scholars (e.g., Tickner 2001; Cohn 2008). However, some more recent mainstream publications have shown a greater awareness of the gender-specific impact of armed conflict (e.g., Keen 2008). The chapter will also draw on an ever-expanding body of material from the field of practice, including policy documents intended to guide the institutions of the international community and evaluations of projects carried out for international donors. This category of material, generally referred to as "gray literature," contains empirically grounded information on what is happening to gender relations in postwar/post-political settlement societies. Much of this literature is not generally produced for publication in the academic domain, but it is important in reflecting major challenges and constraints which are not always integrated into more theoretically oriented frameworks originating in the academic field.[1]

The principal objective of this chapter is to follow through the thematic threads of previous chapters by examining, for example, what happens in the immediate postwar context when women who have been forced to flee (chapter 4) return to their homes? What happens about the health needs of women and girls (chapter 3)? How can women rebuild secure livelihoods (chapters 2 and 9)? How does the particular model of liberal democracy advocated by international donors impact on women who have forged a public or political voice through the crucible of armed conflict? This chapter will thus look at a range of institutions that impact on women and girls, ranging from global financial institutions down to much more local institutions in the conflict-affected society.

The first section of this chapter, "Toward an Analytical Framework," undertakes some essential groundwork in terms of the analytical and associated methodological challenges. "Gendered Aspects of Post-Political Settlements" follows through some of the principal gendered elements of the "first stage" environment such as disarmament, demobilization and reintegration (DDR) packages for former combatants or the return of displaced populations. The following section, "The Neoliberal Project, Conditionality, and Gender: A War against Poor Women?," focuses on the funding context in which postwar institutions of the international community, particularly the International Financial Institutions (IFIs), have the power to impose policies at the level of individual nation-states emerging from conflict. This section is complemented by examination of postwar national-level political transformations, generally known as "democratic transition," which also demonstrate the impact of pressures and demands from the international community. Across this canvas of transformation, there is substantial evidence of significant forces serving to marginalize or even disempower the women who have sustained the socioeconomic fabric of their communities during the conflict – or, to use Donna Pankhurst's term, there is a "gendered peace" (Pankhurst 2008c). In order to examine this process from a different perspective, the chapter's focus then shifts away from economic and political fields to look at the role that civil society has played in the search for justice and reconciliation through various forms of truth commissions. The final section moves closer in toward the grassroots, examining first the phenomenon of postwar backlash against women, and then, women's agency, despite all the challenges, in building a sustainable peace.

Toward an analytical framework

The initial analytical challenge in understanding the gender dimensions of any "post-conflict" environment is the sheer diversity of state formations, global institutions, regional, national, and sub-national agencies and actors that are involved. In contrast to the model of the nation-state originating in Europe, the appellation "post-conflict" is variously applied to at least three state formations. Firstly, there are former colonial states of the global South (e.g., Sierra Leone, Liberia, East Timor) that have experienced forms of civil wars that have wreaked havoc on economic and political structures which were already weak in the prewar context. As a result, the entire social fabric of society has been affected, while the state is heavily dependent on the support of international institutions, especially those providing funding essential for the first stages of economic recovery. There is another distinct category of states in Central and Latin America[2] where the nation-state and overall economic life has not been endangered, but where there have been intense, localized periods of brutality and oppression by the state against its own people; for example, in Guatemala, these were principally against indigenous communities. These periods have also had a profound and current impact on the relationship between the nation-state and its citizens, but there is generally less of a need for major interventions from international institutions. A third distinctive category can be found in the reconfigurations of nationhood in post-Cold War Europe, such as the successor states of the former Yugoslavia which have emerged from the 1990s wars still carrying unresolved and intense contestation around statehood.

At the least, therefore, *any* meaningful attempt to understand a "post-conflict" society must engage with these multiple facets of statehood and state capacity and how they interact with the dimensions of gendered complexities. For example, as demonstrated in this volume, contemporary armed conflicts have seen significant participation of women and girls in the actual fighting forces – estimated at as many as one third in Sierra Leone. In many contexts, former military experience is seen as a positive element for claiming political office, but the experience of former female combatants seeking to claim a public voice has been much more problematic.

Moving from state formations to the institutions and actors that are involved in postwar interventions, we find an equally complex picture. For those unfamiliar with the field, it is difficult to convey the number and diversity of the organizations that "parachute" into areas in transition from combat to non-combat; it includes UN international negotiators, a global mix of security personnel (including private military and security forces), a plethora of humanitarian agencies and nongovernmental organizations (NGOs). Table 10.1 can only give a schematic representation of the most important actors – those institutions and networks whose policies and actual programs are most likely to have a significant impact on the population. (As internationally linked criminal networks have become an important factor both during and after many wars, they are included in the table.) Although it would be helpful to be able to grasp the interrelationships of all these forces, this chapter will give priority to the "top layer" of Table 10.1 – the International Financial Institutions (IFIs). This is because, in the great majority of postwar societies of the global South, and in several contexts in the North, such as Kosovo, it is simply not possible to grasp the gendered realities of postwar experience without an understanding of the macro-economic context.

Having examined at least two of the essential elements of an analytical framework, we must add a third. The preceding chapters have established the need to avoid universalizing women's experiences. To take just one example, that of displacement: poor, rural women/girls in non-industrialized societies experience very different forms of displacement than those middle-class/elite women who are able to escape to other countries or to safer areas within their own country. On return, the latter may find employment with one of the incoming humanitarian agencies because of their language or administrative skills; the former must struggle to re-establish a bare livelihood. At the same time, we cannot assume that there are not enormous burdens of grief and emotional loss which they both share.

Having presented some of the major analytic challenges which must be grappled with when attempting to understand the complex situation in any transitional or "postwar" society, we now turn to international peace support operations and their impact on the lives of women and girls. Uniformed, armed, blue-helmeted UN peacekeepers may be the most familiar image of peace support operations (PSOs), but PSOs also have important civilian components which we will explore.

Peace support operations

The UN first started deploying peacekeeping operations during the Cold War; at the time, their main function was to monitor cease-fire agreements. The end of the Cold War led to a new optimism about possibilities

Table 10.1 Who does what in the postwar environment?[3]

Level of operation	Who are they?	What do they do?
Macro-level: external	International Financial Institutions (IFIs)	Responsible for setting terms of funding of postwar economic reconstruction
	UN military/security agencies, e.g., Department of Peacekeeanding Operations and contingents of national militaries mandated by UN	Responsible for implementation of DDR, maintaining security during elections, etc.
	UN humanitarian agencies, e.g., UNHCR, World Food Program Large international humanitarian organizations, e.g., Red Cross/Red Crescent	Responsible for safe return of refugees and displaced populations, civilian protection, etc.
Macro-level: illegal	Global criminal networks	Establish/maintain illegal trading, e.g., diamonds, timber, people
Meso-level: external	Individual nation-states, e.g., USA, UK, Scandinavian countries, Japan Big International NGOs (BINGOs), e.g., Oxfam International CARE	Responsible for funding and overseeing programs of postwar and longer-term "post-conflict" reconstruction
National-level	National state institutions e.g., parliaments, formal court systems, security forces including military and police	Responsible for implementing the political settlement/ transition
	National civil society, e.g., faith groups, legal networks, women's organizations	Contribute to political transition, advocates for reconciliation, e.g., truth commissions
National-level: illegal networks	National power holders, including some holders of political office, former military, etc.	Establish/maintain links with international networks, cross-border activities, etc.

for transformation of conflict-affected societies, and the UN took on what is known as the "second-generation" approach to peacekeeping, as represented in the 1992 publication *An Agenda for Peace* by the then UN secretary-general Boutros Boutros-Ghali (Report of the Secretary-General 1992). This new approach went much further than just the disarmament of combatants. It envisaged the rebuilding of communities and longer-term conflict prevention. This broad shift to the concept of "peace-building" remains in place within the UN and other regional actors such as the Organization for Security and Co-operation in Europe (OSCE) and the African Union.

   When an international peacekeeping force arrives after a cease-fire, their immediate priorities are tasks such as carrying out the disarmament of combatant forces and overseeing the first stages of return of displaced populations. This period is characterized by the need for swift decision making and action on tasks such as ensuring that arrangements are in place to transport, accommodate, feed, and process armed combatants as they arrive at the designated assembly points to start the process of demobilization. This period

---

Box 10.1 United Nations Peace Support Operations: where and who?

By February of 2011, the UN Department of Peacekeeping Operations (UNDPKO) operated fifteen missions (one of which was administered in partnership with the UN Department of Political Affairs), most located in Africa, the Middle East and Eastern Europe. Most missions now focus on internal rather than international conflicts and the numbers of personnel involved in peacekeeping missions remain high, with 98,022 military personnel (over 83,000 troops, 13,124 police and approximately 1,800 military observers) and over 5,000 international civilian personnel, 13,000 local civilian personnel and nearly 2,400 United Nations volunteers deployed on missions around the world in 2011 (UNDPKO 2011a).

Where do the "peacekeepers" come from?
The "blue helmets": It is important to note that there is no "UN army." Instead, there are national contingents from Troop Contributing Countries (TCCs), operating under UN mandate. These TCCs are very widely distributed: in 2011, the list of contributors is topped by Bangladesh, followed by Pakistan, India, Nigeria, Egypt, Nepal, Jordan, Rwanda, Ghana, and Uruguay (UNDPKO 2011b). These contingents generally include police forces drawn from both the military and nonmilitary establishments of the TCC concerned.
The police: UN peace operations also field some 14,700 police officers. These are selected on the basis of their expertise to contribute to UN missions for 6–18 month periods. "Formed Police Units" are dedicated contingents of some 140 officers contributed to a UN mission by a national police service, usually for tours of duty of 6–12 months. In 2007, the deployment of an Indian all-female police unit to Liberia made headlines; as of this writing, there is also an all-female Bangladeshi police unit in Haiti.
The civilians: There are personnel from the permanent UN institutions that are most directly involved in PSOs such as the UNHCR and the UNDP's Bureau for Crisis Prevention and Recovery. The necessary additional civilian personnel are generally recruited through channels of member-states for the duration of the PSO.

is often described in the field of practice as "the tyranny of the urgent" – an acknowledgment of the barriers to integrating *any* kind of longer-term perspectives under the pressure of the hour-by-hour demands. This has been illustrated, for example, in field documentation of the difficulties of achieving correct registration of women and girls in the turbulent context of assembly points, where there are successive arrivals of wary and mistrustful combatants who have to surrender their weapons (Jacobson 2005). Despite these pressures, however, there are substantial grounds for accepting that the visible presence of "the blue helmets" – patrolling neighborhoods previously terrorized by armed gangs, for example – can give the civilian population a sense that, at long last, there is the promise of an end to living under threat. It is therefore all the more bitterly ironic that there is also substantial and repeated evidence of peacekeepers' failure to protect women and girls – not only from local men's sexual violence, but also from sexual exploitation and abuse (SEA) at the hands of UN forces themselves.

There is nothing new about concerns over the abusive nature of sexual relationships in what are now generally known as PSOs; in the early 1990s, Cambodian women's organizations started reporting rises in the rate of prostitution of girls in the vicinity of UN missions.[4] In 2003, the UN secretary-general issued a Bulletin which addresses acts of abuse and exploitation in unequivocal terms: "Sexual relationships between United Nations staff and beneficiaries of assistance, since they are based on inherently unequal power dynamics, undermine the credibility and integrity of the work of the United Nations and are strongly discouraged" (Secretary-General's Bulletin 2003).[5] The Bulletin stresses the responsibilities of every member of the UN mission not only to refrain individually from SEA but also to not be complicit by "turning a blind eye." It contains specific provision for the protection of younger girls (and boys), such as the clause prohibiting "sexual activity with children (persons under the age of 18) . . . regardless of the age of majority or age of consent locally. Mistaken belief in the age of a child is not a defence" (Secretary-General's Bulletin 2003). The Bulletin also contains provisions for disciplinary measures. If fully implemented, therefore, this "zero tolerance" approach would have had a significant impact on the well-being of women and girls who might otherwise be at risk. However, two years later, in 2005, the UN's own investigation, known as the Zeid Report, established that SEA continued to be widespread (UNGA 2005). The Zeid Report found, among other things, that peacekeepers had engaged in enticing desperate women and children to engage in sexual acts for a pittance of money or a small piece of food, or even sometimes giving them money or food after raping them to make the intercourse appear consensual. Beyond these forms of abuse, the report noted complicity of contingent commanders in their resistance to cooperating with investigations.

In other words, while the "boys will be boys" attitude now contravenes official UN policy, it has been hard to erase in the field (Refugees International

2005). Even while SEA continues, however, the "zero tolerance" approach appears to have had some unintended consequences. Field studies, such as Marsha Henry's on Liberia, have noted that the UN's "zero tolerance" approach has, in effect, been taken as a "no fraternization" rule; even if they were motivated to carry out their duty of protection, some peacekeepers would avoid stopping their vehicles at the side of the road or in villages when they saw women who looked as if they were in difficulty (Higate & Henry 2009, p. 147).

The UN's two principal gender equality policies are "gender balance" (equal representation of women and men, a goal which was originally supposed to be met by 2000, and which is still very, very far off) and "gender mainstreaming" (the requirement that all policies and programs be assessed for their differential impacts on men and women and their responsiveness to women's and men's different needs and interests). The UN response to both the evidence of the Zeid Report and widespread negative publicity about peacekeeper SEA has relied, in significant part, on attempting to reach something closer to gender balance – i.e., recruiting more women into the military and police components of PSOs (see Text Box 10.2). This has complex, and not necessarily positive, gender implications. On the one hand, there is at least a higher probability that women/girls who have suffered/are suffering SEA will feel more able to report this to a woman peacekeeper rather than a male one. This also applies to situations of domestic violence and sexual assault more broadly, where the blue helmets are in a position to respond. At the same time, researchers such as Simic (2010) emphasize that "Women are being encouraged to join peacekeeping operations as sexual violence problem-solving forces while simultaneously undertaking a complex role as 'protectors' of local women from local men and from male peacekeepers"(p. 1). This obviously has major implications for all the female personnel deployed in any particular PSO, not least of which is the career risks they run should they decide to challenge their colleagues or superiors.

While the focus on SEA by PSO personnel in recent years is both understandable and at least potentially constructive, both that focus and the emphasis on "more women" as the solution have had the disadvantage of masking some other vital areas. Gender analysis needs to be mainstreamed into PSOs in areas far beyond (what should be the minimum) "do no harm" aspect of not abusing the women the peacekeepers are meant to protect. Gender mainstreaming can mean ensuring that equality provisions are incorporated into the constitutions made by newly formed governments, or responding to the needs of female former combatants in DDR programs, or figuring out the different voter-education needs of men and women, or recognizing the differences in the economic situation and societal and cultural attitudes faced by women and girls as compared to men and boys, to name only a few. To briefly look at one example in more detail – this kind of analysis would have an impact on the operational priorities and practices of civilian

Box 10.2 Where are the women in PSOs?

In 2008, the UN's own analysis of gender balance statistics throughout the UN noted that improvements in gender balance on peace support missions were minimal and in some cases declining. Of the 18 peace support operations deployed on four continents with 77,492 troops, only 1,539 (1.98%) of the military component were women (with Ghana, South Africa, Nigeria, and India as the major TCCs for female blue helmets). In the civilian sector, the recruitment of women into peacekeeping was more obvious, with about 30% of internationally recruited staff and 24% of locally recruited staff being female (Willett 2010, p. 152). However, it is probable that many of both international and local female staff were not operating at higher, decision-making levels. As of 2010, the tenth anniversary of UNSCR 1325, women represented approximately 30% of the civilian staff, 30% of international staff, and 20% of national staff in peacekeeping missions; however, "there has been a substantial decrease in the proportion of women in managerial levels in field missions . . ." (UNDPKO 2010, p. 38).

Gender breakdown of combined military and police components of UN Peacekeeping Operations as of March 2012[6]

	M	F	Total
Military experts	1,987	70	2,057
Military troops	80,280	2,226	82,506
Individual police	5,790	1,206	6,816
Formed police units	7,204	406	7,610
Totals	95,261	3,728	98,989

policing. In many contexts, large numbers of women depend for their livelihoods on small-scale trading, and so it is vital that local markets can be re-established as secure places. The upheavals of the conflict may have left these women particularly vulnerable to irregular demands for payment for licenses or fines from market officials or neighborhood police (who might themselves be demobilized soldiers). An operational emphasis on this aspect should prioritize skills in understanding the local power dynamics, and the nonviolent defusing of tense confrontations rather than the use of arms.

Overall, however, what is striking about both gender balance and gender mainstreaming in peacekeeping is how little progress has been made. The complex reasons for these failures of implementation lie beyond the remit of this chapter but have been summarized (in a journal that specializes in the field of international peacekeeping) as follows:

> Existing attempts to mainstream gender within the UN rarely go to the heart of the institutional inequities and power relations that structure gender relations within the organization. Rather, gender mainstreaming has been grafted onto existing power structures that are circumscribed by the essentialist nature of binary opposites in which gender has been interpreted as woman . . . [t]he portrayal of women as victims in need of protection persists, while men are constructed as protectors and policymakers.

> Meanwhile, women's active roles in conflict resolution and peacemaking continue to be idealized and undervalued. (Willett 2010, p. 143)

This theme of undervaluation of women's knowledge and capacities will be one that occurs with remarkable frequency in the remainder of this chapter. With this in mind, the focus shifts to the first stages of transition.

Gendered aspects of post-political settlement societies

When wars end, there is a characteristic immediate phase of return – of former fighters, exiles, and refugee/displaced households. During the last three decades, these processes have been experienced all over sub-Saharan Africa (e.g., Mozambique, Angola, Liberia, and Sierra Leone), in the former Yugoslavia, Latin America (e.g., Guatemala), and South Asia (e.g., East Timor). Among the principal features to take into account are: the demobilization of fighting forces; the demographic shift toward female-headed households; health issues; and the search for postwar livelihoods.

Combatants

In the context of negotiated endings for large-scale internal armed conflicts such as those of sub-Saharan Africa and Nepal, a political settlement cannot be reached without first dealing with the existing combatants. (This was also the case with the members of the Iraq military after the fall of Saddam Hussein.) Where will they be accommodated? Will it be possible to get their weapons off them without provoking further outbreaks of fighting? Above all, what will we do with them once they have been disarmed? As described in chapter 9, the most common response to these questions starting in the later 1980s has been a process known as DDR (disarmament, demobilization and reintegration), in which "cantonments" are created to contain the armed forces, and international peacekeeping troops carry out the process of disarmament. The process is facilitated by promises given by the international community that, in return for their compliance, former fighters will receive immediate material support, as well as a more substantial package of support to aid their reintegration into civilian life.

Chapter 9 establishes the manifold ways in which women and girls associated with armed forces have been marginalized or excluded from DDR processes. It also notes the frequency with which their skills are ignored in the longer-term processes of reconstruction. In recent years, these shortcomings have come under scrutiny (Farr, Myrttinen, & Schnabel 2009), not least from the point of view of ensuring maximum "value for money" in terms of financial investment. As a result, some major institutions, such as the UN Department of Peacekeeping Operations (UNDPKO) and the European Union's security arm, have made significant policy changes, and the forces that actually implement disarmament and demobilization are now supposed to establish the status of women/girls in armed forces through processes of separate registration and other forms of evidence, rather than taking the word of male commanders. Some international donor funding has been established specifically for the reintegration of these women and girls. This is a positive demonstration that there is always potential for change even in those deeply embedded attitudes that have historically excluded women from claiming knowledge and experience of "the business of war." However, the gray literature and reports from the field suggest that there are still major obstacles in terms of actual implementation, e.g., there is no careful registration of women and girls, nor provision of appropriate facilities for them and their children (Olonisakin, Barnes, & Ikpe 2010). As a result, there is an even higher likelihood that they will not gain from even the limited benefits available and will simply "reintegrate themselves." The most common rationale given by field personnel for not paying consistent attention to gender issues is the need for immediate action (again, "the tyranny of the urgent"), shortage of resources, and absence of expertise. However, underlying this there are strong indications of what can be called "institutional resistance." This form of resistance is another manifestation of chapter 1's analysis of gendered institutions: DDR-implementing institutions have embedded within them assumptions and values which shape what is seen as most urgent, important or significant to do – assumptions which are taken as "objective" within the organization but which are actually highly gendered.

Transformed households

Another unmistakable characteristic of the postwar trajectory and political settlement phase is that it enables the safe return of displaced populations. This is often a time of great celebration as families reunite, discover that missing relatives are still alive and take up the threads of their lives. At the same time, the war will have had a toll on the makeup of the civilian population, which is very likely to contain higher numbers of female-headed households than existed pre-conflict. At least in the immediate postwar phase, there can be a significant percentage of households made up of: (a) war widows or women abandoned by their partners, plus their dependent children; (b) women living on their own, for example, older women whose children have been killed or dispersed as a result of the war; and/or (c) households with no resident adult parent or guardian. The welfare of these households is critically impacted by the existence of preexisting gender norms that disadvantage women in a "non-conflict" context. For example, women may not have the rights to own land or property, to travel independently, to speak in public meetings, or even simply to appear in mixed settings. Although some gender norms may be suspended or refigured in the actual combat period, there is now accumulating evidence that this shift is not permanent (El-Bushra 2008; Pankhurst 2008a). As a result, households headed by women or girls may find themselves more vulnerable than other households. In the immediate postwar period, these women may be hampered from accessing the resources made available as part of reconstruction initiatives and this disadvantage can then extend into the longer term. A longitudinal study in Uganda, for instance, notes the persistently high levels of both material poverty and psychosocial distress experienced by widows and abandoned women arising from their losses: "[s]eventeen years on, conflict still casts a long shadow" (Bird & Shinyekwa 2003, p. 29).

Health

Turning to issues of health, there is also a distinction to be made between short- and long-term impact. War is obviously capable of destroying both rudimentary health care systems and the material infrastructure and human resources and expertise that are needed for large-scale health improvements, such as an immunization campaign. At the same time, it is necessary to recognize that women and girls who were fortunate enough to find refuge in well-organized and adequately funded camps may in fact have had *better* access to health services, such as maternal health care and child immunization, than they received prewar. What then are the priorities for women in terms of health during the postwar period? On the one hand, it has become increasingly clear that in many contexts, the postwar needs of women and girls[7] are inseparable from their exposure to sexual violence/coercive sexual relationships during the war period. These may include, *inter alia*, the long-term health effects of vaginal and anal penetration by objects, the impact of early pregnancy and labor for girls who might have otherwise been protected by social norms, and the spread of sexually transmitted diseases (STDs) including HIV/AIDS. To these must be added a whole range of psychosocial effects specifically associated with sexual violence (Duggan & Jacobson 2009). At the same time, several other vital aspects of postwar health need to be taken into account. Malnutrition and crowded living conditions in refugee and displacement camps contribute to higher risks of contracting tuberculosis (TB) and other infectious diseases. Throughout the health field, the health of older women is also a very low priority.

These shortcomings can be directly related to the fact that the larger project of postwar (re)construction of health services for women's health needs are subject to two powerful constraints. The first is the prevalent neoliberal model of "reconstruction" that demands severe restrictions on state spending in all public services, including health services; this will be discussed in more detail below. This constraint, which has been operative for several decades, has more recently been compounded by a second: all aspects of health service reconstruction have experienced cuts in external donor funding as a result of the global economic recession. As of early 2012, there are no indications that these cuts are going to be significantly restored.

Livelihoods

The single most important feature of the period around political settlement is the desperate search for livelihoods to replace dependency on army salaries, extortion from civilians, precarious wartime activities and/or external emergency aid. In both non-industrialized and developed societies, families returning to their rural home area may find that their land, houses and other property have been "grabbed" by powerful local figures such as former rebel or government commanders. All forms of households are at risk, but male heads of household may be in a position to risk a challenge in order to secure their own and their families' future well-being. Households without a male "protector" and spokesperson, however, may find that the challenge is too great, particularly if the traditional or communal-based institutions for settling such disputes are dominated by patriarchal norms.

Livelihoods in urban areas are also affected by gender. In many war settings, families fled from rural areas to the relative safety of peri-urban settlement areas around major towns. Once political settlements make a return to the countryside feasible, male household heads often decide to stay on in their new settings, frequently with a new partner and family. This has also been the case with young single men unwilling to return to the burdens of rural life. As a result, postwar rural areas in non-industrialized societies such as Mozambique have very scant numbers of adult men, further adding to the labor burdens of women and girls.

On the other hand, there are contexts where women and girls find that they are able to attain a degree of economic independence by using the new livelihood skills and associated self-confidence that they have acquired directly as a result of war. They may have learned how to manage independently as petty traders, or acquired dressmaking skills through training programs offered to refugees and displaced women. Girls, in particular, may have benefited from literacy programs that would not have been available in the prewar context of early marriage. The issue here therefore is the manner in which these livelihood skills and capabilities carry through into family and community gender relations in the more immediate postwar period.

One additional important issue in the search for postwar livelihoods, as discussed earlier, is the presence of international peacekeepers and the wide range of other international actors who "parachute" into areas in transition. It is now recognized that there is an association between the presence of international peacekeeping troops and institutions overseeing the immediate postwar phase and an increase in prostitution and/or trafficking[8] of women/girls. In some contexts, such as Kosovo, the availability of weapons and the complicity of some of the international peacekeepers and the national police forces have contributed to a situation where internal and cross-border sex trafficking can flourish with little risk for the traffickers (Corrin 2000). Given the nature of the trade, it is virtually impossible to establish any realistic picture of the degree and nature of female involvement as "business women" rather than victims. However, the underlying issue is the interrelationship between the highly fragile environment of many postwar political settlements, war-related impoverishment, and the desperate search for livelihoods.

Earlier chapters of this book addressed many features of war itself, including the mobilization of fighting forces, displacement, and the destruction of infrastructures and livelihoods. In this chapter so far, we have seen some of the ways that each of these elements plays out during the aftermath of armed conflict. But in order to more fully understand postwar settings, we need not only to look at effects directly produced by the context of war itself, but also at the larger set of political and economic relations within which both the conflict and the transition are situated. Here, an understanding of the workings of international financial institutions and neoliberal economic policies will be crucial.

The neoliberal project, conditionality, and gender: a war against poor women?

It is generally accepted that the later 1970s saw the emergence of a very specific model of how economies "ought" to work to ensure growth, replacing previous models which rested heavily on the involvement of the state. This model, generally referred to as "neoliberalism," has had a profound global impact spanning both the industrialized North and the developing South (Cramer 2006; Duffield 2008). As Peterson and Runyan (2010) note, although the advocates of neoliberalism claim only to be proposing a "technical fix" for economies, neoliberalism is inextricable from a particular ideological position. "Since approximately the 1970s, globalization has been driven primarily by neo-liberal economic policies favored by geopolitical elites (mostly men), and especially, economists trained in the global North and acting as policy makers in international economic institutions (IMF, World Bank, WTO)" (Peterson & Runyan 2010, p. 192). Furthermore, Peterson and Runyan point out that advocates of the neoliberal project (also known as market fundamentalism) claim that "unconstrained markets 'naturally' foster liberty, democracy and more peaceful societies" (Peterson & Runyan 2010, p. 192).

The two institutions most responsible for implementing the model are the International Monetary Fund (IMF) and the World Bank (the name used to refer to the International Bank for Reconstruction & Development and the International Development Association). Both war and the economic crises of the 1980s meant that national governments across the regions of the developing world had to turn for loans to these two international financial institutions based in the West. These loans were *only* provided on condition that the neoliberal model was implemented – hence the term "conditionality." Moreover, with few exceptions, other leading external donors such as the USA, the UK, Japan, and the European Union also made their funding conditional on the acceptance of the IFI model. Thus, although national governments nominally had freedom to make their own policy decisions, in effect, huge areas of national economic policy were effectively set by external financial institutions.

There is a large body of critique of the neoliberal model in general, and of its gendered impacts in particular, including from leading feminist economists such as Diane Elson (1991) and Lourdes Beneria (2003). The neoliberal model not only has specifically gendered impacts, it also rests on fundamentally gendered assumptions; for example, it views women's unpaid labor as a "free good" that is: (a) not economically productive; and (b) infinitely expandable in the face of reduction of public services. These critiques support Peterson and Runyan's conclusion about the imposition of neoliberal programs in developing countries across all the major regions of the South, namely that "[t]hese programs have eroded whatever gains were made earlier in getting public and private development lending agencies to recognize the importance of women's work and gender issues to successful economic development" (Peterson & Runyan 2010, p. 193).

From its outset in the late 1970s and through to current times, neoliberalism has been critiqued as effectively constituting "a war against the poor." Undeterred by criticism even from their former Chief Economist and holder of the Nobel Prize for Economics, Joseph Stiglitz, the IMF and the World Bank have insisted on the implementation of the model in postwar countries as diverse as Mozambique, Bosnia-Herzegovina, and El Salvador – even though neoliberalism in its initial form was not designed for postwar settings. It is important to reiterate that there has been virtually no area of choice for postwar governments in desperate need of funding for reconstruction. Funds have *only* been made available on condition of acceptance of the neoliberal package.

Against this backdrop, what then is the gender relevance of neoliberal conditionality for war-shattered economies? The neoliberal insistence on "shrinking the state" requires severe cutbacks and controls on public expenditure in exactly those areas that could be most transformatory for women and girls affected by conflict. For example, it is well established across the regions of the South that an entire generation of girls has lost out on access to education due to conflict. International donors can support states and communities endeavoring to rebuild local schools and health clinics, but, at the same time, restrictions on state spending may well mean they remain unstaffed or without resources; this has proved to be the case, for example, in postwar Mozambique (Hanlon & Smart 2010).

Another essential condition of the neoliberal package is privatization of public goods and services such as water and power supplies. While it needs to be recognized that many of these services were not previously delivered by the state in ways that benefited women, there is evidence that postwar privatization has intensified women's time and work burdens regarding water

Box 10.3 Gaps between gender rhetoric and funding

The organization Gender Action's 2009 study on the gender aspects of post-conflict financing noted that "Financiers like the World Bank may produce excellent gender studies and use powerful gender rhetoric, but failing to incorporate them into investments then undermines their returns" (Greenberg & Zuckerman 2009, p. 21). The study examined Post-Conflict Reconstruction (PCR) projects at the World Bank (WB) and concluded that despite the generous monetary support that these programs receive, little funding is assigned to women-focused activities. "An example is the World Bank Sierra Leone Economic Rehabilitation and Recovery Credit Project (III) . . . did not ensure that women will be borrowers. . . . In Timor-Leste, two independent Commissions identified ex-combatants and veterans, and elaborated programmes to assist them. More than 10,000 men registered. Yet the programme excluded women ex-combatants." (Greenberg & Zuckerman 2009, pp. 14–15).

and fuel. As a result of analysis of these sorts of problems, "there is a growing lobby supported by some eminent economists that such conditions ought to be loosened in postwar economies since they severely undermine the chances of economic recovery. The needs of women and other vulnerable groups should be given a higher priority than macro-economic probity" (Pankhurst 2008a, p. 17). Yet this argument and the IFIs' own self-critiques of previous programs do not seem to have radically changed the actual implementation of programs in relation to gender issues. The figures in Text Box 10.3 are drawn from the World Bank's *own* Post-Conflict Reconstruction Fund. They indicate that actual allocation of funding is not consistent with the Bank's rhetoric about women's vital role in reconstruction. Neoliberal conditionalities constitute a tremendously important external force bearing on gender and postwar reconstruction. They are macro-level impositions whose impacts filter down to everyday experiences: Can a woman procure clean water for her family? Will there be anyone to staff a school or a health clinic? Will there be public transportation to get to a market? Will she be unemployed because the entire public service sector of the state has been shrunk? We now turn to a second aspect of the larger political and economic relations within which postwar reconstruction takes place: international policies designed to foster "transitions to democracy."

Democratic transitions, postwar politics, and gender

Contrary to what may be assumed, postwar reconstruction programs funded by the international community are *not* designed solely for the rebuilding of material infrastructure such as roads and electrical grids. In post-Cold War thinking about war and its aftermath, donors also have the objectives of permanent transformation of the institutions of government. This is particularly the case where prewar regimes have been authoritarian and/or oppressive. In taking responsibility for funding these kinds of programs, the range of international, regional, and national donors identified in Table 10.1 are demonstrating their vision of priorities for the post-conflict state. Until recently, this vision was almost synonymous with the holding of multi-party elections to a representative legislature. The transition may often also involve requirements for constitutional reform, separation of the military from political power so as to preclude reversion to military rule, separation of the executive and judicial arms of government, etc. There may be specific attention to the constitutional rights of women. Taken altogether, this vision can be summed up as "the liberal peace" (Duffield 2008).

It is undeniable that substantive democracy within a formal political structure of accountability has the potential to substantially improve the well-being of postwar populations. There are, however, some significant flaws in the form in which it is implemented. This version of "democracy" is derived from the historical western combination of liberal political development with capitalist economic growth. Thus it largely fails to take into account the different conditions of contemporary postwar societies in the non-industrialized world, particularly in the context of shattered economies and dependence on external funding. Yet programs for democratic transition have been implemented in the form of a "short cut" toward the kind of systems achieved over centuries by the western political systems. This kind of optimism – or even triumphalism – was prevalent amongst the political community of the West during the decade following the collapse of the Soviet Union.

Not surprisingly, therefore, the kind of formal democratic structures brought into existence in postwar conditions have been assailed by problems, ranging from weak institutions, the impact of national and global economic recession, and the prevalence of forms of corruption arising from the previous conflict. Thus, for example, an election can assist former military leaders to use their position within the new regime to maintain or expand illegal activities. In many such cases, this form of corruption is actively abetted by global economic forces, as noted in chapter 1 with reference to the DRC. As a result of these problems, the ambitious project of "democratic transition" has more recently been replaced by a concern among international donors with building up government institutions in postwar societies over the longer term. However, this shift of emphasis has not fundamentally altered the constraints of neoliberal conditionality.

Given its embedded nature, it is not surprising to find that gender can be relevant across the spectrum of actual political transformation, whether in relation to fundamental constitutional reform, quotas for political parties, or the distribution of actual decision-making powers within the postwar government. Clearly, however, this chapter cannot explore all these aspects in depth, so it will limit itself to two issues that are salient to several political contexts: gender quotas and land reforms.

Quota systems

There are a number of different types of postwar quota systems – including constitutional reforms that reserve a specific number of parliamentary seats for ethnic groups particularly affected by the conflict. Quota systems for women generally involve setting a requirement for any party contesting the postwar election to have a given percentage of female candidates. In most contexts where they have been adopted, the first set of postwar elections has seen the entry of unprecedented numbers of women into the formal political sphere. The reasons quotas are adopted are not always self-evident; they may indicate a substantial change of heart amongst the previously all-male political leadership who recognize the importance of women in the process of national reconstruction. But they may also be linked to the need to gain women's votes, or to comply with external donors' expectations. Thus each context requires careful "unpacking." Whatever the reasons, though, the result is that women have taken their place in national legislatures in countries as diverse as Mozambique, El Salvador, Iraq, and Afghanistan. There is, however, another side to this picture. To reiterate yet again, women are not a homogenous category, and elected female representatives will not necessarily share the same political positions. This has been the case with regard to the process of constitutional reform in Iraq. Here, there are major divisions between the positions of female secular, political activists and those of the female political representatives associated with Islamist parties (Al-Ali & Pratt 2009, p. 79).

Similarly, it cannot simply be assumed that female political representatives will take a "pro-women" stance in relation to the central political task of setting a national budget. For example, improving resources for primary health services in rural areas can reduce maternal mortality, and immunization programs can reduce the care burden on women. Under these conditions, it is particularly relevant to see whether female representatives are more willing than their male colleagues to prioritize spending on these areas over, for example, more "hi-tech" medical facilities in urban areas.

Land reform

One of the most important tasks for a postwar government concerns land reform. Secure access to land is essential for a very large proportion of women in non-industrialized postwar societies. In many societies of the South, including non-urbanized regions of Latin America and South Asia, historical forms of ownership have often been some form of collective or communal ownership. Even though neither women nor men had individual rights of ownership, these systems allowed women to cultivate the land to meet at least some of their subsistence food needs. The system could also offer some degree of security for housing on or near the farmed land, or for forms of small-scale economic activity such as cooking food for sale. In addition, land often carries important emotional and symbolic connotations, for example, as the burial place of family members and ancestors. Some postwar transitions have explicitly recognized the connection between postwar reconstruction and women's land ownership needs. In Rwanda, the preponderance of widows in the post-genocide population was a factor behind altering the formal legal system to allow married women and widows to own land in their own right (albeit not covering the situation of single women and those in nonformalized marriages).

The larger picture of postwar political dispensations around land is less positive. There have been strong pressures to adopt systems of individual land ownership backed up by codified systems of legal documentation that disproportionately favor men. In particular, the World Bank promotes "market-friendly" land reform in postwar societies (Pankhurst 2008a). All existing evidence suggests that this kind of system drastically reduces or even removes completely the multiple and collective forms of land use on which rural women have relied. It can also have implications for women who have spent years working on small parcels of land to supply the urban market. Mozambique provides a relevant case study (see Text Box 10.4). In the Mozambique case, eventually there were some positive outcomes for women, but there are many less encouraging examples. In her study of global land reform, Susie Jacobs (2010) finds numerous instances of women's marginalization from land reform programs as a result of indifference or active hostility from male-dominated political institutions in post-conflict contexts such as Guatemala.

Security sector reform and women's security

Security sector reform (SSR) provides another example of the gendered implications of postwar politics. It is the fundamental requirement of the state to protect its citizens and residents. In a postwar context, this is likely to involve reform of all the arms of the previous "security forces," including not only the military, but also police, border guards, and prison personnel, many of whom themselves are likely to have been abusers of human rights rather than protectors. There has been extensive investment by the international community in the field of postwar security sector reform. To what extent has this investment recognized the gender-specific abuses experienced by women and girls at the hands of these forces? The situation is highly context specific. Some political settlements, such as that in Afghanistan, allow those responsible for authorizing and/or carrying out these abuses to continue to hold high office, including posts in the postwar regime's security apparatus. Others have been barred from holding office (Iraq) or even indicted in international courts (former Yugoslavia).

The trajectory of donor-funded projects in SSR is similar to that outlined for

Box 10.4 Land reform in Mozambique: the battle to protect women's rights[9]

Background

Mozambique is repeatedly cited as "the" success story of international intervention, whether by the UN, the IFIs, or the northern civil society involved. At one level, this is certainly the case: the 1992 Rome Peace Accord political settlement that put an end to two decades of war has been sustained up into 2012 and there seems very little likelihood of a return to armed conflict. Women from all regions of the country greeted the end of the war with enormous jubilation and set to the task of reconstruction – literally, in terms of rebuilding homes. They also entered into the postwar legislative assembly in unprecedented numbers, partly as a result of a quota system adopted by the former ruling party, Frelimo.

Women, men, the World Bank, and land reform

In common with rural Southern Africa as a whole, the concept of individual land ownership was never practiced in rural areas. Instead, traditional local leaders, known as *regulos*, had the authority to allocate specific areas of land for cultivation and pasture. These plots could be passed down through the generations, and also allocated to newcomers when sufficient land was available. The ideology formerly adopted by Frelimo meant a notional shift toward all land being the property of the state – thus both women *and* men were excluded from individual ownership or inheritance. In practice, the structural gender regime of Mozambican society meant that women's rights to land use were always dependent on husbands or male kin – even non-adult sons. Their position prewar was to some extent protected by gendered norms that placed a value on women's ability to provide for their households through their farming abilities.

During the war, huge areas of land had to be left uncultivated, but rural communities retained clear memories of the prewar patterns of usage. However, the neoliberal international dispensation required that land could no longer be the property of the state and this was one of the conditions of the Rome Peace Accord. The new postwar legislature therefore had to formulate a land law. During this process, it became clear that the World Bank's "technical advisors" were exerting enormous pressure to assure that the law would follow western-style individual ownership. They made common cause with leading political figures, many of them former military commanders from both sides, who had acquired substantial land themselves, sometimes at the point of a gun. Initially, the proposed legislation claimed to be "gender neutral" since it would give women the same rights to acquire land as men. However, it became clear that such a law would potentially be very harmful to women in rural areas, who would lose the traditional rights of access. In peri-urban areas, women who had been displaced by the war had succeeded in forming successful horticultural cooperatives, and they would also be threatened.

Remarkably, a determined coalition of forces achieved a modification of the law, allowing some provisions for collective ownership. This coalition involved female political representatives from all the parties, including former enemies, plus a range of civil society organizations and faith groups. The membership was overwhelmingly, although not exclusively, female; very few male politicians spoke out in favor of protecting women's rights and some opposed them as contrary to "Mozambican culture and tradition."

DDR. Earlier interventions effectively ignored gender issues – for example, programs for police training may have included instruction on the obligation to observe human rights included in the ban on torture/maltreatment of suspects or prisoners, but not on the obligation to avoid sexual violence/harassment of women and girls. Trainers have not considered the possibility that women, including young women, might offer valuable insights on reform. Energetic feminist advocacy has led to this marginalization being addressed, to some extent, within international institutions (Bastick & Valasek 2008).

It is important to bear in mind that substantial areas of women's experiences of postwar insecurity are not effectively controlled by *any* of the national state's formal bodies. For example, the reach of formal legal systems based on constitutional law is often virtually nonexistent over rural (and sometimes urban) areas of the global South and the more isolated areas within the successor states of the former Yugoslavia, such as Kosovo. Instead, there are the institutions of customary law, such as hereditary chiefdoms, councils of elders, or religious figures. These bodies characteristically categorize women/girls as legal minors.[10] This means that, in the context of postwar insecurities, women often have nowhere to turn for justice or legal redress. Economic recession seems likely to intensify this situation.

In several postwar contexts, we can note the emergence of new forms of gendered institutions that consider themselves entitled in some way to patrol and punish women/girls. A recent example is the growing prevalence of state or state-sanctioned forces monitoring women's clothing and conduct, as in postwar Aceh. Another recent development is the expansion in private military and security companies (PMSCs)[11] to protect private, business, and even government premises and personnel. They are of particular concern since there are neither accepted regulatory standards with regard to their treatment of women/girls, nor structures within which to hold them accountable (Higate 2009).

What conclusions can be drawn from this section on democratic transitions and postwar politics? We find that political transformations in the postwar context have the potential to be transformative for women, but that this "transformation" cannot be assumed to be uniformly positive. Historically, one defining characteristic of high-level politics is as "men's business." Even if women succeed in breaching this in the first postwar phase, they have gender-specific obstacles to confront. From Northern Ireland to Central America, from South Africa to East Timor and Iraq, female political representatives recount being belittled, sexually harassed, patronized, or even threatened with violence. In addition, their male colleagues consider that *anything* related to "women's business" can be allocated to their female colleagues. Despite these constraints, many have battled on and even achieved the highest political office, such as Presidents Michelle Bachelet of Chile and Ellen Johnson Sirleaf of Liberia, and important government positions, such as Esperança Bias, the minister for mineral resources in Mozambique. When taking a longer view, however, it is noticeable how many Mozambican women who were elected in the 1994 postwar election have decided not to stand in subsequent elections. They attribute this at least in part to their unwillingness to face the "gender barrage" of difficulties outlined above (Jacobson 2008). In place of formal politics, women of this generation are investing their energies into civil society organizations (CSOs) or may have even withdrawn, exhausted, from any form of public life.

In view of this, it is appropriate to switch our focus to CSOs, which fall outside formal government structures but are integral to facilitating a longer-term transition from conflict. CSOs include a huge range of initiatives, from village associations working with former child soldiers to national- and international-level organizations of jurists and other specialists. For reasons of length, the final section of this chapter will first focus on just one aspect, civil society initiatives for transitional justice. It will then conclude with an example of everyday experiences of transformation toward what might reasonably be considered a "post-conflict" society.

Justice or gendered silences? The role of truth commissions

The last decade has seen unprecedented progress in the construction of an international legal framework for the criminalization and prosecution of gender-based crimes perpetrated against women and girls during armed conflict or state repression.[12] The visibility of gender-based violence in recent decades, especially sexual violence, is now an important part of the legacy of international criminal law. Rape is included in the definitions of a "grave breach" of the Geneva Conventions, of crimes against humanity, and of genocide. Sexual slavery, rape, forced prostitution, forced pregnancy, and forced sterilization and other forms of sexual violence are listed as war crimes and as crimes against humanity in the Rome Statute of the International Criminal Court. There have also been significant changes in the rules and procedures for prosecuting gender crimes in international criminal tribunals, including for the protection of female witnesses. Thus even with delays and failings in the actual operation of international law, there is reason to believe that there have been significant moves toward gender justice in the field of international justice institutions. However, this is only a part of the picture. There is a large field of processes at the regional, national, and sub-national level that are attempting to grapple with the legacy of war, internal conflict, and oppression. Broadly speaking, these can be classified as "transitional justice mechanisms."

One major element of transitional justice is the variety of "Truth and Reconciliation Commissions" as carried out in individual postwar countries. These commissions share some essential features: they have been established by civil society actors, rather than the postwar state or by an international body; they do not rely on processes of indictment, formal prosecution, and defense; they are attempting to deliver forms of justice that are appropriate to a deeply damaged society and which make a collective contribution to a long-term project of social recovery. How have these bodies approached the issue of gender justice? The Gender and Reparations Project (GRP) of the International Center for Transitional Justice (ICTJ) has stated (in 2007) that "the difference that gender should make when conceptualizing, designing, or implementing reparations has been practically absent until now . . ." (Rubio-Marin 2007a, p. 23). This is a startling claim, but it is substantiated by empirical studies of formal reparative processes across three continents, including in South Africa, Rwanda, Sierra Leone, Guatemala, Peru, and East Timor (Rubio-Marin 2007b).

One of the most consistent findings across all these contexts was that women's voices (across all age groups and classes) were only heard in relation to the suffering of males – husbands, sons, brothers, or other kin. Even with incontrovertible evidence of consistent sexual violence, sometimes carried out deliberately in public, women's experiences remained "un-named." The reasons for this silence are complex, but in a further study the GRP concludes, "In some cases, individual victims [of sexual violence] may be treated with sympathy, but still be considered irretrievably 'damaged.' More commonly, there is a process in which social stigma is transferred from (male) perpetrators to victims. In particular, in some societies women/girls can be stigmatized as 'unmarriageable' within their communities" (Duggan & Jacobson 2009, p. 128). It is clear, therefore, that any long-term progress toward postwar sustainable justice will require much more substantial investment in achieving a gendered framework.

This chapter now arrives at the final section, which attempts to relate the gendered experience of war and postwar conditions more closely to individual social lives of women and men. In order to do so, it has to explore the notion of "backlash."

Toward "post-conflict" social transformation: confronting backlash

The concept of "backlash" against women in postwar contexts crosscuts the entire social spectrum. What happens when men who have had power through their command of weapons have to reintegrate into everyday life? As noted at the outset of this chapter, the conventional representation of the "happy return" with the soldier thankfully embracing his wife and children, has always been problematic. In recent conflicts, the lived experiences of women and men increasingly challenge this idealized picture (see Text Box 10.5). For example, after the Dayton Peace Agreement ended the war in the former Yugoslavia, women's organizations in the successor states of Serbia and Croatia reported a marked increase in domestic violence against women

Box 10.5 Returning to normal life or encountering backlash?

In a comprehensive survey of gender relations in postwar societies, Donna Pankhurst sets out the tensions between contested visions of what constitutes "normal" gender relationships. She observes: "The post-conflict environment cannot be characterized as one in which life for women invariably returns to 'normal' – even if a return to previous patterns of gender and social relationships, as if no war had occurred, were desirable or even possible" (Pankhurst 2008a, p. 3). The upheaval of war is bound to have had an impact on gender relations, especially where women have, for whatever reasons, taken on new roles and responsibilities. As a result, she states "women not only face a continuation of some of the aggression they endured during the war, but may also face new forms of violence. . . . Together, the continued and new forms of violence, and the attacks on women's newly assumed rights and behaviours, constitute what frequently amounts to a post-war backlash against women." (Pankhurst 2008a, p. 3).

carried out by demobilized soldiers and paramilitaries, sometimes using small arms retained from the war. It came to be known as "9:00 pm violence," since the attacks followed the 9:00 pm television news which covered the dismantling of the former militaries and paramilitiaries under the auspices of UN peacekeeping troops. Women's organizations in sub-Saharan Africa, the Pacific region, and Latin and Central America have demonstrated comparable patterns of postwar domestic violence.

Can we posit some direct and causal relationship between the postwar context, the reconstruction of social relationships, and increased violence from ex-military husbands or partners, sometimes leading to fatalities? Some feminist scholars have averred that the postwar period is just one more phase in an ongoing "war on women" (Kelly 2000). However, this author believes that such a broad claim is not sustainable. At the same time, it *is* becoming increasingly evident from the literature on postwar gender relationships that there are huge obstacles arising from deeply embedded patterns of gender relations that may remain relatively unaffected even by sustained periods of war (Pankhurst 2008b).

Although most of the chapter so far has emphasized problems and constraints, it has attempted to avoid suggesting that women are simply helpless victims, devoid of any agency. Even a casual observation of postwar societies demonstrates that women are determined to make a contribution to social transformation in the ways that are feasible and significant for themselves (many of which may be associated with their individual religious beliefs, especially where the church or mosque represents the one stable or safe space.) This determination constitutes peace-building, definable as "activities undertaken over the medium and long term to address the underlying causes of violent conflict and/or to enhance resilience against risks that violence will result from tensions, provocations or acts by any actors that try to provoke violent conflict" (Byron & Jacobson 2009, no page). Although this type of grassroots activity is not always acknowledged as political, the way in which

Box 10.6 Peace-building in postwar Kosovo[13]

The women's organization Ruka Ruci (Hand in Hand) works on gender equality issues in postwar Kosovo, and encourages Kosovar Albanian and Kosovar Serbian women's organizations to cooperate. One of the communities where Ruka Ruci has had an impact is the village of Priluzje, a Kosovar Serbian village of 3,000 inhabitants. The village is isolated and lacks major services, such as a municipal sewage system. Water and electricity supplies are not reliable. This creates extra work for the women of the village, who are all hampered by limited education and the constraints of traditional society. Due to postwar economic conditions, there is an almost total lack of employment opportunities for their male partners within the village. The women consider that this has exacerbated the situation with regard to domestic violence.

In the past, none of the village inhabitants interacted with Kosovar Albanians in neighboring communities, and, in 2008, there remained a general postwar atmosphere of hostility toward any engagement with cross-community organizations. However, faced with the urgent need to find livelihood opportunities, the women of Serbian background in the village decided to take the risk of engaging with the larger network of post-conflict women's organizations, such as the Kosovo Women's Network. With this help, they were able to set up small-scale income-generating schemes, continue their education, and in general move beyond their traditional "place." The village women recount their experience in 2008, when a group went by taxi to the capital city, Pristina, something they had not dared to do in many years (instead, they would have taken a much longer route to access a Kosovo Serbian city). "We sold our handicrafts and traditional food, such as bread and peppers, in the market," the women recounted, "and were amazed at how much the city had changed and grown since the war." They then planned for ten women to get their driver's licenses in order to further break out of their isolation. They have even dared to hold their meetings in the village café, historically a male preserve.

Relationships within their households are also changing. "We are helping each other, and by doing so, earning some income so we don't have to ask our husbands for money," one of the women observes. "This makes us more independent." They feel that this has had an impact on domestic violence. All these changes have made the women of the village much more open to cooperation with the Kosovar Albanian communities – for example, socializing with other women through the Ruka Ruci network in their area – which would previously have been unthinkable.

It is reasonable to argue, therefore, that at the wider political level, these women are playing an active role in the long-term process of conflict mitigation through their cooperation. During the war, any cooperation with Kosovar Albanian women's organizations would have been unthinkable. Ruka Ruci has also focused on building up a good relationship with the local police and social services. This is contrary to prevailing Albanian Serb opinion which still categorizes any form of cooperation with the Kosovar government as "treachery." All this will contribute to helping to diffuse conflict in the event of an escalation of tensions between the Serb and Albanian populations.

Long-embedded gender relations are beginning to shift. The women were initially afraid of male reactions. "They saw us as a feminist sect. Then we decided to hold our meetings at the cafe where the men usually gathered. After the first shock, they became curious, and began listening. Later they complimented us, and said that we were strong because we knew the law."

women have set about rebuilding their lives so that their children do not have to experience the same horrors is unmistakably transformative. So the picture of women "after" war is complex but by no means solely negative. This can be well illustrated by one final example (see Text Box 10.6).

Conclusion

The violence arising from armed conflict can and does come to an end. Rebels finally come out of the bush, violent ethno-nationalist projects fail (with or without international intervention), oppressive regimes are overthrown, or dictators die in their beds. These endings are experienced by the popula-tion at large with enormous waves of relief and joy, albeit accompanied by deep sadness at the losses experienced. Observation of decades of war in Mozambique from 1983 through to the political settlement of 1992 and post-conflict election of 1994 makes this author cautious about any claims that "men" as a singular category experience less heartfelt relief than "women" about the ending of war. The central concerns remain those posed through-out this volume. The notion of gendered endings, beginnings, and continui-ties should therefore underpin our understanding of what happens "after" war.

QUESTIONS FOR DISCUSSION

1 What do you consider to be the essential elements of a "post-conflict" society?

2 Which of the institutions/agencies in Table 10.1 is most likely to have an impact in terms of changing gender relations in a postwar context? (Remember that this kind of change is not necessarily "progressive"!)

3 What kind of support could be given to female political representatives in postwar governments and who should be responsible for supplying it?

4 How should institutions such as truth commissions ensure that women and girls can voice their concerns in safety and with respect?

SUGGESTIONS FOR FURTHER READING

Online resources: examples of gray literature

There are important distinctions between the kind of gray literature that is at least aiming at a gender analysis, and those that are primarily just "adding women" or are even gender-blind. Priority should therefore be given to those kinds of gray literature available via the newly established umbrella organiza-tion, UN Women.

- Other UN agencies have websites on which they post reports on their activi-ties in post-conflict societies and, sometimes, independent evaluations of their work. Among the most relevant are the following: Department of Peacekeeping Operations (UNDPKO); Bureau for Crisis Prevention and Recovery (BCPR) of the United Nations Development Programme (UNDP).

- Major government donor agencies similarly have websites (in various languages) including: Department for International Development (DFID) in the UK; Swedish International Development Agency (Sida); Norwegian Agency for Development Cooperation (NORAD).
- Large nongovernmental organizations (NGOs) operating in post-conflict countries will also generally have their own websites, including the various national branches of Oxfam; Christian Aid; Save the Children; International Alert.

Publications

Afshar, Haleh, and Eade, Deborah (eds.) (2004) *Development, Women, and War: Feminist Perspectives*. Oxford: Oxfam.

Kandiyoti, Deniz (2007) "Political Fiction Meets Gender Myth: Post-Conflict Reconstruction, 'Democratization' and Women's Rights," in Andrea Cornwall, Elizabeth Harrison, and Ann Whitehead (eds.), *Feminisms in Development: Contradictions, Contestations and Challenges*. London: Zed Books.

Meintjes, Sheila, Pillay, Anu, and Turshen, Meredith (eds.) (2001) *The Aftermath: Women in Post-Conflict Transformation*. London: Zed Books.

Pankhurst, Donna (ed.) (2008) *Gendered Peace: Women's Struggles for Post-War Justice and Reconciliation*. New York: Routledge and United Nations Research Institute for Social Development.

Zarkov, Dubravka (ed.) (2008) *Gender, Violent Conflict and Development*. New Delhi: Zubaan/Kali for Women, pp. 191–200.

Notes

CHAPTER 1 WOMEN AND WARS: TOWARD A CONCEPTUAL FRAMEWORK

I wish to thank Malathi de Alwis, Dyan Mazurana, Sandra McEvoy, Laura Sjoberg, and Inger Skjelsbæk for their helpful comments and suggestions on earlier drafts of this chapter. I only regret the limits of my ability to more fully integrate their advice.

1 Enloe, personal communication, 2007. For further discussion of this point, see Enloe (2004, pp. 243–6).
2 See also Peterson (1997).
3 Kimberlé Crenshaw (1991) was influential in introducing the idea of "intersectionality" as a key lens through which to see overlapping structures of power. See also: Collins (2000); Brah and Phoenix (2004); McCall (2005); and Yuval-Davis (2006).
4 This formulation is close to V. Spike Peterson's concept of "triad analytics," which posits "identities, meaning systems, and social practices/institutions as co-constituting dimensions or processes of social reality" (Peterson 2003b, p. 111). On "triad analytics," see also Peterson (2003a).
5 Much of the material in this section is based on Cohn (1993) and Cohn and Ruddick (2004).
6 There are, of course, exceptions to this lack of attention from the northern theorizing and regulating communities – notably the work of the International Action Network on Small Arms (IANSA) and of a small group of scholars. Also, any account of the failure to deal with the proliferation of SALW has to centrally address the vast and varied financial interests served by the unbridled manufacture, licit and illicit trade, and use of SALW. In this instance, the economic motives many actors have for not limiting the availability of SALW can remain unchallenged in part because SALW seem to lack the manly allure that nuclear weapons have for so-called defense intellectuals.
7 See, for example: McClintock (1995); Sinha (1995, 2003); Chowdhry and Nair (2002).
8 The concept of "gendered organizations" has its roots in works on gender and bureaucracy and gendered workplaces by scholars such as Dorothy Smith (1979), Kathy Ferguson (1984), and Cynthia Cockburn (1983). Joan Acker's (1990) paper "Hierarchies, Jobs, Bodies: A Theory of Gendered Organizations" crystallizes the term and becomes the basis for feminist exploration, development, and contestation of the concept since.
9 Cynthia Enloe has alerted us to the gendered dimensions of what counts as "serious" (Enloe 2004, pp. 69–82).
10 This section draws heavily upon Cohn and Ruddick (2004).
11 This is primarily a description of after-effects on societies whose territories have been the site of warfare. But even those societies whose soldiers fight in distant lands suffer related effects. Surviving soldiers may bring home the effects of violence: injured bodies and minds; remorse, rage, and despair; habits of aggression and abuse; syndromes of suffering.

12 For further discussion of what is problematic about the term "postwar" from the perspective of women's experiences, see Chinkin (2003), Meintjes, Pillay, and Turshen (2001), and Jacobson (chapter 10 in this volume).

13 Goldstein (2001) was, until very recently, the sole widely read exception. Of course, among feminist writers and activists there is a much longer tradition of analyzing the ways in which wars are gendered.

14 Cynthia Enloe (1988, 1990, 1993, & 2000) has been a pioneer in showing us militaries' dependence on a wide range of women. See also Kathy Moon (1997).

15 This quote from General Barrow appears in an article by Michael Wright (1982) about the future of the US Marine Corps.

16 The discussion that follows is indebted to Cooper (2002), Duffield (2001), Keen (2008), Mazurana (2005a), Nordstrom (2004), Peterson (2008), Zarkov (2008a).

17 This UN report portrays a far more complex picture of relationships between individuals, governments, armed groups and corporations than can possibly be done justice here, and is well worth reading in full.

18 As in most other wars, men and boys have also been victims of sexual violence in the DRC, although in smaller numbers, and this fact is overlooked or downplayed in most media accounts.

CHAPTER 2   WOMEN AND THE POLITICAL ECONOMY OF WAR

1 A consideration of the new drivers of globalization, such as China and India, will ultimately need to be factored in.

2 Citing McDougall (1998).

3 Useful discussions of this point include Federici (2000), Ferguson (2006), and Marchand and Runyan (2010).

4 See V. Spike Peterson's (2003a) conceptualization of the "reproductive economy."

5 These are tolerated because states come to be complicit and dependent on (il)legitimate forms of transnational economic activities and a neocolonial international division of labor, which is both highly gendered and racialized (Foucault 1995).

6 For an introduction to this literature, see Peterson (1997) and Morgan (2006).

7 See, for example, Baaz and Stern (2009).

8 President Mobutu Sese Seko ruled the DRC for 32 years in the period after it gained independence from Belgium.

CHAPTER 3   SEXUAL VIOLENCE AND WOMEN'S HEALTH IN WAR

1 The degree of and reasons for variation in the prevalence of war-related sexual violence has increasingly received scholarly attention. See, for example: Wood (2006, 2009); Baaz and Stern (2009); Cohen (2010); and Nordås (2011).

2 The topic of war-related sexual violence against men and boys, while outside the scope of this chapter, is an important area of inquiry which has, until recently, received little scholarly or humanitarian attention. While little is known about rates of war-related sexual violence against men and boys, or its lasting psychological and social effects, recent research and news accounts suggest it is far more prevalent than many had assumed. For recent news accounts, see, for example, *Al Jazeera* (2011) and Storr (2011). For scholarly attention to the issue, see, for example: Carpenter (2006b); Sivakumaran (2007); Russell (2008); and Johnson et al. (2010).

3 This material has been adapted from www.womenwarpeace.org/ and www.unwomen.org/ (both last accessed February 2012).

4 For more on the "comfort women", see Hicks (1994) and Sancho (1997).

5 The Geneva Conventions and its Additional Protocols are treatises on the treatment of

civilians, prisoners of war (POWs), injured or sick soldiers and other groups during "all cases of declared war or of any other armed conflict" (Geneva Conventions Article 2 1949). It is most famous for its provisions on the protection of those groups from inhumane treatment, including "attack, execution without judgment, torture, and assaults upon personal dignity" (Geneva Conventions Article 3 1949). For more information and links to the full text of the Conventions and Protocols, see: http://topics.law.cornell.edu/wex/geneva_conventions (accessed February 2012).

6 For more information on the ICTY and ICTR, see Campanaro (2001).

7 The Hague Conventions refer to two international treaties developed in 1899 and 1907. These treaties represent some of the first efforts to develop laws of war and to define war crimes.

8 For transcripts and documentation of all proceedings, see the official website of the ICTR at www. unictr.org.

9 See Gottschall (2004) for a defense of a biosocial explanation for rape during war.

10 See Brownmiller (1975) for a foundational text promulgating this analysis.

11 See, for example, Allen (1996) and Leaning and Gingerich (2004).

12 Charli Carpenter has done extensive research on the plight of such children. For example, see Carpenter (2000 & undated).

13 See, for example, Friedman (1992); Usta, Farver, and Zein (2008); and Annan and Brier (2010).

14 These include the IASC "Guidelines for Gender-based Violence Interventions in Humanitarian Settings," available at: www.humanitarianreform.org/humanitarian-reform/Portals/1/cluster%20approach%20page/clusters%20pages/Gender/tfgender_GBVGuidelines2005.pdf and the WHO, UNFPA, and UNHCR publication "Clinical Management of Rape Survivors," available at: http://whqlibdoc.who.int/publications/2004/924159263X.pdf (accessed February 2012).

15 Pamela DeLargy, fieldwork in Monrovia, Liberia, August 2003.

16 Pamela DeLargy, interview with anonymous woman RUF abductee, Freetown, Sierra Leone, September 14, 2004.

17 Dominique Serrano, unpublished interview, Albania, 1999.

18 See Interagency Standing Committee Guidelines on Management of Gender-based Violence in Humanitarian Settings at www.humanitarianinfo.org/iasc/pageloader.aspx?page=content-subsidi-tf_gender-default.

19 For a discussion of the problems with the court system in the DRC, see Carlsen (2009).

20 Pamela DeLargy, interviews held in Goma, DRC, October 2007.

21 Coupland and Korver (1991) are often cited as the source of this estimate, but their work is not uncontroversial; for example, Murray et al. (2002) have criticized Coupland and Korver for not citing empirical data to support their claim.

22 For this history and for related documentation, see the website for the Interagency Working Group for Reproductive Health in Crises at www. iawg.org.

CHAPTER 4   WOMEN FORCED TO FLEE: REFUGEES AND INTERNALLY DISPLACED PERSONS

1 A video about Halima can be accessed at this website: http://video.nytimes.com/video/2006/11/19/timesselect/1194817120983/halima-needs-your-help.html (accessed February 2012).

2 The language in the 1951 Convention is male-centered, and has remained so since.

3 A good source for information about internal displacement is the website of the Internal Displacement Monitoring Centre: www.internal-displacement.org. For information specifically focused on internally displaced women, look under "Thematic."

4 The United Nations Relief and Works Agency (UNRWA) is responsible for Palestinian refugees, who have experienced the longest protracted situation in the world.

5 In this chapter, I use Enloe's *womenandchildren* (Enloe 1990a) to refer to the way that refugee women are often grouped with children in statistics, in the design of service delivery and in policy making. However, women and children normally have very different needs and identities and it is not useful to group them as if they are one and the same.

6 A modernization framework takes the approach that societies evolve or progress over time from less "civilized" to more "civilized." The latter are usually represented by western market economies of the global North and the former by countries in poor regions of the world. Proponents of this framework take an ahistorical approach that ignores the impact of imperialism and globalization on poor regions of the world and does not admit to the unequal, exploitative interrelationship between the global North and South.

7 The Protection of Refugee Women in the 1980s was discussed in the following places among others: The Intergovernmental Committee for Migration (ICM) in 1983, the 1984 Women in Development (WID) conference at Harvard, the Dutch Refugee Association (DRA) meeting of NGOs, and the UNHCR Roundtable on Refugee Women (Baines 2004, pp. 25, 26).

8 A neoliberal approach espouses economic liberalism towards economic development and "liberty." It is a "free market" approach which includes, for example, the promotion of private property and the freedom of the market to price itself. Opponents of neoliberalism argue that it is exploitative and is linked to the worst aspects of globalization. Inderpal Grewal (2005) argues that "[h]uman rights have become a key mode through which governmental technologies have come into existence through discourses of liberal democracy as a source of freedom" (p. 125).

9 See *Guidelines on the Protection of Refugee Women*, prepared by the Office of the United Nations High Commissioner for Refugees, Geneva, July 1991, available at http://www.unhcr.org/publ/PUBL/3d4f915e4.pdf.

10 Baines (2004) describes attempts to "mainstream gender equality" in the UNHCR as confusing and misleading: "a lack of clarity in the overall strategy to mainstream gender equality contributed to confusion in the field, where 'women's projects and initiatives' continued, often without recognizing new policies on gender mainstreaming" (p. 69). Gender mainstreaming in the UNHCR was instituted in the early 1990s through an approach called "People-Oriented Planning" (POP) by the then Senior Coordinator of Women's Issues (see Hyndman 2000, p. 73n; Baines 2004, p. 44n).

CHAPTER 5   WOMEN AND POLITICAL ACTIVISM IN THE FACE OF WAR AND MILITARIZATION

The authors would like to thank Cynthia Cockburn, Malathi de Alwis, Jill Williams, Ayala Wineman, and Caitlin Lucey for their contributions to this chapter.

1 The questions are derived from the work of feminist theorists who have produced a far richer exploration of "the political" than this brief paragraph can suggest. See, for example, Laclau and Mouffe (1985); Butler (1992, 2004); Butler and Scott (1992); Chatterjee (1997, 2001, & 2004); Menon (2004); Benhabib et al. (1995); Mouffe (2005); de Alwis (2012); Walker (forthcoming).

2 Indeed, it is not only civilian men who enact multiple masculinities, few of which match the aggressive, violent masculinity associated with war making. It is also true that many of the masculinities enacted by men *in* militaries stray far from that image. While some military men are, indeed, engaged in direct combat, wars also require men who, *inter alia*, cook, clean, do clerical work, counsel, heal, maintain equipment, stare at screens all day,

and sit in suits, behind desks, planning and strategizing. On the multiple masculinities required by war making, see, for example, Ruddick (1989); Enloe (1990b, 1993); Cohn (1998). Regarding those men who are involved in direct combat, it has been noted that it takes a tremendous amount of work to get men and boys to be willing to fight in wars – including, *inter alia*, intensive training, drilling, propagandizing; initiation processes aimed at breaking down identities and creating new ones; the creation and maintenance of hierarchical power structures; the creation of small group bonds; gendered taunts; threats, coercion, use of drugs, punishments, and systems of rewards (e.g., Goldstein 2001, p. 253; Whitworth 2008, p. 114). For an extensive, balanced assessment of the debate about the relation between masculinity, aggression, and war, see Goldstein (2001).

3 Carol Cohn's interviews with members of the Mano River Women's Peace Network, between 2001 and 2005.

4 "Preservative love" is Ruddick's term (Ruddick 1989, ch. 3).

5 On militarized motherhood, see Enloe's discussion in *Maneuvers* (2000), with special attention to its valuable and extensive endnotes.

6 For recent comprehensive assessments of the impact of the US War on Terror on women and sexual minorities, see: Scheinin (2009); CHRGJ (2011).

7 See, for example, Jayawardena (1986); Yuval-Davis and Anthias (1989); Yuval-Davis (1997); Pettman (1996); Cockburn (1998); Anand (2010); D'Costa (2010).

8 See, for example, Basu (1993); Menon and Bhasin (1998); Mukta (2000); Butalia (2001); Bacchetta and Power (2002); Alison (2007); Sjoberg and Gentry (2007); McEvoy (2009), as well as chapter 7 in this volume.

9 This quote is from Cynthia Cockburn's interview with a member of Amargi Kadın Akademisi (Cockburn 2007, p. 207).

10 For more on WILPF, see: Berkman (1990); Alonso (1993); Cohn, Kinsella & Gibbings (2004); Cockburn (2007).

11 Women in Black has a very informative website: http://womeninblack.org/. For more on Women in Black in Israel/Palestine and the former Yugoslavia, see also: Zajović (1992); Svirsky (1996); Korac (1998); Shadmi (2000); Mladjenović (2003); Cockburn (2007).

12 IWNAM was formerly known as the East Asia-US-Puerto Rico Women's Network against Militarism. The quotation is from www.genuinesecurity.org/aboutus/index.html. For more on IWNAM, see: Kirk & Okazawa-Rey (1998); Kirk & Francis (2000).

13 Ruth Jacobson, personal observation.

14 Dan Plesch as cited in Fairhall (2006).

15 See notes 7 and 8 above.

CHAPTER 6 WOMEN AND STATE MILITARY FORCES

1 The statistics in this table are adapted from WREI's *Women in the Military: Where They Stand* (6th edn, 2008 and 7th edn, 2010).

2 Jennifer Mathers, personal communication with anonymous female students in British officer training corps, March 2009.

3 Statistics in this table are from WREI's *Women in the Military: Where They Stand* (7th edn, 2010).

CHAPTER 7 WOMEN, GIRLS, AND NON-STATE ARMED OPPOSITION GROUPS

This chapter was written with inputs from co-authors Lucija Bajzer, Lily Bower, Rachel Brown, Hana Cervenka, Kirstin Ellison, Jeremy Harkey, Sara Hellmueller, Lisa Inks, Aya Miyasaka, Rebecca Perlmutter, and Leigh Stefanik. Special thanks to Jeremy Harkey for sharing his primary research data on and analyses of the FARC. Thanks to Cynthia Enloe and

Matteo Tomasini for their reviews of this chapter and to Carol Cohn for her assistance in strengthening the work.

1 Dyan Mazurana, interview with anonymous woman commander from the SPLA, location undisclosed, August 2004.
2 Dyan Mazurana, interview with anonymous woman commander from the CNDD-FDD, location undisclosed, August 2004.
3 Dyan Mazurana, interview with anonymous woman commander of the Widow's Battalion from GAM, location undisclosed, August 2004.
4 The LTTE was founded in 1976, and waged a violent secessionist campaign that evolved into one of the longest-running wars in Asia. The LTTE was militarily defeated in 2009. However, the international network that maintained the insurgency remains intact though heavily fractured with three different leaders located in different parts of the globe vying for sole control.
5 Jeremy Harkey, interview with children's rights organization, location undisclosed, Colombia, July 2010.
6 Jeremy Harkey, interview with children's rights organization, location undisclosed, Colombia, July 2010.
7 While seemingly rare, the FARC is known to sexually assault some women prior to killing them. Jeremy Harkey, personal communication with indigenous rights organization, August 2010.
8 Jeremy Harkey, interview with indigenous rights organization, location undisclosed, Colombia, July 2010.
9 Jeremy Harkey, interview with gender and development organization, location undisclosed, Colombia, July 2010.
10 The AUC is not technically an armed opposition group, as it was originally created by the Colombian government as a militia force to fight the rebels. However, not long after its creation, the AUC began battling both the rebel and Colombian armed forces in a fight over land and territory to control the drug trade.
11 This conclusion owes a great deal to the feminist analysis that Cynthia Enloe (2000) brings to try to understand state militaries. We drew upon key concepts within Enloe's work to help us think smarter about how armed groups attempt to access, wield, and consolidate power.

CHAPTER 8 WOMEN AND PEACE PROCESSES

1 These statements are based on de Alwis's observation of the peace process in Sri Lanka which finally ended in a military resolution in 2009, and various interviews de Alwis conducted in 1999–2006 with international aid workers who had observed peace processes in Africa and Latin America during her research into humanitarianism and displacement.
2 See Abbassi and Lutjens (2002). Social ostracization for participation in armed conflict has not only been experienced in the conflicts of Latin America, such as Colombia, El Salvador, Nicaragua, and Guatemala, but former female combatants in African conflicts have also been treated as social outcasts. Here again, the list is extensive – Sierra Leone, Uganda, Liberia, and so on. See Harsch (2005, p. 17). Also see chapter 9 in this volume for further discussion of this point.
3 See also Sjoberg and Gentry (2007).
4 This video can be viewed on M4P's website: www.mindanaowomen.org/mcw/?page_id=42.
5 Substantial sections of this paragraph are excerpted from de Alwis (2012).
6 Women, too, have mobilized such rhetoric, as in the statement made by Somali peace

activist Asha Hagi Elmi who notes that "as in all conflicts, women and children are the first victims" (as quoted in Fisher-Thompson 2006).

7 *Pray the Devil Back to Hell* (2008) is a film which vividly documents these activities.

8 Sexual violence, in particular rape, was a policy systematically applied by the Guatemalan army as a counterinsurgency strategy at the height of the civil war in the early 1980s.

9 Spivak (2003) seeks to reorient human rights discourses within the UN by pointing out that divisions between elites and subalterns – which cut across race and North–South divides – lead to a certain kind of Social Darwinism where the "fittest must shoulder the burden of righting the wrongs of the unfit," leading to the creation of a top-down power structure (p. 169).

10 This description draws on material including Joya (2009) and Hassan (2010).

11 The terms of reference of the CPC includes UN Security Council Resolutions 1325 and 1820 (Arnado 2011).

12 Edita Tahiri was the foreign minister of the alternative Kosovan political institutions between 1991 and 2000, and the special representative of the Kosovan leader Ibrahim Rugova between 1998 and 2000 (Villellas Ariño 2010, p. 35).

13 Personal communication with Carol Cohn, September 26, 2011.

14 Luz Méndez took part in the debates at the UN ahead of the ratification of Resolution 1325 as witness and actor of the Guatemalan process (Godoy 2010). She was also part of an international group of women activists who met with Burundian peace negotiators to share her insights and experiences, with the support of UNIFEM, in June 2000.

15 Unfortunately, the LTTE refused to allow the government to appoint any Tamil women as part of its delegation.

16 Conversation with Malathi de Alwis, Colombo, Sri Lanka, July 2003.

CHAPTER 9   WOMEN, GIRLS, AND DISARMAMENT, DEMOBILIZATION AND REINTEGRATION (DDR)

This chapter is written with inputs from Lisa Inks, Dmitri Lieders, and Jennifer Marron.

1 This section draws from Dyan Mazurana's previous work and writing for the United Nations Secretary-General (UN 2002a).

2 The descriptions in this table are drawn from UNECHA (2000) and UNDDR (2006b).

3 Mazurana, interview with two national DDR officials in Freetown, Sierra Leone, August 2002.

4 For other stories from WICM, see: Walker (2005) and UNFPA (2005a).

5 Participants came from Angola, Burundi, Democratic Republic of the Congo, Liberia, Rwanda, Sierra Leone, Somalia, Somaliland, South Africa, Sudan, Uganda, and Zimbabwe.

6 List reproduced from Mazurana (2005b, p. 41). Vanessa Farr and Tsjeard Bouta led the group on DDR and were the ones responsible for compiling this list.

CHAPTER 10 WOMEN "AFTER" WARS

1 See Byron and Jacobson (2009) for an example of "gray literature" in the area of gender and conflict that is only available as online publication, as well as the websites at the end of this chapter.

2 This region was also, of course, colonized but has had a much longer period of independent statehood than the countries of sub-Saharan Africa.

3 Please note that this is not a comprehensive list; it is intended to demonstrate some of the multiplicity of institutions and forces in operation.

4 There has been no comparable process in relation to SEA against boys/men to date, although there is no prima facie reason to assert that it does not also occur.

5 For a copy of the full text of the Bulletin, see http://daccess-dds-ny.un.org/doc/UNDOC/GEN/N03/550/40/PDF/N0355040.pdf?OpenElement (accessed September 30, 2011).

6 Statistics from this table are from UNDPKO (2012).

7 It is recognized that there is a major gap in our knowledge of the effects of sexual violence against boys and men. This issue is starting to be addressed by authors such as Dolan (2009).

8 Due to the complexities around "prostitution," the usage of "trafficking" will be reserved for situations that are marked by the use of violence, e.g., kidnapping of women/girls, imprisoning for sexual purposes, smuggling across borders, etc.

9 The material contained in this case study is derived from the author's own fieldwork in Mozambique from 1986 to the current day, supplemented by Joseph Hanlon's extensive work on the impact of IFIs (Hanlon 2003; Hanlon & Smart 2010).

10 Although there may be informal consultative processes, especially with older married women.

11 These companies are often composed of ex-military personnel.

12 This section is largely based on the work of the Gender and Reparations Project of the US-based International Center for Transitional Justice. The ICTJ is acknowledged as one of the lead institutions in this field (see website list).

13 The material contained in this case study is derived from a range of secondary documentation on the organization Ruka Ruci including: www.kvinnatillkvinna.se/en/, www.womensnetwork.org and http://reliefweb.int/node/290323 (accessed over April 2010).

References

Abbassi, Jennifer, and Lutjens, Sheryl L. (2002) *Rereading Women in Latin America and the Caribbean: The Political Economy of Gender*. Lanham, MD: Rowman and Littlefield.

Acker, Joan (1990) "Hierarchies, Jobs, Bodies: The Theory of Gendered Organizations." *Gender and Society* 4(2): 139–58.

Africa Recovery, United Nations (2000) "Burundi: Women Strengthen Peace Talks." *Africa Recovery* 14(2). www.un.org/ecosocdev/geninfo/afrec/subjindx/142wm3. htm (accessed April 15, 2011).

Al-Ali, Nadje Sadig, and Pratt, Nicola (2009) *Women and War in the Middle East*. London: Zed Books.

Alison, Miranda (2003) "Cogs in the Wheel? Women in the Liberation Tigers of Tamil Eelam." *Civil Wars* 6(4): 37–54.

Alison, Miranda (2007) "Wartime Sexual Violence: Women's Human Rights and Questions of Masculinity." *Review of International Studies* 33: 75–90.

Alison, Miranda (2010) *Women and Political Violence: Female Combatants in Ethno-National Conflict*. New York: Routledge.

Al Jazeera (2011) "The Silent Male Victims of Rape," *Al Jazeera*. http://english.aljazee ra.net/programmes/insidestory/2011/07/2011728101626315380.html (accessed October 4, 2011).

Allen, Beverly (1996) *Rape Warfare: The Hidden Genocide in Bosnia-Herzegovina and Croatia*. Minneapolis: University of Minnesota Press.

Alonso, Harriet Hyman (1993) *Peace as a Women's Issue: A History of the U.S. Movement for World Peace and Women's Rights*. Syracuse: Syracuse University Press.

Altinay, Ayşe Gül (2004) *The Myth of the Military-Nation: Militarism, Gender and Education in Turkey*. New York: Palgrave Macmillan.

Anand, Dibyesh (2010) "Nationalism," in Laura J. Shepherd (ed.), *Gender Matters in Global Politics: A Feminist Introduction to International Relations*. New York: Routledge.

Anderlini, Sanam Nagarhi (2000) *Women at the Peace Table: Making a Difference*. United Nations Development Fund for Women, Rwanda. www.unifem.org/materials/ item_detail.php?ProductID=15 (accessed September 22, 2011).

Anderlini, Sanam Naraghi (2007) *Women Building Peace: What They Do, Why It Matters*. London: Lynne Rienner Publishers.

Ann, Adele (1993) *Women Fighters of the Liberation Tigers*. Jaffna: LTTE Publication.

Annan, Jeannie, Blattman, Christopher, Carlson, Khristopher, and Mazurana, Dyan (2008) *The State of Female Youth in Northern Uganda: Findings from the Survey of War Affected Youth: Phase II*. A Report for the United Nations Children's Fund, Uganda. Tufts University, MA: Feinstein International Center.

Annan, Jeannie, and Brier, Moriah (2010) "The Risk of Return: Intimate Partner Violence in Northern Uganda's Armed Conflict." *Social Science and Medicine* 70(1): 152–9.

Aranburu, Xabier Agirre (2010) "Sexual Violence beyond Reasonable Doubt: Using Pattern Evidence and Analysis for International Cases." *Law and Social Inquiry* 35(4): 85–79.

Arnado, Mary Ann (2011) "A Victory for Women, A Reason to Celebrate," *Isis International: we! e-Newsletter.* www.isiswomen.org/index.php?option=com_content&view=article&id=1456:a-victory-for-women-a-reason-to-celebrate&catid=20:intermovements&Itemid=231 (accessed May 7, 2011).

AusAID (2008) Violence against Women in Melanesia and East Timor: Building on Global and Regional Promising Approaches. Canberra: Office of Development Effectiveness, Australian Agency for International Development, www.ausaid.gov.au/publications/pdf/vaw_cs_full_report.pdf (accessed October 5, 2011).

Baaz, Maria Eriksson, and Stern, Maria (2008) "Making Sense of Violence: Voices of Soldiers in the Congo." *Journal of Modern African Studies* 46: 57–86.

Baaz, Maria Eriksson, and Stern, Maria (2009) "Why do Soldiers Rape? Gender, Violence and Sexuality in the Armed Forces in the Congo (DRC)." *International Studies Quarterly* 53(2): 495–518.

Bacchetta, Paola, and Power, Margaret (eds.) (2002) *Right-Wing Women: From Conservatives to Extremists around the World.* New York: Routledge.

Baines, Erin (2004) *Vulnerable Bodies: Gender, the UN and the Global Refugee Crisis.* Aldershot: Ashgate.

Baldauf, Scott, and Mohamed, Ali (2010) "Somalia's Al Shabab Recruits 'Holy Warriors' with $400 Bonus," *Christian Science Monitor Online*, April 15. www.csmonitor.com/World/Africa/2010/0415/Somalia-s-Al-Shabab-recruits-holy-warriors-with-400-bonus (accessed August 18, 2010).

Barkalow, Carol with Raab, Andrea (1990) *In the Men's House.* New York: Poseidon Press.

Barry, Jane (2005) *Rising Up in Response: Women's Rights Activism in Conflict.* Boulder, CO: Urgent Action Fund for Women's Human Rights.

Barth, Elise (2002) "Peace as Disappointment: The Reintegration of Female Soldiers in Post-Conflict Societies: A Comparative Study from Africa." *PRIO Report 3.* International Peace Research Institute, Oslo. www.prio.no/Research-and-Publications/Publication/?oid=157396 (accessed September 2011).

Bastick, Megan, and Valasek, Kristin (eds.) (2008) *Gender and Security Reform Toolkit.* Geneva: Geneva Centre for the Democratic Control of Armed Forces. www.dcaf.ch/Publications/Publication-Detail?lng=en&id=47789 (accessed October 13, 2011).

Basu, Amrita (1993) "Feminism Inverted: The Real Women and Gendered Imagery of Hindu Nationalism." *Bulletin of Concerned Asian Scholars* 25(4): 25–36.

Bayard de Volo, Lorraine (1998) "Drafting Motherhood: Maternal Imagery and Organizations in the United States and Nicaragua," in Lois Ann Lorentzen and Jennifer Turpin (eds.), *The Women and War Reader.* New York: New York University Press, pp. 140–253.

Bayard de Volo, Lorraine (2004) "Mobilizing Mothers for War: Cross-National Framing Strategies in Nicaragua's Contra War." *Gender and Society* 18(6): 715–64.

BBC Monitoring International Reports (2008) "Al-Arabiya TV Discusses 'Phenomenon' of Female Suicide Bombers in Iraq," *BBC Monitoring International Reports*, August 3. www.accessmylibrary.com/article-1G1-188592596/al-arabiya-tv-discusses.html (accessed November 16, 2010).

Bell, Christine (2005) "Women Address the Problems of Peace Agreements," in Radhika Coomaraswamy and Dilrukshi Fonseka (eds.), *Women, Peacemaking and Constitutions*. New Delhi: Women Unlimited.

Benedict, Helen (2009) "The Plight of Women Soldiers," *The Nation* and *National Public Radio*, May 6. www.npr.org/templates/story/story.php?storyId=103844570 (accessed November 16, 2010).

Beneria, Lourdes (2003) *Gender, Development, and Globalization: Economics as if all People Mattered*. New York: Routledge.

Benhabib, Seyla, Butler, Judith, Cornell, Drucilla, and Fraser, Nancy (1995) *Feminist Contentions: A Philosophical Exchange*. London: Routledge.

Berger, Susan (2003) "Guatemaltecas: The Politics of Gender and Democratization," in Susan Eckstein and Timothy P. Wickham-Crowley (eds.), *Struggles for Social Rights in Latin America*. New York: Routledge, pp. 193–208.

Berkeley, Bill (1998) "Judgement Day," *The Washington Post*, October 11.

Berkman, Joyce (1990) "Feminism, War and Peace Politics: The Case of World War I," in Jean Bethke Elshtain and Sheila Tobias (eds.), *Women, Militarism and War: Essays in History, Politics and Social Theory*. Lanham, MD: Rowman and Littlefield, pp. 141–62.

Berko, Anat, and Erez, Edna (2007) "Gender, Palestinian Women and Terrorism: Women's Liberation or Oppression?" *Studies in Conflict and Terrorism* 30(6): 493–519.

Bhattacharyya, Gargi (2008) *Dangerous Brown Men: Exploiting Sex, Violence and Feminism in the War on Terror*. London: Zed Books.

Bird, Kate, and Shinyekwa, Isaac (2003) "Multiple Shocks and Downward Mobility: Learning from the Life Histories of Rural Ugandans." CPRC Working Paper, No. 36. London: Chronic Poverty Research Centre.

Bloom, Mia (2005) "Mother. Daughter. Sister. Bomber." *Bulletin of the Atomic Scientists* 61(6): 54–62.

Boldry, Jennifer, Wood, Wendy, and Kashy, Deborah A. (2001) "Gender Stereotypes and the Evaluation of Men and Women in Military Training." *Journal of Social Issues* 57(4): 689–705.

Bouta, Tsjeard (2005) *Gender and Disarmament, Demobilization and Reintegration: Building Blocs for Dutch Policy*. The Hague: Netherlands Institute of International Relations "Clingendael". www.clingendael.nl/publications/2005/20050300_cru_paper_bouta.pdf (accessed December 21, 2011).

Brah, Avtar, and Phoenix, Ann (2004) "Ain't I a Woman? Revisiting Intersectionality." *Journal of International Women's Studies* 5(3): 75–86.

Brittain, James J. (2010) *Revolutionary Social Change in Colombia: The Origin and Direction of the FARC-EPI*. New York: Pluto Press.

Brooks, Andy (2005) *The Disarmament, Demobilization and Reintegration of Children Associated with the Fighting Forces: Lessons Learned in Sierra Leone*. Dakar: United Nations Children's Fund.

Brown, Melissa T. (2006) "'A Woman in the Army is Still a Woman': Recruiting

Women into the All-Volunteer Force." Paper delivered at the annual conference of the International Studies Association. www.allacademic.com//meta/p_mla_apa_research_citation/1/0/0/9/1/pages100916/p100916-1.php (accessed September 13, 2011).

Brownmiller, Susan (1975) *Against Our Will: Men, Women and Rape*. New York: Ballantine Books.

Bumiller, Elisabeth (2010) "Sex Assault Reports Rise in Military," *The New York Times*, March 16. www.nytimes.com/2010/03/17/us/17assault.html (accessed September 12, 2011).

Bunster, Ximena (1993) "Surviving Beyond Fear: Women and Torture in Latin America," in Marjorie Agosin (ed.), *Surviving Beyond Fear: Women, Children and Human Rights in Latin America*. New York: White Pine Press, pp. 99–125.

Burke, Carol (2004) *Camp All-American, Hanoi Jane and the High and Tight: Gender, Folklore and Changing Military Culture*. Boston: Beacon Press.

Burke, Enid de Silva, Klot, Jennifer, and Bunting, Ikaweba (2001) *Engendering Peace: Reflections on the Burundi Peace Process*. Nairobi: United Nations Development Fund for Women.

Burton, Fred, and Stewart, Scott (2007) "On the Cusp: The Next Wave of Female Suicide Bombers?" *Stratfor Global Intelligence*, September. www.stratfor.com/cusp_next_wave_female_suicide_bombers (accessed December 10, 2009).

Buscher, Dale, and Makinson, Carolyn (2006) "Protection of IDP Women, Children and Youth." *Forced Migration Review*: 15–16. *Women's Refugee Commission*. http://womensrefugeecommission.org/docs/fmr_protection.pdf (accessed June 14, 2011).

Bush, George W. (2001) "Radio Address by Mrs. Bush." *The American Presidency Project*, November 17. www.presidency.ucsb.edu/ws?pid=24992 (accessed December 14, 2011).

Butalia, Urvashi (2000) *The Other Side of Silence: Voices from the Partition of India*. Durham: Duke University Press.

Butalia, Urvashi (2001) "Women and Communal Conflict: New Challenges for the Women's Movement in India," in Caroline O. N. Moser and Fiona C. Clark (eds.), *Victims, Perpetrators or Actors? Gender, Armed Conflict and Political Violence*. London: Zed Books, pp. 99–114.

Butler, Judith (1990) "Performative Acts and Gender Constitution: An Essay in Phenomenology and Feminist Theory," in Sue-Ellen Case (ed.), *Performing Feminisms*. Baltimore: Johns Hopkins University Press, pp. 270–82.

Butler, Judith (1992) "Contingent Foundations: Feminism and the Question of 'Postmodernism,'" in Judith Butler and Joan Scott (eds.), *Feminists Theorise the Political*. New York: Routledge, pp. 3–21.

Butler, Judith (2004) *Precarious Life: The Power of Mourning and Violence*. London: Verso.

Butler, Judith, and Scott, Joan (eds.) (1992) *Feminists Theorise the Political*. London: Routledge.

Byron, Gabriela, and Jacobson, Ruth (2009) "Women and Peacebuilding in the Southern Caucasus." *Sida Evaluation Study 10*. Stockholm: Swedish International Development Agency. Available on request from the author.

Caldicott, Helen (1985) *Missile Envy*. New York: Bantam Books.

Campanaro, Jocelyn (2001) "Women, War, and International Law: The Historical

Treatment of Gender-Based War Crimes." *Georgetown Law Journal* 89(8): 2557–92.

Campbell, D'Ann (1990) "The Regimented Women of World War II," in Jean Bethke Elshtain and Sheila Tobias (eds.), *Women, Militarism and War: Essays in History, Politics and Social Theory*. Lanham, MD: Rowman and Littlefield, pp. 107–220.

Campbell, D'Ann (1993) "Women in Combat: The World War II Experience in the United States, Great Britain, Germany, and the Soviet Union." *The Journal of Military History* 57(2): 301–23.

Carlsen, Erika (2009) "Ra/pe and War in the Democratic Republic of the Congo." *Peace Review* 21(4): 474–83.

Carpenter, R. Charli (undated) *War's Impact on Children Born of Rape and Sexual Exploitation: Physical, Economic and Psychosocial Dimensions*. http://people.umass.edu/charli/childrenbornofwar/Carpenter-WP.pdf (accessed October 6, 2011).

Carpenter, R. Charli (2000) "Surfacing Children: Limitations of Genocidal Rape Discourse." *Human Rights Quarterly* 22(2): 428–77.

Carpenter, R. Charli (2005) "'Women, Children and Other Vulnerable Groups': Gender, Strategic Frames and the Protection of Civilians as a Transnational Issue." *International Studies Quarterly* 49(2): 295–334.

Carpenter, R. Charli (2006a) *"Innocent Women and Children": Gender, Norms and the Protection of Civilians*. Farnham: Ashgate.

Carpenter, R. Charli (2006b) "Recognizing Gender-Based Violence against Civilian Men and Boys in Conflict Situations." *Security Dialogue* 37(1): 83–103.

Chambon, Adrienne (2008) "Befriending Refugee Women: Refracted Knowledge and Shifting Viewpoints," in Maroussia Hajdukowski-Ahmed, Nazilla Khanlou, and Helene Moussa (eds.), *Not Born a Refugee Woman: Contesting Identities, Rethinking Practices*. Oxford: Berghahn Books, pp. 101–12.

Charny, Israel W. (2007) *Fighting Suicide Bombing: A Worldwide Campaign for Life*. Westport, CT: Praeger Security International.

Chase, Cheryl (1998) "Hermaphrodites with Attitude: Mapping the Emergence of Intersex Political Information." *GLQ: A Journal of Lesbian and Gay Studies* 4(2): 189–212.

Chatterjee, Partha (1997) "Beyond the Nation? Or Within?" *Economic and Political Weekly* 32(1–2): 30–4.

Chatterjee, Partha (2001) "On Civil and Political Society in Post-Colonial Democracies," in Sudipta Kaviraj and Sunil Khilnani (eds.), *Civil Society: History and Possibilities*. Cambridge: Cambridge University Press, pp. 165–78.

Chatterjee, Partha (2004) *The Politics of the Governed: Reflections on Popular Politics in Most of the World*. New York: Columbia University Press.

Chenoy, Anuradha M. (2002) *Militarism and Women in South Asia*. New Delhi: Kali for Women.

Chinkin, Christine (2003) *Peace Agreements as a Means for Promoting Gender Equality and Ensuring Participation of Women: A Framework of Model Provisions*. EGM/PEACE/REPORT/2003. Report of the Expert Group Meeting, November 10–13, 2003. Ottawa, Canada: United Nations Division for the Advancement of Women: Office of the Special Adviser on Gender Issues and Advancement of Women and the Department of Political Affairs, New York. www.un.org/womenwatch/daw/egm/peace2003/reports/Finalreport.PDF (accessed November 20, 2010).

Chowdhry, Geeta, and Nair, Sheila (eds.) (2002) *Power, Postcolonialism, and International Relations: Reading Race, Gender, and Class*. London: Routledge.

CHRGJ (2011) *A Decade Lost: Locating Gender in U.S. Counter-Terrorism*. New York: Center for Human Rights and Global Justice, NYU School of Law. www.chrgj.org/pro jects/docs/locatinggender.pdf (accessed January 11, 2012).

Clinton, Hillary Rodham (2009) *Roundtable with NGOs and Activists on Sexual and Gender-Based Violence Issues*, August 11. Goma, Democratic Republic of the Congo. www.state.gov/secretary/rm/2009a/08/127171.htm (accessed October 4, 2011).

Cock, Jacklyn (1994) "Women and the Military: Implications for Demilitarization in the 1990s in South Africa." *Gender and Society* 8(2): 152–69.

Cockburn, Cynthia (1983) *Brothers: Male Dominance and Technological Change*. London: Pluto Press.

Cockburn, Cynthia (1998) *The Space between Us: Negotiating Gender and National Identities in Conflict*. London: Zed Books.

Cockburn, Cynthia (2004) "The Continuum of Violence: A Gender Perspective on War and Peace," in Wenona Giles and Jennifer Hyndman (eds.), *Sites of Violence: Gender and Conflict Zones*. Berkeley: University of California Press, pp. 24–44.

Cockburn, Cynthia (2007) *From Where We Stand: War, Women's Activism and Feminist Analysis*. London: Zed Books.

Cohen, Dara Kay (2010) "Explaining Sexual Violence during Civil War." PhD dissertation, Stanford University.

Cohn, Carol (1987) "Sex and Death in the Rational World of Defense Intellectuals." *Signs* 12(4): 687–718.

Cohn, Carol (1993) "Wars, Wimps, and Women: Talking Gender and Thinking War," in Miriam Cooke and Angela Woollacott (eds.), *Gendering War Talk*. Princeton: Princeton University Press.

Cohn, Carol (1998) "Gays in the Military: Texts and Subtexts," in Marysia Zalewski and Jane Parpart (eds.), *The "Man Question" in International Relations*. Boulder, CO: Westview Press, pp. 129–49.

Cohn, Carol (2002) "Technologies of Terror." Unpublished paper prepared for TACT Symposium, Watson Institute, Brown University, Providence.

Cohn, Carol (2008) "Mainstreaming Gender in UN Security Policy: A Path to Political Transformation?" in Shirin M. Rai and Georgina Waylen (eds.), *Global Governance: Feminist Perspectives*. Basingstoke: Palgrave Macmillan, pp. 185–206.

Cohn, Carol, and Ruddick, Sara (2004) "A Feminist Ethical Perspective on Weapons of Mass Destruction," in Sohail H. Hashmi and Steven P. Lee (eds.), *Ethics and Weapons of Mass Destruction: Religious and Secular Perspectives*. Cambridge: Cambridge University Press, pp. 405–35.

Cohn, Carol, Kinsella, Helen, and Gibbings, Sheri (2004) "Women, Peace and Security: Resolution 1325." *International Feminist Journal of Politics* 6(1): 130–40.

Cohn, Carol, Hill, Felicity, and Ruddick, Sara (2005) "The Relevance of Gender for Eliminating Weapons of Mass Destruction." *Disarmament Diplomacy* 80. www. acronym.org/uk/dd/dd80/80ccfhsr.htm (accessed January 3, 2012).

Collins, Patricia Hill (2000) "Gender, Black Feminism, and Black Political Economy." *The ANNALS of the American Academy of Political Social Science* 568(1): 41–53.

Conaway, Camille Pampell, and Martinez, Salome (2004) *Adding Value: Women's*

Contribution to Reintegration and Reconstruction in El Salvador. Washington, DC: Hunt Alternatives Fund: Women Waging Peace.

Connell, R. W. (1987) *Gender and Power*. Stanford, CA: Stanford University Press.

Cooper, Neil (2002) "State Collapse as Business: The Role of Conflict Trade and the Emerging Control Agenda." *Development and Change* 33(5): 935–55.

Corbett, Sara (2007) "The Women's War," *The New York Times*, March 18. www.nytimes.com/2007/03/18/magazine/18cover.html?scp=2&sq=military%20sexual%20assault%20ptsd%20iraq&st=cse (accessed August 8, 2011).

Correia, Maria (2009) *Disarm, Demobilize, and Reintegrate: Transforming Combatants into Citizens to Consolidate Peace*. Washington, DC: World Bank Institute, http://site resources.worldbank.org/WBI/Resources/213798-1253552326261/do-oct09-corre ia.pdf (accessed October 3, 2011).

Corrin, Chris (2000) *Gender Audit of Reconstruction Programmes in South Eastern Europe*. Boulder, CO: Urgent Action Fund and Women's Commission for Refugee Women and Children.

Coughtry, Sarah Elspeth (2011) "Patriachy and the Trap of Masculinity: A Post-Colonial Analysis of Violence against Sexual Minorities in Uganda." MA thesis, Northampton, MA: Smith College.

Coulter, Chris (2009) *Bush Wives and Girl Soldiers: Women's Lives through War and Peace in Sierra Leone*. Ithaca: Cornell University Press.

Coupland, Robin M., and Korver, Adriaan (1991) "Injuries from Antipersonnel Mines: The Experience of the International Committee of the Red Cross." *British Medical Journal* 303: 1509–12.

Cramer, Christopher (2006) *Civil War Is Not a Stupid Thing: Accounting for Violence in Developing Countries*. London: Hurst.

Crenshaw, Kimberlé (1991) "Mapping the Margins: Intersectionality, Identity Politics, and Violence against Women of Color." *Stanford Law Review* 43(6): 1241–99.

CSMR (2011) *Committee of Soldiers' Mothers of Russia*. Committee of Soldiers' Mothers of Russia, Moscow. www.soldiers-mothers-rus.ru/index_en.html (accessed May 13, 2010).

Cutter, Ana (1998) "Tamil Tigresses: Hindu Martyrs." *Columbia Online*.

Daily Mail (Pakistan) (2009) www.dailymailnews.com/0909/08/FrontPage/ FrontPage5.php

Daley, Patricia (2007) "The Burundi Peace Negotiations: An African Experience of Peace-Making." *Review of African Political Economy* 34(112): 333–52.

D'Amico, Francine (1998) "Feminist Perspectives on Women Warriors," in Lois Ann Lorentzen and Jennifer Turpin (eds.), *The Women and War Reader*. New York: New York University Press, pp. 119–25.

Davis, Karen D. (1997) "Understanding Women's Exit from the Canadian Forces: Implications for Integration?" in Laurie Weinstein and Christie C. White (eds.), *Wives and Warriors: Women and the Military in the United States and Canada*. Westport, CT: Bergin and Garvey, pp. 179–98.

D'Costa, Bina (2010) *Nationbuilding, Gender and War Crimes in South Asia*. New York: Routledge.

De Alwis, Malathi (1998) "Motherhood as a Space of Protest: Women's Political Participation in Contemporary Sri Lanka," in Patricia Jeffery and Amrita Basu (eds.), *Appropriating Gender: Women's Activism and Politicized Religion in South Asia*. London: Routledge, pp. 185–202.

De Alwis, Malathi (2004) "Feminism," in Joan Vincent and David Nugent (eds.), *A Companion to the Anthropology of Politics*. Boston: Blackwell, pp. 121–34.

De Alwis, Malathi (2012) "Feminist Politics and Maternalist Agonism," in Ania Loomba and Ritty A. Lukose (eds.), *South Asian Feminisms*. Durham: Duke University Press, pp. 162–80.

Defensoría del Pueblo de Colombia (2001) *La Niñez en el Conflicto Armado Colombiano: Boletin La Niñez y sus Derechos No. 8*. Geneva: UNICEF. www.unicef.org/colombia/pdf/boletin-8.pdf (accessed August 31, 2010).

Defensoría del Pueblo de Colombia. November (2006) *Caracterización de las Niñas, Niños y Adolescentes Desvinculados de los Grupos Armados Ilegales: Inserción Social y Productive Desde un Dnfoque de Derechos Humanos*. www.unicef.org.co/conocimiento/estudio-defensoria.htm (accessed August 31, 2010).

De Waal, Alex, Klot, Jennifer F., Mahajan, Manjari, et al. (2009) *HIV/AIDS, Security and Conflict: New Realities, New Responses*. AIDS Security and Conflict Initiative (ASCI): Clingendael, The Hague, and Social Science Research Council, Brooklyn. http://asci.researchhub.ssrc.org/HIVAIDS%20Security%20and%20Conflict%20New%20Realities%20New%20Responses.pdf (accessed November 13, 2011).

Diamond, Milton and Sigmundson, H. Keith (1997) "Management of Intersexuality: Guidelines for Dealing with Individuals with Ambiguous Genitalia." www.ukia.co.uk/diamond/diaguide.html (accessed January 4, 2012).

Dickey, Christopher (2005) "Women of Al-Qaeda," *Newsweek Online*, December 12. www.newsweek.com/id/51391 (accessed January 15, 2009).

Disch, Estelle (2000) *Reconstructing Gender: A Multicultural Anthology*, 2nd edn. Mountain View: Mayfield Publishing.

Dolan, Chris (2002) "Collapsing Masculinities and Weak States – A Case Study of Northern Uganda," in Frances Cleaver (ed.), *Masculinities Matter! Men, Gender and Development*. London: Zed Books, pp. 57–83.

Dolan, Chris (2009) *Social Torture: The Case of Northern Uganda, 1986–2006*. New York: Berghahn Books.

Duffield, Mark (2001) *Global Governance and the New Wars: The Merging of Development and Security*. London: Zed Books.

Duffield, Mark (2008) *Development, Security and Unending War: Governing the World of Peoples*. Cambridge: Polity Press.

Duggan, Colleen, and Jacobson, Ruth (2009) "Reparation of Sexual and Reproductive Violence: Moving from Codification to Implementation," in Ruth Rubio-Marin (ed.), *The Gender of Reparations: Unsettling Sexual Hierarchies while Redressing Human Rights Violations*. Cambridge: Cambridge University Press, pp. 121–61.

Dyfan, Isha, Haver, Katherine, and Piccirilli, Kara (2004) *No Women, No Peace: The Importance of Women's Participation to Achieve Peace and Security*. New York: NGO Working Group on Women, Peace and Security. http://womensrefugeecommission.org/docs/ngowgpno.pdf (accessed May 8, 2011).

The Economist (2011) "Violence against Women: War's Overlooked Victims," January 13. www.economist.com/node/17900482 (accessed October 4, 2011).

El-Bushra, Judy (1995) *Thematic Paper 3: Gender Planning in Conflict Situations*. Oxford: Oxford University, Refugee Studies Centre.

El-Bushra, Judy (2008) "Feminism, Gender, and Women's Peace Activism," in Andrea Cornwall, Elizabeth Harrison, and Ann Whitehead (eds.), *Gender Myths and Feminist Fables: The Struggle for Interpretive Power in Gender and Development.* Oxford, UK: Blackwell, pp. 127–44.

El-Bushra, Judy, and Sahl, Ibrahim M. G. (2005) *Cycles of Violence: Gender Relations in Armed Conflict.* Nairobi: Agency for Co-operation and Research in Development.

Electronic Intifada (2010) "Why Violence against Palestinian Women is Widespread," March 17, *The Electronic Intifada.* http://electronicintifada.net/content/why-violence-against-palestinian-women-widespread/8731#.To3SH97iGU9 (accessed October 5, 2011).

Elshtain, Jean Bethke (1987) *Women and War.* Chicago: The University of Chicago Press.

Elson, Diane (ed.) (1991) *Male Bias in the Development Process.* Manchester, UK: Manchester University Press.

Engle, Karen (2005) "Feminism and Its (Dis)contents: Criminalizing Wartime Rape in Bosnia and Herzegovina." *The American Journal of International Law* 99(4): 778–816.

Enloe, Cynthia (1988) *Does Khaki Become You? The Militarization of Women's Lives.* London: Pandora Press.

Enloe, Cynthia (1990a) "Women and Children: Making Feminist Sense of the Persian Gulf Crisis," *The Village Voice*, 25 September.

Enloe, Cynthia (1990b) *Bananas, Beaches, and Bases: Making Feminist Sense of International Politics.* Berkeley: University of California Press.

Enloe, Cynthia (1992) "The Politics of Constructing the American Woman Soldier as a Professionalized 'First Class Citizen': Some Lessons from the Gulf War." *Minerva: Quarterly Report on Women and the Military* 10(1): 14–31.

Enloe, Cynthia (1993) *The Morning After: Sexual Politics and the End of the Cold War.* Berkeley: University of California Press.

Enloe, Cynthia (1994) "Afterword," in Alexandra Stiglmayer (ed.), *Mass Rape: The War against Women in Bosnia-Herzegovina.* Lincoln: University of Nebraska Press, pp. 219–30.

Enloe, Cynthia (2000) *Maneuvers: The International Politics of Militarizing Women's Lives.* Berkeley: University of California Press.

Enloe, Cynthia (2002) "Demilitarization – Or More of the Same? Feminist Questions to Ask in the Post-war Moment," in Cynthia Cockburn and Dubravka Zarkov (eds.), *The Post War Moment: Militaries, Masculinities and International Peacekeeping.* London: Lawrence & Wishart, pp. 22–32.

Enloe, Cynthia (2004) *The Curious Feminist: Searching for Women in a New Age of Empire.* Berkeley: University of California Press.

Enloe, Cynthia (2007) *Globalization and Militarism: Feminists Make the Link.* Lanham, MD: Rowman and Littlefield.

Enloe, Cynthia (2010) *Nimo's War, Emma's War: Making Feminist Sense of the Iraq War.* Berkeley: University of California Press.

Fairhall, David (2006) *Common Ground: The Story of Greenham.* London: I.B. Tauris, p. 199.

Farr, Vanessa (2002) *Gendering Demilitarization as a Peacebuilding Tool.* Bonn: Bonn International Center for Conversion.

Farr, Vanessa, Myrttinen, Henri, and Schnabel, Albrecht (eds.) (2009) *Sexed Pistols: The Gendered Impacts of Small Arms and Light Weapons*. Tokyo: United Nations University Press.

Fausto-Sterling, Anne (2000) *Sexing the Body: Gender Politics and the Construction of Sexuality*. New York: Basic Books.

Federici, Silvia (2000) "War, Globalization and Reproduction." *Peace and Change* 25(2): 153–65.

Feinman, Ilene Rose (2000) *Citizenship Rites: Feminist Soldiers and Feminist Antimilitarists*. New York: New York University Press.

Ferguson, James (2006) *Global Shadows: Africa in the Neoliberal World Order*. Durham: Duke University Press.

Ferguson, Kathy E. (1984) *The Feminist Case against Bureaucracy*. Philadelphia: Temple University Press.

Ferris, Elizabeth (2008) "Protracted Refugee Situations, Human Rights and Civil Society," in Gil Loescher, James Milner, Edward Newman, and Gary Troeller (eds.), *Protracted Refugee Situations: Political, Human Rights and Security Implications*. Tokyo: United Nations University Press, pp. 85–107.

Finnström, Sverker (2008) *Living with Bad Surroundings: War, History, and Everyday Moments in Northern Uganda*. Durham: Duke University Press.

Fisher, Siobhán K. (1996) "Occupation of the Womb: Forced Impregnation as Genocide." *Duke Law Journal* 46(1): 91–133.

Fisher-Thompson, Jim (2006) "Somali Women Hope to Affect Khartoum Peace Talks," *The Washington File*, October 16. www.america.gov/st/washfile-english/2006/October/200610161651141EJrehsiF0.1500208.html (accessed April 9, 2011).

Forest, James F. (ed.) (2006) *The Making of a Terrorist: Recruitment, Training, and Root Causes*. Westport, CT: Praeger Security International.

Foucault, Michel (1995) *Discipline and Punish: The Birth of the Prison*, 2nd edn. New York: Random House.

Fried, Norman (2008) "Female Suicide Bombers in Iraq: The Effect on the Survivors," *Encyclopedia Britannica Blog*, July 11. www.britannica.com/blogs/2008/07/female-suicide-bombers-in-iraq-the-effect-on-the-survivors (accessed November 19, 2010).

Friedman, Amy R. (1992). "Rape and Domestic Violence: The Experience of Refugee Women." *Women and Therapy* 13(1–2): 65–78.

Fukuyama, Francis (1998) "Women and the Evolution of World Politics." *Foreign Affairs* 77(5): 24–40.

Global Justice Center (2010) "The Right to an Abortion for Girls and Women Raped in Armed Conflict – States' Positive Obligations to Provide Non-Discriminatory Medical Care under the Geneva Conventions." New York: Global Justice Center. http://globaljusticecenter.net/publications/Reports/GJCbrief-final.pdf (accessed November 13, 2011).

Godoy, Julio (2010) "Guatemala: Crude Awakening in the Cradle of Resolution 1325: Interview with Luz Méndez," *Visionews*. www.visionews.net/guatemala-crude-awakening-in-the-cradle-of-resolution-1325/ (accessed April 16, 2011).

Goldstein, Joshua (2001) *War and Gender: How Gender Shapes the War System and Vice Versa*. Cambridge: Cambridge University Press.

Gottschall, Jonathan (2004) "Explaining Wartime Rape." *Journal of Sex Research* 41(2): 129–36.

Graeff-Wassink, Maria (1994) "The Militarization of Women and 'Feminism' in Libya," in Elisabetta Addis, Valeria E. Russo, and Lorenza Sebesta (eds.), *Women Soldiers: Images and Realities*. New York: St. Martin's Press, pp. 37–49

Grayzel, Susan R. (2002) *Women and the First World War*. New York: Longman.

Greenberg, Marcia E., and Zuckerman, Elaine (2009) *The Gender Dimensions of Post-Conflict Reconstruction: The Challenges in Development Aid*. Washington, DC: Gender Action, www.genderaction.org/images/GenderDimensionsPCR_2009.pdf (accessed October 3, 2011).

Grewal, Inderpal (2005) "Women's Rights as Human Rights: The Transnational Production of Global Feminist Subjects," in *Transnational America: Feminisms, Diasporas, Neoliberalisms*. Durham: Duke University Press, pp. 121–57.

Guy, Samantha, Austin, Judy, Lee-Jones, Louise, McGinn, Therese, and Schlechte, Jennifer (2008) "Reproductive Health: A Right for Refugees and Internally Displaced Persons." *Reproductive Health Matters* 16(31): 10–21.

Hadid, Dina (2008) "3 Female Bombers in Weeks Raises Concerns that Al-Qaida is Trying to Recruit More Women," *The Associated Press*, January 4. LexisNexis Academic (accessed November 18, 2010).

Hadjipavlou, Maria (2006) "No Permission to Cross: Cypriot Women's Dialogue across the Divide." *Gender, Place and Culture* 13(4): 329–51.

Hagen, Kristen, and Yohani, Sophie C. (2010) "The Nature and Psychosocial Consequences of War Rape for Individuals and Communities." *International Journal of Psychological Studies* 2(2): 14–25.

Hale, Sondra (2001) "Liberated but Not Free: Women in Post-War Eritrea," in Sheila Meintjes, Anu Pillay, and Meredith Turshen (eds.), *The Aftermath: Women in Post-Conflict Transformation*. London: Zed Books, pp. 122–41.

Hanlon, Joseph (2003) *Peace Without Profit: How the IMF Blocks Re-building in Mozambique*. African Issues Series. London: James Currey.

Hanlon, Joseph, and Smart, Teresa (2010) *Do Bicycles Equal Development in Mozambique?* Rochester, NY: Boydell and Brewer.

Hansen, Stig J. (2008) "Misspent Youth: Somalia's Shabab Insurgents." *Jane's Intelligence Review*, September. http://jir.janes.com.

Harsch, Ernest (2005) "Women: Africa's Ignored Combatants." *Africa Renewal* 19(3): 17. www.un.org/ecosocdev/geninfo/afrec/vol19no3/193women.html (accessed May 5, 2011).

Hartsock, Nancy C. M. (1984) "Masculinity, Citizenship and the Making of War." *Political Science and Politics* 17(2): 198–202.

Hartung, William D., and Moix, Bridget (2000) *Deadly Legacy: US Arms to Africa and the Congo War*. New York: World Policy Institute: Arms Trade Resource Center, www.worldpolicy.org/projects/arms/reports/congo.htm (accessed November 20, 2010).

Hassan, Palwasha (2010) *Afghan Peace Jirga: Ensuring that Women are at the Peace Table*. Washington, DC: United States Institute of Peace, www.usip.org/publications/the-afghan-peace-jirga-ensuring-women-are-the-peace-table (accessed May 7, 2011).

Hayden, Robert M. (2000) "Rape and Rape Avoidance in Ethno-National Conflicts: Sexual Violence in Liminalized States."*American Anthropologist* 102(1): 27–41.

Hayward, Lynda, Hajdukowski-Ahmed, Maroussia, Ploeg, Jenny, and Trollope-Kumar,

Karen (2008) "We Want to Talk, They Give Us Pills: Identity and Mental Health of Refugee Women from Sudan," in Maroussia Hajdukowski-Ahmed, Nazilla Khanlou, and Helene Moussa (eds.), *Not Born a Refugee Woman: Contesting Identities, Rethinking Practices*. New York: Berghahn Books, pp. 196–214.

Henkel, Heiko, and Stirrat, Roderick (2001) "Participation as Spiritual Duty; Empowerment as Secular Subjection," in Bill Cooke and Uma Kothari (eds.), *Participation: The New Tyranny*. London: Zed Books, pp. 168–84.

Henry, Nicola (2010) "The Impossibility of Bearing Witness: Wartime Rape and the Promise of Justice." *Violence Against Women* 16(10): 1098–119.

Herbert, Melissa S. (1998) *Camouflage Isn't Only for Combat*. New York: New York University Press.

Herrera, Natalia, and Porch, Douglas (2008) "'Like Going to a Fiesta': The Role of Female Fighters in Colombia's FARC-EP." *Small Wars and Insurgencies* 19(4): 609–28.

Hicks, George (1994) *The Comfort Women: Japan's Brutal Regime of Enforced Prostitution in the Second World War*. New York: W. W. Norton.

Hider, James (2008) "Girl of 13 Becomes Youngest Suicide Bomber in Day of Carnage," *The Times*, November 11. www.timesonline.co.uk/tol/news/world/middle_east/article5126873.ece (accessed January 2, 2010).

Higate, Paul (2009) "Private Military Security Companies and the Problem of Men and Masculinities." Paper presented at the annual meeting of the ISA's 50th Annual Convention "Exploring the Past, Anticipating the Future," February 15–18, 2009, New York. www/allacademic.com/meta/p314176_index.html (accessed November 15, 2010).

Higate, Paul, and Henry, Marsha (2009) *Insecure Spaces: Peacekeeping, Power and Performance in Haiti, Kosovo and Liberia*. London: Zed Books.

Hobfoll, Stevan E., et al. (2007) "Five Essential Elements of Immediate and Mid-Term Mass Trauma Intervention: Empirical Evidence." *Psychiatry* 70(4): 283–315.

Hobson, Matt (2005) *Forgotten Casualties of War: Girls in Armed Conflict*. London: Save the Children.

Hooper, Charlotte (1998) *Manly States: Masculinities, International Relations and Gender Politics*. New York: Columbia University Press.

HRW (2003) *"We'll Kill You If You Cry": Sexual Violence in the Sierra Leone Conflict*. New York: Human Rights Watch. www.hrw.org/sites/default/files/reports/sierleon0103.pdf (accessed October 1, 2011)

HRW (2010) *"They Own the People": The Ampatuans, State-Backed Militias, and Killings in the Southern Philippines*. New York: Human Rights Watch.

Hu, Hua-ling (2000). *American Goddess at the Rape of Nanking: The Courage of Minnie Vautrin*. Carbondale, IL: Southern Illinois University Press.

Hughes, Donna M., Chon, Katherine Y., and Ellerman, Derek P. (2007) "Modern-Day Comfort Women: The U.S. Military, Transnational Crime and the Trafficking of Women." *Violence against Women* 13(9): 901–22.

Hyndman, Jennifer (2000) *Managing Displacement: Refugees and the Politics of Displacement*. Minneapolis: University of Minnesota Press.

Hyndman, Jennifer (2011) *Dual Disasters: Humanitarian Aid after the 2004 Tsunami*. Sterling: Kumarian Press.

Hyndman, Jennifer, and de Alwis, Malathi (2003) "Beyond Gender: Towards a

Feminist Analysis of Humanitarianism and Development in Sri Lanka." *Women's Studies Quarterly* 4(3–4): 212–26.

IAWG (2010) *Inter-Agency Field Manual on Reproductive Health in Humanitarian Settings*. Inter-Agency Working Group on Reproductive Health in Crises. www.iawg.net/IAFM%202010.pdf (accessed January 17, 2012).

IDMC (2006a) *Global Overview of Trends and Developments in 2006*. Geneva: Norwegian Refugee Council: Internal Displacement Monitoring Centre. www.internal-displacement.org/8025708F004BE3B1/(httpInfoFiles)/9251510E3E5B6FC3C12572BF0029C267/$file/Global_Overview_2006.pdf (accessed November 20, 2010).

IDMC (2006b) *Internally Displaced Women*. Geneva: Norwegian Refugee Council: Internal Displacement Monitoring Centre. www.internal-displacement.org/8025708F004D404D/(httpPages)/953DF04611AD1A88802570A10046397B? (accessed November 20, 2010).

IDMC (2008) *Global IDP Estimates (1990–2007)*. Geneva: Norwegian Refugee Council: Internal Displacement Monitoring Centre. www.internal-displacement.org/8025708F004CE90B/%28httpPages%29/10C43F54DA2C34A7C12573A1004EF9FF?OpenDocument&count=1000 (accessed November 15, 2010).

IDMC (2010) *Global Estimates for IDPs 1990–2010*. Geneva: Internal Displacement Monitoring Centre. www.internal-displacement.org/8025708F004CE90B/(httpPages)/22FB1D4E2B196DAA802570BB005E787C?OpenDocument (accessed April 22, 2011).

Indra, Doreen (ed.) (1999) *Engendering Forced Migration: Theory and Practice*. New York: Berghahn Books.

International Alert (2006) *Local Business, Local Peace: The Peace Building Potential of the Domestic Private Sector. Case Study: Burundi*. London: International Alert. www.international-alert.org/sites/default/files/publications/13_section_2_Burundi.pdf, (accessed September 16, 2011).

International Women's Mission to the North East of Sri Lanka (2003) "Women's Concerns and the Peace Process. Recommendations, October 12–17, 2002," *Lines Magazine*. http://issues.lines-magazine.org/indexfeb03.htm (accessed April 25, 2011).

IRB (1996) *Women Refugee Claimants Fearing Gender-Related Persecution*. Ottawa: Immigration and Refugee Board of Canada.

Itto, Ann (2006) "Guests at the Table? The Role of Women in Peace Processes." *Accord* 18. www.c-r.org/accord-article/guests-table-role-women-peace-processes (accessed March 1, 2012).

Jacobs, Susie (2010) *Gender and Agrarian Reform*. Abingdon, UK: Routledge.

Jacobson, Ruth (2000) "Women and Peace in Northern Ireland: A Complicated Relationship," in Susie Jacobs, Ruth Jacobson, and Jennifer Marchbank (eds.), *States of Conflict: Gender, Violence and Resistance*. London: Zed Books, pp. 179–99.

Jacobson, Ruth (2005) "Gender, War, and Peace in Mozambique and Angola: Advances and Absences," in Dyan Mazurana, Angela Raven-Roberts, and Jane Parpart (eds.), *Gender, Conflict, and Peacekeeping*. Oxford: Rowman and Littlefield, pp. 134–49.

Jacobson, Ruth (2008) "Gender, Development and Conflict in Mozambique: Lessons of a 'Success' Story," in Dubravka Zarkov (ed.), *Gender, Violent Conflict and Development*. New Delhi: Zubaan/Kali for Women.

Jacoby, Tami Amanda (2010) "Fighting in the Feminine: The Dilemmas of Combat Women in Israel," in Laura Sjoberg and Sandra Via (eds.), *Gender, War, and Militarism: Feminist Perspectives*. Santa Barbara, CA: Praeger, pp. 155–92.

Jaggar, Allison M. (2005) "Arenas of Citizenship: Civil Society, State and the Global Order." *International Feminist Journal of Politics* 7(1): 4–7.

Jansen, Golie G. (2006) "Gender and War: The Effects of Armed Conflict on Women's Health and Mental Health." *Affilia* 21(2): 134–45.

Jansz, Frederica (1998) "Why Do They Blow Themselves Up?" *The Sunday Times*, March 15. http://sundaytimes.lk/980315/plus4.html (accessed November 20, 2010).

Jayawardena, Kumari (1986) *Feminism and Nationalism in the Third World*. London: Zed Books.

Jeffery, Patricia, and Basu, Amrita (eds.) (1998) *Appropriating Gender: Women's Activism and Politicized Religion in South Asia*. New York: Routledge.

Jeffreys, Sheila (2007) "Double Jeopardy: Women, the U.S. Military and the War in Iraq." *Women's Studies International Forum* 30(1):16–25.

Jenkins, Robert (2001) "Mistaking 'Governance' for 'Politics': Foreign Aid, Democracy, and the Construction of Civil Society," in Sudipta Kaviraj and Sunil Khilnani (eds.), *Civil Society: History and Possibilities*. Cambridge: Cambridge University Press, pp. 250–68.

Johnson, Kirsten, Scott, Jennifer, Rughita, Bigy, Kisielewski, Michael, Asher, Jana, Ong, Ricardo, et al. (2010) Association of Sexual Violence and Human Rights Violations with Physical and Mental Health in Territories of the Eastern Democratic Republic of the Congo. *The Journal of the American Medical Association*. 304(5): 553–62.

Jok, Jok Madut (2001) *War and Slavery in Sudan*. Ethnography of Political Violence Series, Cynthia Keppley Mahmood (series ed.). Philadelphia: University of Pennsylvania Press.

Jong-Hean, Lee (2011) "Downside for N. Korean Women in the Military: Rampant Sexual Abuse," *World Tribune.com*, April 8. www.worldtribune.com/worldtribune/WTARC/2011/ea_nkorea0407_04_08.asp (accessed July 25, 2011).

Jordan, Kim, and Denov, Myriam (2007) "Birds of Freedom? Perspectives on Female Emancipation and Sri Lanka's Liberation Tigers of Tamil Eelam." *Journal of Women's Studies* 9(1): 42–62.

Josse, Evelyne (2010) "'They came with Two Guns': The Consequences of Sexual Violence for the Mental Health of Women in Armed Conflicts." *International Review of the Red Cross* 92(877): 177–95.

Joya, Malalai (2009) "Excerpt: 'A Woman among Warlords,'" *National Public Radio*. www.npr.org/templates/story/story.php?storyId=114207995 (accessed May 8, 2011).

Kaldor, Mary (1999) *New and Old Wars: Organized Violence in a Global Era*. Cambridge: Polity Press.

Kamaruzzaman, Suraiya (2008) "Agents of Change: The Roles of Women in Aceh's Peace Process." *Accord* 20. www.c-r.org/our-work/accord/aceh/women.php (accessed April 10, 2011).

Kandiyoti, Deniz (1991) "Identity and Its Discontents: Women and the Nation." *Millennium: Journal of International* Studies 20(3): 429–43.

Katzenstein, Mary Fainsod (1990) "Feminism within American Institutions: Unobtrusive Mobilization in the 1980s." *Signs* 16(1): 27–54.

Keegan, John (1993) *A History of Warfare*. New York: Knopf.

Keen, David (2008) *Complex Emergencies*. Cambridge: Polity Press.

Kelley, Ninette (1989) "Report on the International Consultation on Refugee Women Geneva, 15–19 November 1988, with Particular Reference to Protection Problems." *International Journal of Refugee Law* 1(2): 233–41.

Kelly, Daniel (2009) "Congo-Kinshasa: US Pledges $17 Million to Aid Rape Survivors," *AllAfrica Global Media*, August 12. http://allafrica.com/stories/200908130504.html (accessed November 20, 2010).

Kelly, Liz (2000) "Wars against Women: Sexual Violence, Sexual Politics and the Militarised State," in Susie Jacobs, Ruth Jacobson, and Jennifer Marchbank (eds.), *States of Conflict: Gender, Violence, and Resistance*. London: Zed Books, pp. 45–65.

Kessler, S. J., and McKenna, W. (1978) *Gender: An Ethnomethodological Approach*. Chicago: University of Chicago Press.

Kingsbury, Alex (2008) "The Rising Number of Female Suicide bombers in Iraq," *US News and World Report*, July 28. www.usnews.com/articles/news/iraq/2008/07/28/the-rising-number-of-female-suicide-bombers-in-iraq.html (accessed November 20, 2010).

Kinsella, Helen M. (2006) "Gendering Grotius: Sex and Sex Difference in Laws of War." *Political Theory* 34(2): 161–91.

Kirk, Gwyn, and Francis, Carolyn Bowen (2000) "Redefining Security: Women Challenge US Military Policy and Practice in East Asia." *Berkeley Women's Law Journal* 229(15): 229–71.

Kirk, Gwyn, and Okazawa-Rey, Margo (1998) "Making Connections: Building an East Asia–US Women's Network against US Militarism," in Lois Ann Lorentzen and Jennifer Turpin (eds.), *The Women and War Reader*. New York: New York University Press, pp. 308–22.

Klot, Jennifer, and DeLargy, Pamela (2007) "Sexual Violence and HIV/AIDS Transmission." *Forced Migration Review* 27: 23–4.

Knight, Mark, and Özerdem, Alpaslan (2004) "Guns, Camps and Cash: Disarmament, Demobilization and Reinsertion of Former Combatants in Transitions from War to Peace." *Journal of Peace Research* 41(4): 499–516.

Kodikara, Chulani (2010) "Article 7: Political Participation and Representation," in Women and Media Collective (ed.), *Sri Lanka Shadow Report to CEDAW*. Columbo, Sri Lanka: Women and Media Collective.

Korac, Maja (1998) *Linking Arms: Women and War in Post-Yugoslav States*. Uppsala: Life and Peace Institute.

Korac, Maja (2003) "Women Organizing against Ethnic Nationalism and War in the Post-Yugoslav States," in Wenona Giles, Malathi de Alwis, Edith Klein, and Neluka Silva (eds.), *Feminists under Fire: Exchanges across War Zones*. Toronto: Between the Lines, pp. 25–33.

Koven, Seth, and Michel, Sonya (eds.) (1993) *Mothers of a New World: Maternalist Politics and the Origins of Welfare States*. New York: Routledge.

Kristof, Nicholas (2006) "The Face of Genocide," *New York Times*, November 19. http://select.nytimes.com/2006/11/19/opinion/19kristof.html (accessed November 20, 2010).

Krog, Antjie (2009). *Begging to be Black*. Cape Town: Random House.

Kronsell, Annica (2005) "Gendered Practices in Institutions of Hegemonic Masculinity." *International Feminist Journal of Politics* 7(2): 280–98.

Kronsell, Annica, and Svedberg, Erika (2001) "The Duty to Protect: Gender in the Swedish Practice of Conscription." *Cooperation and Conflict* 36(2): 153–76.

Laclau, Ernesto, and Mouffe, Chantal (1985) *Hegemony and Socialist Strategy: Towards a Radical Democratic Politics*. London: Verso.

Lautze, Sue (2008) "Social Dynamics in Militarised Livelihood Systems: Evidence from a Study of Ugandan Army Soldiers." *Journal of Eastern African Studies* 2(3): 415–38.

Leaning, Jennifer, and Gingerich, Tara (2004) *The Use of Rape as a Weapon of War in the Conflict in Darfur, Sudan*. Prepared for the Program on Humanitarian Crises and Human Rights. Cambridge, MA: Harvard School of Public Health.

Lehmann, Aimee (2002) "Safe Abortion: A Right for Refugees." *Reproductive Health Matters* 10(19): 151–5.

Lentin, Ronit (1999) "The Rape of the Nation: Women Narrativising Genocide." *Sociological Research Online* 4(2). www.socresonline.org.uk/4/2/lentin.html (accessed October 5, 2011).

Li, Xiaolin (1993) "Chinese Women in the People's Liberation Army: Professionals or Quasi-Professionals?" *Armed Forces and Society* 20(1): 69–83.

Liborakina, Marina (1996) *Women Fight to be Heard in Chechen War Dialogue*. Washington, DC: Resources for Environmental Activists. www.isar.org/pubs/ST/Chechwomen44.html (accessed May 13, 2010).

Loescher, Gil, and Milner, James (2008) "Understanding the Problem of Protracted Refugee Situations," in Gil Loescher, James Milner, Edward Newman, and Gary Troeller (eds.), *Protracted Refugee Situations: Political, Human Rights and Security Implications*. Tokyo: United Nations University Press, pp. 20–42.

Longombe, Ahuka Ona, Claude, Kasereka Masumbuko, and Ruminjo, Joseph (2008) "Fistula and Traumatic Genital Injury from Sexual Violence in a Conflict Setting in Eastern Congo: Case Studies." *Reproductive Health Matters* 16(31): 132–41.

Luciak, Ilja A. (2001) *After the Revolution: Gender and Democracy in El Salvador, Nicaragua and Guatemala*. Baltimore: Johns Hopkins University Press.

Lynn II, John A. (2008) *Women, Armies, and Warfare in Early Modern Europe*. Cambridge: Cambridge University Press.

Mackenzie, Megan (2010) "Securitizing Sex? Toward a Theory of the Utility of Wartime Sexual Violence." *International Feminist Journal of Politics* 12(2): 202–21.

Macklin, Audrey (2004) "Like Oil and Water, with a Match: Militarized Commerce, Armed Conflict, and Security in Sudan." in Wenona Giles and Jennifer Hyndman (eds.), *Sites of Violence: Gender and Conflict Zones*. Berkeley: University of California Press, pp. 75–107.

Mamdani, Mahmood (1996) *Citizen and Subject: Contemporary Africa and the Legacy of Late Colonialism*. Princeton, NJ: Princeton University Press.

Mamdani, Mahmood (2009) *Saviors and Survivors: Darfur, Politics, and the War on Terror*. New York: Pantheon.

Manji, Firoze, and O'Coill, Chris (2002) "The Missionary Position: NGOs and Development in Africa." *International Affairs* 78(3): 567–83.

Marchand, Marianne H., and Runyan, Anne Sisson (eds.) (2010) *Gender and Global Restructuring: Sightings, Sites and Resistances*, 2nd edn. New York: Routledge.

Marshall, Amy D., Panuzio, Jillian, and Taft, Casey T. (2005) "Intimate Partner Violence among Military Veterans and Active Duty Servicemen." *Clinical Psychology Review* 25(7): 862–76.

Martin, Susan, and Callaway, Amber (2008) "The Link between Internal Displacement and Internal Trafficking: Developing a New Framework for Protection." Paper presented at the Conference of the International Association for Forced Migration, Cairo.

MARWOPNET (2005) "History." Mano River Women's Peace Network. www.marwop net.org/history.htm (accessed December 24, 2011).

Mathers, Jennifer G. (2006) "Women, Society and the Military," in Stephen L. Webber and Jennifer G. Mathers (eds.), *Military and Society in Post-Soviet Russia*. Manchester: Manchester University Press and Palgrave Macmillan, pp. 207–27.

Mazurana, Dyan (2004) *Women in Armed Opposition Groups Speak on War, Protection, and Obligations under International Humanitarian and Human Rights Law*. Geneva: Geneva Call and the Program for the Study of International Organization(s).

Mazurana, Dyan (2005a) "Gender and the Consequences of Armed Conflict," in Dyan Mazurana, Angela Raven-Roberts, and Jane Parpart (eds.), *Gender, Conflict, and Peacekeeping*. Oxford: Rowman and Littlefield, pp. 29–42.

Mazurana, Dyan (2005b) *Women in Armed Opposition Groups in Africa and the Promotion of International Humanitarian Law and Human Rights*. Report of a workshop organized in Addis Ababa by Geneva Call and the Program for the Study of International Organization(s), November 23–26, University of Geneva.

Mazurana, Dyan E., and Carlson, Khristopher (2004) *From Combat to Community: Women and Girls of Sierra Leone*. Washington, DC: Women Waging Peace.

Mazurana, Dyan E., McKay, Susan A., Carlson, Khristopher C., and Kasper, Janel (2002) "Girls in Fighting Forces and Groups: Their Recruitment, Participation, Demobilization, and Reintegration." *Peace and Conflict: Journal of Peace Psychology* 8(2): 97–124.

McCabe, Coco (2007) "Ethiopian Women Rediscover Role as Peace Builders," *Oxfam International*. www.oxfam.org/en/programs/development/hafrica/ethiop ia_peacebuilding (accessed May 11, 2011).

McCall, Leslie (2005) "The Complexity of Intersectionality." *Signs* 30(3): 1771–800.

McClintock, Anne (1995) *Imperial Leather: Race, Gender, and Sexuality in the Colonial Context*. New York: Routledge.

McDougall, Gay J. (Special Rapporteur) (1998) *Contemporary Forms of Slavery: Systematic Rape, Sexual Slavery and Slavery-like Practices during Armed Conflict*. E/CN.4/Sub. 2/1998/13. New York: United Nations Economic and Social Council. www.unhchr.ch/huridocda/huridoca.nsf/0/3d25270b5fa3ea998025665f0032f22 0?OpenDocument (accessed October 1, 2011).

McEvoy, Sandra (2009) "Loyalist Women Paramilitaries in Northern Ireland: Beginning a Feminist Conversation about Conflict Resolution." *Security Studies* 18(2): 262–86.

McKay, Susan (2005) "Girls as 'Weapons of Terror' in Northern Uganda and Sierra Leonean Rebel Fighting Forces." *Studies in Conflict and Terrorism* 28(5): 385–97.

McKay, Susan, and Mazurana, Dyan (2004) *Where are the Girls? Girls in Fighting Forces in Northern Uganda, Sierra Leone and Mozambique: Their Lives during and After War*. Montreal: Rights and Democracy.

McKay, Susan, Robinson, Malia, Gonsalves, Maria, and Worthen, Miranda (2006) *Girls Formerly Associated with Fighting Forces and Their Children: Returned and Neglected*. London: Coalition to Stop the Use of Child Soldiers. www.humansecuritygateway.com/documents/CHILDSOLDIER_returnedneglected.pdf (accessed November 20, 2010).

MDRP and UNIFEM (2005) *Taking a Gender-Perspective to Strengthen the Multi-Country Demobilization and Reintegration Program (MDRP) in the Greater Great Lakes Region*. Rwanda: Multi-Country Demobilization and Reintegration Program and United Nations Development Fund for Women. www.mdrp.org/PDFs/MDRP_UNIFEM_Gender_DDR_010207_en.pdf (accessed October 5, 2011).

Meger, Sara (2010) "Rape of the Congo: Understanding Sexual Violence in the Conflict in the Democratic Republic of Congo." *Journal of Contemporary African Studies* 28(2): 119–34.

Mehreteab, Amanuel (2002) *Veteran Combatants Do Not Fade Away: A Comparative Study on Two Demobilization and Reintegration Exercises in Eritrea*. Bonn: Bonn International Center for Conversion.

Meintjes, S., Pillay, A., and Turshen, M. (eds.) (2001) *The Aftermath: Women in Post-Conflict Transformation*. London: Zed Books.

Menon, Nivedita (2004) *Recovering Subversion: Feminist Politics Beyond the Law*. Champaign: University of Illinois Press.

Menon, Ritu, and Bhasin, Kamla (1998) *Borders and Boundaries: Women in India's Partition*. New Delhi: Kali for Women.

Milner, James, and Loescher, Gil (2011) "Responding to Protracted Refugee Situations: Lessons from a Decade of Discussion. Refugee Studies Centre." *Forced Migration Policy Briefing 6*. Oxford: Oxford University Department of International Development. www.rsc.ox.ac.uk/publications/policy-briefings/RSCPB6-RespondingToProtractedRefugeeSituations.pdf (accessed May 19, 2011).

Mladjenović, Lepa (2003) "Women in Black against War (Belgrade)," in Wenona Giles, Malathi de Alwis, Edith Klein, and Neluka Silva (eds.), *Feminists under Fire: Exchanges across War Zones*. Toronto: Between the Lines, pp. 41–4.

Mohanty, Chandra Talpade (1988) "Under Western Eyes: Feminist Scholarship and Colonial Discourses." *Feminist Review* 30: 61–88.

Moon, Katherine H. S. (1997) *Sex among Allies: Military Prostitution in US–Korea Relations*. New York: Columbia University Press, pp. 115–35.

Moore, Brenda L. (1996) "From Underrepresentation to Overrepresentation: African American Women," in Judith Hicks Stiehm (ed.), *It's Our Military, Too! Women and the US Military*. Philadelphia: Temple University Press.

Moore, Jina (2008) "In Africa, Justice for 'Bush Wives.'" *The Christian Science Monitor*, June 10. www.csmonitor.com/World/Africa/2008/0610/p06s01-woaf.html (accessed May 6, 2011).

Morgan, David (2006) "The Crisis of Masculinity," in Kathy Davis, Mary Evans, and Judith Lorber (eds.), *Handbook of Gender and Women's Studies*. London: Sage, pp. 109–24.

Mouffe, Chantal (eds) (2005) *On the Political*. New York: Routledge.

Mpoumou, Doris (2004) "Women's Participation in Peace Negotiations: Discourse in the Democratic Republic of the Congo," in Julie Ballington (ed.), *The Implementation of Quotas: African Experiences*. Stockholm: International Institute for Democracy and Electoral Assistance, pp. 120–3. www.idea.int/africa/upload/women_drc.pdf (accessed November 20, 2010).

Mukta, Parita (2000) "Gender, Community, Nation: The Myth of Innocence," in Susie Jacobs, Ruth Jacobson, and Jennifer Marchbank (eds.), *States of Conflict: Gender, Violence and Resistance*. London: Zed Books, pp. 163–78.

Murray, Christopher, et al. (2002) "Armed Conflict as a Public Health Problem." *British Medical Journal* 324: 346–9. http://gking.harvard.edu/files/armedph.pdf (accessed October 5, 2011).

Nakaya, Sumie (2003) "Women and Gender Equality in Peace Processes: From Women at the Negotiating Table to Postwar Structural Reforms in Guatemala and Somalia." *Global Governance* 9(4): 459–76.

Ness, Cindy D. (2008) "The Name of the Cause: Women's Work in Secular and Religious Terrorism," in Cindy D. Ness (ed.), *Female Terrorism and Militancy: Agency, Utility and Organization*. London: Routledge, pp. 11–36.

Newland, Kathleen (2004) *Seeking Protection: Women in Asylum and Refugee Resettlement Processes*. CM/MMW/2003/EP.8. United Nations Division for the Advancement of Women (DAW) Consultative Meeting on "Migration and Mobility and how this Movement Affects Women", December 2–4, 2003, Malmö, Sweden. www.un.org/womenwatch/daw/meetings/consult/CM-Dec03-EP8.pdf (accessed November 20, 2010).

Nikolić-Restanović, Vesna (1998) "War, Nationalism and Mothers in the Former Yugoslavia," in Lois Ann Lorentzen and Jennifer Turpin (eds.), *The Women and War Reader*. New York: New York University Press, pp. 234–9.

Noakes, Lucy (2006) *Women in the British Army: War and the Gentle Sex 1907–1948*. London: Routledge.

Nordås, Ragnhild (2011) "Sexual Violence in African Conflicts." *CSCW Policy Brief* 1. Centre for the Study of Civil Wars, Peace Research Institute, Oslo (PRIO).

Nordstrom, Carolyn (2004) *Shadows of War: Violence, Power, and International Profiteering in the Twenty-first Century*. Berkeley: University of California Press.

Nusair, Isis (2008) "Gendered, Racialized and Sexualized Torture at Abu Ghraib," in Robin Riley, Chandra Talpade Mohanty, and Minnie Bruce Pratt (eds.), *Feminism and War: Confronting U.S. Imperialsim*. London: Zed Books, pp. 179–83.

Olonisakin, Funmi, Barnes, Karen and Ikpe, Eka (eds.) (2010) *Women, Peace and Security: Translating Policy into Practice*. London: Routledge.

Ortiz, Román D. (2006) "The Human Factor in Insurgency: Recruitment and Training in the Revolution Armed Forces of Colombia (FARC)," in James J. F. Forest (ed.), *The Making of a Terrorist: Recruitment, Training, and Root Causes*. Westport, CT: Praeger Security International.

Pankhurst, Donna (2004) "The 'Sex War' and Other Wars: Towards a Feminist Approach to Peacebuilding," in Haleh Afshar and Deborah Eade (eds.), *Development, Women, and War: Feminist Perspectives*. Oxford: Oxfam, pp. 8–42.

Pankhurst, Donna (2008a) "Introduction: Gendered War and Peace," in Donna Pankhurst (ed.), *Gendered Peace: Women's Struggles for Post-War Justice and Reconciliation*. New York: Routledge and United Nations Research Institute for Social Development.

Pankhurst, Donna (2008b) "Post-War Backlash Violence against Women: What Can 'Masculinity' Explain?" in Donna Pankhurst (ed.), *Gendered Peace: Women's*

Struggles for Post-War Justice and Reconciliation. New York: Routledge and United Nations Research Institute for Social Development.

Pankhurst, Donna (ed.) (2008c) *Gendered Peace: Women's Struggles for Post-War Justice and Reconciliation*. New York: Routledge and United Nations Research Institute for Social Development.

Park, Jennifer (2007) "Sexual Violence as a Weapon of War in International Humanitarian Law." *International Public Policy Review* 1(3): 13–18.

PeaceWomen (2010) "SA Women: Hard Time in Military," *Dispatch Online*, November 24. www.peacewomen.org/news_article.php?id=2454&type=news (accessed July 25, 2011).

Perry, Jennifer (2004) *Small Arms and Light Weapons Disarmament Programs: Challenges, Utility, and Lessons Learned*. Fort Belvoir, VA: Defense Threat Reduction Agency.

Pessin, Al (2009) "US Troops Watch for Female Suicide Bombers in Iraq," *Voice of America Online*, January 5. www.voanews.com/english/2009-01-05-voa50.cfm (accessed January 20, 2009).

Peterson, V. Spike (1997) "Whose Crisis? Early and Post-Modern Masculinism," in Stephen Gill and James H. Mittleman (eds.), *Innovation and Transformation in International Studies*. Cambridge: Cambridge University Press, pp.185–201.

Peterson, V. Spike (1999) "Sexing Political Identities/Nationalism as Heterosexism." *International Feminist Journal of Politics* 1(1): 34–65.

Peterson, V. Spike (2003a) *A Critical Rewriting of Global Political Economy: Integrating Reproductive, Productive and Virtual Economies*. New York: Routledge.

Peterson, V. Spike (2003b) "Shifting Ground(s), Remapping Strategies and Triad Analytics," in Eleonore Kofman and Gillian Youngs (eds.), *Globalization: Theory and Practice*. London: Continuum.

Peterson, V. Spike (2008) "'New Wars' and Gendered Economies." *Feminist Review* 88(1): 7–20.

Peterson, V. Spike, and Runyan, Anne Sisson (2010) *Global Gender Issues in the New Millennium*, 3rd edn. Boulder: Westview Press.

Pettman, Jan Jindy (1996) *Worlding Women: A Feminist International Politics*. New York: Routledge.

Pittaway, Eileen (2008) "The Rohingya Refugees in Bangladesh: A Failure of the International Protection Regime," in Howard Adelman (ed.), *Protracted Displacement in Asia: No Place to Call Home*. Aldershot: Ashgate, pp. 83–106.

Plumper, Thomas, and Neumayer, Eric (2006) "The Unequal Burden of War: The Effect of Armed Conflict on the Gender Gap in Life Expectancy." *International Organization* 60(3): 723–54.

Potter, Antonia (2005) *We the Women: Why Conflict Mediation is Not Just a Job for Men*. Geneva: The Centre for Humanitarian Dialogue.

Potter, Antonia (2008) *Gender Sensitivity: Nicety or Necessity in Peace Process Management?* Geneva: The Centre for Humanitarian Dialogue.

Powell, Sian (2006) "UN Verdict on East Timor," *The Australian*, January 19. www.yale.edu/gsp/east_timor/unverdict.html (accessed October 4, 2011).

Pray the Devil Back to Hell. Film. Directed by Gini Reticker. 2008. Fork Films LLC, New York. DVD.

Puechguirbal, Nadine (2005) "Gender and Peace Building in Africa: Some Analysis of Structural Obstacles," in Dina Rodriguez and Edith Natukunda-Togboa (eds.),

Gender and Peace Building in Africa. San Jose, Costa Rica: University for Peace, pp. 1–12.

Radio Free Asia (2010) *Bangladesh: Rohingya Rejected Again,* April 12. www.unhcr.org/refworld/docid/4c05091526.html (accessed January 17, 2012).

Ramose, Magobe (1999) *African Philosophy through Ubuntu.* Harare: Mond Publishers.

Refugees International (2005) *Must Boys Be Boys? Ending Sexual Exploitation and Abuse in UN Peacekeeping Missions.* Washington, DC: Refugees International, http://refugeesinternational.org/policy/in-depth-report/must-boys-be-boys-ending-sexual-exploitation-abuse-un-peacekeeping-missions (accessed November 20, 2010).

Rehn, Elisabeth, and Sirleaf, Ellen J. (2002) *Women, War and Peace: The Independent Experts' Assessment of Armed Conflict on Women and Women's Role in Peacebuilding.* New York: United Nations Development Fund for Women.

Reno, William (1998) *Warlord Politics and the African States.* Boulder, CO: Lynne Rienner.

Report of the Secretary-General (1992) *An Agenda for Peace: Preventive Diplomacy, Peacemaking and Peace-Keeping.* A/47/277 – S/24111. New York: United Nations. www.un.org/Docs/SG/agpeace.html (accessed September 29, 2011).

Report of the Secretary-General (2000) *The Role of United Nations Peacekeeping in Disarmament, Demobilization and Reintegration.* S/2000/101. New York: United Nations Security Council.

Report of the Secretary-General (2002) *Report of the Secretary-General on Women, Peace and Security.* S/2002/115. New York: United Nations Security Council. http://daccess-dds-ny.un.org/doc/UNDOC/GEN/N02/634/68/PDF/N0263468.pdf?OpenElement (accessed October 5, 2011).

Reuter, Christophe. (2004) *My Life is a Weapon: A Modern History of Suicide Bombing.* Princeton: Princeton University Press.

Richards, Paul (1996) *Fighting for the Rainforest: War, Youth and Resources in Sierra Leone.* Portsmouth: Heinemann Press.

Ricks, Thomas E. (2009) "Women in COIN (II): How to Do it Right." *Foreign Policy,* October 9. http://ricks.foreignpolicy.com/posts/2009/10/09/women_in_coin_ii_how_to_do_it_right (accessed July 25, 2011).

Right Livelihood Award (1996) *Right Livelihood Award: 1996 – CSMR.* Stockholm: Right Livelihood Award. www.rightlivelihood.org/csmr.html (accessed May 13, 2010).

Roy, Arundhati (2001) "The Algebra of Infinite Justice." *The Progressive.* www.progressive.org/node/1713 (accessed December 19, 2011).

Royal Norwegian Ministry of Foreign Affairs. (2003) *First Meeting of the Sub-Committee on Gender Issues (SGI), Held in Kilinochchi,* March 5–6. Press Release. www.peace-in-srilanka.org/negotiations/rng-051 (accessed May 8, 2011).

Rubio-Marin, Ruth (2007a) "Introduction: The Gender of Reparations: Setting the Agenda," in Ruth Rubio-Marin (ed.), *What Happened to the Women? Gender and Reparations for Human Rights Violations.* New York: International Center for Transitional Justice, pp. 20–47.

Rubio-Marin, Ruth (ed.) (2007b) *What Happened to the Women? Gender and Reparations for Human Rights Violations.* New York: International Center for Transitional Justice.

Ruddick, Sara (1989) *Maternal Thinking: Towards a Politics of Peace.* Boston: Beacon Press.

Russell, Wynne (2008) "A Silence Deep as Death: Sexual Violence against Men and Boys in Armed Conflicts." Background paper prepared for OCHA experts' meeting "Use of Sexual Violence in Conflict," New York.

Russo, Ann (2006) "The Feminist Majority Foundation's Campaign to Stop Gender Apartheid: The Intersections of Feminism and Imperialism in the United States." *International Feminist Journal of Politics* 8(4): 557–80.

Salzman, Todd A. (1998) "Rape Camps as a Means of Ethnic Cleansing: Religious, Cultural, and Ethical Responses to Rape Victims in the Former Yugoslavia." *Human Rights Quarterly* 20(2): 348–79.

Sancho, Neila (1997) "'The Comfort Women' System World War II: Asian Women as Targets of Mass Rape and Sexual Slavery by Japan," in Ronit Lentin (ed.), *Gender and Catastrophe*. London: Zed Books, pp. 144–54.

Sangari, Kumkum, Malik, Neeraj, Chhachhi, Sheba, Sarkar, Tanikar et al. (2001) "Why Women Must Reject the Bomb," in Movement in India for Nuclear Disarmament (ed.), *Out of Nuclear Darkness: The Indian Case for Disarmament*. New Delhi: MIND, pp. 47–56.

Santiago, Irene (2011) "The Mindanao Peace Talks: What has Gender Got to do with It?" *PeaceTalks*. Geneva: Centre for Humanitarian Dialogue. http://peacetalks. hdcentre.org/2011/03/the-mindanao-peace-talks-what-has-gender-got-to-do-with-it/ (accessed April 15, 2011).

Sasson-Levy, Orna (2007) "Contradictory Consequences of Mandatory Conscription: The Case of Women Secretaries in the Israeli Military." *Gender and Society* 21(4): 481–507.

Sasson-Levy, Orna, and Amram-Katz, Sarit (2007) "Gender Integration in Israeli Officer Training: Degendering and Regendering the Military." *Signs* 33(1): 105–33.

Schalk, Peter (1994) "Women Fighters of the Liberation Tigers in Tamil īlam: The Martial Feminism of Atēl Palacinkam." *South Asia Research* 14(2): 163–95.

Scheinin, Martin (Special Rapporteur) (2009) *Protection of Human Rights and Fundamental Freedoms while Countering Terrorism*. A/64/211. New York: United Nations General Assembly. www.chrgj.org/projects/docs/A64211.pdf (accessed January 11, 2012).

Scheper-Hughes, Nancy (1992) *Death Without Weeping: The Violence of Everyday Life in Brazil*. Berkeley: University of California Press.

Scheper-Hughes, Nancy (1996) "Maternal Thinking and the Politics of War." *Peace Review* 8(3): 353–8.

Schmidt, Rachel (2007) "No Girls Allowed? Recruitment and Gender in Colombian Armed Groups." *Focal Point* 6(10): 5–7.

Schroeder, Emily (2003) "A Window of Opportunity in the Democratic Republic of the Congo: Incorporating a Gender Perspective in the Disarmament, Demobilization and Reintegration Process." *Peace, Conflict and Development* 5: 1–45.

Scott, Joan (1986) "Gender: A Useful Category of Historical Analysis." *American Historical Review* 91: 1035–75.

Scott, Joan Wallach (1996) *Only Paradoxes to Offer: French Feminists and the Rights of Man*. Cambridge, MA: Harvard University Press.

Secretary-General's Bulletin (2003) *Special Measures for Protection from Sexual Exploitation and Sexual Abuse*. ST/SGB/2003/13. New York: United Nations

Secretariat. http://daccess-dds-ny.un.org/doc/UNDOC/GEN/N03/550/40/PDF/N03/5 5040.pdf?OpenElement (accessed September 30, 2011).

Sewonet, Abraham, and Taouti-Cherif, Ratiba (2004) *Crossing the Border: Demobilization and Reintegration of Rwandan Boys and Girls Associated with Armed Groups in the Democratic Republic of Congo.* Save the Children, UK.

Shadmi, Erella (2000) "Between Resistance and Compliance, Feminism and Nationalism: Women in Black in Israel." *Women's Studies International Forum* 23(1): 23–4.

Shay, Shaul (2004) *The Shahids: Islam and Suicide Attacks.* New Brunswick, NJ: Transaction.

Shephard, Michelle (2008) "Sad End for Young Refugee," *Toronto Star*, December 21. www.thestar.com/article/556919 (accessed September 27, 2011).

Simic, Olivera (2010) "Does the Presence of Women Really Matter? Towards Combating Male Sexual Violence in Peacekeeping Operations." *International Peacekeeping* 17(2): 188–99.

Singh, Shreyasi (2010) "'Women Not Worth the Money,'" *The Diplomat*, February 1. http://the-diplomat.com/2010/02/01/women-not-worth-the-money-2/ (accessed July 25, 2011).

Sinha, Mrinalini (1995) *Colonial Masculinity: the "Manly Englishman" and the "Effeminate Bengali" in the Late Nineteenth Century.* Manchester, UK: Manchester University Press.

Sinha, Mrinalini (2003) "Reconfiguring Hierarchies: The Ilbert Bill Controversy, 1883," in Reina Lewis and Sara Mills (eds.), *Feminist Postcolonial Theory: A Reader.* New York: Routledge, pp. 427–59.

Sivakumaran, Sandesh (2007) "Sexual Violence against Men in Armed Conflict." *European Journal of International Law* 18(2): 253–76.

Sjoberg, Laura (2007) "Agency, Militarized Femininity and Enemy Others: Observations from the War in Iraq." *International Feminist Journal of Politics* 9(1): 82–101.

Sjoberg, Laura, and Gentry, Caron E. (2007) *Mothers, Monsters, Whores: Women's Violence in Global Politics.* London: Zed Books.

Skaine, Rosemarie (2011) *Women in Combat: A Reference Handbook.* Santa Barbara, CA: ABC-CLIO.

Skjelsbæk, Inger, and Tryggestad, Torunn L. (2009) "Women in the Norwegian Armed Forces: Gender Equality or Operational Imperative?" *Minerva Journal of Women and War* 3(2): 34–51.

Slim, Hugo (2008) *Killing Civilians: Method, Madness, and Morality in War.* New York: Columbia University Press.

Smith, Dorothy E. (1979) "A Sociology for Women," in Julia A. Sherman and Evelyn Torten Beck (eds.), *The Prism of Sex: Essays in the Sociology of Knowledge.* Madison: University of Wisconsin Press.

Snyder, R. Claire (1999) *Citizen-Soldiers and Manly Warriors: Military Service and Gender in the Civic Republican Tradition.* Lanham, MD: Rowman and Littlefield.

Solaro, Erin (2006) *Women in the Line of Fire: What You Should Know About Women in the Military.* Emeryville, CA: Seal Press.

Sorensen, Brigitte (1998) *Women and Post-Conflict Reconstruction: Issues and Sources.* WSP Occasional Paper No 3. Geneva: United Nations Research Institute for Social

Development (UNRISD) and Programme for Strategic and International Security Studies (PSIS). www.unrisd.org/unrisd/website/document.nsf/d2a23ad2d50cb2a 280256eb300385855/631060b93ec1119ec1256d120043e600/$FILE/opw3.pdf (accessed May 9, 2011).

Soysa, Champika K. (2011) "Women in Sri Lanka's War: Participants and Peacebuilders." Paper presented at The Consortium on Gender, Security and Human Rights, University of Massachusetts, Boston, April 14, 2011.

Spears, Sally (1998) *Call Sign Revlon: The Life and Death of Navy Fighter Pilot Kara Hultgreen*. Annapolis, MD: Naval Institute Press.

Spivak, Gayatri Chakravorty (1988) "Can the Subaltern Speak?" in Cary Nelson and Lawrence Grossberg (eds.), *Marxism and Interpretation of Culture*. Chicago: University of Illinois Press, pp. 271–316.

Spivak, Gayatri Chakravorty (2003) "Righting Wrongs," in Nicholas Owen (ed.), *Human Rights, Human Wrongs*. Oxford: Oxford University Press.

Stack-O'Conner, Alisa (2007) "Lions, Tigers, and Freedom Birds: How and Why the Liberation Tigers of Tamil Eelam Employs Women." *Terrorism and Political Violence* 19(1): 43–63.

Stanski, Keith (2006) "Terrorism, Gender, and Ideology: A Case Study of Women Who Join the Revolutionary Forces of Colombia (FARC)," in James J. F. Forest (ed.), *The Making of a Terrorist: Recruitment, Training, and Root Causes*. Westport, CT: Praeger Security International.

Stiehm, Judith Hicks (1982) "The Protected, The Protector, The Defender." *Women's Studies International Forum* 5(4): 367–76.

Storr, Will (2011) "The Rape of Men," *The Observer*, July 16. www.guardian.co.uk/ society/2011/jul/17/the-rape-of-men (accessed October 4, 2011).

Svirsky, Gila (1996) *Standing for Peace: A History of Women in Black in Israel*. www.gilas-virsky.com/wib_book.html (accessed January 18, 2012)

Thompson, Carol B. (1999) "Beyond Civil Society: Child Soldiers as Citizens in Mozambique." *Review of African Political Economy* 26(80): 191–206.

Tickner, J. Ann (1992) *Gender in International Relations*. New York: Columbia University Press.

Tickner, J. Ann (1999) "Why Women Can't Run the World: International Politics According to Francis Fukuyama." *International Studies Review* 1(3): 3–11.

Tickner, J. Ann (2001) *Gendering World Politics: Issues and Approaches in the Post-Cold War Era*. New York: Columbia University Press.

UN (1993) *Declaration on the Elimination of Violence against Women*. A/RES/48/104. New York: United Nations. www.un.org/documents/ga/res/48/a48r104.htm (accessed October 1, 2011).

UN (1995) *Platform for Action*. A/CONF/177/20. United Nations Fourth World Conference on Women, Beijing, China. www.un.org/womenwatch/daw/beijing/ platform/plat1.htm (accessed October 1, 2011).

UN (2002a) *Women, Peace and Security*. Study submitted by the United Nations Secretary-General pursuant to Security Council Resolution 1325 (2000). New York: United Nations.

UN (2002b) "Disarmament, Demobilization and Reintegration," in *Women, Peace and Security*. Study submitted by the United Nations Secretary-General pursuant to Security Council Resolution 1325 (2000). New York: United Nations, pp. 129–34.

UNDDR (2006a) *Integrated Disarmament, Demobilization, and Reintegration Standards: Glossary: Terms and Definitions.* New York: United Nations Disarmament, Demobilization and Reintegration. www.unddr.org/iddrs/01/download/IDDRS_120.pdf (accessed October 3, 2011).

UNDDR (2006b) *Integrated Disarmament, Demobilization, and Reintegration Standards: Glossary: Terms and Definitions.* United Nations Disarmament, Demobilization and Reintegration, New York. www.unddr.org/iddrs/framework.php (accessed October 3, 2011).

UNDPKO (1999) *Disarmament, Demobilization and Reintegration of Ex-combatants in a Peacekeeping Environment: Principles and Guidelines.* New York: United Nations Department of Peacekeeping Operations.

UNDPKO (2010) *Ten-year Impact Study on Implementation of UN Security Council Resolution 1325 (2000) on Women, Peace and Security in Peacekeeping.* New York: United Nations Department of Peacekeeping Operations. www.peacewomen.org/assets/file/PWandUN/UNImplementation/Secretariat/DepartmentAndOffices/DPKO/dpko_10yearimpactstudy1325_.pdf (accessed October 10, 2011).

UNDPKO (2011a) *Peacekeeping Fact Sheet.* New York: United Nations Department of Peacekeeping Operations. www.un.org/en/peacekeeping/resources/statistics/factsheet.shtml (accessed September 30, 2011).

UNDPKO (2011b) *UN Peacekeeping Background Note.* New York: United Nations Department of Peacekeeping Operations. www.un.org/en/peacekeeping/documents/backgroundnote.pdf (accessed September 29, 2011).

UNDPKO (2012) *Gender Statistics for the Month of March.* New York: United Nations Department of Peacekeeping. www.un.org/en/peacekeeping/contributors/gender/2012gender/March12.pdf (accessed May 16, 2012).

UNECHA (2000) *Harnessing Institutional Capacities in Support of Disarmament, Demobilization and Reintegration of Former Combatants.* New York: United Nations Executive Committee on Humanitarian Affairs (Working Group on Disarmament, Demobilization, and Reintegration). www.undp.org/cpr/documents/DDR/ECHA_Harnessing%20Institutional%20Capacity%20for%20DDR%20July%202000.pdf (accessed November 20, 2010).

UNESCO (2010) *Violence against Palestinian Women and Girls Fact Sheet: A Summary of Findings* Palestinian Women Research and Documentation Center, UNESCO, West Bank.

UNFPA (2005a) *UNFPA State of World Population 2005: Journalists' Press Kit.* www.unfpa.org/swp/2005/presskit/index.htm (accessed October 3, 2011).

UNFPA (2005b) *Gender-Based Violence in Occupied Palestinian Territory.* New York: United Nations Population Fund. www.unfpa.org/women/docs/gbv_opt.pdf (accessed October 5, 2011).

UNFPA (2005c) *Gender-Based Violence in Timor-Leste.* New York: United Nations Population Fund. www.unfpa.org/women/docs/gbv_timorleste.pdf (accessed October 5, 2011).

UNGA (2005) *Letter Dated 24 March 2005 from the Secretary-General to the President of the General Assembly.* A/59/710. New York: United Nations General Assembly. http://cdu.unlb.org/Portals/0/Documents/KeyDoc5.pdf (accessed October 2, 2011).

UNHCR (undated) *Stateless People – Searching for Citizenship.* Geneva: United Nations

High Commissioner for Refugees. www.unhcr.org/pages/49c3646c155.html (accessed June 19, 2011).

UNHCR (1985) *Refugee Women and International Protection*. No. 39 (XXXVI) – 1985. Geneva: United Nations High Commissioner for Refugees. www.unhcr.org/refworld/docid/3ae68c43a8.html (accessed September 11, 2011).

UNHCR (2002) "Section IV." *Resettlement Handbook*. Geneva: United Nations High Commissioner for Refugees.

UNHCR (2007) *Convention and Protocol Relating to the Status of Refugees*. Geneva: United Nations High Commissioner for Refugees. www.unhcr.org/protect/PROTECTION/3b66c2aa10.pdf (accessed November 20, 2010).

UNHCR (2009) *UNHCR Eligibility Guidelines for Assessing the International Protection Needs of Asylum-Seekers from Eritrea*. Geneva: United Nations High Commissioner for Refugees. www.unhcr.org/refworld/docid/49de06122.html (accessed November 20, 2010).

UNICEF (2005) *The Impact of Conflict on Women and Girls in West and Central Africa and the UNICEF Response*. New York: United Nations Children's Fund. www.unicef.org/publications/files/Impact_final.pdf (accessed November 20, 2010).

UNIFEM (2005) *Securing the Peace: Guiding the International Community towards Women's Effective Participation throughout Peace Processes*. New York: United Nations Development Fund for Women. www.unifem.org/attachments/products/Securing_the_Peace.pdf (accessed May 3, 2011).

UNSC (2001) *Report of the Panel of Experts on the Illegal Exploitation of Natural Resources and the Other Forms of Wealth of the Democratic Republic of the Congo*. S/2001/357. New York: United Nations Security Council.

Unterhalter, Elaine (1988) "Women Soldiers and White Unity in Apartheid South Africa," in Sharon Macdonald, Pat Holden, and Shirley Ardener (eds.), *Images of Women in Peace and War: Cross-Cultural and Historical Perspectives*. Madison: The University of Wisconsin Press, pp. 100–21.

USCRI (2009) "Refugee and Asylum-Seekers Worldwide (as of December 31, 2008)." *World Refugee Survey, 2009*. Arlington: US Committee for Refugees and Immigrants.

USCRI (2010) *Refugees and Asylum Seekers Worldwide*. Arlington: US Committee for Refugees and Immigrants. www.uscrirefugees.org/2010Website/5_Resources/5_5_Refugee_Warehousing/5_5_4_Archived_World_Refugee_Surveys/5_5_4_7_World_Refugee_Survey_2009/5_5_4_7_1_Statistics/RefugeesandAsylumseek.pdf (accessed May 19, 2011).

USDOD (2005) *Military Enlisted Personnel by Broad Occupational Category and Branch of Military Service*. Washington, DC: United States Department of Defense and Defense Manpower Data Center.

Usta, Jinan, Farver, Jo Ann, and Zein, Lama (2008) "Women, War, and Violence: Surviving the Experience." *Journal of Women's Health* 17(5): 793–804.

Vandergeest, Peter, Idahosa, Pablo, and Bose, Pablo (eds.) (2007) "Introduction," in *Development's Displacements: Ecologies, Economies and Cultures at Risk*. Vancouver: UBC Press, pp. 3–32.

Van Devanter, Lynda (1984) *Home before Morning: The True Story of an Army Nurse*. New York: Warner Books.

Veale, Angela (2003) "From Child Soldier to Ex-Fighter: Female Fighters,

Demobilisation and Reintegration in Ethiopia." *ISS Monograph Series* 85. Pretoria: Institute for Security Studies.

Veale, Angela, and Stavrou, Aki (2003) "Violence, Reconciliation and Identity: The Reintegration of the Lord's Resistance Army Child Abductees in Northern Uganda." *ISS Monograph Series* 85. Pretoria: Institute for Security Studies.

Verhey, Beth (2001) "Child Soldiers: Preventing, Demobilizing and Reintegration," Africa Region Working Paper Series No. 23. World Bank.

Verhey, Beth (2004) *Reaching the Girls: Study on Girls Associated with Armed Forces and Groups in the Democratic Republic of Congo*. Save the Children UK and the NGO Group: CARE, IFESH and IRC, London.

Villellas Ariño, María (2010) *The Participation of Women in Peace Processes: The Other Tables*. Barcelona: ICIP Working Papers. Institut Català Internacional per la Pau.

Villellas Ariño, Ana, and Redondo de la Morena, Gema (2008) *An Approach to the Kosovo Post-War Rehabilitation Process from a Gender Perspective*. Quaderns de Construcció de Pau, No. 2. Barcelona: Escola de Cultura de Pau.

Vlassenroot, Koen, and Van Acker, Frank (2000) "Youth and Conflict in Kivu: 'Komona Clair.'" *Journal of Humanitarian Assistance* 5: 1–17.

VPU of East Timor Police Service, OPE, and UNFPA (2002) *Training of Trainers: Police Basic Training on Domestic Violence – Strengthening Response Capacity to Gender-Based Violence*. New York: Vulnerable Persons Unit, Office for the Promotion of Equality and United Nations Population Fund.

Walker, Angela (2005) "Sharing the Secret: Rape Survivors Find Solace and Skills with UNFPA-Sponsored Programme," in *UNFPA State of World Population 2005: Journalists' Press Kit*. New York: United Nations Population Fund. www.unfpa.org/swp/2005/presskit/index.htm (accessed October 3, 2011).

Walker, Margaret Urban (2009) "Gender and Violence in Focus," in Ruth Rubio (ed.), *The Gender of Reparations: Unsettling Sexual Hierarchies While Redressing Human Rights Violations*. Cambridge: Cambridge University Press.

Walker, Rebecca (forthcoming) "'Speak to the Women as the Men Have All Gone': Exploring Networks of Support amongst Women in Eastern Sri Lanka," in Srila Roy (ed.), *New South Asian Feminisms: Paradoxes and Possibilities*. London: Zed Books.

Walsh, Sean P. (2007) "The Roar of the Lion City: Ethnicity, Gender and Culture in the Singapore Armed Forces." *Armed Forces and Society* 33(2): 265–85.

Waylen, Georgina October (2000) "Gender and Democratic Politics: A Comparative Analysis of Consolidation in Argentina and Chile." *Journal of Latin American Studies* 32(3): 765–93.

WCRWC (2001) *Out of Sight, Out of Mind: Conflict and Displacement in Burundi*. New York: Women's Commission for Refugee Women and Children. http://repository.forcedmigration.org/show_metadata.jsp?pid=fmo:2437 (accessed September 16, 2011).

WCRWC (2006) *Displaced Women and Girls at Risk: Risk Factors, Protection Solutions and Resource Tools*. New York: Women's Commission for Refugee Women and Children.

Weaver, Mary Anne (2000) "The Real Bin Laden," *The New Yorker*, January 24.

Weinstein, Laurie, and Mederer, Helen (1997) "Blue Navy Blues: Submarine Officers and the Two-Person Career," in Laurie Weinstein and Christie C. White (eds.), *Wives and Warriors: Women and the Military in the United States and Canada.* Westport, CT: Bergin and Garvey, pp. 8–14.

West, Candace, and Zimmerman, Don H. (1987) "Doing Gender." *Gender and Society* 1(2): 125–51.

Whitworth, Sandra (2008) "Militarized Masculinity and Post-Traumatic Stress Disorder," in Jane Parpart and Marysia Zalewski (eds.), *Rethinking the Man Question: Sex, Gender and Violence in International Relations.* London: Zed Books.

Willett, Susan (2010) "Introduction: Security Council Resolution 1325: Assessing the Impact on Women, Peace and Security." *International Peacekeeping* 17(2): 142–58.

Williams, Suzanne (2002) "Conflicts of Interest: Gender in Oxfam's Emergency Response," in Cynthia Cockburn and Dubravka Zarkov (eds.), *The Postwar Moment: Militaries, Masculinities and International Peacekeeping.* London: Lawrence and Wishart, pp. 90–1.

Wood, Elisabeth Jean (2006) "Variation in Sexual Violence during War." *Politics and Society* 34(3): 307–42.

Wood, Elisabeth Jean (2009) "Armed Groups and Sexual Violence: When is Wartime Rape Rare?" *Politics and Society* 37(1): 131–61.

WREI (2008) *Women in the Military: Where They Stand,* 6th edn. Arlington, VA: Women's Research and Education Institute.

WREI (2010) *Women in the Military: Where They Stand,* 7th edn. Arlington, VA: Women's Research and Education Institute.

Wright, Michael (1982) "The Marine Corps Faces the Future," *The New York Times,* June 20, Sunday, Late City Final Edition. LexisNexis Academic.

Young, Iris Marion (2003) "The Logic of Masculinist Protection: Reflections on the Current Security State." *Signs: Journal of Women in Culture and Society* 29(1): 1–25.

Yuval-Davis, Nira (1997) *Gender and Nation.* London: Sage Publications.

Yuval-Davis, Nira (2006) "Intersectionality and Feminist Politics." *European Journal of Women's Studies* 13(3): 193–210.

Yuval-Davis, Nira, and Anthias, Floya (eds.) (1989) *Woman–Nation–State* (consultant ed. Jo Campling). Basingstoke, UK: Palgrave Macmillan.

Zajović, Staša (1992) "Women Resist Militarization of Former Yugoslavia." *Off Our Backs* 22(4): 7–10.

Zamkanei, Shayna (2008) "Marrying Motherhood with Martyrdom: The Politics of Women and Jihad in Hamas." Paper presented at the Midwest Political Science Association's Annual National Conference, April 3–6, 2008, Chicago, Illinois.

Zarkov, Dubravka (ed.) (2008a) *Gender, Violent Conflict and Development.* New Delhi: Zubaan/Kali for Women.

Zarkov, Dubravka (2008b) "On Militarism, Economy and Gender: Working in Global Contexts," in Dubravka Zarkov (ed.), *Gender, Violent Conflict and Development.* New Delhi: Zubaan/Kali for Women, pp. 1–19.

Zarkov, Dubravka (2008c) "Globalizing Gender? Militarization, 'New Wars' and the Global Economy." Talk given at the Five College Women's Studies Research Center, March 31, 2008, South Hadley, MA.

Zavis, Alexandra (2008) "Grooming a Female Suicide Bomber," *Los Angeles Times,*

August 21. http://articles.latimes.com/2008/aug/21/world/fg-women21 (accessed January 15, 2009).

Zawilski, Valerie (2006) "Saving Russia's Sons: The Soldiers' Mothers and the Russian–Chechen Wars," in Stephen L. Webber and Jennifer G. Mathers (eds.), *Military and Society in Post-Soviet Russia*. Manchester: Manchester University Press and Palgrave Macmillan, pp. 228–40.

Zedalis, Debra (2004) "Female Suicide Bombers." *Carlisle Papers in Security Strategy*. Carlisle: Security Strategy Institute of US Army War College.

Zeigler, Sara L., and Gunderson, Gregory G. (2005) *Moving Beyond G.I. Jane: Women and the US Military*. Lanham, MD: University Press of America.

Index

Bold entries refer to tables, italic entries to text boxes

abduction/kidnapping 26, 75, 93, 107
  of women and girls 43, 46, 55, 56, 59, 147, 150,
    151, 194, *208*
Aberdeen Proving Ground scandal 142
abortion *39*, 63, 64, 75–6; *see also* forced
    termination of pregnancy
accountability *57*, 60, 172, 183, 231, 235
Aceh
  peace agreement *177, 191*
  women's activism in *191*
  women in NSAGs 150
  women postwar *191*, 235
Acker, Joan 15 n.8
Acquired Immunodeficiency Syndrome (AIDS) *see*
    HIV/AIDS
activism/activists 69, 77, 108
  anti-apartheid 133
  celebrity 56
  human rights 56, 72, 73, 74
  political 32, 83, 102, 181
activism, women's political 32, 102–22, 127, 181,
    187–9, 232
  anti-militarization 109, *110*, 117. 117 n.12
  antiwar 102, 106–7, 111, 116–18, 120–2
  costs/dangers of 107, 108, 122, *185*, 235
  feminist 103, 117, 121, 181, 187
  feminist antinuclear 118–19, *119*, 176, 179
  maternal identity as basis of 102, 106–11, *110*,
    175–6
  opposing government violence 102, 107–8, 176
  pacifist 104, 121
  peace 16, 36, 102, 169, 175, 176 n.6, 179, *179*,
    180–2, 183, 185, 188–9, 192
  "political action," meaning of 103
  supporting armed violence 109–11, 116, 121,
    129–30
  transnational 116, 117, 122, 181, 183, 185, 191
  transversal 120–1
  see also women's organizations and networks
advocacy 59, 116, *142*, 173, 183, 235
Afghan women *40*, 114–15, *115*, 120, **131**, 148, **149**,
    185, 185
  in government 185, 232
  threats against *185*
Afghanistan 75, 78, 88, 120, 196, 233
  CIA role in 115
  gender roles in *40*, 148
  National Assembly *185*
  peace negotiations in *185*
  Soviet occupation of *40*, *110*, 115, 129
  US war in 25, 64–5, 86, 114, 115, *115*, 129, 130,
    137, 142, 143
Africa 41, 49, 52, 59, 74, 89, 120, 148–9, 172 n.1,
    220

DDR in 194, 196, 203–5
  Eastern Africa 87
  sub-Saharan 55, 217 n.2, 224, 238
  see also specific countries
African Union 59, 70, 164, 220
African Union/United Nations Hybrid operation
    in Darfur (UNAMID) 70
African leaders 59
African women 116, 117, **149**, 175 n.2, 210, *211*
agency, women's 2, 28, 30, 31, 35, 37, 52, 73, 117,
    164, 224, 238
  political 50, 52, 108, 116, 120, 183, 217
  see also victim/agent dichotomy, problem of
aid *see* development, aid; humanitarian aid
AIDS *see* HIV/AIDS
Akeyesu, Jean-Paul 58–9
al-Aqsa Martyrs' Brigade (AMB) 159
al-Bashir, Omar 59
al-Qaeda 115, 159, 161, 163
al-Shabaab *see* Harakat al-Shabaab al-Mujahideen
Albania 187, *239*
All-Manipur Social Reformation and Development
    Samaj 176
All-Women Contingent of the Mindanao Peoples
    Caucus 177
Amargi Kadın Akademisi 117
Americas
  Central America **149**, 215, 217, 235
    women's organizations in 238
  Latin America 103, 108, 117, 120, 147, **149**, 149,
    172 n.1, 204, 215, 217, 224, 232
    DDR in 196, 204
    peace processes in 172 n.1
    women's political organizing in 107–8, 238
  North America 86, 117, 125
  South America 49, 117, **149**
  see also specific countries
Amnesty International 94
Angola 134, **149**, 150, *177*, 203, 210 n.5, 215, 224
apartheid 133–4, 135, 183
"Arab Spring" 102
Argentina 102, 176, 215
  women's political activism in 102, 107–8, 176
arms
  control 13, 198, *199*, *200*
  manufacturers 14 n.6, 15, 28
  trade/transfers 14 n.6, 24–8, 41, 46, 49–50
  see also weapons
armed conflict *see* war(s)
armed forces *see* militaries
armed groups *see* non-state armed groups (NSAGs)
Arnado, Mary Ann 177–8
Arusha, 1998 peace talks 187, 190
Arusha, All-Party Women's Peace Conference 190

Asia 27, 89, 148, **149**
  Asia-Pacific, women's activism in 117
  Central Asia 148
  South Asia 107, 117, 131, 181, 224, 232
  Southeast Asia 49
asylum 99
  seekers 80, 82, 86
  women's claims for 96, 97, 97, 99
  women and 94
AUC see United Self-Defense Forces of Colombia
Australia 84, 86, 97–9, **131**, **139**

Bachelet, Michelle 235
backlash see post-conflict/postwar
Balkans, rape as strategy in war 56, 62–3, 68
Bangladesh 92, **131**
  rape during 1971 war of liberation 14, 55, 63
  Rohingya refugees 89
  as troop contributing country in PSOs 220
Barakzai, Shukria 185
Barrow, General Robert H. 23
Basque women 181
Bayard de Volo, Lorraine 109
Beijing Platform for Action 39
Belgium 27, **139**, 189
Ben-Gurion, David 140
Bias, Esperança 235
biological explanations
  for differences between men and women 6–8,
    138, 229
  for men being "warlike" 23, 112–13
  for racial categories 5
  for rape 60
  for women's "peacefulness" 106, 108, 111
  for women's vulnerability in war 29, 54, 77, 78
Birds of Freedom 151–2
body(ies) 11, 29, 65, 113
  female 6, 16, 17, 33, 65, 91, 113, 120, 138, 159,
    176
  male 6, 17, 19
  women's, as symbol of nation 14
borders 20, 24, 25, 54, 80, 81–2, 86, 88, 91, 94, 99,
    121, 181–2, **219**, 227, 233
Bosnia 14, 43, 59, 63, 65, 120–1, 229
Bosnia-Herzegovina 120–1, 229
Bosnian women 63, 121, 181
Boutros-Ghali, Boutros 220
boys 22, 27 n.18, 42, 56, 82, 87, 91, 221
  in fighting forces 147, 152, 155–6, 160, 167, 194,
    202, 205, 222
Brazil 109, **131**, **139**, 215
British American Security Council (BASIC) 119
Brownmiller, Susan 55
Bukavu 65–6
Burke, Carol 135
Burma/Myanmar 89, 126, **149**
Burundi
  peace process, women and 174, 185, 187, 187
    n.14, 189–1
  women's activism in 189–1
  women and girls in NSAGs **149**, 150, 203, 203
  see also Arusha
Bush, George W. administration of 114, 115
Bush, Laura 115
"bush wives" see forced wives

Cambodia **149**, 221
camps, refugee and IDP 2, 8, 13, 42, 44, 47, 58,
    80, 83, 85, 87, 89–91, 92–3, 94, 98, 100, 184,
    190, 226

design and supplies 20, 70
  as entrenching gender inequalities 20, 90
  gendered vulnerability in 8, 76, 89
camps, rape 58, 63
camps, women's peace 119; see also Greenham
    Common Women's Peace Camp
"camp follower" 130
Canada 84, 93, 97, 98, 99, **131**, **139**, 139–40, 144,
    189
  as country of resettlement 86, 92, 93, 99
  military, women in **131**, 139–40, 144
Canadian Working Group on Refugee Women 97
cantonment (in DDR) 194, 200–1, 203, 206, 224
capitalism/ist 231
  global capitalism 100, 182
  globalization of capitalist production trade and
    finance 26
  see also neoliberalism
care see labor, caring
caste 2, 4, 5, 7, 10, 15, 16, 37, 100, 120, 151, 189,
    192
Catholicism/Catholics 121, 169, 181
cattle see livestock
Caucasus 49; see also specific countries
cease-fire 151, 171, 172, 177, 179, 218, 220
CEDAW see Convention on the Elimination of All
    Forms of Discrimination against Women
Chad 80, 84, **149**
Chambon, Adrienne 93
chastity/virtue, patriarchal constructions of 197
Chechnya, conflict in 110, 129, 149, 159, 160, 176
Chechen women 110, 129, 159, 160
childcare 11, 17, 206, 207, 208
child soldiers 87, 147, 152, 155–6, 160, 167, 177,
    194, 200, 201, 202, 222, 236; see also boys;
    girls
children 1, 4, 6, 9, 13, 28, 36, 42, 50, 66, 70, 85,
    99, 158, 194–5, 208
  born of rape 29, 63, 64, 64 n.12, 65, 112
  child-headed households 22, 225
  commoditization of 45–7, 91, 95, 98
  displacement and 20, 74, 80, 82, 83, 87, 91, 98
  educational possibilities for 43, 207
  of ex-combatants 207, 208
  labor of, wars effect on 42–3, 43
  left behind by soldiers 117
  orphaned by war 43, 103
  SEA of 39, 46, 91, 221
  trafficking of 43, 45, 82, 84
  vulnerabilities of 225–6
  "womenandchildren" 95, 99
  as women's responsibility 8, 29, 40, 47, 72, 84,
    86, 99, 106, 164, 174, 176
  see also abduction/kidnapping; boys; child
    soldiers; DDR programs; girls; protection
Chile 97, **139**, 235
China 27, 38 n.2, 55, 58, 95, 120, 130, 134, **139**, 183
Christian 36, 182, 186
citizenship 2, 128
  displacement and 82, 85, 89–90, 91
  gendering of 14, 32, 104, 128
  militarization of 14, 128, 132, 140
civil society 58, 106, 169, 173, 182–3, 187, 217,
    219, 234
civil society organizations (CSOs) 187, 234
  faith groups 219, 234
  women's civil society organizations 172, 173,
    174–6, 181, 187, **219**, 236
  see also activism/activists; nongovernmental
    organizations

civil war 14, 36, 54, 55, 84, 88, 91, 92, 180, 181, *208*, 217
civilian(s) 45, 49, 61, 62–3, 85, 128, 135, 176, 198, *199–200*, 209, *220*, 221, 225, 227
  casualties 25, 26, 74, 83
  civil/military divide 126, 135
  civilian/combatant binary, problem with 25, 199
  civilian control of armed forces *110*, 125, 126, 144
  civilian life, reintegration of ex-combatants 195, 196–7, 200–2, 207, 224
  protection of 46, *57*, 58, 62, 196, *211*, **219**, 56 n.5, 58 n.7
  in PSOs *184*, *218*, *220*, 222–3, *223*
  SEA of 46, 91
  targeting of 25, 41, 54, 55, *57*, 62–3, 74
  women's lives, militarization of 128–9, 145
  see also protection
Civilian Protection Component–Mindanao (CPC) 177–8, 185–6, 204
civilized/uncivilized dichotomy 5–6, 10, 27, 96 n.6, 115, 182
clan 2, 169, 180–1, 192
Clinton, Hillary Rodham 55, 102
CNDD-FDD *see* National Council for the Defense of Democracy/Forces of Defense of Democracy (Burundi)
Cockburn, Cynthia 15n.8, 88, 117 n.9, 120, 120 n.16
Cold War 113, *119*, 119, 218
  end of, effects on armed conflict 24–8, 41, 148, 215, 217, 230
  proxy wars 26
Colombia 56, 91, 148–50, 154–7, 163, 165, 196, 202, 209; *see also* FARC
colonialism 4–5
  anticolonial liberation movements 119–20, 148
  colonial and postcolonial politics 89
  colonial and postcolonial racial hierarchies 15
  colonial relations, impact on war of 25–6, 38, 85
  and "crisis of masculinity" 51
  former colonial states 217
  land tenure and local governance, impact on 51
  role of former colonial powers 172, 189
  wars of conquest 114
  see also neocolonial relationships; postcolonial
coltan 26–7, 45
combat 23
  "combat exclusion" (of women) 23, 136–9, 140, 155
  masculine preserve of 136
  women in combat positions 16, 22, **139**, 139–40, 141, *142*, 145
combatants 11, 19–22, 39, 46, 48, 55-6, 59, 74, 171, 194, 197–203, *230*, 237
  combatant/civilian binary 25, 199
  ex-combatants 21, 34, *184*, 195, 197–203, 205, 212, 216, 220, 224, *230*, 238
  female ex-combatants *184*, 195, 197–212, *203*, *208*, *211*, 218, 221, 222, *230*
  and international law 50, 58–60
  masculinities of 14, 61, 105 n.2
  socialization of 61–2
  women and girls as 2, 23, *47*, 89, 132–3, 150, 151–3, 155, 158, 163, 167, 175, 175 n.2, 200, 205, 218, 222, *230*
"comfort women" 56, *58*, 58 n.4, 130, 181
  see also slavery, sexual
Committee of Soldiers' Mothers of Russia (CSMR) 109, *110*, 129, 176

commodities, global trafficking of 24, 26, 50–1
community(ies) 9, 12, 28, 33, 40, 41, 48, 51, 62, 84, 105
  conflict transformation, women's work in 172, *179*, 180, 181, 190–1, *233*
  and DDR 14, 195–6, 197, 198, 201–2, 206–7, *208*, 209–11
  effects of sexual violence on 54, 56, 59, 62–3, 66, 67, 72, 73, 89
  leaders 68, 91, 96, 209
  and NSAGs 146, 147, 148, 153, 154, 156–8, 161–7
  rebuilding of 2, 21, 210–11, 220
  and refugees and IDPs *39*, 44, 54, 80–90, 96
  relationships/networks 21, 37, 43, 44, 68, 89, 97, *97*, 207, 209
  women and girls' relation to 1, 2, 7, 12, 22, 37, 64, *66*, 67, 87, 97, 106, 112, 122, 151, 161, 175, 176, *179*, 217, 237
  war's damage to 36–7, 41, 42–5, 54, 72
  see also international community
conflict prevention, women's role in *57*, 220
conflict resolution 12, 171–2
  specialists who "parachute" in 171–2, 186, 202
  women's role in *57*, 211, 224, *239*
  see also peace processes
Connell, R. W. 4, 10
continuum of violence 21, 88, 141–2
Convention on the Elimination of All Forms of Discrimination against Women (CEDAW) 59, *83*
Convention on the Rights of the Child (CRC) *83*
corruption 26, 71, *110*, 173, 205, 231
Côte d'Ivoire **149**, 177, 196, 215
credit, access to 42, 43, 46, 187, 202, *208*, 211, *230*
crimes against humanity 55, 58–9, 236
criminal networks 41–2, 50, 196, 218, **219**
"crisis of masculinity" 50–2
Croatian women 110, 181, 237
CRSV *see* sexual violence, conflict-related
cultural relativism 96, 98–9, 174
Cyprus 181

Daley, Patricia 190
Darfur 70, 80, 84
  sexual violence in 14, 56, 66, 69, 74
Dayton Peace Agreement 237
DDR programs (disarmament, demobilization and reintegration) 171, 194–213, 216, 220–1, 224
  actors in 198–9, *199–200*, 201, 218, **219**
  in Angola 203
  in Burundi 203, *203*
  in Colombia 196
  context and definitions of 195–202
  in El Salvador 204
  gender norms, transitions of 196–7
  in Kosovo 198
  in Mozambique 194
  planners, gendered assumptions of 194–5, 205, 212–13
  in Republic of Congo 203–4
  in Rwanda 203–4
  in Sierra Leone 196, 198, 205
  women's and girls' access to and exclusion from 151, 178, *203*, 203–5, 224–5
  women and girls, challenges for 194–5, 204–11, *208*
  women and girls in *57*, 195, 202–11, 183, *184*, *211*, 222
  see also cantonment; combatants; UNSCR 1325

de Alwis, Malathi 100
demilitarization *184*; *see also* DDR programs
demobilization *199–200*, 200–1, 220, 224, 237–8
    challenges for women and girls 204–6
    self-demobilization 151, 207
    see also DDR programs
democracy, liberal 172, 186, 228; *see also*
        democratic transitions
    democratic processes 122, 172
    democratic rights 178
    democratization, liberal model of 216
democratic transitions 96 n.8, 172, 215, 230–2
    accountability 172, 183, 231
    critiques of 182–3, 231
    electoral processes 188, 231
Democratic Republic of the Congo (DRC) 51–2,
        65–6, 70, 91, **149**, 150, 174, 182, 189, 210,
        210 n.5, 231
    coltan 25–7, 45; *see also* resources, natural,
        conflict-related
    drivers of conflict 27
    eastern Congo 56, 63, *66*, 71
    masculinities in DRC war 27
Denmark 100, **139**
dependents, classification of women as 87, 93, 97,
        99, 194
development, economic 75, *177*, 198, 210
    aid *85*, 85, 95, 182, 187, 202
    as driver of conflict 84
    gendering of 95, 100, *177*, 229
    -induced disasters 80, 84
    -induced displacement 91
"developing regions" *see* global South
diaspora 24, 190, 196
Dinka 50, *179*
"dirty war," in Argentina 102, 107
disabilities/disabled 13, 20, 130, 176, 200, 201
"disappeared" 107–8, 122, 176
disarmament, demobilization and reintegration
        see DDR programs
disasters 24, 80, 84, 85, 86, 88–9, 91, 100
discourse(s)
    gender as a 11–16
    gendered 16
    feminist 38
    human rights 183 n.9
    nationalist 14, 116, 120
    war discourses, gendering of 12–14, 20–2,
        104–6, 113–16
    see also women, "peacefulness" of
discrimination 16, 33, *40*, 120
    gender discrimination 47, 59, 140–5, 177, 187–8
disempowerment 10–11, *40*, 52
    political and economic 51
    of women 2, 35, 111, 217
displacement 22, 41–4, 80–100, *83*, 171, 172 n.1
    categories/terminology 81–3
    feminist responses 94–100
    gender relations of 86–100
    gendered consequences of 64, 73, *97*, 153
    health and 54, 74–7, 226
    internal 80, 82, 88, 91–2, 97
    long-term 81, 86, 89–91, 92
    repatriation 93–4, *184*
    resettlement 44, 86, 87, 92–3, 94, 97–9, 171,
        184, 189
    return 196, 202, *208*, 216, **219**, 220, 224, 225
    roots of 25, 41, 62–3, *83*, 84–6, 91–2
    women and girls, 80–1, 86–100, *184*, 218, 227,
        234

urban 91
    see also camps, refugee and IDP
division of labor
    ethnicized 16
    gendered 7–8, 11, 15–20, 29, 42–3, *43*, 46,
        106, 153–5, 158, 164, 227, 229–30, *see also*
        gendered institutions; labor, caring
    household 42–3, *43*, 46, 164
    international 45 n. 5
domestic violence *39*, 98, 155–7
    postwar 21, *40*, 196, 237–8, 222, 237–8, *239*
    war's impact on 36, 64–5, 88, 90, 95–6
donors, international 72, 74, 77, 216, 241
    democratic transition, and 230–2
    engagement with peace processes 172, 181, 186,
        189, 191, 212, 225
    neoliberal conditionality, and 226, 228–31,
        233, *234*
    restrictions on reproductive health funding
        76, 78
    short term, problem of 71, 212
    SSR, and 233–5
dowry *39*, 189
DPA *see* United Nations Department of Political
        Affairs
DPKO *see* United Nations Department of
        Peacekeeping Operations
drivers of conflict 27, 84–5
drug trafficking/ers 24, 26, 28, 45, 46, 50, 165
        n.10, *185*, 196, 215
Dushirehamwe 190–1
Dutch Refugee Council 98

East Timor conflict 75, **149**
    sexual violence in 56, 62, 64
    postwar 64, 217, 224, *230*, 235, 237
economic recession, global 226, 231, 235
economic inequality *see* inequality, economic
economy(ies)
    domestic *see* reproductive
    formal 45
        effects of armed conflicts on 44–5, 52
        women's access to/exclusion from 8, 12,
            45
    global 38, 49–50
    household 42, 46, 52
    illicit, illegal and shadow 14 n.6, 26–7, 41,
        44–50, 147, 148
        women in 45–8, 68; *see also* trade, in
            commodities, illegal
    informal, women's labor in 12, 44–8
    postwar 196, 217, **219**, 229–30, 231, 239
    reproductive 42, 42 n.4
    war 38, 41, 44–50
    see also capitalism/ist; livelihood(s);
        neoliberalism; trade
ECOWAS (Economic Community of West African
        States) 180
education, formal 44, 126
    in DDR 199, *200*, 201, 211
    disruption of, by displacement 76, 82, 83, 85,
        90, 91, 93, 153
    disruption of, by war 36, *43*, 68, 195–6, 229
    educational institutions 5, 6, 9, 15
    SAP's negative effects on 45
    war's destruction of education infrastructure
        25, 44, 201
    of women and girls *40*, 46, 68, 100, *115*, 134, 150,
        187, 188, *191*, 207, 210, 211, 229, *239*
Egypt 120, *220*

elections 36, 102, 169, 178, 188, **219**, 231–2, 236, 240
  electoral laws 185, 188
  electoral systems *184*, 188
  voter education 222
elites
  geopolitical 183, n.9, 228
  international policy 28
  local 26, 227, 231, *234*
  marginalized ethnic 190
  military and national security 106, 118
  political 125, 131, 149
  post-Soviet 41
  women 218
Elmi, Asha Hagi 169, 176 n.6, 180
El Salvador 60, 75, **149**, 204, 210, 229, 232
Elshtain, Jean Bethke 127
emergencies 87, 96, 210
  complex political or protracted 24, 41–2
  emergency assistance 76, *85*, 85, 87, 90, 227
  "emergency excuse" 99–100
  humanitarian 77, 81, 82
  national 131, 132
emerging political complexes 41
employment, paid 16, 43, 189, 201
  refugees and IDPs 90, 91, 92, 93
  women's 8, *43*, 133, 134, 136, 218
  unemployment, men's 64, 164, *239*
  unemployment, women's 37, 45, 206, 230
"The Enemy" 23, 29, 50, 56, 63–4, 110
  representations of 10–11, 62
England *see* United Kingdom
Enloe, Cynthia 4, 18 n.9, 19–20, 23 n.14, 38–9, 49, 95 n.5, 114, 128–9, 145, 162, 166 n.10, 175
environmental costs of militarization 117, 118
environmental degradation 26, 215
environmental disasters 80, 84, 85, 88–9
Eritrea 25, 60, *177*, 190, 215
  women in armed forces and groups 48, 132, 144, **149**, 206, 209
Eritrean People's Liberation Front (EPLF) 209
essentialism 38, 99, 176, 223
Ethiopia 132, **149**, 175, 177, 206
ethnic boundaries/lines 86
women's political action across 103, 110, 120, 173, *179*, 181–2, 190
"ethnic cleansing" 14, 56
  rape as tactic of 14, 29, 63–4, 72, 120, 190–1
ethnic conflict(s) 36, 63, 82, 84, 85, 90
ethnicity(ies) 2, 5, 7, 10, 15, 16, 37, 54, 100, 108, 134, 151, 154, 192
ethnic fundamentalism 94
ethnic groups 65, 73, 83, 91, 232
ethnicity-based political parties 173
ethnicized animosities 27, 41, 110
ethnic(ized) identity(ies) 27, 51, 102, 103, 120
  women's bodies as repository and reproducers of 14, 29, 50, 63–4, 120
ethnicized subordinated masculinities 10–11, 15
ethnocentric biases 182
ethno-nationalist conflict(s) 83, 88, 115–16, 120, 240
ethno-nationalist movements, women's relation to 116, 119–21, 182, 187
Europe 27, 41, 99, 117, 125, 130, **149**, 220, 215, 217
  Eastern Europe 55, *220*
  Western Europe 84, 86, 107
  see also specific countries
European Union (EU) 99, 224, 228

ex-combatants *see* combatants
exile 80–1, 85–90, 92–5, 98, 100–1, 224

failed states 36, 50, 51
faith-based groups 67, 76; *see also* religion
Falklands/Malvinas 102
Farabundo Martí National Liberation Front *see* FMLN
FARC (Fuerzas Armadas Revolucionarias de Colombia – Ejército del Pueblo) 154–8, 202
Female Engagement Teams 135
female-headed households 22, 42–4, 46, *97*, 224–7; *see also* men, absence of
female youth 52, 91, 167, 197
femininity/ies 3–15, 18–20, 120, 122, 125, 209
  militarized 21, 24, 136, 145, 146, 151, 163, 167, 196, 197, 212
  privileging of masculinity over 28, 30, 135–6, 145
  social construction of 6–8, 11, 38, 41, 51, 108–9, 128, 135
feminist(s) 81, 100, 103, 151, 153, 183, *239*
  activism 103, 117–22, 188–9, 191, 235
  analysis/scholarship 14–16, 21, 23, 38, 88, 94–5, 97–8, 100, 103, 106, 117, 130, 135, 146, 166, 178, 191; *see also* feminist(s), researchers and theorists
  curiosity 130, 159, 162, 212
  on maternalist organizing 108–9, 176
  networks, international 122, 181–2
  NGOs 96, 115, 180
  postcolonial 15, 38
  researchers and theorists 3, 6, 15–16, 26, 28, 110, 114, 124, 127–8, 169, 188–9, 216, 229, 238; *see also* feminist(s), analysis/scholarship
  feminist agendas vs. nationalist agendas 187
  within the UN 183
  see also activism, women's; activism, women's, feminist
feminization
  of peace 12, 175
  as means of disempowering 10–11, 135
  of subordinated groups 10, 15, 30
feminize(d), as devalued 13, 15, 30, 103, 126, 173, 178
  civil society 173
  informal level of peace processes 178
  "private sphere" 103
  sectors 126
field studies 221–2, *234* n.9, 225–6
Finland 86, 100
firewood 8, 29, 70, 74, 80, 87, 89–90, 150, 202
First World War 127, 132–3, 141, 196, 215
fistula, obstetric and traumatic *66*
FMLN (Farabundo Martí National Liberation Front) 204
food 25, 118, 135, 150, *200*, 200, 201, 232–3, *239*
  access to *47*, 48, 76, 83, 84, 86, 87, 90, 91, *110*, 130, 134, 150, 207, *208*, *211*, 221
  aid, humanitarian 81, 87, 90, 92, 95
  gathering, as site of CRSV 87, 89
forced marriage *43*, *47*, 89, 98, 150
forced migration 81–6
  gender relations of 82, 83–4, 86–101
  see also IDP; refugee(s)
forced pregnancy *39*, 56, 63, 65, 76, 120, 236
forced prostitution *39*, 236
forced sterilization *39*, 56, 98, 236
forced termination of pregnancy *39*, 56, 65, 76, 98, 120, 166, 236; *see also* abortion

forced use of contraception 166
forced wives ("bush wives") 47, 59
Foro Nacional de la Mujeres (FORO) 188
Foucault, Michel 45, 45 n.5
France 27, 55, **139**, **149**, 183, 189
Free Aceh Movement (GAM) 150
Frelimo (Frente de Libertação de Moçambique)
　194, *234*
Front pour la démocratie au Burundi (FRODEBU)
　189–90
Fukuyama, Francis 106

GAD (gender and development) 95–6
Gaddafi, Muammar 132
GAFM (gender and forced migration) 95–6,
　99–100
GAM *see* Free Aceh Movement
Gandhi, Indira 106
Gandhi, Rajiv 153, 159
Gbowee, Leymah 102
GBV *see* gender-based violence
gender
　as a discourse 11, 13, 16, 29; *see also* discourses,
　　gendered
　equality/equity 17, 57, 131–2, 149, 153, 155,
　　156–8, 175, 187, *203*, 207, 209, 222, *239*
　as motive for joining armed forces or groups
　　48, 134, 149, 153–4, 160–1, 204
　hierarchies 3, 4–5, 10, 15–16, 126, 171
　ideas about, societal and cultural 4, 15, 19–20,
　　28, 30, 104, 105, 108–9, 111–12, 113, 121–2,
　　125, 127, 128, 135, 136, 152, 159–60, 162,
　　163, 165, 174–5, 176, 182, 197, 209–10, 222
　ideologies 4, 20, 29, 37, 38, 42, 45, 46, 163, 166,
　　187
　inequality 5–7, 10, 20, 43, 46, 88, 92, 100
　　justifications for 5–7, 11–12
　and intersectionality 5, 5 n.3, 7, 10, 28, 100, 108,
　　120, 192
　as a meaning system 11–15, 29
　meanings of, multiple 3–20
　militarization of 19–20, 23–4, 49–52, 61–2, 88,
　　114, 117–18, 124, 126–8, 145, 146, 151–4,
　　159–168, 175, 195–7, 212–13
　stereotypes 105, 113, 178, 186
　and nuclear weapons 13, 118–19, *119*
　as primary way of signifying power 3, 15
　and sex, relation of 6–8
　as socially constructed 6–8, 11, 19–20
　as structural power relation 3–6, 10, 14–15, 29,
　　37, 99, 151
　　co-constituting of other forms of structuring
　　power 5, 10, 14–15
　subordination 4, 61, 95, 117
　symbolic gender coding 5, 11–15, 29, 137
　and war as mutually constitutive 1, 22–4
gender analysis xv–xvi, 5, 8, 18–19, 28–30,
　　51–2, 146, 189, 222–3; *see also* gender
　　mainstreaming *and passim*
gender balance, policy of 222–3, *223*
gender-based violence (GBV) 38, *39*, *57*, 59, 87, 89,
　　92, 94, 95–6, 98, 154–6, 166, 183, *184*, 236–7
gender equality policies 222; *see also* gender
　　balance; gender mainstreaming
gender identities/subjectivities 8–11, 19–20, 30,
　　50–51, 135–6, 146
gender justice *58*, 236–7
gender mainstreaming *57*, 99, 99 n.10, 184, *184*,
　　189, *191*, 222–3; *see also* peace support
　　operations

gender-neutrality, myth of 16–19, 48, 52, 104,
　　234
gender relations
　postwar re-entrenchment of traditional *43*, 48,
　　64, 154–5, 197, 207, 216, 225–6, 227–8,
　　237–40, *238*
　prewar, importance of 27, 51
　restructured/reinscribed during peace talks 71,
　　170, 171
　shifts in due to war 30, 33, *43*, 43, 48, 50, 52,
　　64, 87, 112, 164, 192, 196, 207, 209–11, *211*,
　　213, *238*, *239*
　as source of women's vulnerabilities in war 8,
　　28–30, *39*, 45–6, 47, 54, 82, 84, 86–8, 89, 90,
　　96, 97, *97*, *142*, 176–7, 206–7, 223, 225–6
Gender and Reparations Project (GRP) 237, 236
　n.12
Gender Working Group (GWG) *191*
gendered division of labor 7–8, 11, 15–20, 29,
　　42–3, *43*, 46, 74, 106, 153–5, 158, 164, 227,
　　229–30; *see also* gendered institutions;
　　labor, caring
gendered institutions/organizations 12–13, 15–20,
　　15 n.8, 27–8, 216, 235
　armed forces and groups/militaries as 15, 19,
　　30, 124–8, 135–45, 165
"gendered peace" 216–17
gendered power relations/dynamics 4, 15–16, 29,
　　37, 80, 158
Geneva Conventions 58, 58 n.5, 236
genocide 120
　rape as 14, 29, 58, 63, 236
　Rwandan 63, 103, 233
Germany 27, **131**, **139**
girls 8, 11, *39*, 42, *43*, 52, *57*, 70, 132, 215, 216, 227,
　　235, 236
　access to education 229
　commoditization of 46
　and DDR 194–213, 221, 224–5
　and forced migration 82, 86–94, *184*
　health 20, 65–6, 74–8, 226,
　in NSAGs 23, 146–68, 217
　sexual violence against 21, 54, 56, 59, 65–6, 68,
　　184, 221, 222, 233, 235, 237
global corporations 26, 27, 28, 84; *see also*
　　globalization; PMSC
global economic inequality 84–5, 95, 117, 215
global North 13–14, 95 n.6, 100, 169, 228
　as location of resettlement 86, 92–3, 97
global South 38, 50, 100, 169, 217–18, 232, 235
economies, neoliberal restructuring of 41, 228–9
　as host countries for forced migrants 84–5, 99
　as origin of forced migration 84–5, 91
globalization 3, 24, 27–8, 40–1, 49, 182
　of capitalist production, trade and finance
　　26–8
　of commodities trade 50–1
　as driver of conflict 27, 37, 41, 83
gendered relations of poverty 95
global criminal networks 42, 50, 218, **219**
　global economy, licit and illicit 38, 45, 49–50,
　　84
　militarization, linked to 26, 38, 49
　of popular culture, and violent masculine
　　identities 50–1
　see also global corporations
Goldstein, Joshua 22 n.13
Goma 65–6
governance 41, 51, *57*, 78, 103, 112, 116, 148, 172,
　　183, 185

government(s), post-conflict 18, 36, 148, 173–4, *185*, 222, 229, 230–6, *234*
grassroots political action, women's 106, 147–8, *179*, 180–2, *191*, 238; *see also* activism, women's
"gray literature" 216, 216 n.1, 221, 225, 240–1
Greenham Common Women's Peace Camp *119*
Guatemala, conflict in 60, **149**, 181, 181 n.8, 187, 190, 215, 217, 224, 233, 237
   Defensoría de la Mujer Indígena (Office for the Defence of Indigenous Women) 188
   Foro Nacional de la Mujeres (National Women's Forum, FORO) 188
   Guatemalan National Revolutionary Unity (URNG) 187
   National Union of Guatemalan Women 187
   peace processes, and women 174, 187–8
   violence against women 181
   women's activism in 181, 187–8

Hague Conventions 58, 58 n.7
Haiti **149**, *220*
Hamas 159–60, 163–4
Harakat al-Shabaab al-Mujahideen 163–4
HEAL Africa Hospital 65–6
health care 45, 126, *142*, *208*, 222
   DDR, and 200, 206–7, 210
   effects of loss of access to 54, 65, 75, 77
   forced migrants, and 81, 82, 90–1, 100, 226
   maternal and reproductive 200, 206, 226
   services 36, 65, 72, 81, 91, 100, 201, 210, 226, 229–30, 232
   war's damage to health services 25, 36, 44, 46, 65, 75, 78, 226
   workers/providers 56, 70, 74–5, 78
health, women's and girls' 54–6, 65, *66*, 74–8, 226
   effects of CRSV on 65–8
   maternal mortality 75, 232
   mental 54, 75, 90, 142, 210, 226
   reproductive 20, 31, 39, 53, 54–5, 63, 64, 65, *66*, 74–7, 77 n.22, 89, 166, 200, 206, 226
   see also forced use of contraception; forced pregnancy; forced sterilization; forced termination of pregnancy; pregnancy
hegemonic masculinities 4, 10–11, 13–14, 30, 127
Helms Amendment 76
Herbert, Melissa 141
heterosexuality, as part of hegemonic masculinity 17, 24, 29–30, 136, 138
hierarchical forms of structuring power 5, 14–16, 171
   in armed forces and groups 33, 143, 151
   colonial and postcolonial racial hierarchies 15
   gendered 3–5, 14–16, 126, 171
Hiroshima 25, 119
HIV/AIDS 54, *57*, 65–6, 68, 73, 76–7, *184*, *208*, 226
   in UN Security Council resolutions *57*
   as weapon 63, 148
honor 29, 56, 63–4, 86, 120
   honor killings 182
   redemption of, as motive for female NSAG participation 153, 161
   women as symbols of men's 50
household(s), effects of war on 43, 52, 87, 90, *239*
   child-headed 22, 225
   female-headed 22, 42–4, 46, *97*, 224–7
   see also division of labor; household(s); economies, household
Hultgreen, Kara 141

human rights 41, 69, 77, 82, *110*, 115, 172, *184*, 203, 233, 235
   activists 56, 72–4
   conventions 83, *83*
   organizations 69, 71, 78, 143, *144*, 176
   see also international law, human rights; women's rights
human trafficking *see* trafficking, human
humanitarian aid/assistance 24, 41, 45–6, 56, 71–2, 78, 81–2, *85*, 85, 88–92, 182
humanitarian assistance organizations/agencies 24, 41, 70, 76, 77, 85, 87, 100, 218, **219**
   as gendered organizations 12–13, 15
   staff, gendered assumptions of 87–8, 90, 176
   staff, SEA by 46, 56, 92
humanitarian emergencies/crises 99–100
humanitarian intervention(s)/response 49, 67, 69
humanitarian law *see* international law, humanitarian
humanitarianism 88, 96, 172 n.1
humiliation 11, 167
   rape as a tactic to humiliate men 56, 61–4, 66–8
Hussein, Saddam 224
Hyndman, Jennifer 100

ICC *see* International Criminal Court
ICRC *see* International Committee of the Red Cross
ICTR *see* International Criminal Tribunal for Rwanda
ICTY *see* International Criminal Tribunal for the former Yugoslavia
identity
   as constructed by social, historical, economic, political processes 50–1
   influence of global popular culture 50–1
   militarization of 50–2, 60, 61
   war's transformations of 92, 98
   women as reproducers of collective identities 14, 29, 50, 63–4, 120
   see also ethnic(ized) identity(ies); gender identities/subjectivities; nationalism(s)
ideology(ies), gender(ed) 4–5, 20, 29, 37, 38, 42, 45, 46, 152, 163, 166, 187; *see also* nationalism(s); *and specific armed groups*
IDP *see* internally displaced person(s)
IFI *see* international financial institutions
IMF *see* international financial institutions
imperialism 38, 85, 114, 182, 186
impunity, problem of 56, *57*, 62, 70–1, 73, 144, 177, 188
independence movements *see* national liberation movements/forces
indentured servitude *see* slavery
Indo-Chinese refugee women 95
India 92, 120, **149**, 153, 179, *220*, *223*
   military SEA by 46–7, 176
   partition of 14, 55, 63
   women in military **139**, 141, 144
   women's activism in 118, 176, 179–80
indigenous communities *39*, 157, 187–8, 217
indigenous modes of healing 67
indigenous women 187–8
Indonesia 62, 120, **149**, 150
inequality 10, 15, 120
   gender 6, 10, 20, 43, 46, 82, 100
   economic 15, 26, 84–5, 95, 117
   see also global economic inequality

infrastructure, war's destruction of 21, 25, 37, 42, 44–6, 65, 70–1, 75, 77–8, 84, 118, 201, *211*, 226, 228, 230, *239*, 239; *see also* education
institutional resistance 99, 221, 225
insurgent groups *see* non-state armed groups
internally displaced person(s), women as 42, 80–101, 177, 202
    see also camps, refugee and IDP; displacement
International Alert 189, 191, 241
International Committee of the Red Cross (ICRC) *66*, *85*, *200*, **219**
international community 35, 56, 69, 71, 85, 100, 199, *199*, 216, 224, 229–31, 233
International Criminal Court (ICC) 59, *83*, *184*, 236
International Criminal Tribunal for Rwanda (ICTR) 58, 58 n.6, 63, 59 n.8
International Criminal Tribunal for the former Yugoslavia (ICTY) 58, 58 n.6, 121
international financial institutions (IFIs) 26, 28, 216–18, **219**, 227–30, *234*
    IMF 228–9
    World Bank 228, *230*
    see also neoliberalism
international intervention 32, *234*, 240
international law 38, *58*, 58–60, 78, *184*, 236
    criminal *58*, 58–9, 63, 67, 236; *see also* ICC; ICTR; ICTY
    human rights 41 82, *83*; *see also* CEDAW; Convention on the Rights of the Child
    humanitarian 41, 50, *58*, 58, 121
    refugee 81, 96; *see also* United Nations Convention Relating to the Status of Refugees
    see also Geneva Conventions; Hague Conventions; international tribunals and special courts
International Monetary Fund (IMF) *see international financial institutions*
international tribunals and special courts *58*, 58–60, 58 n.6, 181, 236
    International Military Tribunal for the Far East 58
    Special Court for Sierra Leone 47, 59
    "Tribunal of Consciousness" (Guatemala) 181
    Women's International War Crimes Tribunal for the Trial of Japan's Military Sexual Slavery *58*, 181
    see also ICC; ICTR; ICTY
International Women's Network against Militarism (IWNAM) 117, 117 n.12
intersectionality 5, 5 n.3, 7, 10, 28, 100, 108, 120, 192
Iran 86, 88, 92, 120, **149**
Iraq 25, 115, 235
    US war in 25, 38–9, 64–5, 86, 130, 137, 142, *142*, 143, 148, **149**, 149, 159, 182, 196, 224
    women's activism in 232
Islam
    and "global war on terror" 115
    Islamist groups and parties 115, 159, 163–5, 175, 232
    women's rights as "un-Islamic" 185
Israel 92, **149**, 159, 165, 170
    military, women in 132, **139**, 140, 144
    women's activism in 117, 120, 181
Itto, Ann *179*, 180

janjaweed 80
Japan 49, 50, 58, 117, 120, 130, **139**, 181, **219**, 228
    "comfort women" 56, *58*, 58 n.4

military of *58*, 130
    see also international tribunals and special courts
Jayawardena, Kumari 120, 189
Jordan 86, **149**, *220*
Joya, Malalai *185*
jihad, jihadist 159, 164
    role of women in 160, 161, 164–5
judicial system 70, 93, 178, 181, **219**, 231
    training 71, 181
justice 94, 108, 112, 116, 121, 122, 149, 152, 167, 209, 210, 217, 235
    gender 149, 236–7
    justice system, formal 71, 74, 233, 235
    justice system, traditional 73–4
    rule of law 71
    sexual violence and *58*, 73–4, 144, 181
    transitional 236–7
    see also ICTR; ICTY; impunity, problem of; international tribunals and special courts; law; truth commissions

Kaldor, Mary 24
Keegan, John 124, 144
Kenya 76, 87, 92, 94, **139**, 189
kidnapping/abduction 26, 46, 107, 227 n.8
    of children 43, 93, 195
    of girls 59, 84, 89, 94, 147, 150–1, 194, *208*
    into armed groups 2, 46, 56, 59, 67, 89, 147, 150–1, 194, 195, *208*
    of women 2, 55, 56, *58*, 59, 67, 89, 150–1, 194, *208*
Kivu 71, 174
Konteh, Juliana *208*
Korean War 130
Kosovo/a 56, 182, 185, 218, 227, 235, *239*
    DDR in 198
Koven, Seth 176
Kronsell, Annica 125
Kurdistan Workers' Party (PKK) 159–61

labor 5, 26, 93, 211
    caring, women's 8, 11, 17, *40*, 46, 54, 83, 90, 106, 130, 174, 201, 206, 207, *208*, 232; *see also* division of labor; employment; livelihood(s); NSAGs, women's and girls' roles and experiences in
    women's, as central to war making 22–3
    women's paid 8, *43*, 133, 134, 136, 173, 218
    women's unpaid 12, 173, 227, 229
land, forcible displacement for resource access 26, 56, 84, 89, 225
land, women's right to own 8, 42, 46, 187, 188, 225, 233
land reform 202, 232–3, *234*
    marginalizing effect on women 233
    in Mozambique 233, *234*
    transition from traditional forms of use to individual ownership 51, 232–3, *234*
Latin America *see* Americas, *and specific countries*
latrines 70, 89
Lautze, Sue 49
law(s) 69, 181, *191*, *239*
    constitutional 235
    customary 235
    electoral 185, 188
    formal legal systems 233, 235
    restrictive to women *40*, 235
    sexual violence and 70–1, 78

see also international law; justice; judicial
system; land reform; law, Sharia
leadership 210
  in NSAGs 26, 59, 151, 152, 155, 158. 160, 161,
    165, 167, 210
  political 129, 132, *185, 199*, 232; *see also* political
    leaders
  in US military 23, 59, 133, 137, 140
  women's 137, 140, 179, *185*, 209, 210
  see also male leaders
Lebanon 44, **149**, 158
leftist ideology 151
leftist movements in Latin America 174, 204
legislature(s) (includes parliaments) 15, 18, 169,
    173, *185*, 185, 188, **219**, 231, 232, *234*
legitimacy 152, 166, 175, 186, 197, 212
liberal constructions of gender 103, 192
liberal democracy *see* democratic transitions
"liberal" peace 190, 231
liberation, women's 154, 209; *see also* national
    liberation movements
Liberation Tigers of Tamil Eelam (LTTE) 151 n.4,
    151–4, 159–61, 174, 181, 187–9
Liberia 102, 177, 210 n.5, 217, 235
Liberian women 102
Liborakina, Marina *110*
Libya 54, 63, 102, 132, **149**, 182
literacy 99, 173, *208*, 210, 227
livelihood(s) 22, 72
  after war 189, 195, 197, 207, *208*, 211, 216, 218,
    223, 224, 227–8, *239*
  displacement and 83, 91, 93, 97
  gender analysis of 42–50, *43, 47, 203*, 207, 223,
    227–30
  humanitarian interventions and 67, 227
  militarization of 49-52, 134, 195–6
  rural 42, 43–4, 227
  urban 227
  war's effects on 36, 41–9, 54, 64, 100, 112, 134
livestock 25, 42–4
lobbying 74, 169, 173, 180, 186, 188
local–global linkages 2, 3, 25, 37, 41, 50, 51, 84,
    92
local political, social and economic dynamics 49,
    72, 223
Lord's Resistance Army (LRA) 150–1
loss 218, 240
  of communities 152–3
  displacement and 100
  emotional 90, 109, 218, 226
  of families *43*, 43, 93–4, 109, 152–3, 160
  of health access 54, 75
  of infrastructure 43
  of livelihoods 22, 36, 44, 64, 84
"Lost Boys" and "Lost Girls" of Sudan 87, 88
LTTE *see* Liberation Tigers of Tamil Eelam
Lynn, John 130

machismo 155, 165–6
Madres of the Plaza de Mayo 102, 107–8, 176
male dominance 6, 10, 61, 162
  justifications for 6, 10
  role of 162, 163,
  see also patriarchy
male ex-combatants *see* combatants
male leaders 105–6, 112–13, 175
male youth 50–2, 196, 197, 227
Mandela, Nelson 189, 190
manhood *see* masculinity/ies
manliness *see* masculinity/ies

Mano River Women's Peace Network
    (MARWOPNET) 106, 116
Maoists (Nepal) 150–1, 202, 209
marginalization 41, 190, 191, 207
  of children *43*
  of girls 68, 161, 194–5, 207, 224
  of women 35, 48, 68, 161, 173, 179, 194–5, 207,
    217, 224, 233, 235
markets 89
  global 27, 42, 45, 46, 50, 182
  local 42, 44, 84, 86, 87, 144, 223, 230, 233, *239*
  market economy 100; *see also* capitalism/ist
  "market friendly" land reform 233
  neoliberal market fundamentalism 228; *see also*
    neoliberalism
  see also economy(ies), illicit, illegal and shadow
marriage 50, 65, 73,189, 209–10, 233, 235 n.10,
    237
  early 227
  forced *43, 47*, 89, 98, 150
Marshall, George C. 139
MARWOPNET *see* Mano River Women's Peace
    Network
masculine, privileging of over feminine 12–13,
    28, 30, 126, 128, 145
masculinism 4
masculinity/ies 3–15, 18–20, 28, 105 n.2, 122, 125,
    161, 164
  as associated with bellicosity 23, 105–6, 111–13
  combat as masculine preserve 136–9
  "crisis of masculinity" 51–2
  ethnicized subordinated 10–11, 15
  hegemonic 4, 10–11, 13–14, 24, 29–30, 125, 127
  identification of militaries with 126–8, 131,
    135, 145
  masculine protection as justification for war
    113–16, 127
  militarized 19–20, 21, 23, 24, 27, 50, 51–2, 61, 88,
    114, 117–18, 125–8, 146, 151, 162, 165–7,
    175, 196, 212
  multiple 4, 9–11, 27, 105, 113
  and nationalist projects 120–1
  "postwar" *40*, 197
  social construction of 6–8, 11, 23, 41, 117, 120,
    126
  as shaped by war 38, 50–2
  targeting of manliness 10–11
  violent or predatory 27, 50, 51–2, 113–14
  and war in DRC 26–7
  war, as integrally linked to 1, 18–19, 22–4, 105
    n.2, 108–9, 121, 124, 175, 225
  see also DDR programs; feminization; men;
    militaries; NSAGs
masculinized spheres 103, 107, 109, 173, 184–5
maternalist political movements 108–9, *110*, 129,
    176
McWilliams, Monica 169
media, mass 9, 102, 141, 146
  coverage of peace processes 170, 180
  representation of CRSV 27, 56, 74
  representation of women in NSAGs 151, 152,
    158, 203
  transnational spread of violent ideals of
    masculinities 50–1
mediation 70, 171–2, *211*
Medica Women's Therapy Centre 120–1
Meir, Golda 106
men 24, *40*, 43, 47, 52–3, *119*, 196
  absence of 46, 64, 87, 225, 228
  as default category 15–20, 98

men *(cont.)*
  in NSAGs 152, 160, 163, 164, 165
  in peace processes 170, 171, 174, 186, 192
  postwar 48, 64–5, 196, 206, 227, 233, *234*,
    237
  as protectors 113–14, 223, 227
  and sexual violence 56, 60–5, 67
  and state militaries 126–8, 129, 133, 137–8
  see also masculinity/ies; "men as warlike" trope;
    NSAGs
"men as warlike/women as peaceful" trope 23,
  105–6, 111–13, 121, 175
Méndez, Luz 1887, 187 n.134
mercenary/ies 25, 41, 130; *see also* private military
  and security company(ies) (PMSC)
Mexico 45, **149**, 215
Michel, Sonya 176
Middle East 117, 148, **149**, *220*
militant groups *see* non-state armed groups
militaries, state 19, 28, 48, 56, *58*, 60, 124–45, 233
  and citizenship 128
  civilian control of 125, 126
  gays in 24
  as gendered organizations 124–7, 135, 140–1
  as linked to masculinity/ies 19, 126–8, 131,
    136–9
  prostitution 46–7, 56, 130–1
  reliance on civilian women 128–31
  reliance on and construction of ideas about
    gender 124–6, 135–9, 144–5
  sexual harassment and assault in 141–4, 222
  variations among 124, 144
  women in 23, 48, 124–5, 131–45, 217–18
  women's reasons for joining 48, 134
  see also DDR programs; masculinity/ies,
    militarized
militarism 105, 108, 109, *110*, 111, 117, 135
militarization 3, 32, 49, 128, 135, 154
  as driver of conflict 27
  and gender 41, 45, 49–52, 158, 166–7, 212–13
  globalization, linked to 26
  and sexual violence 61–2
  women's activism and 102–22
  of women's lives 128–31
militarized livelihoods *see* livelihood(s),
  militarization of
militarized masculinity *see* masculinity/ies,
  militarized
military aid 27, 115
military budgets 117, *191*, 232
military culture 117, 122, 128, 135, 139
military leaders 23, 56, 59, 114, 125, 126, 133,
  137, 140, 209, 231; *see also* leadership, in US
  military
military service and political legitimacy 217–18
military training 10, 23, 25, 27, 47–8, 61–2, 114,
  135–6, 144
  of female soldiers 132, 134–6, 141, *142*, 145
  misogyny in 135, 141
militias 28, 41, 43, 45, 48, 49–50, 80, 165 n.10,
  165, 196
Mindanao Peoples Caucus (MPC) 177–8
misogyny 27, 50, 61
Mobutu Sese Seko 51, 51 n.4
modernity 115, 118
modernization 95, 95 n.6, 132
Mothers' Front (Sri Lanka) 108
"Mothers' Movement" (former Yugoslavia) 108,
  110
Mothers for Peace (M4P) (Mindanao) 175–6, 180

motherhood, political mobilization of 106–9, *110*,
  110 n.5, 110, 111, 176, 178
Mozambique **149**, 150, 194, 209, 224, 227, 229,
  232–3, *234*, 235, 236, 240
mujahideen 164
multinational corporations *see* transnational
  corporations
Muslim women 36, 164, 188
Mwalimu Nyerere Foundation 190

Nagaland conflict, women's peace-building
  179–80
Nagasaki 25
Nairobi *see* United Nations World Conferences on
  Women
nation- and state-building processes 140, 175
nation, woman as embodiment of 14, 29, 114,
  116, 120
National Council for the Defense of Democracy/
  Forces of Defense of Democracy (CNDD-
  FDD) 150
national liberation movements/forces 120, 132,
  133–4, 151, 167, 179
  and women's rights 48, 153–4, 120, 167, 207,
    209
  see also non-state armed groups
nationalism(s) 110, 117, 153, 154, 172
  discourses of 14, 116, 120
  feminist analysis of 14, 120
  as motivation for joining armed forces/groups
    48, 152–4, 160
nationalist conflicts 115–16, 151; *see also*
  conflict(s); ethno-nationalist movements
nationalist versus feminist agendas 154, 187
natural resources, global trade in, 26, 45, 84, *219*;
  see also resources, natural, conflict-related
neocolonial relationships 45 n.5, 171, 172
neoliberalism 26, 27, 41, 49, 51, 96, 96 n.8, 216,
  226, 228–30
  as driver of conflict 27
  negative effects on women 45, 228–30
  neoliberal conditionality 216, 228–30, 231, *234*
  World Bank promotion of neoliberal policies
    230, 233, *234*
Nepal 196, 215, *220*
women and girls in armed forces and groups **131**,
  149, **149**, 150–1, 202, 209, 224
Netherlands 100, **139**
networks
  local community support 37, 43–4, 89, 97, *97*,
    207, 209
  women's antiwar and anti-militarization 106,
    116–18, 117 n.12, 121, 122, 129, *179*, 181–2,
    183; *see also* peace-building, women's
    informal
New Zealand 97, **131**, **139**
Newland, Kathleen 97
NGO *see* nongovernmental organization
NGO Forum (1985 Nairobi Conference) 95–6
Nicaragua 48, 109, **149**
Nobel Peace Prize 102, 170
nongovernmental organizations (NGOs) 15, 24,
  40, 85, 87–8, 95–6, 98, 176, 179, 189, 200–1,
  208, 218–19, **219**
  effects of gender assumptions of NGO workers
    87–8, 176
  as gendered institutions 12–13, 15
  humanitarian 24, 85, 87, 218, **219**
  international (INGOs) 15, 69, 98, 176, 180, 189,
    199–200, **219**

local 15, 69, *179*, 182, 201, *208*
national 98, *200*, **219**
see also feminist(s), NGOs; women's
organizations and networks
non-state armed groups (NSAGs) 9, 15, 25–6, 30,
33, 47–8, 49, 56, 102, 146–68, 169, 195, 196,
202–3, 205, 213
female commanders in 148–50, 153, 165
gender ideologies of 48, 151, 166
recruitment strategies of 146, 152, 154–6, 160,
161, 163–4, 167
regulation of sexual relationships within 150–1,
156
reliance on and manipulations of gender by
146–7, 154–60, 163–5, 166
reliance on women and girls 23, 146–7, 152,
155, 159–62, 164, 212
religiously identified 159–63
training and socialization 61–2, 114, 150, 160,
166, 202
women's exclusion from roles in 162–6
women's and girls' roles and experiences in 32,
47, 60, 146–68, 203
effects on NSAG tactics and ideologies
153–7
reasons for participation 48, 82, 146, 148–50,
152–3, 156–7, 160–1
see also Liberation Tigers of Tamil Eelam; FARC
nonviolence 21, 47, 61, 109, 117, 119, *119*
nonviolent conflict resolution 12, 223–4
women in 109, 224
North Korea 132, 144, *144*
Northern Ireland 120, **149**, 169, 176, 180–1, 215,
235
Northern Ireland Women's Coalition (NIWC) 121,
169, 181
Women's Support Network in Belfast 121
Norway 86, 100, **139**, *139*, 170, 188
NSAGs *see* non-state armed groups
nuclear weapons 13–14, 14 n.6, 118–19, *119*, 176
Nuer *179*
nutrition/malnutrition 75, 77, 109, *203*, 226
Nyerere, Julius 189

Ortiz, Jacqueline 143
ostracism
as cost of women's political activism 122, 175
of female ex-combatants 148, 151, 161, 175 n.2,
197, 207, 209
as result of CRSV 64, *66*, 67–8, 148, 161
see also stigmatization
"Othering" 135, 186
Ottoman Empire 133
Oxfam 12–13, **219**

Pacific Islands 49, 117, 238
pacifist/pacifism 104, 121
Pakistan 55, 63, 88, 92, 126, **139**, **149**, 220
Palestine 64, 120, 159, 170
Palestinian Islamic Jihad (PIJ) 159
Palestinian refugees 44, 89, 92, 165
Palestinian women 181
Pankhurst, Donna 106, 217, *238*
Panzi Hospital 65–6
paramilitaries 107, 155, 165, *199*, *200*, 237–8
parliaments *see* legislature(s)
patriarchal 120, 122, 160, 165, 196
constructions of family honor 14, 29, 50, 56,
63–4, 86, 120, 161, 162
culture 63, 119

gender arrangements 29, 61, 107, 118, 164, 165,
175, 186, 227, 235
religiously identified armed groups 162–4
structures of power 173, 182, 196
systems 4, 149, 165, 172
patriarchy 29, 63–4, 107, 119–20, 151, 160, 164,
182
as explanation for CRSV 61
as a factor in war 61, 122
meaning of 4
"predatory patriarchy" 50–2
patronage 49, 51, 173
peace
feminization of 12, 175
"gendered peace" 216–17
"liberal peace" 190, 231
see also peace agreements; peace-building; peace
negotiations (formal); peace processes;
women, "peacefulness" of
peace agreements/accords 151, 188, 192, 196,
197, 215
addressing inequalities and justice 171
drafting and signing of 21, 169–70, *177*
gender-sensitive 180
grassroots peace accords *179*
implementation of 170, 172, *184*, 184, 186, *191*
as site of restructuring postwar society 171
sustainability of 170, 171–2
see also specific peace agreements 169, 170, *177*, *185*,
187, 194, *234*, 237
peace-building, women's informal 57, 116, 120–1,
169, 173, 178–82, *179*, 183, 184, 186, 190,
192, 210, 238, *239*
networks/organizations *179*, *179*, 181, 182,
190–1, *191*, *239*
peace negotiations (formal)
actors in 169, 170, 176, 180–1, 182, 185, 188, 190,
191, 202, 212
as gendered 18, 170–1, 173–92
importance for women 71, 171, *177*, 191–2, 204
restructuring/reinscribing gender hierarchies
71, 170, 171
women's participation/exclusion 57, 111–12,
116, 169, 172, 174–6, 177, *179*, 179–81, 183,
185–7, 189, 190, *191*, 202; *see also* UNSCR
1325
women's pressure on men to reach agreements
169, 176
women's representation, dilemmas of 178,
186–7, 191–2
women's right to be included in 173–8
see also peace processes; UNSCR 1325; *and specific
countries* 169, 170, 174, 176, *177*, *185*, 187
n.14, 187
peace organizations *see* activism, women's
political; peace-building, women's
informal
peace processes
African regional initiatives 189
neocolonial relationships in, danger of 172
overview of 170–3
women's participation in 173–92
terminology 171–3, *177*
see also conflict resolution
peace support operations (PSOs) 57, 69, *184–5*, 218,
220–3, 227, 238
gender mainstreaming in 222–3
personnel 57, 218, *220*, 222, *223*
SEA *see* peacekeepers
women in 57, 222, *223*

peace support operations (PSOs (*cont.*)
　zero-tolerance policy 57, 221–2
　see also Troop Contributing Countries
peacekeepers 46, 57, 91, 218, 224
　sexual exploitation and abuse by 221–2, 227
　training 57, *184*
peacekeeping operations *see* peace support
　operations
peace talks *see* peace negotiations
Pentagon, US 17–18
persecution, gendered forms of 94, 96–8, *97*
Peru **131, 149,** 237
Peterson, Spike 4 n.2, 228–9
Philippines 49, 58, 115, 117, 120, 130, **149,** 175–6,
　180, 185–6
PKK *see* Kurdistan Workers' Party
PMSC *see* private military and security
　company(ies)
Poland **131,** 132
police/ing, civilian 11, 15, 74, 93, 98, 148, *184,* 198,
　203, 239
　gender dimensions of 64, 69–71, 223, 233
　in PSOs 185, 218–24, **219,** *220,* 223, *223*
　　all-female formed police units 185, *220*
　post-conflict reform 233, 235
policy makers 3, 8, 13, 31, 56, 78, 91, 98, 126, 175,
　212, 223, 228
political economy of war, gendered 36–7, 40–53
political institutions 113, 117, 169, 172, 233
political leaders 8, 59, 73, 105–6, 109, 114, 126,
　129, 132, 153, 209
political movements 108–9
　communalist 110, 116, 204
　ethno-nationalist 110, 116, 119–21, 182, 187
　religious fundamentalist 110, 115, 147
　sectarian 116
　see also national liberation movements/forces
political participation of women 33, 34, *57,* 82,
　112, 169–70 173, 188, 206
political parties 169, 173, 181, *185,* 187, 190, 196,
　209, 231, 232, *234; see also* quotas
political representation of women 169–70, 173–8,
　179, 180, 186–7, 188, 189, 191–2, 232
political settlements *see* peace agreements
post-Cold War *see* Cold War, end of, effects on
　conflict
postcolonial
　feminists 15, 38
　patronage systems 51
　racial hierarchies 15, 51
　scholars and activists 182
　see also colonialism
post-conflict/postwar 22, 65, 172, 175, *184,* 196,
　209, 215–40
　actors, multiplicity and diversity of 218,
　　219
　backlash against women's wartime gains 154,
　　164, 167, 237–40, *238*
　constitutional reform 171, 178, 185, *185,* 222,
　　231, 232
　economies 229–30, 231
　family reunification 225, 227
　gender relations, shifts in 64, 196–7, 206–11,
　　208, 211, 225–6, 227–8, 237–40, *238, 239*
　gendered realities of 222–36
　gender-specific needs 222
　governance 18, 36, 112, 116, 148, 185, *185,* 222,
　　229, 230–6, *234*
　health, women's and girls' 226
　households, transformed 225–6, *239*

land reform 232–3, *234*
livelihoods 227
neoliberal conditionality, gendered 228–30, *230*
"parachuting in" of experts 171–2
political transformation 230–2
problem with the term "post" 22 n.12, 215–18
reconstruction 71, 170, 184, *184,* 230–1, 233,
　241
return phase 224–7
transitional justice 236–7
"tyranny of the urgent" 220–1
women's security and SSR 233, 235
　see also DDR programs; democratic transitions;
　　justice; neoliberalism; peace-building;
　　peace support operations; quotas
post-traumatic stress disorder (PTSD) 142, *142*
poverty
　gender relations of 92, 95, 188, 194, 206, *208,*
　　226, 228
　neoliberal economic policies 26, 228
　war, links with 44, 65, 71, 85, 88, 156, 206, *208,*
　　226, 228
power relations, structural 3–7, 10, 14–15, 29,
　37, 151
　see also colonialism; ethnicity(ies); gender;
　　patriarchy
pregnancy 53, 54, 64, *66,* 75, 76, 77, 89, 166, 206
　early 226
　forced *39,* 56, 63, 65, 76, 120, 236
　as weapon (of war) 63, 120
　see also health, women's
prevention of armed conflicts *57,* 116, 122, 220
prevention of CRSV 55, 60, 70, 78, 122
prevention of infection and disease 65, 75, 76,
　77, *208*
prison(s) 70–1, 176, 223
private military and security company(ies) (PMSC)
　15, 25, 26, 28, 197, 201, 218, 235, 235 n.11
private/public divide *see* public/private divide
property rights 22, 29, 42, 46, 225, 227, 227 n.8
prostitution 39, 46–7, 68, 86, 89, 92, 97, 221, 227
　n.8, 236
　military prostitution 2, 117, 130–1; *see also*
　　"comfort women"
　and PSOs 221–2
　see also sex industry and war economies
protection 86–91, 94–5, *97, 97,* 109
　of citizens, by state 233
　of civilians 46, 58, **219**
　contestation of military as source of 116–19
　as justification for war 113–15
　and masculinity 11–12, 28, 127–8
　men as protectors 1, 6, 11, 14, 28, 56, 61, 127–8
　nuclear weapons and 13–14, 118–19, *119*
　peacekeeper, failures of 221–2
　as reason females join armed groups 48–9, 148
　of refugee women 95, 95 n.7
　under international law 82
　of witnesses 59, 236 69, 71–4
　of women and girls 56, 61, 113–16, 127, 176, 177,
　　184, 206
"protector/protected" trope 28, 32, 121, 223
　as justification for subordination 117, 127
　as legitimization for war 14, 114, *115,* 116
Protestant 121, 169, 181
protracted refugee situations 88, 89, 92
PSO *see* peace support operation
PTSD *see* post-traumatic stress disorder
public/private divide 22, *39,* 51, 95–7, 103, 107,
　109, *110,* 111–12, 128, 163, 164–5, 176

public services/sector, under neoliberalism 226,
        229, 230
Puechguirbal, Nadine 177
Puerto Rico 117
Putin, Vladimir *110*

quotas 169, 231, 232, *234*
    for women 169, 180, *185*, 231, 232

racism 5, 52, 109–10, 188
rape *see* sexual violence, conflict-related
Rassemblement Congolais pour la Démocratie
        (RCD) 174
RAWA *see* Revolutionary Women of Afghanistan
rebels 36, 63, 67, 194, *208*, 240; *see also* non-state
        armed groups
reconciliation 178, 179, 189–90, *191*, 217, **219**
reconstruction, postwar 116, *177*, 178, *184*, 184,
        189, *191*, 210, **219**, 229–30, 238
recruitment
    forced conscription 156, 157, 161
    manipulation of gender as part of 19, 154–67
    of men and boys into NSAGs 156, 162–3
    of men into state militaries 19–20, 127, 138, 167
    of women and girls into NSAGs 147, 152,
        155–62, 164–7
    of women into PSOs 16
    of women into state militaries 125, 127–8,
        132–4
refoulement 93, *97*; *see also* repatriation, gendered
        experiences of, forced
refugee(s), women as 44, 75–6, 80–101, *208*, 227;
        see also camps, refugee and IDP
rehabilitation 172, *177*, 178, *184*, 188, *191*; *see also*
        DDR programs
reintegration *57*, 171, 178, *184*, 194–213, 224, *238*
    of women and girls 195, 201–2, 206–11
    women's under-utilized skills 210–11, *211*
    see also DDR programs
Relatives' Action Committee in Northern Ireland
        176
relief agencies *see* humanitarian assistance
        organizations
relief aid *see* humanitarian aid
religion 2, 9, 10, 37, 62, 81, 192
    fundamentalism 94, 110, 182
    leaders 56, 68, 165, 201, 235
religious beliefs 140, 186, 238
religious identities 14, 29, 83, 100, 102, 108, 120,
        166, 181, 182
religious institutions 4, 6, 9, 15, 103, 201
religiously based conflicts 50
    religiously configured armed opposition groups
        159–60, 161–5
    see also individual religions
Renamo *see* Resistência Nacional Moçambicana
reparations 181, 237
repatriation, gendered experiences of 31, 81, 88,
        93–100, 184
    forced 93, *97*
reproductive health *see* health, women's and
        girls', reproductive
Republic of Congo, DDR in 203
Republic of South Sudan 65, 66, 75, 78
Réseau des Femmes pour la Defense des Droits et
        la Paix 174
resettlement 44, 86, 171, 189
    countries of 84–5, 86, 87, 89–90, 92–4, 97, 99
    gendered experiences of 87, 92–3, 94, 97–9, *184*
resistance, institutional 99, 221, 225

resistance, women's 55, 103, *111*, *119*
resistance movements 115, 163, 165; *see also*
        NSAGs
Resistência Nacional Moçambicana (Renamo) 194
resources, natural, conflict-related 26–7, 45, **219**
revenge 49, 56, 150, 160–1
Revolutionary United Front (RUF) 67, 151, 210
Revolutionary Women of Afghanistan (RAWA) 115
right-wing regimes/factions 117, 147–8, 165, 174
rights *see* democracy, democratic rights; human
        rights; property rights; women's rights
Rohingya 89
Rome General Peace Accords 194, *234*
Rome Statute of the ICC, 59, *184*, 236
Ruddick, Sara 13, 105, 108–9, *111*
RUF *see* Revolutionary United Front
rule of law 71, 74, 171–2
Runyan, Anne 228–9
rural areas *39*, 42, 155, 227, 232, *234*, 235
rural women 29, 218, 233
Russia, 41, 132–3, 231
    military 133, 160
    mother's movements in 109, *110*, 129, 176
    women in military 132–3, **139**, 144
    see also Chechnya, conflict in; the Committee of
        Soldiers' Mothers of Russia
Rwanda 26–7, 75, 102–3, 189, *220*, 233, 237
    sexual violence, genocidal 14, 56, 58–9, 62–3
    women and girls in NSAGs **149**, 150, 203–4

SADF *see* South African Defense Force
Sagar, Pearl 169
SALW *see* small arms and light weapons
Save Somali Women and Children (SSWC) 180–1
SEA *see* sexual exploitation and abuse
Second World War *58*, 98, 130, 132, 133, 138, 215
security sector reform (SSR) *57*, 64, **219**, 233
    gender and 185, *203*, 233, 235
security studies 12, 216
self-determination 152, 197
self-reintegration 206, 225
Serbia 187, **149**
    rape by armed forces 63, 68, 237–8
    women's activism 110, 120–1, 181, 182, *239*
sex, relationship to gender 5–7
sex industry and war economies 45–7, 82, 84; *see
        also* prostitution, military
sexual exploitation and abuse (SEA) 46, 56, 68, 76,
        89, *97*, 140, *184*, 201, 209–10, 221–2
    of children 221
    as a destroyer of cultures and communities 54
    as motive for joining NSAGs 150, 153, 155–7, 161
    by NGO personnel 46, 54, 56, 221
    as a peace and security issue 54–5, 183
    by peacekeepers 221–20
    response and prevention policies 55, 78
    see also "survival sex"
sexual harassment 39, *97*, 140, *185*, 206, 235
    of women in state militaries 141–4
sexual relationships, coercive 226; *see also* forced
        wives; sexual violence; slavery
sexual servitude *see* slavery
sexual violence, conflict-related (CRSV) 21, 25, 30,
        54–74, *97*, 181 n.8, 190, 201, *208*, 235–7
    as crime against humanity *58*, 58, 59, 236
    definition of *39*, 56
    documentation and research *57*, 69, 73
    effects of
        on community 59, 66
        on family 59, 66, 68

sexual violence (*cont.*)
  on health 54, 65–6, *66*, 226
  on marriageability 68, 143, *144*, 237
  psychological 54, 66–7, 142, *142*, 226
  stigmatization and ostracism 64, *66*, 66, 67–8,
    70, 72–3, 78, 143, 148, 161, *208*, 237
explanations of 60–4
impunity 56, *57*, 62, 70–1, 73, 144, 177, 188
justice, barriers to 70–1, 73
  against men and boys 27 n.18, 56, 56 n.2, 221
    n.4, 226 n.7
  as peace and security issue 54–5, 56, 57,
    183–4
perpetrators of *39*, 55–6, *57*, 59, 70–1
policy responses/care and treatment 69–70,
    71–4
prevalence, variation in 55–6, 59, 60–2
prevention of 55, 60, 70–3, 78
prosecution of 58, 59, 69, 70–1, 73
  see also international law
protection of survivors and witnesses 59, 69,
    71–4, 236
rape 22, 27, *39*, *47*, 51–2, 55–6, 60, 65–6, 95, 120,
    150–1, 157, 161, 176, *184*, 185
  by aid workers 65, 91
  camps *58*, 130
  children born of 64, 68, 112
  as "ethnic cleansing" 14, 29, 63–4, 72
  gang rape 10, 27, 63, 65, 80, *142*
  as genocide 14, 29, 58, 63
  as international crime *58*, 58, 59
  mass rape 14, 58
  opportunistic 56, 61, 72
  as public spectacle 63, 66
  as weapon of war *see* sexual violence; as tactic
    of war
as reason for joining armed forces or groups 32,
    150, 153, 155–7, 161
right to protection against *see* international law;
    ICTR; ICTY; CEDAW
in specific countries
  Balkans 56, 62, 63
  Bangladesh 55, 63
  Colombia 56; DRC 27 n.18, 55, 63
  East Timor 62
  El Salvador 60
  Eritrea 60
  French revolution 55
  Guatemala 60
  Kosovo 56, 68
  Libya 63
  Nanjing 55
  Rwanda 62
  Sierra Leone 66
  Sri Lanka 60
  former Yugoslavia 58
as tactic of war *57*, 60, 181 n.8, *208*
  to displace 62–3, 88–9
  as "ethnic cleansing" 14, 29, 63–4, 72
  of men and boys 56
  to terrorize 14, 62–3, *208*
  of women and girls, to attack men 11, 29, 56,
    61–4, 66–8
as torture 27, 56, *58*, 65–6, *66*, 93, 95, 97, 148, *208*
training for health workers 69–70
against women in militaries 140–4, *142*
zero-tolerance policy *57*, 221–2
  see also "comfort women"; forced pregnancy;
    forced sterilization; forced termination
    of pregnancy; slavery, sexual; trafficking,

human; United Nations Security Council
    Resolution, on Women, Peace, and Security
sexuality
  changes in wartime 51, 76
  of females in armed forces or groups 141, 151,
    197, 210
  male 29–30, 127
  targeting of *39*
sexually transmitted disease/infection (STD/I) 54,
    76, 226
shadow economies *see* economies, illicit, illegal
    and shadow
Sharia law *40*, 94
Sheper-Hughes, Nancy 109
Sierra Leone 70, 75, 78, 177, 224, 237
  DDR in 196, 199, 205, 207, *208*, 209–10
  Lomé Peace Accord *177*
  sexual violence as tactic of war 56, 66–8
  Special Court for Sierra Leone *47*, 59
  women and girls in *47*, 106, **149**, 150–1, *177*, 205,
    207, *208*, 209–10, 217, *230*
  see also Mano River Women's Peace Network
Sinhalese/Sinhala women 108, 134, 152, 188
Sirleaf, Ellen Johnson 36, 102
Skjelsbaek and Tryggestad 139–40
slavery 4, 5, 82
  indentured labor 26, 43, 45, *47*, 82, 84, 86–7
  sexual *39*, 45, *47*, 47, 50, 56, *58*, 58 n.4, 82, 89,
    130, 150–1, 201, 227 n.8, 236
small arms and light weapons (SALW) 13–14, 14
    n.6, 41, 49–50, 74, 198, 205, *234*, 237
  definition of 49–50
  and masculinity 13–14
  soldier *see* combatants
Somalia 94, **149**, 210 n.5
  al-Shabaab in 163–4
  women and girls 43, 94, **149**, 150, 164, 169
  women in peace talks, "sixth clan" 169,
    180–1
South Africa **149**, 183, 189–90, 194, 210 n.5, 223,
    235, 237
South African Defense Force (SADF), women in
    133, 135, 139, 144
South America *see* Americas, *and specific countries*
South Asia *see* Asia
South Korean women 117, 130–1, **139**
Southeast Asia *see* Asia
sovereignty *96*, 190
Soviet Union, collapse of 41, 231
Spain **139**, **149**
Special Representative of the Secretary-General
    (SRSG) 57, *200*
Spivak, Gayatri Chakravorty 114, 183, 183 n.9
SPLM/A *see* Sudanese People's Liberation
    Movement/Army
Sri Lanka 60, 84, 88, 120, 215
  feminists 189
  peace process, women and 172 n.1, 174, 181,
    185, 187, 188–9
  tsunami 84, 88
  women's activism 108, 181, 188
  women in military 134, **139**
  women in NSAGs 149, **149**, 151–4
  women's political representation 173–4, 189
  see also Liberation Tigers of Tamil Eelam
SSR *see* security sector reform
state(s)
  emerging from conflict 48, 216, 233, *234*, 235–7
  European nation-state model 217
  gendered understanding of 120, 190

"failed states" 36, 41, 50
formations, diversity of 217–18
"hollowed out" by neoliberal restructuring 41, 228–30
state-building processes 120, 175
state militaries *see* militaries, state
stateless people 82–3, 85, 89, 91, 93, 100
STD/I *see* sexually transmitted disease/infection
Stiehm, Judith Hicks 114, 127
Stiglitz, Joseph 229
stigmatization
of female ex-combatants 143, 151, 161, 175 n.2, 197, 207, 209–10, 211
as result of CRSV 64, *66*, 66, 67–8, 70, 72–3, 78, 143, 161, *208*, 237
see also ostracism
stoning 94
structural adjustment programs 41; *see also* neoliberalism
subalterns 183, 183 n.9
Sudan 25, 59, 80, 84, 91, 149, **149**, 182, 210 n.5
"Lost Boys"/"Lost Girls" 87
south Sudan 50, 65, *66*, *179*
Sudanese women *43*, 92, *179*, 180
Sudanese women's movement 74, *179*
see also Darfur; janjaweed; Republic of South Sudan; SPLM/A
Sudanese People's Liberation Movement/Army (SPLM/A) 149, *179*, 180, 198
suicide bombers, female *153*, 158–65
"survival sex"/"transactional sex" 86, 92
sustainable peace and security 172, 183, 190, 215, 217
Sweden 86, 97–9, 100, 127, **139**, 141
Swerdlow, Amy 119
Switzerland **131**, 189
Syria 86, **149**, 158–9, 182

Tailhook Scandal 142
Taliban *40*, *115*, 115, 163
Tamil values 151–2
Tamil women and girls 108, 152–4, 188
Tanzania 92, 189
Taylor, Charles 36, 102
terrorism/terrorist, problem with terms 115, 147; *see also* "war on terror," global
Thailand 44, 92, 95, **149**
Thatcher, Margaret 102, 106
"Third World" 84; *see also* global South
"Third World Women" 38, 186
Tickner, Ann 114
torture 148, 235; *see also* sexual violence, conflict-related (CRSV)
trade
arms 14 n.6, 24–8, 41, 49–50
in commodities, illegal 24, 45, 46, 49, 50
drugs 14 n. 6, 24, 26, 27–8, 41, 45–6, 50, 165 n.10, 196, 215
petty 45, 133, 223, 227, 233
sex 45–7, 82, 84, 86–7, 88–9
see also arms trade; economies, illicit, illegal, and shadow; globalization; trafficking, human
trafficking, human 24, 26, 28, 41, 82, 84, 227 n.8, 227–8
of children 45, 46, 80, 82, 84, 88–9, 227
as indentured laborers 84, 88–9
peacekeepers, police and US soldiers as traffickers 131, 227
sex trafficking *39*, 45–7, 82, 84, 86–7, 88–9, 227

of women *39*, 45–7, 59, 68, 80, 82, 84, 88–9, 92, 131, 227
training, skills/vocational 93, 133, 134, *191*, 227
in DDR 199, *200*, 201, 207, 211
transformation 26
conflict 12, 172, 182, 200
of gender relations 116, 178, 120
of identity in exile 92
postwar structural 191, 192, 215–40
transitional justice 236, 235 n.12, 237
transitional processes 184–5, 196, 215–16, 218, **219**, 224–8, 235–6; *see also* democratic transitions
transnational corporations, as driver of conflict 26–7
transnational women's networks 117; *see also* Women in Black
transparency 172, 183
transportation, systems 25, 42, 44
transportation, effects of women's lack of access 46, 92, 93, 199, 206, 230
transversal feminist politics 110, 119–21, 179, 180–2
trauma 66–8, 72, 77–9, 84, 92, 95, *97*, *142*, 142, 208
"triad analytics" 5 n.4
Troop Contributing Countries (TCCs) *220*, 223
major contributors of women 223
see also peace support operations
truth commissions 35, 178, 217, **219**, 236
tsunami 84, 88
tuberculosis (TB) 77, 226
Turkey 117, 120, 133, 135, **139**, 165, 169
"tyranny of the urgent" 221, 225

ubuntu 183
Uganda 26–7, *43*, 49, 51, 91, **149**, 150–1, 189, 190, 210 n.5, 226
UN *see* United Nations
UNDDR *see* DDR programs
UNDPKO *see* United Nations Department of Peacekeeping Operations
UNHCR *see* United Nations High Commissioner for Refugees
UNIFEM *see* United Nations Development Fund for Women
UNITA (National Union for the Total Independence of Angola) 203
unintended consequences
of focus on gender balance 222
of sexual violence response and prevention policies 71–4
of zero-tolerance policy 222
United Kingdom (UK) 98, 102, *119*, 119, 127–8, **131**, 132, 133, 135, **139**, 141, 183, **219**, 228
United Nations (UN) 20, 24, 26–7, 34, *40*, 57, 59, 91, 95–6, 164, 172, 176, 180, 183, *184*, 185, 189, 191, 198, *199–200*, *208*, 218–24, **219**, 220, *220*, *223*, *234*, 238, 240
Commission on the Status of Women 183
Declaration on the Elimination of Violence against Women *39*, 59
as a gendered organization 18, 185, 221–3
see also peace support operations
United Nations agencies, departments, and organizations 34, *66*, *85*, 92 n.4, 169, 176, 180, 184, 194, *199*, *200*
United Nations Convention Relating to the Status of Refugees 81, 81 n.2, 82, 83, 91, 94, 96, *96*, 98

United Nations Department of Peacekeeping
     Operations (UNDPKO) 18, *199*, 199–201, 218,
     219, *220*, 220–5, *223*, 227–8
United Nations Department of Political Affairs
     (DPA) 18, *199*, *220*
United Nations Development Fund for Women
     (UNIFEM) 187 n.14, 190
United Nations High Commissioner for Refugees
     (UNHCR) 20, 85, 88, 89–90, 91, 93, 95–9, *96*,
     97, 99 n.10, 164, **219**, *220*
United Nations Human Rights Conventions 82, *83*
United Nations Secretary-General 18, 56, *57*, 220,
     221
United Nations Security Council (UNSC) 56, *57*,
     59, 116,183, 184
United Nations Security Council Resolution(s)
     (UNSCR) 69, *57*, 176–7
   on Women, Peace and Security 28, 34, *57*, 59,
     116, 117, 182–6, *184*, *185*, 186 n.11, 187, 187
     n.14, *223*
United Nations World Conferences on Women
   Beijing (1995) 99, 183
     1995 Beijing Platform for Action 39
   Copenhagen (1980) 95
   Nairobi (1985) 95–6
United Self-Defense Forces of Colombia (AUC)
     165–6
United States (USA) 12, 27, 36, 38, 49, 55, 56, 59,
     84, 97, 98, 102, 109, 113, 115, 119, 128, 132,
     133, 134, 170, 176, 183, *185*, 189, 194, **219**,
     228–9
   as country of resettlement 86, 87, 99
   see also Afghanistan, US war in; Iraq, US war in;
     Vietnam, war in
United States military 23–4, 26–7, 37, 102, 115,
     117, 126, 130–1, 142–3, *142*, 203
   domestic violence and 64–5
   prostitution 130–1
   sexual abuse within 141–4, *142*
   women in 134–9, 141–4, *142*
   see also Afghanistan, US war in; Female
     Engagement Teams; Iraq, US war in;
     Vietnam, war in
UNSC *see* United Nations Security Council
UNSCR *see* United Nations Security Council
     Resolution(s)
UNSCR 1325 *see* United Nations Security Council
     Resolution(s) on Women, Peace and
     Security
URNG *see* Guatemala,Guatemalan National
     Revolutionary Unity

victim/agent dichotomy, problem of 31–2, 37, 47,
     52, 90, 116–17, 120, 121, 124, 146, 176–7,
     177, 183, 223–4, 238
Vietnam, war in 55, 133, 136, 170
violence 22 n.11, 24, 26, 30, 37, 83, 85, 110, 147,
     198, 204, 213, 235
   against women *39*, 59, 64, 80, 90, *97*, 98, *111*, 117,
     164, 181, 182, 188, *238*
   armed 12, 21, 22, 25, 33, 38, 74, 95, 103, 104,
     109, 166, 190, 195–6, 238
   association with men/masculinity 12, 22, 23,
     105–6, 114
   definition of *39*
   domestic 21, 36, *39*, *40*, 64–5, 88–9, 95-6, 98,
     155–7, 196, 222, 237–8, *239*
   gender-based (GBV) 38, *39*, *57*, 59, 87, 89, 92, 94,
     95–6, 154–6, 166, 183, *184*, 236–7
   and militarization 49–52, 61–2, 195

see also male youth; sexual violence, conflict-
     related; trafficking, human; torture
"vulnerable groups" 28, 176–7, 201, 230
vulnerability 87, 97, 127, 136
   of boys 82, 84
   of female-headed households 8, 46, 225–6
   gender analysis of 28–30
   of girls 82, 84, 86–8, 89, 90, 206–7
   of women in war 8, 28–30, *39*, 45–6, 47, 54,
     82, 84, 86–8, 89, 90, 96, 97, *97*, *142*, 176–7,
     206–7, 223, 225–6

WAD *see* Women and Development
Walker, Margaret Urban 22
war
   "after" war *see* post-conflict/postwar
   casualties, gender differences in 36, 54, 74
   centrality of women's labor to 22–3, 128–31; *see
     also* non-state armed groups
   as changing social norms 53
   discourses/narratives 1, 12–14, 20–2, 28, 104–6,
     113–16, 124
   drivers of conflict 27, 84–5
   economies *see* economies, illicit, illegal and
     shadow *and* economies, war
   funding of 24–7, 45, 146, **219**
   gains possible for women 43, 48, 52, 100, 133,
     134, 153–4, 170, 171, 207, 209, 210–11, *211*,
     238
   and gender as mutually constitutive 1, 22–4
   as a gendered practice 22–4
   global/local processes formative of war 3–4,
     24–8, 37, 38, 40–1, 45–6, 49–51, 117, 228
   impacts
     on communities 21, 36–7, 41, 43–4, 45, 49, 51,
        54, 56, 59, 66, 67–8, 75, 78, 89, 90, 164, 167,
        195, 201, 206, 211
     on families/households 43–4, *43*, 52, 87, 90,
        225–6, *239*
     on gender relations 30, 33, *43*, 43, 48, 52, 64,
        87, 112, 196, 207, 209–10, 213, 216, *238*
     on infrastructure 21, 24, 25, 36, 37, 42 , *43*,
        44–5, 46, 65, 70, 75, 84, 118, 201, 226, 228,
        230
     psychological 43, 46, 65, 66–8, 122, *142*, *142*,
        208
     on (local) support structures/networks, 37,
        43–4
   and masculinity/ies 1, 17–19, 22–4, 105–6,
        108–9, 121, 124–5, 175, 225
   political economy and 40–2, 47–53
   prevention *57*, 116, 122, 220
   "protection" as justification for 113–15
   as reshaping power structures 37
   spatial and temporal boundaries of 21–2, 22
        n.11, 40, 53
   specificity and context, importance of 2, 27, 28,
        30, 37, 40, 41, 60, 108, 147, 151, 164, 169–70,
        172, 228
   symbolic gender coding of 11–14
   types of 15, 24–7, 63, 64, 84, 85, 88, 91–2, 102,
        103, 107
     civil 15, 36, 84, 88, 91–92, 180, 181, 217
     "dirty war" 102, 107
     ethnically constructed 14, 36, 50, 63–4, 82,
        179
     intra-state, problem of concept of 25–7
     national liberation 15, 85, 120, 206, 209
     "new wars," characteristics of 24–7
   women's experiences of 21–2

as dependent on broader processes out of which wars arise 27–8, 30
as dependent on preexisting gender arrangements 7–8, 27–30, 48, 86, 89, 92
diversity/specificity/complexity of 1-2, 7–8, 15, 22, 28, 29, 37, 38–9, 54, 92, 100, 102–3, 119–20, 146, 151, 182, 204, 206, 218
see also international law; non-state armed groups; post-conflict/postwar; sexual violence, conflict-related; militaries, state
war crimes tribunals *see* international tribunals and special courts
"war on terror," global 114–15, 115 n.6, 147, 163
war system 32, 117–18, 121–2
water 8, 13, 29, 70, 74, 109, 118, 138, 150, 200, 202, 211, 229–30, *239*, 239,
Waylen, Georgina 108
"weak states" 26, 51
weapon(s) 2, 12, 13, 21, 23, 27, 28, 40, 121, 131, 132, 143, 146, 150, 165, *211*, 215, 223–4, 227, 237, 238
  attacks on masculinity as 10–11
  collection and destruction of 195–9, 205, 221, 224 *see also* DDR programs
  rape as 60–1, 120
  see also arms; DDR programs; landmines; nuclear weapons; small arms and light weapons
"the West" 115, 182, 228, 231
Western Europe *see* Europe
western political systems 231
WFP *see* World Food Program
WHO *see* World Health Organization
WICM *see* Women in Crisis Movement
WID *see* Women in Development
widows/widowhood 1, 36, 39, *43*, 43, 46, 83, 94, 102, 112, 150, 225–6, 233
Williams, Suzanne 12–13
WILPF *see* Women's International League for Peace and Freedom
wives 4, 9, 11, 23, 43, 46, *47*, 47, 59, 64, 65, 68, 104, 129, 130, 162, 164, 174, 187, 190, *208*, 237; *see also* widows/widowhood
women
  agency of *see* agency, women's
  bodies of *see* body(ies), female
  as caregivers *see* labor, caring, women's
  and combat *see* combat; combatants
  commoditization of 45–7
  disempowerment of 2, 35, 111, 217
  diversity among 2, 5, 15, 16, 29, 38, 108, 115, 182, 186–7
  employment *see* employment, paid
  experiences in war, diversity of 1–2, 7–8, 15, 22, 28, 29, 37, 38–9, 54, 92, 100, 102–3, 119–20, 146, 151, 182, 204, 206, 218, *passim*
  as leaders 105, 153, 175, 179, *185*, 190–1, 209, 210
  "peacefulness" of 32, 105, 107–9, *111*, 111–13, 121–2, 175–6, 178, 192
  peace-building activities of *see* peace-building, women's informal
  processes formative of conditions of women's lives 2
  representation of *see* peace negotiations (formal), women's representation, dilemmas of; political representation of women
  as reproducers of collective identities 14, 29, 50, 63–4, 120
  rural 29, 218, 233
  subordination of 4, 61, 95, 117, 165
  as supporters of armed violence 109–11, 116, 121, 129–30; *see also* non-state armed groups; national liberation movements/ forces
  as symbol of nation 14, 29, 114, 116, 120
  as symbols of family or group honor 14, 29, 50, 56, 63–4, 86, 120, 161, 162
  vulnerability of *see* vulnerability, of women in war
Women in Black 117, 117 n.11, 182
Women in Crisis Movement (WICM) *208*
Women and Development (WAD) 95
Women in Development (WID) 95
Women in Forced Migration (WIFM) 95–7
Women Strike for Peace (WSP) 119, 176
women's access to
  economic opportunities 42, 43, 46, 187, 202, 207, *208*, 211, 227, *230*
  food *47*, 48, 76, 83, 84, 86, 87, 90, 91, *110*, 130, 134, 150, 207, *208*, *211*, 221
  land 8, 42, 46, 187, 188, 225, 233
  property 42, 46, 225, 227, 227 n.8
  transportation 46, 92, 93, 199, 206, 230
Women's International League for Peace and Freedom (WILPF) 117
Women's International War Crimes Tribunal for the Trial of Japan's Military Sexual Slavery *58*
"women's issues"/interests 174–5, 178, 181, 189, *191*
  ghettoization of 189
women's liberation 154, 209
women's organizations and networks 69, 71, 96, 116, 117, 122, 183, 185, 187, **219**
  in Aceh *191*
  in Afghanistan 115, 185
  Ahotsak (Voices) 181
  All-Manipur Social Reformation and Development Samaj 176
  All-Women Contingent of the Mindanao Peoples Caucus 177
  Amargi Kadın Akademisi 117
  in Argentina 102, 107–8, 176
  in Bosnia-Herzegovina 120–1
  in Burundi 185, 189–1
  in Cambodia 221
  in Chechnya 129
  in Columbia 185
  Committee of Soldiers' Mothers in Russia (CSMR) 109, *110*, 129, 176
  in Cyprus 181
  in DRC 174
  Dushirehamwe 190–1
  in Europe 181
  in former Yugoslavia 108, 110, 117, 117 n.12, 120–1, 182, 185, 237, *239*
  Foro Nacional de la Mujeres (FORO) 188
  Gabriela 115
  ghettoization of 189
  Greenham Common Women's Peace Camp *119*
  in Guatemala 181, 187, 188
  in Guinea 106, 116
  Hands Across the Divide 181
  in India 176, 179–80
  International Network of Women's Network against Militarism (IWNAM) 117, 117 n.12
  in Israel 117, 181
  Kosova Women's Network 182, *239*

women's organizations and networks (*cont.*)
in Liberia 102, 106, 116, 180
Madres of the Plaza de Mayo 102, 107–8, 176
Mano River Women's Peace Network
    (MARWOPNET) 106, 116
Medica Women's Therapy Centre 120–1
in Mindanao 115, 175–6, 180
Mothers for Peace (M4P) 175–6, 180
Mothers' Front (Sri Lanka) 108
"Mother's Movement" 108, 110
Naga Mothers' Association (NMA) 179–80
Naga Women Union of Manipur (NWUM)
    179–80
National Union of Guatemalan Women 187
New Sudan Women's Association *179*
New Sudan Women's Federation *179*
in Northern Ireland 121, 169, 176, 181
Northern Ireland Women's Coalition 169, 181
in the Pacific region 117
in Palestine 181
in the Philippines 185
Relatives Action Committee 176
Réseau des Femmes pour la Defense des Droits
    et la Paix 174
Revolutionary Women of Afghanistan (RAWA)
    115
Ruka Ruci 239
in Russia 109, *110*, 129, 176
Save Somali Women and Children (SSWC)
    180–1
in Sierra Leone 106, 116, *208*
in Somalia 180–1
in Sri Lanka 108, 181, 185, 188
in Sudan 74, *179*
Sudanese Women's Voice for Peace *179*
in Turkey 117
in the United Kingdom *119*
in the USA 119, 176
Women in Black 117, 117 n.11, 182
Women in Crisis Movement (WICM) *208*
Women's International League for Peace and
    Freedom (WILPF) 117

women's liberation 154, 209
women's organizations and networks 69, 71, 96,
    116, 117, 122, 183, 185, 187, **219**
Women's Peace Coalition 182
Women's Peace Network (JPuD) *191*
Women's Policy Network (JPuK) *191*
Women Strike for Peace (WSP) 119, 176
Women's Support Network in Belfast 121
Women's Peace Network (JPuD) *191*
Women's Policy Network (JPuK) *191*
women's political organizing
    women-only (protest) groups 107–8,
        119
    women's trans-border organizing 103, 110, 116,
        117, 120, 122, 173, *179*, 181–2, 183, 185,
        190–1
    violent repression of 107–8, 122, *185*
    see also activism, women's
women's political participation 169–70, 173–8,
    179, 180, 186–7, 188, 189, 232
    dilemmas of 177–8, 186–7, 191–2
women's rights 39, *57*, 59, 92, 96, 115, 120, 151,
    183, *184*, *185*, 187, 192, 204, 209, 231, *234*,
    238
World Bank 200, 228–30, *230*, 233, 234
World Food Program (WFP) *85*, 85, 90, *200*, **219**
World Heath Organization (WHO) *200*
World Trade Organization (WTO) 228

Young, Iris Marion 113–14
youth 41, 50, 51–2, 88, 157, 167, 197, 199, *199*; *see
    also* male youth; female youth
Yugoslavia, former 58, 108, 110, 121, **149**, 217, 224,
    233, 235, 237
    International Criminal Tribunal for the former
        Yugoslavia (ICTY) 58, 58 n.6, 121
Yuval-Davis, Nira 182

Zarkov, Dubravka 25
Zedalis, Debra 159
Zeid Report 221–2
Zimbabwe **149**, 210 n.5